On the Trail
of the Legions

The author at Usworth aerodrome, near Sunderland.

On the Trail of the Legions

Raymond Selkirk

Anglia Publishing
Watts House
Capel St Mary
Ipswich
Suffolk, IP9 2JB

First published in 1995.
ISBN 1-897874-08-1

This book is available from:
Anglia Publishing, Watts House, Capel St Mary,
Ipswich, Suffolk, IP9 2JB, U.K.
Telephone: 01473 311138   Fax: 01473 311131

By the same author
The Piercebridge Formula, Patrick Stephens Ltd, 1983.
ISBN 0-85059-621-1
Reprinting with minor revisions, Anglia Publishing, 1995,
ISBN 1-897874-14-6

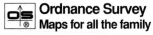 **Ordnance Survey**
Maps for all the family

On the Trail of the Legions - produced in association with Ordnance Survey.

The Ordnance Survey 1:25 000 series includes Pathfinder Maps, Explorer Maps and Outdoor Leisure Maps. An Index is available free of charge by telephoning 01703 792912.

Layout and typesetting by Max Newport.
Dust jacket design by Anthony King.
Illustration scanning and film output by Suffolk Offset, Martlesham, Suffolk. IP5 7RG.

Printed in England by Hillman Printers (Frome) Ltd, Frome, Somerset, BA11 4RW.

Contents

Acknowledgements

My thanks are due to the following people who assisted with this book; All the members of the Northern Archaeology Group of County Durham **to whom this book is dedicated.**

Members of the Association of Northumberland Local History Societies who assisted with archaeological excavations.

Divers Rolfe Mitchinson and Bob Middlemass, who found the Roman treasure on the bed of the River Tees at Piercebridge.

Retired bridge builder Bob Robson for his information on Roman and other period bridges in Northumberland.

Gordon Heald, Institute of Civil Engineers, Northampton, for his advice on the design of the Roman dam/weir at Piercebridge.

Pat Jones, former Commodore of the Ripon Motor Boat Club, for his vast information on inland waterways.

Brenda Locke, aircraft co-pilot/observer.

Tom Wright, air photographer/observer.

Civil engineer John V Smith of Croxton Kerrial for his survey of the Tay.

Dr Eric Clavering for his information on the River Wear.

Andy Davison for his finds of suspected Roman roads.

Geoffrey N Wright, author of *The Northumbrian Uplands,* who discovered the rock-cut paving in the Simonside Hills.

Steve Marchant for his photographic expertise.

Brian Atkinson, for his model of a Roman bridge pier.

Norman Cassidy for his model of the spillway of a Roman dam/weir.

Joe Cassidy for the use of his private archaeological library.

Neville Andison for his advice on engineering subjects.

Gordon Henderson for his help with the exploration of Binchester.

Dr Irene Robinson for her professional use of a metal detector.

Liz Robinson (BBC) also for her expert use of a metal detector.

Elizabeth Anderson who grew rice in her garden.

Margaret Whyte, New College, Durham, historical adviser.

Tom Gray, ex RAF pilot, for his assistance with fieldwork.

Ernest W Sockett, retired university lecturer and archaeologist, for his information on past excavations in Northumberland, and for his assistance with historic references and Latin translations.

Elizabeth Waller of Piercebridge who brought to my notice the post-holes of the hitherto unknown Roman weir (W4) in the bed of the Tees opposite Holme House Farm Roman villa.

Sue Brown for her translations of Professor Grenier's works.

Messrs Faber & Faber for permission to reproduce T S Eliot's Little Gidding.

R B Nelson and P W Norris for permission to reproduce drawings of ancient ships from *Warfleets of Antiquity.*

The Imperial War Museum for permission to reproduce the photograph of R.N.A.S. airship.

All of the farmers and landowners who have allowed me access to their land.

All of those hundreds of members of the general public who have kept up my morale with their letters of support and snippets of valuable information.

Foreword

In 1983, Raymond Selkirk wrote a book entitled *The Piercebridge Formula*. It was one of the most controversial archaeological books of recent years, and was inspired by the author's experiences as an air survey pilot for a professor of archaeology. Because of his background and training, Raymond Selkirk was able to identify evidence missed by most pilots. This experience included several years as a ship's officer prior to entering commercial aviation. He served with many airlines world-wide, and also spent some time flying photographic survey aircraft in central Africa. His interest in archaeology led him to take an honours degree in the subject, and he won the Martin Harrison prize at Newcastle upon Tyne University for his dissertation on the lost Roman roads of northern England.

His *Piercebridge Formula* won an international prize in Switzerland in 1984 - a Rolex Award for Exploration. This was presented in London by Dr Vivian Fuchs, the Antarctic explorer. The views expressed in *The Piercebridge Formula* opposed those of many British archaeologists but the general public received the book enthusiastically and hundreds of supportive letters were received. Many archaeologists are being forced to accept Selkirk's point of view following his increasing volume of new evidence. This is his story.

Tom Wright,

Chairman of the Northern Archaeology Group.

Introduction

This book is about a search for new evidence of the Roman military occupation of Britain. Unexpected archaeological discoveries have altered the whole accepted concept of Roman army logistics. Two thousand year old evidence is often hard to come by, but little changes in armies. It is therefore possible to find parallel answers to Roman problems from the experiences of other armies. No excuse therefore is made for introducing into this work, the solutions and failures which range from those of of Hilter's *Wehrmacht* to Alexander the Great's conquests.

In 1939, the French army and British Expeditionary Force sat behind the extremely well fortified Maginot Line and faced the German army which was equally well protected by its Siegfried Line. Very little happened during the months of what was termed "The Phoney War." It was like a chess game before the first move.

Both the Maginot and Siegfried lines were networks of defences in depth, and two thousand years earlier, the Romans called their own similar frontier grids, *limes*.

In April 1940, the Germans made the first move in the chess game by going off the side of the board to invade neutral Denmark and Norway. In May they disobeyed the rules again, this time on the Western Front, by going round the end of the Maginot Line through neutral Belgium. The German *Blitzkreig* (lightning war) which followed is well remembered by my generation who, after the subsequent fall of France, faced a well organised enemy army across a very narrow sea. In many ways, Hitler's army resembled the Roman army but whereas the German army never attempted to invade Britain, the Romans did it three times. The reasons for the German failure will be explained in detail in due course.

After a very good start to their war, the Germans made mistakes and suffered reverses. Four years after their swift conquest of France and most of Europe and North Africa, they found themselves defending their own German homeland, with the Russians encroaching on the east and the Anglo-Americans and allies on the west. The German military might had lasted only five years. The Roman legions, which both Hitler and Mussolini tried to emulate, had dominated their neighbours for eight hundred years and occupied most of Britain for four hundred.

As the Germans were forced back across their own frontiers in 1945, they withdrew through their own Siegfried *limes* (fortified grid) of 1939. Their strong points were difficult to detect from the air because Mother Nature, in only five years, had provided excellent camouflage in the way of grass and undergrowth. Today's archaeological reconnaissance pilots who search for signs of the Roman army in Britain are faced with sixteen hundred years of such natural camouflage. Even so, for reasons which will be explained shortly, from time to time, under certain conditions, ancient sites reveal themselves to airborne searchers. Most of the time however, the Roman fortifications lie hidden underneath our pleasant countryside, and while an aircraft is a useful tool, its use is not obligatory. This book will attempt to show how any observant field walker can detect from ground level, the most important clues left behind from our four hundred year period of occupation. Those clues are of course, the Roman roads. A few of them are marked by mediaeval and modern roads but many miles still lie unknown and unrecognised. After the Roman military withdrawal from Britain, these roads were unused by the Saxons except as land boundaries. They subsequently became disguised as field walls, hedge lines, footpaths, bridleways and farm tracks.

A combination of research, map interpretation and keen observation is all that is required to convert a field walker into an explorer in his own land. Hundreds, possibly thousands, of miles of Roman roads remain to be found in Britain (and elsewhere). What was the purpose of this vast network? The main answer is: military police action by an army of occupation for the fast, all-weather deployment of infantry and cavalry. Our impractical historians attempt to depict Roman roads as supply lines with strings of military ox-wagons mixed up with commercial transport. Clearly these gentlemen have neither examined Roman roads closely nor ever tried to move heavy goods across country. Most Roman roads ignore gradients as they switchback up and down the hills and valleys. A recently discovered Roman road in Northumberland goes right over the peak of a hill which is capped by a pre-historic tumulus (NZ 075 768), whereas a deviation of a few hundred yards would have taken it around the base. Three hundred yards further north, a recently discovered fortlet (NZ 075 773) sits on a cliff edge. Beyond the fortlet, the Roman road makes an angled dive down the cliff with a slope of one-in-three. A modern tracked military vehicle would have trouble either climbing this road or controlling a descent.

To compound the mystery, the Roman roads in Britain were surfaced with gravel. It does not take much to stop a wheel which is bearing a heavy load. In a modern factory where a machine is being repositioned on the factory floor by means of rollers, a stone the size of a pea will bring the whole operation to a halt and this is on a smooth horizontal concrete floor; not a one-in-three gradient on gravel-strewn Roman road. The answers to the problems will become apparent to readers in due course.

I know of only two long distance Roman roads which make any attempt to reduce gradients by meanders, and these are special cases. Both roads transit the narrow isthmus of Northern England between the estuary of the River Tyne and the Solway Firth. The first is the Stanegate Roman road, which runs to the south of Hadrian's Wall, and the second, the Roman Military Way which formed an integral part of the Hadrianic frontier, and ran the full length of the multiple barrier, following the strip between the Wall and the north mound of the *Vallum*. This Roman "Military Way" is not to be confused with General Wade's "Military Road" of 1753, (Wade planned it, but he died before work commenced on it). It used Hadrian's Wall as a quarry and a foundation for many miles in the eastern sector. Fortunately, the builders took a different line west of the North Tyne, otherwise the Roman Wall would have been completely destroyed.

The reason for Wade's road was that in the 1745 Scottish rebellion, he had difficulty getting his artillery along the bad roads in the Tyne Gap. His road was intended for quick reaction in any future campaign. It is significant to note that he avoided the length of Roman Wall on the central crags and sought lower ground to ease the way for his heavy artillery.

After the earlier Scottish rebellion in 1715, Wade had built many military roads in the Highlands in the 1720's. These quickly fell into disuse and were useless as commercial roads because he copied the Roman road planning methods of going straight up and over the high ground. These Highland military roads were meant for police action by swiftly moving, lightly loaded "anti-terrorist forces." If the later commercial traffic couldn't use Wade's roads, how did the Roman ox-wagons cope with the earlier but very similar Roman military roads? This book will attempt to provide the answers.

The Rev J Collingwood Bruce, in his *Roman Wall*, 1867, tells us that while the Roman Wall shoots over the highest and steepest summits, the Roman Military Way just behind it takes a slightly easier route as far as the limits of Wall and *Vallum* allowed. Even so, on page 76, the famous historian challenges wagon-drivers of his day to negotiate the steep inclines of this Roman Military Way, with laden vehicles. If this was an "easy-gradient" Roman road, imagine what the difficult ones were like.

To the south of the Wall, the Stanegate Roman road, probably built by Agricola, uncharacteristically meanders here and there in a most un-Roman fashion. Until General Wade's military road of 1753, there was no modern through-road between Newcastle upon Tyne and Carlisle. For the central part of the journey, prior to 1753, carriers resorted to the old Roman Stanegate road and Military Way of the Wall and were forced to use pack-horses as even the the two "easy gradient roads" were unsuitable for wheeled traffic.

In his *Roman Roads in Britain,* David E Johnston comments on similar problems. He discusses the transportation of Roman lead ingots from the Mendip mines to a port in Southampton, and suggests that a steep gradient on the route would have halved the loads and doubled the costs. He thinks that the last part of the journey was by river and that the use of inland water transport by the Romans was far more extensive than is usually portrayed. The truth of this statement will explode into clear view as new evidence is revealed in the forthcoming chapters.

Before the production of new evidence, it is necessary to familiarise potential hunters for signs of the Romans, with the various search techniques available to them. It is also essential that field walkers are able to recognise handiwork of ancient peoples other than the Romans.

Chapter 1

Aerial Searches

OPERTA APERTA

(Hidden things are revealed)
Motto of 16 [Air Reconnaissance] Squadron, Royal Flying Corps

Nature's target markers

It is well known that under certain conditions, tell-tale marks manifest themselves in open country and if viewed from above, the shapes of these marks often reveal the location and identity of buried features. These give-away marks can be seen as differential colouring of vegetation above buried features (crop marks); white-outlined shapes produced by a thin dusting of snow collecting in slight hollows, or drifting along ridges (snow marks); shapes visible in bare ground where the farmer has filled in an old ditch with a different coloured soil (soil marks); and shadowy shapes produced by low angle sunlight outlining undulations almost imperceptible at ground level (shadow marks).

The manifestations were observed long before the development of aeroplanes. About 1715, the antiquarian William Stukeley was ridiculed when he said that from a hilltop, he could see the distinctive shape of a Roman temple in a field of corn. Pioneer balloonists also reported similar sightings but it was not until the tremendous expansion of aviation in the 1914-18 World War that serious notice was taken of the phenomena. The various types of marks are explained as follows.

Crop marks

For crop marks to show, two conditions must be met. Firstly, the right type of crop must be planted in the field which contains the hidden archaeological site (cereal crops give the best results by far) and secondly, a drought or period of dry weather be experienced. The ancient peoples were enthusiastic ditch-diggers and even though infilled, these deep cuttings in the subsoil retain water and during dry weather, the roots of a cereal easily penetrate the loose infill with the result that the crop over the ditch grows taller, thicker and of a deeper shade of green. This is know as a "positive crop mark." Where the hard subsoil has not been disturbed, the crop's roots reach the level of the subsoil and stop, resulting in a uniform shade of medium green.

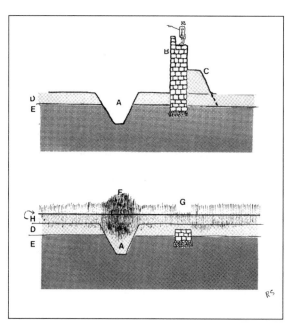

Above

A Roman ditch outside fort wall.
B Fort Wall.
C Earth rampart behind fort wall.
D Topsoil growth since Roman times.
E Subsoil

Below

A The Roman ditch is still there, but full of topsoil, and the fort wall and rampart have gone.
F During a dry spell, the cereal crop can send its roots into deeper and damper topsoil in the old Roman ditch, and the crop grows thicker and higher, causing a positive crop mark.
G The crop's growth is stunted over the Roman foundations, causing a negative crop mark.
H The present level of the surface is about two feet higher than the surface in Roman times. This is caused largely by earthworm action.

Over old foundations or road metalling, the crop grows stunted and of a yellow-green colour. This is a "negative crop mark." When a cereal crop is ripe, the positive crop mark is still visible as a deeper gold colour and the negative mark as a more watery-yellow.

What Stukeley had seen from his hilltop was the crop mark of a Roman temple. About the same period, negative crop marks were reported in France over the ploughed-out remains of circular burial mounds. On these, plant growth was sparse and they were known locally in northern France as *danses de fées* (fairy dances).

Even after the crop is harvested, the thick growth over the infilled ditch can be seen as a deeper colour in the remaining stubble and a suitable name for this would be a "stubble mark."

Crop marks can show up in plants other than cereals, such as peas and beans or sugar beet, but the contrasting marks in these and other crops are much inferior to those produced by wheat, oats and barley.

Identification of sites

The identity of the site is determined by the shape of the crop/snow/shadow/soil mark. If it is square or rectangular with rounded corners, it is highly likely that the constructors were from the Roman army. If it is an irregular quadrilateral with a gateway on the eastern side, then the originators were Roman-period British (Celtic) farmers. Circular ditches usually surrounded the defended pre-Roman Iron Age Celtic settlements. Other archaeological sites such as prehistoric religious monuments (henges) and burial mounds (barrows) had their own distinctive shapes. There will be a more detailed explanation of site identification later.

Old foundations of walls are buried not because the stonework is sinking

The Roman fort at Birrens (Blatobulgium), Dumfries & Galloway. The fort is a standing earthwork but the annexe, normally invisible, is showing as a triple-ditched crop mark.

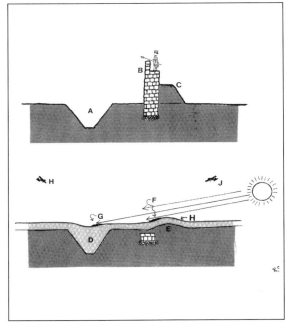

Top

Roman defences with ditch **A**, fort wall **B**, and earth rampart **C**.

Bottom
The same site almost 2,000 years later.

The fort wall **B** has been robbed for building materials.

The ditch **D** has been filled in, but a slight depression, difficult to detect at ground level, still exists.

The earth rampart has almost gone but leaves a slight ridge **E**, also difficult to detect at ground level. In low angle sunlight, shadows are cast by the remains of the rampart at **F** and by the lip of the slight depression at **G**.

The down-sun side of the ancient ditch is also highlighted. An observer in the aircraft at **J** does not see the shadows, but as the aircraft circles into the down-sun position at **H**, the whole shape of the Roman fort is revealed by the shadows.

but by earthworm action. Every night, the worms push up their casts and the end result is approximately an extra foot of soil above the ancient ground level for every thousand years of elapsed time. Windblown debris also assist the build-up. This rate of burial refers to open country. In towns where each generation flattens buildings and starts again on top of the rubble, the ancient habitation layers can be twenty or thirty feet below the modern surface. In the Middle East, this continuous elevation of habitation levels is exaggerated in the *tells* (Arabic for mound or hill) which rise above the plains as artificial hills, produced by a long accumulation of mud bricks. New villages are constantly erected on top of the remnants of the old.

With regard to earthworm action; as the level of the soil rises, the Earth does not increase in diameter; gravity keeps it in shape. Therefore, hundreds of thousands of years of earthworm activities are not increasing our planet's size.

Soil marks

These marks are useful in winter and do not rely on a combination of cereal crops and a drought. Quite often when a farmer has infilled an old ditch, the soil he has used is of a different colour and is easily visible from an aircraft. Sites which show up as soil marks in bare fields in winter invariably produce crop marks in the other seasons if the right conditions are met.

Shadow marks

Many fields are in permanent pasture and have not been cultivated for hundreds of years or even longer. If the surface of such a field contains very slight undulations such as the last remnants of ancient earthworks and ditches, these may be invisible to the observer at ground level, but when viewed from an aircraft in low-angle sunlight in early morning or late evening and especially in winter and spring when the grass is short and the sun's altitude small, the shape of the whole habitation appears as if by magic. One side of the almost flattened earthwork is highlighted and the other casts a shadow. The almost invisible ditch likewise has one side highlighted with the other in shadow. Thus the whole shape of the site is revealed. The marks show best when the aircraft is down-sun of the site so searches for shadow marks should be conducted in a series of advancing circles.

The British archaeologist Sir Leonard Woolley (1880-1960), who excavated Ur in 1922-9 was attempting earlier to locate an ancient Egyptian cemetery below the Second Cataract of the Nile near Wadi Halfa. This site had eluded Sir Leonard and the expedition leader, D R MacIver, but one evening after a hard day's search, the two men climbed a hill to view the sunset. In the low-angled sunlight, strange circles, invisible at ground level, appeared at the base of the hill. As Sir Leonard descended, the circles disappeared, but MacIver who had remained behind was able to direct him to the positions with hand signals. Sir Leonard marked them with small cairns. Next day, workers excavated the marked positions and found a tomb at every one.

When crop mark conditions are present, the corn or barley grows higher over the infilled ditch and in low-angle sunlight, this casts a shadow and an excellent combination of crop marks and shadow marks is obtained.

During the nineteenth century, soldiers who had served at Gibraltar said that when they looked from the top of the rock, towards the Spanish border to the north, they could see the remains of the old Spanish lines which were invisible at ground level.

Snow marks

Snow marks are rather like shadow marks etched with a white paint brush. Faint traces of earthworks are necessary and in a light dusting of snow, the ditch is painted with a bright white band. A bank, even a slight one, causes drifting and a combination of snow marks and low-angle-sun shadow marks can produce a most striking result.

Heavy snow obliterates all signs of the site but during the thaw, the snow remains in the ditch long after the remainder of the field is clear. Possibly the latter would be better called "melt marks." Closely related to melt marks are *"frost marks"* ; when a field is covered by frost, ancient stonework below ground level retains heat better than the surrounding soil and the line of the foundation is revealed by the absence of frost, and shows as a dark line.

Parch marks

Crop marks do not normally show up in grassland but during a period of hot dry weather, lawns and pastures which hide buried roads or stone foundations reveal their secrets when the grass above the stonework or metalling becomes scorched and turns brown.

A suspected Roman fort at Press Mains Farm, NT 883 653, north of Berwick upon Tweed. Half of the rectangle is showing as a crop mark in the field at the left, the other half, as shadow marks in rough pasture at the right. If this site is genuine, then it means that the Devil's Causeway Roman road did not terminate at Berwick.

A suspected double-ditched Roman fort at Elstob, NZ 338 240, County Durham, showing as a soil mark caused by the farmer filling in old ditches with different coloured soil. The Modern road in the background is on top of a Roman road which runs from Brough on Humber to Newcastle upon Tyne. North is to right.

Plant marks

Some wild flowers and weeds like to grow over old stonework and quite often, a field with a buried line of stone develops a prominent line of flowering weeds above the invisible foundations. Poppies have an affinity for the wetter infilled ditches outside the ramparts of Iron Age British hillforts.

Wind marks

When positive crop marks are present, the cereal growth above the ditch is higher than that over the rest of the field. Strong winds can strike the projecting tops and the end result is that the corn is flattened along the lines of the ditches.

Mediaeval "rig and furrow" agriculture on top of the Roman *vicus* (civil settlement) beside Halton (Onnum) Roman fort on Hadrian's Wall.
The foundations of a line of suspected Roman houses can be seen in the corner of the field in the centre of the photograph. This view is to the south and the aircraft is directly above the Roman fort.

Spurious marks

Where horses or goats have been tethered, they may have grazed circles of grass which can look like the marks of Iron Age huts when viewed from an aircraft.

Circular bands of dark grass caused by fungi (fairy rings) can also look like the marks left by ancient rondavels.

A straight track of stunted grass across a field need not be evidence of an ancient road. It may be an animal path, the cattle having been kept in a straight line by a thin electrified wire invisible to the airborne searcher.

In the last few years, strange circles have appeared in cornfields, each year's marks becoming more complex. They are not agricultural marks and have been caused by the corn being flattened by practical jokers, many of whom have admitted their involvement. They are formed by a walker with boards on his feet, making circles of increasing radius from a central spike. On some aerial photographs, stilt-holes can be seen which show how the humorists gained access to the centre of the field without disturbing the crop. The most amazing thing was the acceptance of the sites by some scientists of high standing. These gentlemen are normally the first to resist even genuine new evidence, never mind "duck-board circles" supposedly caused by "impacts of rotating plasma," whatever that means.

Summary

Wherever the hand of man has disturbed the soil, the resulting differences of soil density or colour, water content, undulations (humps and bumps), heat retention etc, periodically show some kind of phenomena which are visible to an airborne observer.

Our search areas can be likened to a "palimpsest." That is a manuscript on which the original script has been effaced to make room for a second writing. Parts of the surface of lowland Britain for example, have Celtic field systems overlain by signs of Roman occupation and this in turn almost obliterated by the mediaeval rig and furrow strip-field system. Modern agriculture obliterates all three except for occasional crop marks. Shadow marks in permanent pasture sometimes show traces of all the periods and then it is up to the photographic interpreter to identify and separate the evidence.

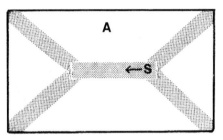
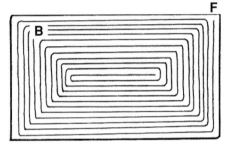

Many fields have in them what are usually referred to as "envelope patterns."
These are caused by the farmer commencing ploughing at point **S** on diagram **A**. The farmer ploughs round and round the initial furrow, and the four diagonal lines result from the plough being lifted at the corners.

In diagram **B**, the farmer has finished ploughing and has left the field, at **F**.

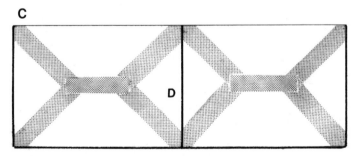

In diagram **C**, two adjoining fields have envelope marks showing as soil or crop marks, and the unwary aerial observer may think that he has located a square archaeological site at **D**.

Classroom simulation of shadow marks

If you wish to demonstrate an archaeological palimpsest to students, it can be done by overlaying two sheets of paper; on the top sheet, draw heavily with a pencil or ball-point, a pattern of irregular squares and rectangles to represent Celtic fields. Then, superimpose on these fields a perfect rectangle with rounded corners; this is the shape of a typical Roman fort. Over the top of all these lines, heavily sketch long parallel strips to depict mediaeval rig and furrow agriculture. Remove the top sheet to reveal a jumble of indented lines on the second. Draw the curtains or dim the lights, and to simulate low-angle sunlight, shine a torch almost horizontally from the side of the paper. All the lines immediately become visible as shadow marks and the student with a knowledge of the various shapes will pick them out.

Stereoscopic photography

Using certain techniques and a simple optical device, pairs of photographs can be arranged to produce three-dimensional images. Two aerial photographs of the same target are taken from, for example, the left-hand window of an aircraft, with a short interval between exposures, during which time the aircraft has travelled some distance thus slightly altering the angle of view. The two photographs are placed side by side on a table with the first to be taken on the left and the second on the right. An instrument with two eyepiece lenses mounted on a bridge is placed over the top of the photographs and the left eye looks at the left photograph and the right eye, the right. The ground-zero features on both photographs will appear identical to both the observer's eyes and the two photographs will be seen as one. Due to the slightly different viewing angle of the two photographs, objects above the ground such as the top of a factory chimney, will appear to be in slightly different positions.

The human eye judges distances by the angle the eyes turn inwards. The degree of cross-eye is greater for a near object than a distant one, when for the latter, the eye directions are almost parallel. This angling of the eyes, signals to the brain the distance of the object and this is nature's equivalent of the rangefinder of a naval gun. In order to get the top of the factory chimney into focus and merge the two displaced images, the eyes unconsciously turn inwards and outwards many times a second as they alternately look at ground-zero and then the chimney top. The brain sees this as a three dimensional image with the factory chimney sticking up out of the photograph.

To a lesser degree, all objects such as trees and bushes appear to rise up out of the photograph. Depressions seem to be sunk into the photograph. If the photographs are accidentally reversed, chimneys look like wells, ditches like walls and hills like hollows.

If the interval between photograph exposures is extended, the height and depth of features are exaggerated and the slightest earthwork, maybe only a few inches high, looks like a high wall and becomes instantly obvious to the observer.

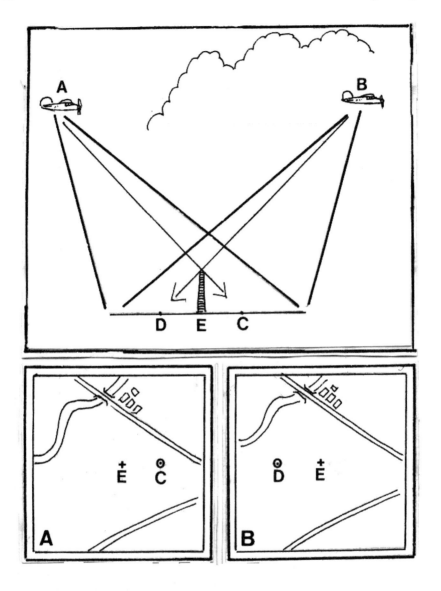

To take stereoscopic pairs of photographs, which give a 3D effect, the aircraft is flown in a straight line, and two photographs of the same target area (or overlapping areas) are taken at positions A and B. The two photographs are identical except that on photo **A**. the top of the tall chimney **E**, is seen at **C**, and on photo **B**, at **D**.

When the photographs are placed side by side and viewed through a stereoscope, with the left eye looking at the left photograph and the right eye, the right, the human brain sees just one photograph. The top of the chimney however, appears as a double image, and the eyes cross slightly to merge them into one image. This constant flexing of the eyes signals a three-dimensional image to the brain. In practice, it works for objects of any height and not just for tall buildings.

If the delay between photographs is increased, the 3D effect is also increased, and a factory chimney can appear as if it is 1,000 feet high, and a moderately tall building looks like a skyscraper. The advantage however, is that a slight mound in open country can be exaggerated to look like a 6 ft high embankment.

Oblique and vertical photographs

We have a choice of two types of photographs, oblique or vertical. Each type has its advantages. Pictures taken from the side window of an aircraft are oblique types but if a steep angle of aircraft bank is used, they can become near-vertical. In an oblique photograph, a tree looks like a tree and a house like a house. In a vertical photograph, a tree looks like a blotch and a house like a square. The vertical photograph is very useful for map-making but to take them, an aircraft has to be specially modified with a hole or hatch in the floor, and a complex mounting to eliminate camera-shake.

Vertical photographs are usually taken by the RAF, for mapping, or by survey companies for mineral prospecting. These surveys are seldom carried out with archaeology in mind and are therefore conducted during the best possible lighting conditions, i.e. midday and in summer. For this reason, neither shadow marks nor snow marks are seen. Now and again crop marks appear. One collection of military photographs does however show many archaeological sites, and these photographs were taken by German reconnaissance aircraft during the 1939-45 war. These aeroplanes sneaked over Britain at dawn and dusk, and as well as military targets, the shadow marks of many archaeological sites can be seen on the photographs. The German government has released hundreds of such photographs to British researchers.

Infra-red photography

Infra-red film can be useful for the detection of buried sites when visible light phenomena are not showing. Also this method detects soil disturbances under crops other than cereals but it is difficult to get the length of exposure correct. The resulting colour photographs do not show the natural colours but in archaeology, it is contrast we are looking for and we do not care if a field shows up as pink as long as the archaeological site is a different shade of pink.

An introduction to aircraft operations

The most suitable aircraft for archaeological searches are single-engine, high-wing types, with opening side windows. One engine means minimum flying costs; the high wing gives the photographer an excellent view of the ground and the opening window avoids perspex degrading the quality of the photographs. Both the two seat Cessna 150 and its bigger brother, the four seat Cessna 172 are suitable aircraft for archaeological reconnaissance, but in the 172, only the left-hand side window opens. The Piper Cub is also a suitable aircraft and in this type, the two crew-members sit in tandem. The advantage of this arrangement is that the photographer can select his targets from either side of the aircraft. Windows on both sides can be opened.

International Law deems all aircraft to be of the left-hand-drive category, so with side-by-side pilot seating, the captain occupies the left-hand seat. In the Cessna 172, the captain must fly from the right-hand seat thus allowing the photographer access to the opening window. This causes few problems but many light aircraft do not have all the main flight instruments repeated in front of the co-pilot so the pilot must frequently glance sideways across the cockpit.

To photograph an archaeological site, the pilot orbits the target at about 1,500 feet (in aviation, in most countries, heights are still quoted in feet and not metres) with a fairly steep angle of bank, and the photographer on the inside of the turn. The photographer keeps his hands well clear of the aircraft structure as vibrations can cause camera-shake. If the pilot has judged the rate of turn correctly, the target remains almost stationary underneath the aircraft, and merely rotates in the photographer's viewfinder. Owing to the slow movement of the relatively distant target below, and the usually good lighting conditions, a fine-grained and fairly slow film with an ASA rating of say, 100 can be used. Two cameras should be carried in the aircraft, one loaded with black and white film to record shadow marks, and one with colour to capture the crop marks. As many sites show a combination of marks, both black and white and colour shots should be taken of every worthwhile target.

Hand signals are generally used by the archaeologist or photographer to indicate to the pilot when to turn, increase or decrease the radius of turn, and when to straighten out.

If a strong wind is blowing, the pilot must execute an egg-shaped turn in the air which will produce a perfect circle relative to the ground. The aircraft at all times must be flown at its normal speed-for-weight and angle-of-bank in the turn (the stalling speed of an aircraft increases in a turn). Archaeologists have been known to ask pilots to fly as slowly as possible during photography but this is a dangerous practice. When we talk about an aircraft stalling, we do not mean that the engine has stopped; the aeronautical use of the word means that the wing has stopped lifting. A wing depends for its lift on a smooth stream of air passing over and under it. Due to the airfoil shape, the air over the top surface is accelerated causing upward suction (lift) and also, a high pressure is created on the undersurface resulting in more lift. Over two-thirds of the lift is supplied by the upper surface. As aircraft speed is reduced, there is a critical airflow speed below which the wing ceases to lift and becomes a useless piece of metal. This is the stalling speed of the wing. In a turn, the inside wing moves slower than the outside one and if the speed is near the critical stalling speed, the inside wing stalls first and becomes useless while the outer one continues flying. The resulting violent rotating descent is known as a "spin" and a lot of height can be lost in the recovery.

Readers must forgive me if I seem to be labouring this technical point but it is intended as a warning to young pilots who, as a result of this book, may consider volunteering for archaeological searches. An American pilot friend of mine used to say: "Ninety-nine per-cent aint a passmark in aviation!"

During the steep turns required for archaeological searches, it must be remembered that centrifugal force increases the weight of the aircraft and therefore also raises the stalling speed. A stall in a steep turn, compounded with inadvertent use of top rudder, can result in violent reactions and is not recommended if one is carrying an archaeologist or photographer of a nervous disposition.

Some readers may be interested in the actual handling of the aircraft, and it is always useful for a crew member to be able to fly the machine if necessary. Most people soon get the hang of straight and level flight and gentle turns, and although the following has nothing to do with archaeology, it may help potential air photographers or air observers to understand the technique of getting the aeroplane back on the ground.

An intentional stall is used when landing an aircraft. On the approach-to-land, flaps are lowered on the trailing edges of the wings and these reduce the stalling speed. The final approach to the runway is made down the extended runway centre-line, at a descent angle of three degrees and with an airspeed of stalling speed plus about ten per-cent. As the aircraft skims over the runway threshold, power is cut right back and the nose is raised so that the machine mushes along just above the runway, nose-high, with the speed decaying towards the stall. If the pilot has judged it right, the wings stop lifting when the main wheels are a couple of inches off the ground and the tyres contact the runway with a satisfying squeal. If the stall occurs several feet above the runway, the aircraft drops with a bone-shattering thud. If the aeroplane contacts the runway with speed in excess of the stall, it is deflected back into the air and this is known as a "bounce."

Once the main wheels have contacted the ground, the nose is lowered with a release of back-pressure on the stick and the nose-wheel then contacts the runway. The flying machine has now become an ungainly ground vehicle.

Some of the aircraft used in archaeology, such as the Piper Cub have the old fashioned "tail-wheel" type undercarriage and on landing, the aircraft is held off the ground, nose-high, in the "mushing-along" stage. The idea is to place all three wheels on the ground together as the aircraft stalls. This is known as a "three-pointer." The main advantage of the tail-wheel type aircraft, better known as a "taildragger," is that it can be operated from fairly rough grass fields and on occasion, this is extremely useful for the flying archaeologist.

At all times during a flight, one of the pilots or crew must keep a lookout for other aircraft. The closing speed of a jet fighter can be a mile in four seconds and air traffic control seldom exists over the countryside away from the airport control zones and airways systems. Most of the worlds airways only start at five thousand feet and military aircraft have a habit of practising in "free-for-all airspace" away from zones and airways and quite often, just where we are looking for archaeological sites.

The use of an aircraft for archaeological searches has an advantage seldom mentioned. That is, permission to cross private land does not have to be obtained. The aircraft sweeps over the high estate walls and gamekeeper-patrolled woods without the need of a single telephone call. The humorous words of Woodie Guthrie express this:

> "Was a big high wall there that tried to stop me. A sign was painted said: Private Property, But on the other side, it didn't say nuthin', That side was made for you and me."

The Pathfinders

No work on aerial archaeology would be complete without a mention of the pioneer searchers. One of these was the famous O G S Crawford who served as a major in the Royal Flying Corps in the 1914-18 war. Major Crawford flew two-seater reconnaissance aircraft and he was the aircraft's observer; that is the old term for the crew member who was a combined navigator/radio operator/ photographer/bombardier and gunner.

Osbert Guy Stanhope Crawford was born in 1886 in Bombay where his father was a High Court judge. Both his parents died when he was in his infancy and he was brought up by two elderly maiden aunts in England. He was a solitary boy and the Hampshire area where he grew up was full of the ghosts of a remote past. The young Crawford was intrigued by the *tumuli,* earthworks and field systems which were scattered across the Downs, and whenever possible, his spare time was spent searching, mapping, drawing, collecting and digging. He was particularly interested in what he thought were the remains of a prehistoric cultivation system, and he made extensive maps of the rectangular *lynchets* (step-like features on a hillside) which he called *Celtic* lynchets to distinguish them from the post-Roman, mediaeval cultivation strips usually known as "rig and furrow" or "ridge and furrow." There is no absolute dating evidence for the beginning of rig and furrow, but Crawford was convinced that it had been introduced into Britain by the Saxon invaders in the post-Roman period. He would return to the subject after his studies at Oxford, and a period of military service in the war which was looming.

Crawford entered Oxford to read classics, but switched to geography. In 1913, he joined the archaeologist Sir Henry Wellcome in the Sudan and first came into contact with aerial photographs which were taken from box-kites. Then the war intervened and he first saw service in the infantry. Later he was employed on mapping and photography, and he finally transferred to the Royal Flying Corps as an observer.

His flying career had introduced him to the phenomena of crop marks which he called *streak marks.* Some of these had probably saved his, and his pilot's life one day when they were disorientated in poor visibility behind the German lines. Crawford recognised the distinctive parallel lines of marks above the side-ditches of a Roman road which he had discovered on a previous flight. They were able to follow this buried Roman road back to the allied lines. He was not so lucky on another occasion and ended up in a German prisoner of war camp. During his many months of captivity at Landshut, from which he escaped but was recaptured, and at Holzminden, he had plenty of time to ponder over archaeological questions. After the war, he became Archaeology Officer at the Ordnance Survey.

Like all explorers and finders of new evidence, Crawford experienced scepticism from disbelievers in some quarters, who regarded his techniques as what today would be called *"fringe archaeology".* A trial excavation of one of his crop mark sites vindicated him and he is now recognised as the father figure of the aerial archaeological discipline.

Unfortunately, we have always had cloister-bound self-accredited experts who belittle new evidence. The German geographical explorers of East Africa in the nineteenth century were lampooned when they reported snow-capped, twenty-thousand-feet mountains almost on the equator. The sages in Berlin, Paris and London said that it was impossible for ice-caps to exist on the equator.

Even the great Ptolemy, the famous Greek geographer of Alexandria, could be mistaken. He had a theory that Africa was connected to India by a land bridge around the southern edge of the Indian Ocean. Writing in the second century AD, he dismissed the findings of the Phoenician sailors who had been sent by Pharoah Necho about 600 BC to find out if Africa could be circumnavigated. These Phoenicians spent three years on the voyage which began in the Red Sea and returned via Gibraltar. They camped for months on end at various suitable places in order to grow crops. Ptolemy rejected their account of the voyage because they had said that on rounding the southern cape of Africa, the midday sun was in the northern sky. This of course was excellent proof that they had indeed sailed well into the southern hemisphere and rounded Africa, beating Bartolomeu Dias to it by over two thousand years. Dias sailed the other way, from west to east, in 1487, and got as far as Algoa Bay before returning home the way he had come. In 1498, Vasgo da Gama made it all the way from Portugal to India and back again.

Not so many years ago, archaeologists from all over Europe immediately dismissed the theory by a French historian that the cave-paintings discovered by children in central France, were the work of Stone Age artists.

Let us forget about those who pour cold water on new knowledge, and return to those magnificent men and their flying machines.

After the 1914-18 war, Crawford continued his work on ancient agriculture. He was sure that the Celtic fields in England had lasted for almost a thousand years, right through the Roman occupation. His aerial photographs revealed that southern England in the Iron Age was definitely under intense agriculture. This disputes the old theory that Britain was just one gigantic forest during the Roman period. It also explains the Romans' extensive use of cavalry and how they were able to exact their taxes in the form of grain.

There is literary evidence to substantiate Crawford's findings. Pytheas, a famous geographer and navigator of the fourth century BC, Julius Caesar (c100-44 BC) and Diodorus Siculus, A Greek writer (c80-c29 BC) all mention British farming. Pliny the Elder, a Roman writer and administrator, writing about AD 70, quotes the use of chalk by British farmers for fertilizing their fields: "The chalk is dug from shafts, often a hundred feet deep, with narrow tops but spreading out below." On some of Crawford's aerial photographs, there are white spots at the end of lynchets. These may mark some of the pits described by Pliny.

On one occasion, Crawford was able to conduct an aerial search for a Saxon fortification on the strength of a reference in a Saxon charter of 982, to an *eorth-burgh* (earthwork-fortification), and rediscovered it from the air as a huge semi-circle of poppies in a field of oats.

Crawford's studies were assisted by members of his former flying service which had changed from an army regiment, the Royal Flying Corps, to an independent service, the Royal Air Force, on 1st April 1918. The RAF made aerial photographs available to Crawford and encouraged its pilots to practice the art of reconnaissance by searching for archaeological sites. The slow-flying, open-cockpit aircraft of the period were very suitable for such searches.

In 1925, Squadron Leader GSM Insall, who had been awarded the Victoria Cross in the war, was on a flight out of his base at Netheravon and from a height of two thousand feet he looked down on what was thought by antiquarians to be the mutilated remains of a very large "disc barrow." To Insall, it looked very much like a much-eroded version of the famous Stonehenge just a couple of miles away. The following year, when the site was under wheat, Insall took a photograph of the crop marks of the so-called "barrow" and the result caused a stir among archaeologists. Insall's photograph suggested that the site had been a wooden version of Stonehenge, and excavations confirmed this and it became known as "Woodhenge." Further monuments of this type, hitherto unknown, were found throughout Britain, and dated to the Neolithic and early Bronze Ages.

During the 14-18 war, a certain Lieutenant-Colonel G A Beazeley of the Royal Engineers, was carrying out an aerial survey of the Tigris-Euphrates plain when about sixty-five miles north-west of Baghdad, he sighted the outlines of canals, and the square grid system of an ancient city. He had discovered the ninth century, "Old Samarra." Beazeley continued to investigate these sites, both from the air and on the ground, but in May 1918, the searches were cut short when he was shot down by an enemy aircraft. Thus another flying archaeologist was awarded ample study time in a prison camp.

After the war, Beazley's accounts were published in the *Geographical Journal* of 1919 and 1920.

Insall, the discover of Woodhenge, arrived in the area and continued Beazley's investigations. He discovered near Baghdad, the former capital, "Seleucia," which had been founded around 300 BC.

During Crawford's visit to the area in 1928-9, Insall was able to fly him over this site and many others in the area with the result that many more blanks were filled in on the maps.

In 1924 help had come to Crawford from a kindred antiquarian, Alexander Keiller, who had been a pilot in the Royal Naval Air Service during the war. An aircraft was hired from the De Havilland company, based at the RAF aerodrome at Weyhill, and a captured German camera installed in the observer's cockpit. The results of this Keiller/Crawford survey were published in *Wessex from the Air* in 1928.

Enter the Priest

In 1925, a French flyer with a very unusual background began investigations in Syria and Mesopotamia. He was Père Poidebard, a Jesuit priest. Father R P Antoine Poidebard, (1878-1955) had worked at the Jesuit Lesser Armenian Mission at Tokar between 1904 and 1907. He had served throughout the war, first as a chaplain in the French army on the Western Front and in 1917 was transferred to the Caucasus as an interpreter.

In 1924, he was appointed to a professorship at the University of St Joseph in Beirut and in 1925, joined the French air force reserve as an observer, with the rank of lieutenant-colonel. Shortly after this, the Geographical Society of France asked him to carry out an investigation of northern Syria. He was to study the economic potential and elucidate the forms of pasturage and agriculture which had once flourished there. He was also to investigate lost irrigation schemes. All this could be best surveyed from the air.

On his very first flight, he was amazed at the number of unknown archaeological sites he could see. Not only was there a profusion of *tells*; in addition he spotted completely unknown evidence of the Roman occupation of the area. During this and subsequent flights, he saw a complete Roman frontier system with forts, fortlets, watchtowers, roads, irrigation channels and field systems. Mostly, the Roman sites were covered by wind-blown sand but still clearly visible as shadow-marks. In the appropriate seasons, areas covered by scrub vegetation produced crop marks and parch marks.

Poidebard used to get his pilot to skim along the lost Roman roads at a height of fifteen feet while he tried to photograph inscriptions on Roman milestones! He thought nothing of landing his old biplane in the middle of the desert in order to dig a quick *sondage* (trial trench) across a buried feature.

Often, he found that once he was on the ground, it was difficult to locate the almost invisible feature seen clearly from above. Initially, his groundwork was not a success and this led to knowing winks and smiles from the sceptics in the learned circles of Paris. There were references to Poidebard's "fantasies of the Jules Verne type."

He was a resourceful man and discovered a unique method of locating Roman roads on the ground, which, from his aerial observations, he knew existed somewhere in the featureless area. He drove a train of camels over the vicinity and soon, the desert beasts established their course along the line of the invisible road. The Roman writer, Vegetius, had also known of the camels' trail-finding abilities; he said: "These animals seemed to have a natural instinct for following in the steps of their long-departed kin."

Poidebard noticed that the Roman frontier roads had evolved from marching routes in a conquered land, into a fortified line, and later formed the basis for a gridwork of defence in depth, or *limes* as the Romans called such a system.

He was also aware that the Roman engineers had often reused Hittite and Assyrian sites and had placed their buildings on the old foundations.

Poidebard found the reason for the alignment of the wide Roman frontier grid. The aerial photographs showed that the Roman *limes* followed the zone of vegetation, and therefore the highest rainfall across the arid desert. This would have given the Romans an effective control over the native Bedouin tribes. He noted the number of impressive barrages and reservoirs, which had fed large-scale irrigation works. He remarked on the way the Romans varied their road construction according to the terrain. Some were paved but others which traversed firm, dry areas merely had kerbstones to mark their courses.

He was truly a remarkable man. His published work *La Trace de Rome dans le désert de Syrie* (Paris, 1934) and *Le Limes de Chalcis* (Paris, 1945) contain pictures and plans of the hundreds of sites he discovered, and remain the standard reference works for the Roman Empire's eastern frontiers.

The French Colonel

Another amazing Frenchman, Colonel Jean Baradez (1895-1969), like Poidebard was a late starter in archaeology. Also like Crawford and Poidebard, he had served in the 1914-18 war. He started his military career in the French mountain brigade. Following serious injuries, he was hospitalised for eighteen months but then applied for training as a pilot. This was denied and he became an observer on captive balloons. After the war, he at last qualified as an air force pilot and also became a navigator and an expert in high altitude reconnaissance and photographic interpretation.

His archaeological searches began in North Africa in 1945 and he was inspired by Poidebard's work. Both aviation and photographic technology had advanced by leaps and bounds, and Baradez used an American-built bomber, a Martin Marauder which could do almost 300 mph with its two 2,000 hp Pratt & Whitney engines, and it could operate on photographic missions at heights of up to 20,000 feet. This class of aircraft was not well suited for the low level photography of individual sites so Baradez used the modern military method of taking grids of high level shots, with the interpretation and search carried out after the flight, with the aid of high powered magnifiers and stereoscopes. Each overlapping photograph covered several square kilometres, and mosaics were built up of the search areas.

When Baradez required medium and low level oblique shots of individual archaeological features, he used a single-engined Piper Cub of the type used by the air force for artillery spotting duties.

Baradez was not a trained archaeologist but he was an expert at picking out enemy camps, vehicles and airstrips so he quickly acquainted himself with the shapes of the various Roman sites and features and then went searching for the Roman army.

In his initial trial programme, he photographed 150 square kilometres in one hour and although this area had been well studied, he confounded the experts with the discovery of a ditch and wall system, similar to Hadrian's Wall in Britain. Baradez was extremely lucky because his *Fossatum Africae*, lay in his trial survey area. His first grid of photographs also produced a hundred kilometres of unknown Roman roads; a Roman fort; thirty fortlets and other buildings associated with these roads; sixty stone towers along the *Fossatum*, many integral with the wall like the turrets on Hadrian's Wall in Britain; several farms and *vici;* and irrigation and field systems. His wonderful finds were published in 1949 in *Fossatum Africae – Vue Aérienne de l'organisation romaine dans le sud-Algérien*. The Algerian war of independence prevented Baradez completing his work and it is extremely unlikely that any future archaeologist will be able to emulate either his skills or his ability to persuade a government department to furnish a powerful bomber.

Britain again

Back in Britain, there had been other aerial surveyors in addition to O G S Crawford. One of the best known was Major George W G Allen, an engineer who owned his own aircraft. His photography was mostly in the Oxford and Thames valley areas, and he must be admired for the excellent results he obtained while flying his De Havilland Puss Moth solo, handling a large,

The Roman complex at Blakehope, on Dere Street , near Elishaw, Northumberland, showing as snow marks. The fort and annexe occupy the centre of an earlier temporary camp. The Roman features are covered with mediaeval rig and furrow agriculture. Towards the River Rede, the rig and furrow has been destroyed by modern ploughing.

unwieldy and complex camera while gripping the aircraft's stick between his knees.

Crawford's work was curtailed during the 1939-45 war and one of his last speaking engagements before the outbreak of hostilities was to a group of *Luftwaffe* officers. A German bomb hit his office during the blitz! The Ashmolean Museum's large collection of Allen's excellent photographs partly compensated for the loss of Crawford's office library at the Ordnance Survey. Crawford said of Allen: "In mere quantity alone, he had discovered more previously unknown ancient sites than any other archaeologist, past or present." Unfortunately, after ten years of aerial searching, Allen was killed in a motorcycle accident at the age of forty-nine.

In 1939, Dr (later Professor) St Joseph carried out some searches but was interrupted by the war. He took up the search again in 1945 and carried out a major aerial search of the whole of Britain on behalf of Cambridge University. Professor St Joseph was particularly interested in the Roman period and discovered from the air, a large number of hitherto unknown Roman forts, *vici*, roads, temporary camps and signal stations. He became the leading archaeological pathfinder in Britain and continued the excellent work of Crawford and Allen.

During the 39-45 war, he served in RAF Coastal Command and in 1960, operated Cambridge University's Taylorcraft Auster aircraft, a single-engined high-wing type, developed during the war for artillery observation. This was replaced in 1965 by a twin-engined Cessna 337 Skymaster. The unorthodox configuration of this aircraft makes it eminently suitable for aerial surveys. The high wing is out of the photographer's view and the undercarriage retracts into the fuselage thus removing a further obstruction to oblique photography. The two engines are cunningly arranged, one in the normal single-engine nose position, and the other in the rear fuselage driving a "pusher" propeller. This system is usually referred to as "push-pull." The tail is carried on two booms which sprout from the wings. A further advantage of this layout is that if an engine fails, the remaining thrust is still along the centre-line of the aircraft thus eliminating the problems of asymmetric power encountered after an engine failure with orthodox wing-mounted engines.

Space here does not allow mentions of the dozens of aerial searchers now at work in Britain. Be it sufficient to say that they are carrying on the excellent work of Crawford, Allen, St Joseph and others. A reference must be made however to Professor Dennis Harding of Edinburgh University, previously a lecturer at Durham University. During the professor's time at Durham, he learned to fly in order to conduct his aerial surveys of Iron Age sites in northern England and southern Scotland.

While he was learning to fly, he recruited two part-time pilots. One was Captain Dennis Ord, a sailing ship master who recently commanded the *Golden Hinde,* a replica of Sir Francis Drake's ship. Captain Ord sailed the galleon to the United States and various other countries. He was also a survivor from the British sailing ship *Marques* which was lost during the Tall Ships Race of June 1984. He was the first mate but was off duty and asleep below decks at the time of the accident when the violent vortex around a waterspout hit the vessel at night near Bermuda.

Professor Harding's other pilot was myself. While flying for the professor, the aircraft was flown on strict schedules and in search areas designated by the university, which paid the bills. Hundreds of previously unknown sites were found.

Between official flights, my fascination for the Roman period led me to take a single-seat aircraft on free-lance searches along the Roman roads and over the large tracts which had remained blank on the Ordnance Survey maps of Roman Britain. This book is a result of those flights.

Chapter 2

Down to Earth

Per Ardua ad Astra
(Through hardships to the heavens)
[Motto of the Royal Air Force]
Per Ardua
(Through hardships)
[Motto of the Royal Air Force Regiment]

Fieldwalking

An aeroplane is extremely useful for locating unknown archaeological sites but once the hidden feature is pinpointed from the air, it must be located on the ground. This is when the art of fieldwalking must be practised. It is an exciting feeling to know, with the help of details seen from above, that one is the first person in fifteen hundred years to realise that the insignificant-looking bump in a certain pasture is what is left of the ramparts of a temporary Roman camp.

The crop mark of an unknown Roman road which ends suddenly at the river bank gives away the position of a long lost and totally unsuspected bridge. A closer look at the map reveals parish boundaries on the other side of the river, on the same alignment. The road has continued south, heading for a destination as yet unknown. The line will be investigated later.

The marks of the foundations of an old building beside the pond in the old clay-pit show buttressed foundations similar to those of a Roman granary, but a little research in the local record office reveals that the site was an old brickworks constructed by French prisoners of war in the Napoleonic period.

The peculiar flower-shaped mark beside the barn turns out to be a 1940 anti-aircraft-gun-emplacement. In the farmhouse kitchen, there is a brass shell-case in use as a poker-stand, which was given to the farmer's grandfather by the gun-crew.

Fieldwalking is a skill which can only be perfected by constant practice. One's eyes become tuned to the landscape, picking up instantly, such obvious features as the strip-fields of the mediaeval rig and furrow agriculture. As experience is gained, more obscure features will be noticed; why is the farmhouse standing on a raised earthwork when it could quite easily have been built on flat ground? What building prior to the farm needed a large earthwork for a base?

Map-reading is an essential part of the skill, and a study of the area to be searched, in the comfort of an armchair, the evening before an expedition, will reveal much information. The straight piece of footpath on the east side of a wood coincides with a parish boundary, and these are usually ancient. On the west side of the wood, the same alignment is followed by a cart-track for a few hundred yards, and this passes a small church.

On the fieldwalk next day, the "long and short" quoinwork in the church tower identifies it to be of Saxon origin, and most of the stonework looks like second-hand stuff rescued from an older building. A word with the reverend gentleman reveals that the church can be traced back to the seventh century but in the graveyard, a Roman altar has been impressed as a headstone and carries a mid eighteenth century date of reuse. The nearest known Roman fort is ten miles away, and the vicar always understood from "experts" that the altar was transported from there. The fieldwalker doubts this and suspects a possible unknown Roman site and a road, closer to hand. Beyond the church, the alignment of this suspected road is now unmarked by any feature so a compass course is followed across ploughed fields to a stream half a mile away. There, the stones of a paved ford, totally ignored by modern paths or tracks, probably because of the steep gradient of the bank, (more on gradients later), lie in flood-torn disarray in the stream bed. The Romans could not pass by water without casting votive offerings into it and confirmation of the road is obtained by the recovery of Roman coins from between the stones.

Over the next few weeks, the road will be further traced by various tricks of the trade (more of this later), to a junction with a major, known Roman road. Another piece of the jig-saw has been found. The most difficult part still lies ahead, and that is to convince the county archaeologist of the authenticity of the newly discovered road. A local eminent antiquarian is quite upset at the news because he has just published a booklet on the Roman roads of the area, and the new find renders his work obsolete.

In this case, the fieldwalker has made important discoveries sparked off originally by the aerial photograph of the Roman marching camp. His finds have outstripped all written sources and he has been transformed into an explorer, not in a strange, foreign, and hostile jungle but among the fields of his home area where he played as a schoolboy. He has found previously unknown evidence of an ancient civilisation, and the cost of the discovery was nothing more than a bit of shoe-leather and a few scratches from brambles. Even if the search had proved negative, much pleasure was still obtained by the accidental discovery of a lapwing's nest with its four pear-shaped camouflaged eggs, as the searcher followed his compass-course over the ploughed fields. The sight of a fox playing with its cubs would also have been a compensation if the paved ford had not materialised in the predicted position.

Eventually, the fieldwalker's eyes become so attuned to the landscape that his skill becomes akin to that of the North American Indian tracker. Little escapes his notice, and aerial photographs, while of great assistance and interest, are no longer essential.

Amateur or professional, who cares?

A string of academic degrees does not turn a person into an archaeologist. There are highly qualified gentlemen who can recite ancient Greek poetry but are completely lost in the countryside. Many philosophers never leave the confines of their libraries and cloisters and there is the case of the historian who gave a brilliant lecture on Roman engineering and then delivered his car to a local garage for an M.O.T. certificate. Seeing an inspection pit with its boards removed, he tried to assist the mechanic by placing it over the pit, and did a nose-dive into it with a Reliant three-wheeler!

There is no stigma attached to being an amateur archaeologist. After all, a degree in the subject was introduced only a few years ago. Most of the famous and successful archaeologists have been unqualified but still extremely competent. It is better to be competent and unqualified than qualified and incompetent.

The extremely learned Professor Hoskins had this to say on the subject of qualifications and fieldwork:

"A basic working knowledge of general English history is obviously desirable; but there is much to be said for being self-taught, for never having sat at the feet of some immense authority laying down the law in unforgettable terms. Instead, everything comes fresh, bright-polished, and newly-minted to the eager eye."

The famous historian went on to say this:

"There is no opposition between fieldwork and documents. Both are essential to the good local historian. Behind a good deal of work in the field and in the street are documents that help to throw more light on what is being studied; and behind a good many documents lies much valuable fieldwork if only the unimaginative 'researcher' had the wit to see it. Most academically-trained historians are completely blind to the existence and value of visual evidence, visually speaking, they are still illiterate."

When anyone mentions archaeology, the average layman conjures up pictures of excavations, with pith-helmeted gentlemen directing the activities of hundreds of workers, some moving soil and sand with shovels and wheelbarrows, while others crouch in holes, apparently removing the soil with toothbrushes. Major excavations are extremeley complex and expensive operations and are only undertaken on virgin sites once in a blue moon. The universities usually dig a bit more out of the same old known site year after year while completely unknown complexes are ripped out of the ground by the giant earth-movers of the motorway builders and the open-cast mines. The developers have been given the go-ahead to destroy the landscape with the words: "There are no archaeological remains in the area." instead of: "There are no *known* archaeological remains in the area." The universities and Royal Commission on Historic Monuments do not have the money or personnel to search the countryside and rely mainly on chance finds. More often than not, landowners keep quiet about suspected sites on their property. An army of volunteer searchers would decrease the rate at which our heritage is being destroyed. Such a body of men does exist but is unco-ordinated as yet, but more of this shortly.

Once the position of the site is known, whether from the air, with fieldwalking or by chance finds, steps can be taken to protect it. Dozens of years may elapse before money can be found to excavate, but the hidden evidence will be safe for future generations to study. If technology continues to advance at the present rate, our future archaeologists will be able to view the underground remains without the process of excavation which produces much information but destroys most of the feature under examination. Before many more years are past, searchers will be able to scan the buried remains with complex earth-probing electro-magnetic devices, the early forms of which are already revolutionising archaeology. All this marvellous equipment of the near future will be useless if the site was destroyed by bulldozers years before.

Some of the scientific aids to searching, and laboratory dating techniques will be mentioned briefly before we move on to the controversial subjects of metal detectors and dowsing.

Resistivity surveys

This is the most commonly used of the geophysical surveying methods. The electrical resistance of the ground is measured with a resistivity meter. Readings are taken in a grid pattern. The resistance between probes varies with high levels through buried stone walls and low levels across infilled and wet ditches. When the readings are plotted on a plan, an outline of the buried site is produced.

The magnetometer

This instrument measures the strength of the Earth's magnetic field. In the tail of an anti-submarine aircraft, an indication is received when the aircraft passes over a submerged craft. Likewise, buried stonework and old ditches cause fluctuations of magnetic field, which can be measured by a suitable surface-crawling machine. When plotted, the readings outline the buried features.

Radar (R-adio A-ngle D-irection A-nd R-ange)

Since the beginning of the 39-45 war, ships and aircraft have been detected by reflections of transmitted radio waves. The archaeological version of this equipment detects buried features with a beam transmitted down into the ground. In maritime and aviation work, the radio pulses are sent out in space from a rotating antenna and the echoes are displayed electronically in plan form on a fluorescent screen. Airfield and ships' radars suffer from a minimum range problem as the same antenna is used for transmission and reception. A radio wave travels at 186,000 miles per second, (300,000,000 metres/second) or 300 metres in a microsecond (millionth of a second). The leading edge of a microsecond-duration pulse will extend outwards from a ship for 300 metres before the trailing edge leaves the antenna. Thus a dead circle devoid of echoes extends for 150 metres around the ship. Shorter pulses are selected for close range work such as river navigation in fog.

With archaeological ground-probing radars, I have not yet managed to extract an explanation of how a pulse-length can be made so short as to allow reflections from a depth of a few feet, but no doubt I shall be informed before long by the new generation of technicians.

Laboratory based dating methods

When a site is under investigation by various archaeological authorities, there are many scientific methods of dating the artefacts found. Most of them are extremely expensive processes and are beyond the scope of the amateur archaeologist who is interested in the actual discovery of the site. A brief mention of them follows before we move back out into the countryside where the site must be found before the boffins can tell us how old it is.

Coin and pottery dating

Scientific dating methods are superfluous if we find Roman coins. Unlike our modern ones, these coins do not carry dates, but the period of reign of the emperor depicted, is known. Likewise, the periods of manufacture of various types of Roman pottery are known and this provides an excellent method of dating the layer of soil in which the ceramics are found.

Radiocarbon dating

All living things, both animal and vegetable absorb carbon. Plants take in carbon dioxide from the atmosphere and retain some carbon in their tissues. The plants are eaten by herbivorous animals some of which are in turn eaten by carnivores.

Carbon dioxide contains a very small proportion of the radioactive isotope, carbon 14, so-called because it has two more neutrons in its nucleus than the normal carbon 12 atom. C14 has eight neutrons, and C12, six. Both carbon 12 and carbon 14 have six protons and six electrons, the electrons in two distinct orbit-shells. Carbon 14 is constantly produced in the upper atmosphere by a reaction involving cosmic radiation. All radioactive materials release energy. In a nuclear bomb, it all happens at once and whole cities can be destroyed. Left on its own, the radioactivity of a substance decays at a known rate for that substance over an extremely long period. For carbon 14, its radioactivity is halved every 5,736 years. When an animal or plant dies, it ceases to absorb carbon and the carbon 12 remains in the dead material while the radioactive carbon 14 decays to carbon 12 at the known rate. Thus the ratio of carbon 12 to carbon 14 can determine the time elapsed since death. The production rate of carbon 14 in the upper atmosphere has not been constant over the last few thousand of years and a correction has to be made to readings. The upper case letters BC or AD denote a calibrated radiocarbon date or a date derived from historical sources that needs no scientific confirmation. The lower case letters bc or ad represent uncalibrated radiocarbon years. BP (calibrated) or bp (uncalibrated) mean "before present" but the "present" refers to the year 1950, the latest date that the atmosphere was sufficiently uncontaminated to act as a standard for radiocarbon dating.

Dendrochronology (tree ring dating)

It is well known that the age of a tree can be determined by counting the rings. One new ring is grown every year. Depending on the weather experienced during the year, the ring growths vary in thickness so that all trees in the same area will have been affected in a similar manner. Using present day trees, and specimens of progressively older timbers from churches and archaeological sites, each with overlapping ring sequences, a table of tree-ring widths has been established and this extends back in time for several thousand years. The Bristlecone Pine of California is particularly long-living and has yielded a sequence extending back to c9000 BP. In Ireland, oak preserved in bogs has produced a table of ring thicknesses going back to c5950 BP.

If wood is kept wet, it can last for thousands of years and the above method of dating can be of considerable use when we examine surviving Roman bridge timbers and piles which still lie on our river beds.

Thermoluminescence

This is a method of dating pottery and other clay-fired objects. All objects, both above and below ground are being constantly bombarded by cosmic rays. Minerals absorb this radiation and store up energy in their crystal lattices. This energy is released in the form of light when the mineral is heated. When pottery is fired, the energy is released and the build-up process starts all over again. If the ancient pottery is re-heated, the energy picked up since its original firing will be released and the amount will tell us how long ago the original firing took place.

Other sophisticated laboratory tests

There are many other methods such as Potassium/argon dating, Fission track dating, and Magnetic dating. The reader who is interested in the whole subject of scientific dating should consult the many and varied specialist books available.

Metal detectors

During recent years much heated discussion has taken place via the media, between a few conventional archaeologists and those whose hobby it is to find hidden, lost or discarded artefacts in the ground, with the use of metal detectors. A few archaeologists have called for a nationwide ban on the use of these instruments but does that make sense? Because motor cars have been used for "ram-raiding" and get-away vehicles in bank robberies, are we to banish them from our roads? It is extremely difficult to wind the clock back and ignore modern technology. We cannot de-invent nuclear bombs and scrapping them in this country would merely invite threats from unstable dictatorships. Likewise, the banning of metal detectors would discriminate against the vast majority of honest practitioners, leaving unscrupulous persons as the sole users.

Let us examine the pros and cons of metal detectors. The anti-lobby claim that scheduled archaeological sites have been robbed by trespassers. That may well be the case but we do not ban narcotics in medicine because of illegal drug-pushers. In any case, scheduled archaeological sites can easily be protected from detector-equipped thieves by spreading sugar-cube-sized nuts of domestic coke or BB-size lead shot. This puts a blanket signal over the whole area and makes life very difficult for any night prowler. I am sure that scientists would be able to come up with even better protective prescriptions if they applied themselves to the problem.

Another criticism levelled at the metal detectorists is that they upset the stratigraphy of potential archaeological sites. A metal detector can detect a coin-sized object at a maximum depth of eight inches. When a university begins an excavation, a bulldozer usually takes the top two feet of soil off the site to begin with. In any case, this top layer has no stratigraphy whatsoever as it has been disturbed and rotated thousands of times by agriculture since the Neolithic period began.

Metal detectorists find great difficulty finding artefacts in rig and furrowed land. These areas have lain undisturbed only since the end of the mediaeval period but the artefacts lie too deep. The detectors rely on repeated ploughing to bring fresh artefacts near the surface each year. The Roman coin which was two feet down last year, may be only three inches deep after this year's ploughing. The argument for the disturbance of stratigraphy is therefore defeated.

If the use of modern chemical fertilisers continues, there will be no metal artefacts at all left in the topsoil in a few years. The corrosion will leave nothing for either the detectorist or the excavator. It is better to find and record the artefacts now before they are gone.

Open cast coal mining

Here in County Durham, an open-cast coal company recently took out a complete Romano-British farmstead in spite of warnings to the authorities of its existence. I find it astonishing to hear detectorists castigated for digging six-inch holes when the open-cast organisations are allowed half-square-mile craters.

Time and time again, I have found stretches of unknown Roman roads in our northern counties, only to be frustrated when they entered open-cast sites. Our history has gone for ever from these tremendous tracts of land. On one occasion, two Roman roads entered the same moonscape area of coal extraction. What Roman building now lost forever, sat at the crossroads? Criticising detectorists here in the north of England is rather like ticking-off a small boy for playing with a catapult in the ruins of Hiroshima.

Archaeologists pride themselves that little gets past the eagle-eyed scan of the trowelling and tooth-brushing students in the bottom of the trenches. Permission was obtained at a large excavation for detectorists to scan the "dead" spoil-heap from which all artefacts had supposedly been extracted. Over two hundred Roman coins were found in this "dead soil." I was astonished and thereafter, in my own excavations, I always ensured that every shovelful of spoil went past the head of a detector before it was consigned to the heap. This precaution has been amply rewarded.

Much of my aerial work involves the search for Roman roads. Flying is an expensive business, and a wild goose chase across country can cost a lot of money. Early in my career as an archaeologist, I discovered that a lot of time and money could be saved by employing an expert detectorist to scan the stream beds where suspected Roman roads crossed. As mentioned previously, the Romans seldom crossed a river or brook without making an offering to the gods of that particular water. The coins thus found satisfied me that a road was genuine and an expensive aerial search was justified along the line.

Open cast
mining in
central
Durham.
The dotted
lines show
Roman roads
from which
long sections
have been lost.
Since this map
was drawn,
several of the
planned areas
have also been
exploited. This
map illustrates
the need for
intense activity
by both
professional
and amateur
archaeologists.

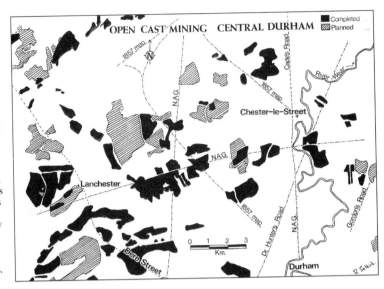

Old Ravensworth, Tyne and Wear. NZ 230 578.
The fields to the right were open cast mined some years ago and have lost ten thousand years of history. The wood, top right has had a near miss. It contains a Roman temporary camp and a suspected road. The square archaeological site in the field bottom left, has been lost recently when this area was also strip-mined. This view is to the east.

In the last three years or so, some 250 miles of unknown Roman roads have been revealed in Northumberland, Durham and Cumbria by the combination of aeroplanes, fieldwalking and metal detectors.

Attitude problems

For every hour I fly, a hundred is spent fieldwalking. During many years of ground searching, I have only ever met one other professional archaeologist out in the countryside and he was digging a hole because he disagreed with a colleague and was trying to prove that in that particular field, there were no Roman remains! With gentlemen of this calibre, we should easily be able to prove that Plautius and Claudius never even came to Britain.

During the same fieldwork, I have met dozens of amateur archaeologists and scores of metal detectorists. Here is our potential army to search for and record our unknown archaeological sites which face destruction over the next few years. Steps have already been taken here in the north of England, to pool information from the various detector clubs. My telephone rings constantly with new snippets of information and the once-empty spaces on my map are covered with find-spots of artefacts. A pattern often emerges which leads to greater discoveries.

I think that the animosity between some archaeologists and detectorists springs from jealousy. A museum employee goes for years without a single discovery of any significance and a young man straight out of school spends his pocket money on a gadget, learns how to use it, and finds dozens of Roman coins which in turn, lead to the discovery of an unknown villa.

Before we leave the subject, I will just refer back to the negative gentleman who dug his hole hoping to find nothing. This reminded me of a time many years ago when I was working in the United States. My attention was attracted by an obelisk on a hill and after my curiosity forced me to make the ascent, I read the inscription which said: "At this spot, during the American Civil War, nothing happened!"

In Britain, we have some of the finest archaeologists in the world, and there are also a lot of competent eccentrics who are great fun to work with. Unfortunately, a few pompous asses have infiltrated the profession and if one of these becomes installed in a museum or in a position of authority, the rate of reporting of new archaeological evidence goes down to zero.

The philosopher Herbert Spencer (1820-1903), summed up the negative attitudes of our disbelievers and pooh-poohers of new evidence with the following words:

"There is a principle which is a bar against all information, which is proof against all arguments, and which cannot fail to keep a man in everlasting ignorance – that principle is contempt prior to investigation."

Dowsing

This brings us to an even more controversial method of archaeological site detection and that is the ancient art of dowsing. The very mention of the subject can cause some traditionalists to go red in the face while others are fanatical in their support of the craft. The human being can be a strange creature and anything he cannot understand, he often dismisses out of hand. I do not pretend to understand the principles behind dowsing but one thing is for certain; it works. Like most people, I had my doubts about it and thought that water-divining may have been good luck, with lots of chances to hit the extensive water table. The discovery of stonework seemed a bit far-fetched. Any doubts I had were eliminated when a most learned scholar and leading expert on early English history carried out a survey of Saxon churches in the north of England. Professor Richard Bailey, assisted by Eric Cambridge, another leading academic, and his expert dowser, H Dennis Briggs, revolutionised our knowledge of these buildings. Earlier structures were discovered under the churches, and where excavations were carried out, the dowsing had been correct to three centimetres. The findings are published in *Dowsing and Church Archaeology.*

Mr Briggs says that the best results are obtained when a dowser sticks to his own period of interest. I had only limited success myself and a few false readings so I enlisted the help of an expert. Andy Davison was given a series of stringent tests to prove his ability. I took him to an area unfamiliar to him and asked to him locate some known Roman roads. He located them without difficulty. I then tried him in another area with a road I had recently discovered from the air. He found that too. There was no visible evidence whatsoever on the surface of the field. Then I tried driving him at night in more territory strange to him. I drove at a steady 30 mph along a road which was crossed by an invisible Roman road. He found the road but his reaction was delayed by about twenty yards. When a run was made in the other direction, his reaction was again delayed by twenty yards. A central point between the delayed reactions coincided exactly with the Roman road.

Before I leave the subject of dowsing, what really threw me was the dowsers' ability to detect stonework which had long been removed. They call this an "imprint." I cannot hazard a guess as to the explanation for this. Nevertheless, after excavation, I have seen the marks left behind by the long-gone stones.

The main object of this book is the search for evidence of the Roman legions and auxiliaries but Britain is just one huge archaeological site and the next chapter will attempt to assist readers with the identification of various features left behind in our landscape by the peoples who lived here from the melting of the ice to the prolific records of the Normans. After that, we can get down to the job in hand of locating some missing evidence of the Roman occupation.

Chapter 3

Who's That Down There?

*"When we compare the present life of man with that time of which we
have no knowledge, it seems to me like the swift flight of a lone sparrow
through the banqueting-hall where you sit in the winter months...This
sparrow flies swiftly in through one door of the hall, and out through
another...Similarly, man appears on earth for a while, but we know
nothing of what went on before this life, and what follows"*

spoken by a Saxon noble at a council of King Edwin
of Northumbria early in the seventh century

Who's who under the ground?
This book is intended for those whose hobby is the search for new evidence
of the Roman occupation of Britain, but before we can isolate and select
information from these four hundred years of our history, we must also learn
to identify the sometimes prolific signs of human activity left by those various
peoples who inhabited our post-glacial landscape in a continuous occupation
for ten thousand years before, and fifteen hundred years after, the period
when Britain was but a province of an Imperial empire which stretched from
Caledonia to Mesopotamia.

The ice retreats
A good place to start is the melting of the last great ice sheet which
covered northern Europe until about twelve thousand years ago. The causes
of the Ice Ages are not known and there have been at least four of them; the
last one, known as the "Devensian" formed about 120,000 BC. When it finally
melted about 10,000 BC, it left the topography much the same as it is now
except for a few adjustments which will be mentioned shortly. In this residual
landscape shaped by the ice-cap, the evidence we seek lies in the top few feet
of soil.

The Old and Middle Stone Ages
The Palaeolithic (Old Stone Age) people who fashioned the first crude

chipped-stone tools and who wandered around gathering berries, hunting mammoths and dodging large sabre-toothed cats, were around the fringes of the ice during the Devensian Glaciation, but only quarry-men, river-gravel diggers, and miners are likely to find any traces of them.

As the ice began to melt and retreat, the Mesolithic (Middle Stone Age) hunting, fishing, communities could wander across what is now the bed of the North Sea because the sea levels were much lower due to much of the Earth's water being locked-up in the glaciers. This link between Britain and Europe was probably not all *dry*-land as the sea was advancing due to the melting ice, flooding up the valleys and inundating low lying plains. The Thames no longer flowed into the Rhine, and about 8000 BC, it broke through the Dover area and formed the English Channel. Britain was now an island. About the same time, over the other side of the North Pole, the land bridge between Asia and America was submerged, forming the Bering Strait.

The North Sea is still very shallow, and mammoth and reindeer bones have been trawled up from the Dogger Bank. The English Channel is also shallow except for the Hurd Deep, which is a trench north of the Channel Islands and the Cherbourg Peninsula. This trench has the typical shape of a sub-glacial valley rather like the melt channels found under the ice in Greenland. Maybe the great ice-cap did not end at the Thames line after all. Huge boulders, known as "erratics" such as the fifty-ton Giant's Rock at Portleven, Cornwall, have been transported from north-west Scotland. How else did they get there but by ice?

Although the hills and valleys are just the way the ice left them, some changes have taken place to coastline shapes, with losses due to erosion, and gains with siltation and shingle deposits. There are also slight changes in the elevation of the land surfaces due to the return to equilibrium after the release of the tremendous weight of ice which was two miles thick over some parts of Britain. This movement is called "isostasy" and is very slow but continues to date. In Norway, some of the Viking landing stages have risen several feet out of the water. In Britain, the movement is much smaller and not uniform over the whole country. North of the Bristol-Humber line, the land is rising extremely slowly while in south-eastern England, for some reason, it is still subsiding. The whole subject is very complex but can be briefly summarised.

Two major processes have been in operation. First, general rises and falls of sea level due to the waxing and waning of the ice sheets, and second, the independent movements of the lands resulting mainly from their reaction to increasing or decreasing weight of ice.

The changes in shorelines due to erosion and siltation must be taken into account when we study coastal archaeological sites. As will be seen later, of great importance to our searches will be the migration of rivers, especially at bends, and also scouring actions. During glaciations, the sea levels are low therefore the gradients of the rivers are increased and this causes deeper beds to be cut. During the intervening periods of high sea levels (such as the present post-glacial period), the rivers are sluggish and are depositing gravel. Due to a misunderstanding of the subject, the opposite is often claimed, but positive proof of a general lack of bed-cutting in the last few thousand years is: the bases of Roman bridge-piers remain intact on our river beds with not even the Roman tool-marks scoured from the stones.

Now let us return to the peoples who occupied the land after the formation of the North Sea and the English Channel.

The Mesolithic people had no knowledge of farming and continued their hunting, fishing and food gathering. One of their sites has been identified at Star Carr, in the Vale of Pickering. Artefacts have been radiocarbon-dated to c7500 bc. The mud deposits on the site preserved wooden objects as well as bone arrow-points and small harpoon-heads.

The coming of the farmers

By about 4000 BC significant changes took place in Britain when settlers with a knowledge of agriculture and animal husbandry arrived.

These "Neolithic" (New Stone Age) peoples are classified under this heading because their improved polished stone axes, with holes drilled for hafts, show their advancing technology. They also used pottery but it was their ability to farm the land which allowed them to follow a totally different life-style from the nomadic hunter-fishers who had been forced to follow herds of wild animals. This significant change is often termed the "Neolithic revolution" and happened in Western Asia about 10,000 BC, but a few thousand years later in Europe and Britain.

The new arrivals must have made the channel crossing in skin boats, bringing their animals and seed with them. They were from tribes which spread right across France and southern Europe. Don't forget, there was no such thing as an Englishman in Britain. The Angles, Saxons and Jutes did not arrive until the end of the Roman period, about five thousand years into the future.

The Neolithic farmers built rectangular timber huts and buried their dead communally in elongated burial mounds which we call "long barrows." While thousands have been destroyed, a great many survive in our countryside and provide the most obvious evidence of the period. If the barrow is of earth and rubble construction, it is usually marked as a "tumulus" on Ordnance Survey maps and "cairn" if it is made entirely of stones. Some of these long barrows are extremely complex and a vast number of man-hours must have been spent in their creation. This tells us that the workers lived in an organised society which could support them on tasks other than the essential ones of food production, habitation buiding and forest clearance.

Perhaps these burial mounds were more than just tombs. It is thought in some circles that the human remains were taken out at intervals for rituals. Maybe the barrows were the first religious monuments in our countryside. The practice of barrow-burial continued for several thousand years. New designs appeared and there were switches from communal to single burials; inhumations to cremations and *vice-versa*, but more of that later.

Neolithic enclosures known as "causewayed camps" (changing archaeological fashions sometimes refer to them now as "interrupted-ditch enclosures") have been found in southern England, dated to the fourth millennium BC and these consist of a number of concentric ditches and internal banks. The ditches were seldom continuous, with uncut ground forming causeways. Their purpose is unclear as there is little evidence for occupation. Windmill Hill in Wiltshire is the best known example and has been dated to c3300 BC.

Late Neolithic man (and early Bronze Age man too) built monuments known as "henges," found only in the British Isles. In addition to the famous Stonehenge which had later additions in the Bronze Age, many crop marks are seen from the air, of circular ditched and banked enclosures, some with one entrance and others with two, diametrically opposed. Henges often have extra features such as circles of upright stones, as at Stonehenge and Avebury, or timber posts which at one time graced Durrington Walls and Woodhenge. Other features include burials, pits, and occasionally a long avenue-type enclosure known as a *cursus*. Henges usually produce Neolithic pottery.

There has been much publicity about the astronomical alignments of stone circles and some henges. At first, archaeologists resisted the new theories (as they invariably do) but now, to varying degrees, the celestial orientations are accepted.

The farmers mined flint for axe-heads, and the mines are quite easy to identify. The miners found that better flints came from seams down to about twenty-five feet, and these seams were reached by vertical shafts. The pits were widened at the bottom.

Britain's first roads seem to have been constructed in the Neolithic period: in Somerset, corduroy timber trackways dating to the late-Neolithic have been found preserved in peat. The trackways had crossed marshy areas, linking settlements on higher ground.

The arrival of the metal-workers; copper to begin with...

More significant changes occurred in Britain around 2500 BC with the arrival of the "Beakers." This beaker is a pottery drinking-vessel, usually without a handle, and is found associated with burials in barrows which had now become circular in shape. The new-style barrows show no signs of periodic removal of the dead after burial.

Some archaeologists argue that there was an "invasion" of Beaker People but others think that the artefacts arrived by trade or a transfer of manufacturing techniques. Skulls found in burials are round, unlike the long ones from earlier periods so the "invasion theory" seems to hold favour. The importance of the Beaker period is that metallurgy was introduced into Britain at this time, proof of which are copper daggers and ornaments found with the beaker burials. The Bronze Age was dawning. Bronze is an alloy of copper and tin and is a much harder material. It is likely that the discovery was made accidentally by using copper ore which contained tin as an impurity.

The Bronze Age

A further influx of settlers known as the "Wessex culture" arrived in Britain in the second millenium BC. No settlements have been found but further changes in barrow fashions identify the culture. The circular tombs have several variations such as "bell," "disc," "saucer," and "pond" barrows. Inhumations predominate in the early Wessex barrows, and cremations in the later ones. Rich grave-goods are found with the burials. These include objects of gold, copper, bronze, amber, faience, shale, bone, and various pottery vessels. Most of these materials are not available in Wessex and demonstrate that the inhabitants were extensive traders.

It is possible that the missing settlements of this period are hidden under the later Iron Age hillforts as it is now thought that this type of defended enclosure was used in the late Bronze Age. Radiocarbon-dating has shown some surprisingly early origins for some hillforts. Examples are: 1470 BC at Mam Tor in Derbyshire and 1100 BC at Dinorben in Denbighshire.

The various fashions of Bronze Age barrows remain in our landscape although thousands have been destroyed by later agriculture. Even so, circular burial mounds usually had ditches around them and the latter occasionally manifest themselves as crop marks, visible from an aircraft or a hilltop.

The barrows are often on high ground but the builders have seldom selected the peaks as sites. Quite often the peaks are out of sight of the immediate valley so the builders have placed their mounds on high shoulders which are easily visible. They would not have been visible if the valleys had been heavily wooded and this is just one more pointer towards extensive early forest clearances.

Small circular copses frequently cover burial mounds but care must be taken not to confuse them with round, tree-covered fox-coverts of fairly recent times. Mediaeval artificial rabbit warrens can also resemble barrows. Other "false barrows" may be "drumlins" which are heaps of ice-transported spoil, dropped during the melting of the glaciers. Spoil-heaps from lead-mining and other such activities also on occasion resemble the genuine articles.

The square and rectangular field-systems called "Celtic lynchets" by O G S Crawford have been in use during the Bronze Age and possibly earlier. Crawford was correct when he said these fields were pre-Roman but it looks as if they were also pre-Celtic.

The Iron Age

Iron is more difficult to produce and work than bronze but its advantages are manifest. Unfortunately for the archaeologist, it corrodes easily.

In Europe, the Iron Age began about 1100 BC when the knowlege of iron-working spread westwards from the Middle East after the collapse of the Hittites which allowed the secret to escape.

Trading probably introduced iron objects into Britain but a comprehensive knowledge of iron production arrived with the coming of the "Belgae," a wave of invaders of Celtic origin, Their home had been northern France in the last few centuries BC, but many of them were evacuating Gaul ahead of the Roman conquest of that land.

It is not possible to state a firm date for the arrival of the first iron-workers in Britain. It looks as if the same tribes had begun immigration into Britain in the Bronze Age as there was a continuation of use of farmland and cemeteries.

The new arrivals brought with them, in addition to the latest skills in iron-working, more sophisticated weaponry, coinage, and the potter's wheel.

From Roman sources, we know that their fortified administrative settlements were known as *oppida*. Some of these, such as Maiden Castle in Dorset, were extremely complex. The *oppidum* at Maiden Castle was the fourth feature on

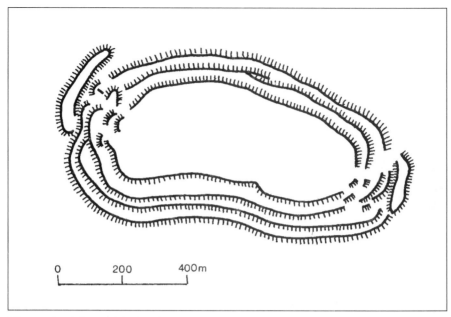

The complex defences of the Iron Age fortification at Maiden Castle, south-west of Dorchester, which was stormed and taken by the Romans. The Romans moved the population to a new settlement at Durnovaria (Dorchester) and Maiden Castle was abandoned.

The crop marks of an Iron Age hillfort, NY 375 585, on a knoll beside the River Eden, opposite Grinsdale, to the north-west of Carlisle. The double hedge-line at left appears to contain a Roman road. Bonnie Prince Charlie and his army also camped here in 1745.

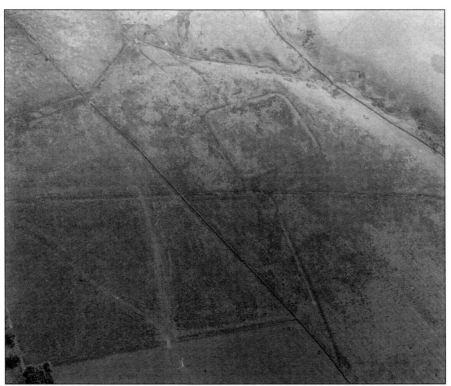

A Roman temporary camp on Haltwhistle Common (NY 646 654), a quarter mile south of Turret 47A on Hadrian's Wall. This photograph shows the characteristic shape of the camp, and the defensive *tuteli* in front of the entrances.

the same site, having been preceded by a Neolithic causewayed camp, a long barrow, and an Iron Age hillfort. This hillfort had developed into an *oppidum*. Right throughout Britain, hundreds of these hillforts survive, most of them on well-selected, easily defended positions. They are generally circular in shape but often follow a hill-contour which produces an oval or irregular perimeter. The design is usually a ditch surrounding a timber-revetted earth and stone rampart. Sometimes dry-stone walling was used to revet the ramparts. Where there were high sea-cliffs, promontories have been fashioned into forts by digging ditches over narrow necks of land.

The entrances of hillforts were cunningly constructed but were not as complex of those of the larger *oppida*. The buildings inside the hillforts were circular huts. It seems that Iron Age Britain was a very warlike place with one tribe against the next. When the Roman occupation took place, inter-tribal conflict was discouraged and evidence of this can be seen from the air in the form of hut circles *outside* the ramparts of the hillforts. *Pax Romana* rendered the fortifications obsolete, but that is leaping ahead...

We have an eye-witness report of Iron Age Britain: about 320 BC, the great navigator Pytheas, from Massilia (Marseilles), evaded the Carthaginian blockade, passed through the Straits of Gibraltar and headed north. Perhaps he was trying to find the trading secrets of the Carthaginians, such as the source of tin they obtained from an island in north-western Europe. He talked of the islands of "Albion" and "Ierne" and described chariots which he saw in operation in Belerium (Cornwall) and bread, cake and mead which he tasted in Kent. He mentioned several geographical peculiarities, notably the tides. He circumnavigated Ireland and then pressed on northwards to an island which he called "Thule" (probably Iceland), six days sailing from Britain and one day south of the great frozen sea. So much for the myth that ancient navigators hugged the land.

There is evidence that the Iron Age tribes used a network of roads which often followed the high ground and are known as "ridgeways." These roads probably originated in much earlier periods. The Romans who would shortly enter the scene in Britain, paved some of these roads and incorporated them into their military network thus explaining why a straight Roman road suddenly meandered for a few miles in a most un-Roman fashion.

Rome prepares to attack

In the last century BC, the Roman emperor Julius Caesar was in the process of conquering Gaul. His written account states that his planned attack on Britain was to stop aid reaching the Gauls from their kinsmen across the Channel. It is likely that his motives also included the seizure of plunder to add to his capital, and the glory of victories to further his political career.

The Roman period

Imagine what Britain would have been like, if in 1940 Adolf Hitler had won the Battle of Britain, successfully invaded, and the German army had remained in occupation until the year 2300. That would be similar to the

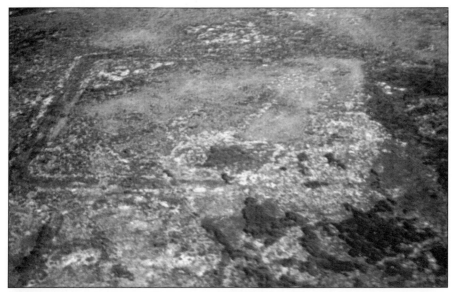

A previously unknown temporary Roman camp at SE 797 976, on Wheeldale Moor, North Yorkshire, close to the known Roman road. After a heath fire, the heather is growing thicker over the Roman ditch.

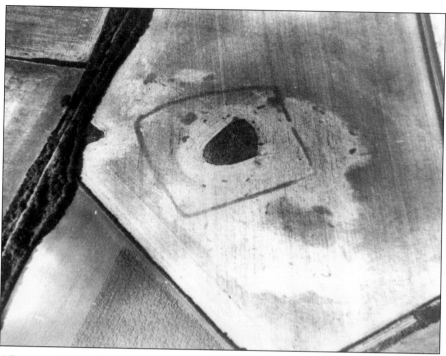

A Roman period Iron Age enclosure at Dene House Farm, NZ 354 388, Thornley, County Durham. These settlements were simple native farmsteads and are usually known as "Romano-British settlements" (or RB sites). This site is known to pilots as "The fried egg site." The yolk of the egg is a rocky outcrop which presumably provided an excellent foundation for a large circular hut. The single entrances to these sites were nearly always in the eastern sides.

A previously unknown Roman fortlet, NZ 143 162, (above centre) at Winston, on the top of the cliff above the River Tees. Dr Gale reported a Roman road here. He was correct. It can be seen descending the hill to the left of the modern road, just right of bottom centre. The mirror image of the Roman road can be seen on the opposite side of the river, running from centre to left-centre.
The Romans must have had a bridge or a ford in this vicinity. The ditch of the fortlet is too regular for a native RB site and there is an entrance on the south side.

traumatic experiences which overtook the Celtic inhabitants of Britain almost two thousand years ago.

The following chapters of this book will deal with certain aspects of the Roman occupation of Britain in great detail so only a brief mention will be made here. First of all, the Roman arrival in Britain marks the end of British pre-history and the beginning of written history. For the most part we have only a few pieces of the jig-saw puzzle and the rest of the picture must be filled in by archaeologists, air survey pilots, detector searchers and chance finds. With the rapid development of motorways, industry and urbanisation, time is running out. Archaeologists and historians have often attempted to obtain a complete understanding of the occupation by expanding the available pieces of the jig-saw to fit the whole frame, thus achieving a distorted picture. Like frustrated children, they have sometimes forced incorrect pieces into place and are most reluctant to take them out when genuine fits are found.

In the past, the study of the Roman period was thought to be simple. After all, the Romans have left us quite a lot of written material and their square and rectangular forts and buildings are easy to identify. Also, much of their magnificent road system either still exists or is followed by more recent roads. This has led many of our scholars to classify them as the Roman equivalent of motorways. Only at the very steep Roman gradients have the mediaeval and modern roads been forced to make diversions. If the mediaeval horse-drawn carts and the modern motor cars could not take the Roman inclines, how did the Roman ox-wagons manage when they could do little more than 1 mph on the flat? Such problems have been glossed-over by our cloister-bound historians. The only way to obtain the answers is to get out there in the countryside and put oneself in the place of the Roman engineers and try to recapture their strategy.

To-date, the great blank spaces on the Roman-period maps are explained away by: "the natives were hostile in that area," and when a long stretch of Roman road has no forts on it, the excuse is: "the road passed through the territory of friendly tribes." Aerial reconnaissance is putting an end to all those old negative theories. There were no great open spaces in the occupation except in the Highlands of Scotland; the roads through so-called "friendly territory" are producing crop marks of unknown fortifications and the road network is proving to be far more complex than anyone ever credited. We will return to all this in great detail very shortly.

The purpose of the present chapter is not only to describe the habitations before and after the Romans so that the searcher will experience minimum confusion; it is also to demonstate how *non-Roman* sites can actually *assist* the searcher to trace and identify hitherto unknown Roman features. With this in mind, we will now move briefly to the end of the Roman period in Britain about AD 406 when the troops were being withdrawn in order to defend Rome.

Towards the end of the fourth century, Roman Britain had been under attack from unfriendly tribes in Caledonia, the Picts and the Scots, and had also suffered seaborne attacks by Saxon pirates. The latter had caused the Romans to build a chain of new-style coastal defence forts, and these operated in conjunction with a fleet of warships.

The Saxons

After the Roman military withdrawal, Britain was wide open for invasion, and the Germanic tribes, mentioned by Bede as "Angles, Saxons, and Jutes," but better known collectively as "Anglo-Saxons," soon arrived in their ships which closely resembled the later Viking ships. The newcomers were warlike, illiterate and pagan. They fought fierce battles against the native Romanised-British Celts.

During the Roman occupation of Britain, the Roman army and administrators had treated the occupied Celtic tribes tolerably well. As long as the Celts paid their taxes (often in corn), obeyed the law, and did not foster political or religious unrest, they were left to live their own lives and worship their own gods. Some British leaders became rich and extremely Romanised. Many Britons joined the Roman army as auxiliary troops though in the first centuries of occupation, they would have been stationed elsewhere in the Empire as the Romans did not like a military presence of soldiery who had a sympathy with the local inhabitants.

From the Roman conquest until the reign of Constantine the Great (Emperor AD 306-37), Christianity was outlawed in the Roman Empire. Constantine's alleged vision of the Cross before the Battle at Ponte Molle (Milvain Bridge) in 312 inspired his "Edict of Milan" of 313 which allowed freedom of worship throughout the Empire to the Christian Church. British bishops were appointed.

Thus, after the Roman military withdrawal, the pagan Anglo-Saxons were fighting Christian Celts. The Celts fought stubbornly but were forced west of Gloucester and most were driven into "Weallas" (Wales); Cornwall (where they later accepted the rule of the Saxon masters); and Scotland. A few stayed behind and many became slaves. Very little is left of the Celtic language or culture in England except the names of some rivers and two or three settlements.

Christianity survived in Ireland and was taken from there into Scotland via Iona by St Columba in 563. Missionaries from the Celtic Church in Ireland, Wales and Scotland attempted, with some success, to Christianise the pagan Saxons. Although Rome had lost military control of England, the Church of Rome also sent missions to England. Thus there was a combined effort from opposite directions and from very different branches of the Church, to convert the Anglo-Saxons.

As will be appreciated shortly, of great importance for the location of unknown Roman sites is a letter sent to Abbott Mellitus in 601 by Pope Gregory. This letter is quoted by Bede in his *Ecclesiastical History of the English Race* and in it, the Pope instructs Abbott Mellitus about the handling of the religious affairs of the English:

"I have decided after long deliberation about the English people, namely that the idol temples of that race should by no means be destroyed, but only the idols in them. Take holy water and sprinkle it in these shrines, build altars and place relics in them. For if the shrines are well built, it is essential that they be changed from the worship of devils to the service of the true God."

Many of these pagan temples were in the now ruinous Roman forts, and this explains why so many Saxon churches grew up right on top of Roman military sites, and reused Roman building materials in the process. When in turn the Saxon churches fell into disrepair, later churches were built on the same sites.

The Vikings

So far, we have the Christianised Anglo-Saxons in England, and Celts in Cornwall, Ireland, Wales and Scotland. The next wave of attacks came from the Vikings in the eighth century, tempted by Britain's wealth. Like the Anglo-Saxons, at first they just raided but later came to stay when they realised that the quarrelling Anglo-Saxon kingdoms could not keep them out.

To describe the story of the Viking settlement in Britain and the subsequent fusion of the Danes and Anglo-Saxons into one people would take up most of the space in this book. This and all the other periods mentioned briefly in this chapter are dealt with in full elsewhere and the object here is merely to familiarise the reader with the various types of settlement which may be encountered during the field searches for the Romans.

Let it suffice to say that the Norwegian Vikings settled in Scotland, Ireland and the Isle of Man, and the Danish Vikings in eastern England. Missing are the Swedish Vikings who concentrated on Russia and penetrated the rivers there and traversed the continent all the way to Constantinople.

The general areas of Viking settlement in Britain are obvious from place names but the actual individual habitations prove to be most elusive.

The Normans

Another Viking invasion is not always recognised as such because the Normans were French-speaking and arrived from France. They were Vikings who had settled in the Normandy peninsula and had adopted the local language. Their successful conquest of England is also too complex to record here. Their impact on archaeology is from their castles, cathedrals and their continued use of the Saxon feudal farming systems.

The Battle of Britain, 1940

Britain almost had another Nordic invasion in 1940 but was saved by a small but very efficient air force, and the melt-waters of the ancient glacier which had flooded the English Channel ten thousand years before. Crop marks of defences against a possible German invasion can still be seen, overlying and mixed up with signs of human handiwork of the preceding six thousand years.

We will next examine the Roman invasions of Britain together with the associated logistical problems which are seldom mentioned by historians.

Chapter 4

The Roman Invaders
(and comparisons with others)

*"The same principles of war which were employed in the past,
appear again and again throughout history..."*

Field Marshal Viscount Montgomery of Alamein

*"We are waiting for the long-promised invasion. So are the
fishes."*

Winston Churchill, 1940

Invasions

Like Adolf Hitler, who contemplated an invasion of Britain after the fall of
France in 1940, it may have seemed to Julius Caesar that the island which was
often in clear view from the French coast, was ill-defended and within grasp.
Hitler never made it and the same unpredictable narrow sea turned both
Caesar's attacks, in 55 and 54 BC, from full-scale invasions into little more
than commando-raids. Another hundred years was to elapse before the
Romans, in AD 43, came, and stayed.

Unlike Hitler, Julius Caesar did not have to gain air superiority before his
seaborne assault. Also, unlike Hitler, he did not have a British navy to face in
"Fretvm Gallicvm." Many of the problems however were the same for Julius
Caesar and Adolf Hitler. One was logistics, a subject hardly mentioned by
historians and archaeologists, and the other was the sailors' number one
enemy in war and peacetime too; the weather.

The swift fall of France in 1940 left Hitler wondering how to transport the
necessary thirty divisions across *der* Kanal once he had gained mastery of the
air (in modern warfare, to land troops on a shore still dominated by an
enemy air force is to invite disaster). Hitler's answer was to collect thousands
of canal barges from all over Europe and the idea was to use captured Dutch
tugs to tow strings of them across the Channel. Half of the German army
transport was still horse-drawn, and the German admirals were horrified at
the thought of trying to escort this totally unsuitable armada, with a very
much smaller navy than the opposing Royal Navy. The RN had available in or
near the Channel: five capital ships, eleven cruisers, seventy-six destroyers and

hundreds of torpedo-boats and armed trawlers. For the escort of the motley armada, the *Kreigsmarine* had only seven destroyers, twenty torpedo-boats plus some fast gun-boats (E boats). Hitler needed a flat calm for his sea-crossing with the low-freeboard canal barges. His admirals warned that British destroyers would race at thity-five knots (40 mph) across the crawling strings of scows and swamp them without the need of gunfire. In the event, Hitler never obtained the necessary air superiority although it was a close-run thing. He was also extremely short of fuel and decided to go for the Caspian oilfields which involved an attack on the Soviet Union. His army suffered a similar fate to that of another dictator who had prepared to cross the English Channel. One hundred and thirty-six years earlier, in 1804, Napoleon Bonaparte had stared with frustration across *la* Manche towards the hated English. Everything was ready for his invasion. Unlike Hitler, he was fully equipped for the assault. His *Grande Armée* comprised 200,000 crack veterans, and the host of sea transports and assault barges were to have been escorted by a fleet of warships. Ammunition, cavalry, artillery, ambulance wagons and even field- bakeries were all ready. Every logistical detail had been carefully planned. For months, Napoleon paced the beach at Boulogne trying to make up his mind and then he turned around and moved his army into the heart of Europe. The deterrent had been the Royal Navy. The Iberians (pre-Celts), Celts, Romans, Scots (who had invaded Caledonia from Ireland), Picts, Saxons, Vikings and Normans were now a unified nation and defended themselves with a formidable navy.   In 1940, the brilliant British war leader, Winston Churchill realised the German logistical problems but fostered the threat of a German invasion in order to rally a spirit of unity in defence, into a previously largely indifferent British public, now bewildered at the swift fall of France. The threat produced a determination to fight to the bitter end, and unified the whole population with an excitement spurred by a common purpose.

Two thousand years earlier, there had been no uniting leader among the mutually hostile tribes of Iron Age Britain who faced the Romans; nor was there a British navy waiting to intercept the Roman invasion fleets.

As France fell in 1940, Churchill had been fortunate to have had a spell of excellent flat calm conditions in the English Channel, and 200,000 troops were rescued from Dunkirk instead of the expected 45,000. An armada of small craft which included yachts, fishing boats, lifeboats and even a Thames fire-fighting float, greatly assisted destroyers, tugs, and ferries, with the evacuation. The Royal Navy used thirty-nine destroyers of which only four were sunk. The English Channel had chosen to be kind to the British.

Unknown to the British people, Churchill was so confident that the Germans had immense logistical problems that at the height of his "invasion scare" he sent three regiments of tanks, and enough 25-pounder guns to equip a field regiment, out of Britain, to the North African theatre. He was also reading the German secret radio signals with the help of a captured *Enigma* coding machine.

The Germans had a method of assault unknown to the Romans, i.e. parachutists. Churchill knew that Hitler had only 357 Junkers 52, trimotored troop-transports, which flew at 140 mph, and each of these could carry only twelve fully-equipped paratroops, or eighteen soldiers if the aircraft landed. Alternatively an empty Ju 52 could tow a glider but the standard German glider, the DFS 230, only carried twelve soldiers so there was no advantage except the short landing-run of the glider and its ability to do so on unprepared terrain. Without German mastery of the air, both sides knew what would happen to the bumbling Junkers transports or gliders if the 300+ mph Spitfires and Hurricanes got among them.

All summer of 1940, the Germans practised invasions on the Dutch coast, trying to coax reluctant mules down improvised gang-planks from unpowered or underpowered canal barges. During all of these rehearsals, they never managed to land successfully a single armoured vehicle even though the tank-transporting craft had been modified with concrete floors and removable bow-doors. Caesar's ship-borne horse-slings were much superior to the 1940 German methods. Why is it that many of our historians refer to the Romans as "landlubbers"? In Britain alone, they managed three times, what Napoleon and Hitler never even attempted. It is true that a high proportion of the seamen on the Roman ships were from seafaring nations conquered by Rome but that does not make the attack any less Roman. In the Battle of Britain of 1940, five hundred of the three thousand Royal Air Force pilots were from the British Commonwealth and Empire, Poland, Belgium, Czechoslovakia, France, Holland, Norway, Palestine, Ireland and America. It was still a British battle.

In 1944, when the turn came for the Anglo-American and allied armies to invade Hitler's Europe, it had taken three years for the combined might of the United States, the British Empire and allies, to prepare for the Normandy landings. Thousands of special landing craft with bow-ramps had been constructed, and two complete floating harbours were towed in sections across the Channel and assembled under the enemy cliffs. The floating harbours took Hitler by surprise as he had assumed that the allies would have to capture a port very early in the invasion for the tremendous amount of supplies that would be needed. The logistical problems were enormous and shortly before the allied armada sailed, the grass verges of major roads at suitable points, all the way from the south coast of England to the Scottish border, were crammed with military vehicles awaiting their turn to move south to embark. The combined Anglo-American invasion fleet contained ninety-three destroyers and 4,024 special landing craft which could discharge tanks, vehicles, guns and infantry directly onto the beach and then return to England for more. Hundreds of merchant ships carried supplies and the cargoes were transported to the beaches by 2,583 amphibious trucks (DUKWS). Several capital ships were also in attendance including the British cruiser *Ajax,* which had damaged the German battleship *Graf Spee* off Montevideo, and the American *Nevada,* once again in service after being raised from the mud of Pearl Harbor.

The Landing of 55 BC

It is not certain whether Julius Caesar's expedition of 55 BC was intended as a full-scale invasion or a reconnaissance-in-force. If the intention had been invasion, then his bad luck with the weather downgraded it to a trial run. Caesar's loss of ships in a storm has been used by some historians to label the

Roman navy as incompetent. As any modern sailor knows, the English Channel can be a hostile place, and modern quarter-million-ton super-tankers are still lost, even though they are equipped with radar, satellite-navigators, echo-sounders, facsimile-weather-chart-read-outs and international voice and telex radiocommunications.

Let us look more closely at the events of 55 BC. A single boat had been sent to scan the British shore and this returned with details of possible landing sites. For the crossing, Caesar needed a wind with a southerly component, and, at midnight on 11th August he departed from Portus Itius (Boulogne). He arrived below the chalk cliffs in the Dover area and selected the best available beach for a landing. The Britons were waiting on the shore. The draught of the ships prevented a dry landing for the troops who didn't like the idea of the deep water. The story of the Eagle-bearer of the Tenth Legion leading the disembarkation by leaping into the water is well known. To preserve the honour of the Legion, the rest of the soldiers had to follow the Eagle. The ensuing battle in the breakers and on the beach was fierce but after a difficult start, the Romans managed to put the enemy to flight, and the Britons sued for peace.

Later, eighteen transport vessels bringing the Roman cavalry were sighted but the wind backed to easterly and increased to gale-force, driving the ships down-channel. Many of the ships of the main force were driven ashore and damaged and some totally wrecked.

On seeing the difficulties of the Romans, the British reneged on their peace treaty and attacked again. Under difficult circumstances, Caesar repaired all but twelve of his ships and still without his cavalry, he decided to call it a day and return to Gaul. The English Channel had been unkind to Julius Caesar.

The synoptic situation which caused such havoc was not unusual for the time of year. A deep depression had moved east-north-east along the coast of Gaul. In June 1944, the floating "Mulberry Harbours" of the Allied invasion of Normandy experienced a similar storm. The American harbour was wrecked and the British one severely damaged yet nobody referred to the British or Americans as "landlubbers."

The Invasion of 54 BC

Caesar was still determined to invade so he rebuilt his fleet. This time his ships which numbered over eight hundred, were of a more suitable type with shallow-draught. He was ready by June of 54 BC, with five legions (25,000 men), two thousand Gaulish cavalry, plus their horses, stores, baggage, artillery, missiles and building material for forts. Persistent northerly winds delayed his departure but on 20th July, he left with a gentle south-westerly breeze. About midnight, the wind dropped away but the flooding tide carried the ships on, and a landing was made on a shelving beach at Deal.

Faced with such a formidable armada, the Britons did not oppose the landing. Caesar marched his troops twelve miles inland and the Britons retired to a fortified position, probably the hillfort at Bigberry, near Canterbury. This hillfort was successfully stormed and taken but once again the English Channel was unkind to Caesar. He received news that a storm had wrecked many of his ships which had been riding at anchor. Instead of pursuing the demoralised Britons, his army worked non-stop for ten days to repair the damaged vessels. They were dragged up the beach into a fortified encampment. The channel weather had cost him an excellent chance of a resounding victory.

The Britons managed to forget their tribal conflicts and had formed a temporary alliance under Cassivellaunus but all they managed to do was fight delaying actions. The British tribes were saved by trouble in Gaul. When Caesar received this news, he ordered a return to Gaul but a fleet of ships expected for the evacuation did not materialise. He packed his men into what ships remained from the storm damage, and calm seas allowed a safe crossing. The British had not defeated the Roman army; on two occasions, the North Atlantic low-pressure systems sweeping up the Channel had done the job for them. Julius Caesar managed to claim his second expedition as a victory but another hundred years were to elapse before the Romans experienced genuine military successes in Britain.

Soldiers' rations

By now, it should be appreciated by the reader, from the accounts of Julius Caesar (and Adolf Hitler) that an invasion is not merely a question of loading troops into ships and setting sail. The same problems apply to land campaigns and military occupations, and the main difficulty is that of *logistics*. The supply of an army is often glossed-over by the phrase: "The Romans foraged for their food." After a day's march is over, you do not feed an army of thirty-five thousand men and thousands of horses, by turning them loose into the fields which barely supported the natives. This book therefore concentrates on the forgotten Roman supply lines, the discovery of which will furnish us with a mass of new information about the reasons for the specific sitings of Roman forts, the discovery of an unknown communications network and the implications of these on the strategy of the Roman army. Julius Caesar and Adolf Hitler had two obvious enemies, the inhabitants of the British Isles and the capricious weather of the English Channel. The third enemy, which does not go away with good weather or an enemy retreat, is the hunger of one's armies. This is summed up very neatly by the Roman military writer, Vegetius, who said: "The threat of starvation is a far greater worry to a soldier than a fierce enemy."

We can now move on to the third and successful invasion of Britain.

The third invasion

In AD 43, during the reign of the Emperor Claudius, a carefully planned assault was made on Britain under the command of Roman general Aulus Plautius Silvanus. The reasons were once again economic and a quest for political success. The lessons from Julius Caesar's attacks were remembered. A hundred years of trading since Julius Caesar's campaigns had also acquainted the Romans with the British shores just as in the 1930's, the peacetime German airline "*Lufthansa*," operating in and out of London's Croydon Airport, had photographed most of the military installations in southern England.

The problems were threefold; first, get the army across the channel; second, defeat the opposition; and third, keep the army supplied and fed while it followed up its initial attacks and occupied the territory of the enemy.

From historical snippets and estimates by military experts, it seems that the invasion force contained about 45,000 men. The breakdown of this figure is:

Four legions (4 x 5,000)	=	20,000 Roman citizens
Ten regiments of cavalry, and auxiliary cohorts all non-citizens from countries within the Empire	=	5,000 horsemen
	=	15,000 infantry
Mule handlers and transport workers	=	<u>5,000</u> supply troops
Estimated total number of men in landing force not counting ships' crews	=	<u>45,000</u>

As well as the 5,000 horses of the cavalry, some 10,000 transport animals would have been required for the movement of tents and baggage, but rations to only two day's march from the beach-head. Longer marches would require an ever-increasing number of pack-animals. The following estimate of shipping space allows for only a modest two weeks' rations for 45,000 men at the landing-site supply base. The Roman norm was to have a year's supply in hand.

Using the size of Caesar's ships of the 54 BC invasion for the calculation, the total number of similar ships required would have been about one thousand.

Paved roads would not have been available for the army advancing from the beach-head area. As the army moved forward, it may have been necessary to prepare temporary tactical roads, clearing scrub and trees where necessary. Many authors at the stroke of a pen tell us that as the Roman army advanced, so did the engineers build a network of roads behind them. The words are quickly written but the work by the army engineers and prisoners of war took much longer. An average permanent Roman road contains 20,000 tons of stone per mile and each mile took several weeks to complete.

It will also be appreciated that as the army moved forward, not only did mules carry supplies for the soldiers; they also needed to feed themselves so that a situation presented itself where extra fodder-mules were necessary to carry food for their ration-carrying kin and themselves. The longer the supply lines, the more fodder-carriers were needed in a mathematical progression which was a nightmare to ancient quartermasters. At the end of a day's work, animals cannot revitalise themselves wholly by grazing. You either graze them or work them but not both. The animals do of course browse in their off-duty hours but this is not sufficient in itself to keep them in a fit working condition. Horses, mules and camels will eat only during the day. If they work, they must be fed. Unlike men, the physical condition of cavalry horses and transport animals cannot be restored by periods of rest and good diet after they have been worked excessively with insufficient food. Such treatment renders them permanently unfit.

In the 1914-18 war, the German General von Kluck made a terrible miscalculation: in his "First Army" alone, he had 84,000 horses and these consumed two million pounds of fodder a day. To carry this, 924 standard fodder-wagons were required. Because of the tremendous transport problem, he decided that during his great advance, his horses would have to live off the country. Even though the season was favourable for this, by the time they crossed the French frontier, the cavalry horses were exhausted and almost useless and the heavy artillery had fallen great distances behind the main army.

Many more comparisons will be made as we consider the problems which faced the Romans. Most of our history books continue to talk of the Romans "supplying themselves" as they went along but clearly this was impossible. No doubt the Romans, like any other army, took was what available along the line of march but to *rely* on such supplies was to invite disaster.

In 1940, Hitler had been talked out of an invasion of Britain by his admirals but he put the blame on his Air Marshal Goering for not defeating the Royal Air Force fighter defence. He attacked the Soviet Union in June 1941. The Russians were taken by surprise even though Winston Churchill, who was reading the secret German signals, had warned Joseph Stalin, the Soviet dictator. Stalin ignored the warning and this cost the Russian forces hundreds of thousands of casualties. The typical German *blitzkreig* (lightning war) pushed the Red Army back at an alarming rate at first but the Russians used a "scorched earth policy" and burned all food and anything else which could be of value to the Germans. As the German supply lines grew in length, the advance slowed and finally the Russian winter turned the tide against a summer-equipped invader.

In southern England in AD 43, the British tribes took their herds of animals with them as they retreated, thus denying them to the advancing Romans. Perhaps they also burned what crops they had even though May and June were early months for a harvest in Britain.

Roman records do not tell us much about the logistics of the advance but let us look at a parallel campaign of more recent times which is well chronicled. In North America, consider the position of the Confederate Army at Gettysburg on July 1-3, 1863. The army consisted of 75,000 troops, mostly infantry, and was under the command of General Robert E Lee. He advanced into southern Pennsylvania in late June which was the harvest date for the winter wheat grown in that region. His army secured an area of three hundred square miles in one of the most productive agricultural regions of the United States. Efficient transport in the area included a railroad and a network of roads which the well-organised army horse and mule-drawn wagons utilised.

In spite of all these advantages, after only two days, the food began to run low. The same rules are valid for all armies of all periods and the main logistical lesson is that when an army remains stationary in a position remote from water transport, either sea, river or canal, it will quickly eat all the supplies from the entire area no matter how many wagons and pack-animals are available.

Because of this, General Lee could not conduct a long defensive action against the Federal troops and was forced to initiate the disastrous attacks of July 2nd and 3rd, 1863.

If the reader will just bear with me a little longer, the reason for the logistical arguments will become apparent and new answers will emerge in our quest for a clearer insight into Roman activities. For the moment, let us return to the task force of Aulus Plautius:

The legions involved were the II Augusta, IX Hispana, XIV Gemina and XX (later "Valeria"), and the embarkation port was Boulogne. The Romans do not mention their destination but archaeological evidence is fairly conclusive that it was Richborough where there was a natural harbour. The landing was unopposed but two skirmishes took place in east Kent after which the Britons retired to the Medway line. The conquest was a series of successes by an organised army against unco-ordinated native tribes. When the Roman army arrived at the Thames, as instructed, it awaited the arrival from Rome of the Emperor Claudius. No doubt Plautius continued unofficial actions in order to make sure that there would be no doubt of Claudius' ulimate victory. The Emperor remained in Britain only sixteen days during which time the Catuvellaunian capital of Colchester capitulated to him. The full accounts of this campaign and others in Britain are discussed in full in many and varied works. The object here is the search for new evidence and to obtain a clearer picture from a jig-saw puzzle, from which, three-quarters of the pieces are missing.

As Aulus Plautius moved out of Richborough, fighting his skirmishes and heading for the Medway and the Thames, probably with about thirty thousand men and thousands of cavalry horses and pack-animals, one of his main worries would have been the provision of supplies for his army. The frightening (for planners and quartermasters) exponential escalation of numbers of supply animals against time and distance has already been stressed. Was there an alternative? Of course there was; what happened to the thousand vessels of the invasion fleet? There were warships equipped with heavy artillery which carried a complement of marines in addition to the operating crew. The fleet also used transports of many types and sizes. Roman merchantmen of 1,000 tons or more were not uncommon. Even a 250 tonner which would be about the size of a very small modern coaster or a trawler, would carry the same amount of cargo as 2,500 mules or 500 ox-wagons. Thus, just two small supply ships, suitably escorted, would dispense with the expedition's impediment of several thousand pack-animals. One small ship arriving every day at some pre-arranged rendezvous would have fed and re-furbished the whole of the invasion force, and Plautius had several hundred ships to choose from.

Tacitus, the Roman chronicler, described Roman ships of the period:

"...some were of shallow draught, pointed bow and stern, and broad-beamed to withstand heavy seas. Others were flat-bottomed to allow grounding. Most of them were equipped with steering-oars at both ends to allow quick movement forward and backwards. Many had decks for the transport of artillery, horses and supplies. They were easy to sail..."

The same writer also had this to say about British rivers:

"I would only add one remark, that nowhere else does the sea make its power more felt: the tide causes long stretches of the rivers alternately to ebb and flow, nor does it simply rise and sink upon the shore, but it runs far inland, and winds about and makes its way into the very heart of the hills and mountain chains, as if the sea were the lord of all."

With that information alone, we can diminish the vacant spaces in our jig-saw puzzle and the new "experimental" pieces will carry pictures of supply ships meeting up with the tired and hungry but victorious troops. What will not show up on our modified picture are several thousand mules and wagons stringing along for miles behind the army thus necessitating a large part of the fighting force being used as an escort.

Comparison with Alexander the Great's army

While trying to fill in missing information from the Roman army of AD 43, we have compared the problems of various modern armies. Before we move on to the next chapter, let us finally look at an ancient army; this time, the army of Alexander the Great, between 332 and 330 BC.

During his long campaigns which stretched from Greece to India, Alexander's army varied in size, but when he crossed the Hellespont on his outward march, he had 48,100 soldiers, 6,100 cavalry horses and about 16,000 servants and non-combatants; a total of about 65,000 personnel. If one pack-animal were needed for every 50 men, to carry non-eatables such as tents, blankets, fuel, personal possessions etc, then an extra 1,300 animals would have been needed. If the army travelled through terrain from which water and forage were available for the horses, then it would have been necessary to carry only grain, and the weight of this grain for one day only would have been 269,000 pounds, i.e. about 120 tons. This would have needed 1,121 grain-carrying animals. If two days' supply of grain had to be carried, then 2,340 grain-carriers would have been needed. Theoretically, 40,350 grain-carriers would have been necessary to move the army for fifteen days, and 107,600 for twenty days. Clearly such numbers of animals were not available in the entire country of transit.

In practice, Alexander's army could not feed itself for more than a few days, so his army had to route between towns which had either seaports or navigable rivers. His supply ships were waiting for him at these points. The itinerary included the coastal towns of Amphipolis, Abdera, Maroneia, and probably Aenos and Sestos. The army averaged nineteen miles per day. The researchers of Alexander's campaigns comment that on many of his stages, the population did not have enough food for themselves, let alone a passing army of 65,000 men plus thousands of animals. Two thousand ships formed a supply chain for Alexander's campaigns.

In Britain and Europe, historians constantly talk about the masses of ox-wagons using the Roman roads. Much more will be said on this subject in the next chapter but it is interesting to note that early in Alexander's campaign, he ordered the burning of all carts except the ones carrying artillery, and the ambulances. He began by burning his own vehicle. His reasons were that carts could not cope with the rough terrain easily negotiated by pack-animals.

Also, ox-wagons were never used by his army because they could not keep up with the army's 2 mph, and the hooves of the oxen were unsuitable for travelling long distances. The ox could work only five hours per day as opposed to eight for a horse or a mule.

We will meet up again with the Roman army of Plautius as it occupied southern England but in the next chapter another supply problem will be highlighted. The much publicised and excellently constructed Roman roads often had a gradient of one in three. We will meet up with typical Roman roads such as Dere Street in Northumberland which runs arrow-straight but switchbacks up and down the hills for miles without the slightest attempt to ease the gradient. These Roman inclines would present huge problems to the later mediaeval teamsters who would attempt to follow them. How did the Roman ox-wagons manage? Let us take a look at a country where ox-transport *was* important – that is South Africa in the eighteenth and nineteenth centuries.

The Afrikaner ox-wagons were pulled by teams of sixteen oxen and had a crew of two, a driver and *voorloper* (bridle-leader). The wagons were small and narrow and a full load was three hogsheads of wine or the equivalent.

Traces of the old *trekpads* (wagon tracks) can still be seen in many parts of the country where they sweep from from one side of the modern road to the other in search of easy gradients. How did the Roman ox-wagons manage without such deviations? The comparison is further highlighted by the facts that the Afrikaner ox-teams contained twice the number of animals as the Roman, and furthermore, the South African oxen were far bigger beasts and one of them, which plied from Capetown is recorded as having a horn spread of 11ft 5 ins (3.5 metres).

Perhaps the answer is that the Romans had no problems at all with the roads because the wagons were used only around the towns and farms, and the heavy cargoes were transported cross-country by a totally different system.

Chapter 5

The Roman Roads
(and associated works)

Great roads the Romans built that men might meet,
And walls to keep strong men apart, secure.
Now centuries are gone, and in defeat
The walls are fallen, but the roads endure. "

Ethelyn Miller Hartwich

Ancient roads in general

Long before Aulus Plautius arrived in Britain, the Romans had an excellent
network of extremely well-engineered roads around their Empire which did
not yet include Britain. Before we rejoin Plautius as he moved across rough
country in Kent, let us examine the subject of ancient roads in general and
their development or lack of it:

The importance of roads to the defence and welfare of nations was very
well known to the ancient peoples. Babylon had a paved road in 2,000 BC,
and the Egyptians used a massive paved road during the construction of the
Great Pyramid. The Chinese, Peruvians, Carthaginians, Persians and
Etruscans were also great road builders, but the greatest of all in the ancient
world were the Romans. The Roman Empire at its height had a vast network
of roads stretching from the Caspian Sea and Mesopotamia in the east, to
Morocco, Portugal, France and Wales in the west, and from Scotland,
Holland, Germany and Roumania in the north to the Sahara Desert and Red
Sea coasts in the south. Many of them survive today as the foundations of
modern roads. Others still exist, but are well camouflaged as cart tracks,
footpaths and field and parish boundaries. Some can be seen only as tell-tale
marks from an aircraft, and thousands of miles of them await discovery. In
the Dark Ages and Middle Ages, the excellent Roman roads were allowed to
decay, and for over a thousand years no new ones were built to take their
place. The mediaeval traveller attempted to follow the Roman roads, but the
disrepair made travel very difficult. When stage-coaches were introduced in
Britain in 1659, there were frequent delays owing to the vehicles overturning
or getting bogged down. Teams of cattle were often procured from

neighbouring farms to drag out the bogged-down coaches. It was not until the nineteenth century that things really began to improve, when John MacAdam and Thomas Telford introduced scientific road-engineering in Britain.

The Roman roads

The Romans learned the art of road-building from excellent teachers, the Etruscans. These people, who settled in the ninth century BC in what today is modern Tuscany, were excellent civil engineers. From the Etruscans, the Romans learned how to construct aqueducts, sewers, bridges and roads. The Etruscans had made well-graded and well-drained dirt roads and the Romans improved on their teachers by adding paving. The Romans were not the first to use paving. All over the ancient world, short distances of special lengths of road were paved, but the Romans used mile after mile of various types of

A previously unknown Roman road (NZ 222 145) to the south of Holme House Farm near Piercebridge. The road ditches are showing as crop marks. A Romano-British farm sits beside the road. This road comes in from the south-east and joins the known Roman road "Dere Street" at Piercebridge.

The suspected Roman road (NY 987 328) from Stanhope, on the River Wear, to Eggleston on the River Tees.

The top photograph shows the Roman road attacking the hill head on, where the later road had to make a detour to lessen the severe Roman gradient.

The bottom picture shows the marked *agger* of the road. This road would have been useless for wheeled vehicles.

hard surface. In Britain, only the roads in the forts and towns would have their tops finished with flags. The arterial roads would be mostly surfaced with rammed-gravel.

Before the Roman roads were built in Britain...

As the invasion force of Aulus Plautius moved towards the River Medway in AD 43, an obvious stop for replenishment would have been Canterbury, fourteen miles distant from the Richborough beach-head. Supply barges could quite easily have followed the flank of the army via the Rivers Stour and Great Stour, so dispensing with about a thousand pack-mules which would have been necessary to carry one day's grain for the army. In the eighteenth century, the Stour was navigable as far as Fordwich (just below Canterbury), but sixteenth century records show river traffic getting up a further twelve miles as far as Wye, where a Roman settlement would be built when the Romans consolidated the area. The Roman town of Durovernum would be founded at Canterbury and a network of roads would radiate from it. Six of these are known to us and there are probably more to be found. It is extremely likely that the first Roman defences here would have been

A junction of two suspected Roman roads (NZ 215 478) near Sacriston, County Durham. The straight farm road from bottom left to top right is called "Long Edge" and is on top of a suspected Roman road from Lanchester to Chester-le-Street. It is joined by another road which has been used by mediaeval farmers as a boundary for their rig and furrows. The second road is believed to be part of "Dere Street North" which linked Dere Street from the sharp turn at Ragpath Wood (NZ 205 422) to Newcastle upon Tyne.
The black spot right-centre is the source of a Roman aqueduct to Chester-le-Street, four miles away. The aqueduct can be seen angling across the field, top left.

The source of the Roman aqueduct to Chester-le-Street (NZ 217 478) on Broomhouse Farm. The channelled stones are identical to those in the latrine at Housesteads on the Wall. Other springs and streams feed this aqueduct on its four mile run.

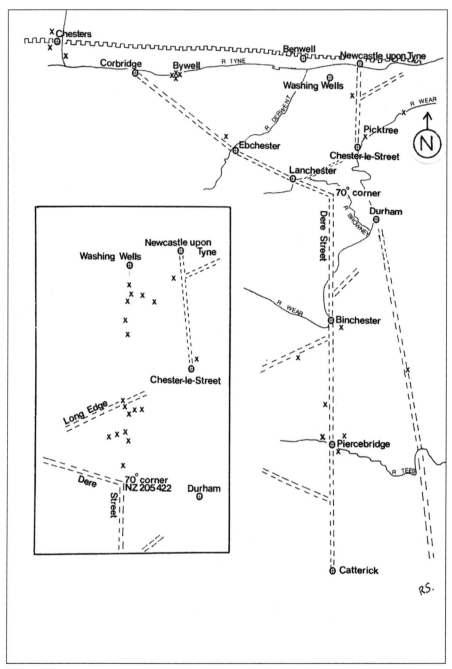

This map shows the line of the suspected Roman road "Long Edge" in relation to Chester-le-Street, Lanchester and the sharp corner of Dere Street at Ragpath Wood. Crosses mark various pieces of evidence such as RB sites, coin finds etc, which point to a further Roman road between Flass Hall below Ragpath Wood (Dere Street Corner) and Newcastle Upon Tyne. Since the map was drawn, this road has been found exactly on the predicted line.

temporary camps. Even for a one-night-stop, the Roman military practice was to construct a fortified square or rectangle and these always had rounded corners. The fortifications consisted of a ditch and the spoil from this was heaped into a rampart on the inner side. A palisade of sharpened wooden stakes topped this bank. Entrances, usually defended by short outlying works, were left in each side. Only when this secure camp was completed could the soldiers pitch their forty-pound, eight-man leather tents, and settle down for a night's sleep. The layout of the tents was always the same so the soldiers knew automatically where the various personnel were located. The size of the temporary camp depended on the number of troops. The single defensive ditch was much narrower than those of the permanent forts which would be built when the army consolidated its territorial gains. The forts were of the same "playing card" shape, either square or rectangular with rounded corners but had massive turf and timber walls and deeper, wider surrounding ditches, sometimes single but often multiple. Towers were built at the gateways and corners. Opposite the gates, causeways were sometimes formed by leaving the ditches uncut but at other locations the ditches were bridged. Later in the occupation, many of the turf-and-timber "permanent" forts would be re-built in stone but the shape and general layout remained the same. The most common types housed five hundred or a thousand auxiliary troops but very large ones could take a whole legion of five thousand men.

Whereas the native-British hillforts were always located on easily defended positions, more than ninety per-cent of the Roman forts were built beside rivers (more of this later).

The advance of the expeditionary force would have been made across open country where possible, with engineers merely filling in gullies, clearing scrub, and laying timber corduroys over swampy ground. Permanent roads would come later but would take a considerable time to construct. Meanwhile, the route to the Thames provided excellent opportunities for the army to be supplied from its right flank by ship or barge. Nine miles west of Canterbury, a small estuary penetrates inland to Faversham. Beyond this, many creeks flank the campaign route and the easily navigable Medway was certainly used, and probably inspired the siting of the later Roman town of Durobrivae (Rochester). To the west of Rochester, the Thames was close to the expedition's right side, and small tributaries intercepting the line of march would have further eased the supply problem.

Pax Romana

It is time to leave the campaign of Claudius' army and look slightly into the future, at the countryside under Roman domination, with the native tribes at peace, even if somewhat sullen. *Pax Romana* had arrived.

By now, a network of permanent, professionally-engineered, well-drained, all-weather roads, was being constructed by sappers, slaves, and prisoners of war. One of these roads would run almost direct from Richborough to London along the line of Plautius' advance. Over sixty miles long, with about twenty thousand tons of stone per mile, it used a minimum of 1.2 million tons. This road and others in the network could not have been created as quickly as the army advanced, as some historians would have us believe. What was the purpose of this Roman road and the thousands of miles of others just

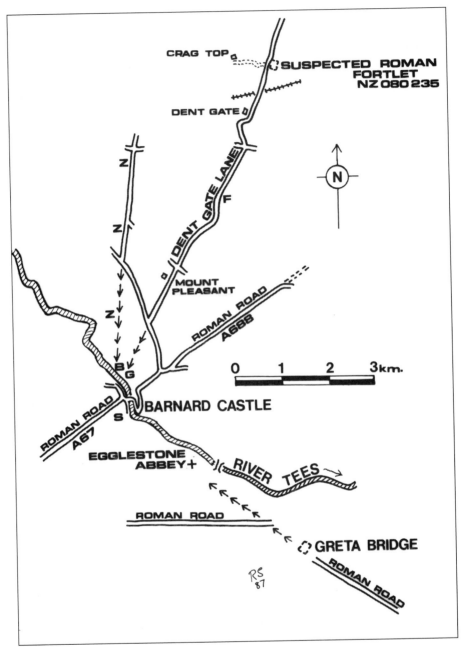

A known Roman road under the modern A688 crosses the River Tees at Barnard Castle. The modern road follows a mediaeval zig-zag down to the bridge. Neither the Roman bridge nor the suspected fort have been found. To descend the cliff, the Roman road deviated the opposite way from the A688 and was found when the gasworks (G) were built many years ago. A pattern of straight roads, all possibly Roman, are lined up on the same point on the river (B). There have been Roman finds at Startforth (S) and this may be the site of a Roman fort. On Dent Gate Lane, a site at NZ 080 235 is an obvious Roman fortlet like it, which were to be built?

It is doubtful if this road was a supply route or a trade road, as Roman records tell us that land transport was fifty-eight times more expensive than sea transport, and sixteen times the cost of river and canal transport. Using the average speed of 4 knots (4.5 mph) for a Roman merchant ship, a five hundred-tonner could have made it to London from abeam Richborough in twenty hours, and its cargo would have been equal to that of a thousand ox-wagons. The *Theodosian Code* informs us that the heavy wagons had a weight restriction of 1,500 Roman pounds (1,000 Imperial pounds, 455 kg) in order to protect the road surfaces. The same records tell us that their *clabularia* (heavy four-wheeled wagons) were drawn by eight oxen in summer and ten in winter. The Roman poet Virgil (70-19 BC), tells us that: "The approach of a heavy wagon was heralded by the squeal of tortured axles." At 2 mph maximum, and working five hours per day, the ox-wagons would have taken six days to reach London. If they were transporting fodder, every day, each ox-team would have consumed at least a third of its own cargo, leaving no payload at the half-way point to London.

The Roman roads took little notice of gradients, further increasing the problem of long distance ox-wagon transport. It can be argued that two or three ox-carts travelling together, could have had their animals unhitched and double or treble-teamed, to drag each wagon in turn up an incline. What a waste of effort when the equivalent of a thousand cart-loads arrived in London five days earlier with no more energy expended than a few sailors trimming sails. The Roman ship was operated by about twenty men whereas the thousand ox-carts would have needed one thousand drivers plus another thousand *cursors* (bridle-leaders). Wagons of any kind were therefore totally unsuitable and far too expensive for long journeys. No wonder Alexander the Great burned all his. The supply of Roman towns and forts remote from the sea will be discussed in due course.

Roman stone-reliefs which depict such wagons, obviously show methods of transport used locally around the towns, villages, farms, and vineyards. The ruts worn into the gateway roads of Roman forts have confused the issue. Historians have assumed that the wagons had travelled long distances whereas they probably came only from the farm or wharf. No Roman records whatsoever mention long journeys by cart.

The most likely purpose of the Roman roads was for the swift movement of Roman troops for police-action against the slightest signs of unrest. Cavalry could dismount for the steep gradients, and accompanying pack-animals were able to negotiate steep inclines but were not restricted to the hard surface should a deviation on an easier gradient become necessary. For Roman troops on the march, an animal-drawn cart *could* accompany them as a few hundred soldiers heaving on ropes would soon assist a vehicle, possibly carrying artillery, up the steepest incline. Further evidence will be presented as we progress, but first we must examine the planning and construction of the roads.

The *Mensores* (Surveyors)

Every Roman legion had a number of surveyors among its ranks, and part of their duties was to establish a military road network. Their job was to find and mark the suitable routes. Engineers would follow behind and carry out the construction. To start with, Roman surveyors marked out the line of the road. Their accuracy was extraordinary. They plotted the line in straight lengths making corrections of heading at high points, not with easy bends but with sudden alterations of up to ten degrees. Sighting-lines were established with surveyors' rods, and fire and smoke signals assisted long-distance alignments. A favourite trick was to aim the line for a distant hill thus saving lots of intermediate observations. Across easy country, the straight lengths were long, and alterations of heading few. On occasion an existing native track was incorporated into the system, resulting in a meandering section.

How did the Roman *mensores* achieve such accuracy? There was more to it than just keeping poles and fires in line. They had to know where they were going, and in which direction to make a start. We are told that the Romans did not have magnetic compasses. This may be true. What the archaeologists should say is that they have not found one yet. Compass-needles must be of iron and such delicate artefacts would easily corrode away to nothing.

The Chinese had magnetic compasses in their Third Dynasty (second millenium BC) and it was called a *Tchi Nan.* Emperor Tcheou gave ambassadors from Cochin China one to find their way home. *Yachting Monthly,* (February 1985) tells us that Pliny the Elder (23-79 AD) wrote about errors caused by the proximity of *alio* (another) compass. The magazine claims that Pliny mistakenly spelt *alio* as *allio,* the latter meaning "garlic." This according to the magazine is why for 1,700 years there was a superstition at sea that garlic affected compasses. I cannot find the original reference but it is certainly true that one compass does affect another one if they are placed too close together.

Whether or not the Romans had magnetic compasses remains to be seen. They certainly did have a type of direction-finder but it did not use the Earth's magnetism. They also knew how to find true north from simple observations, and their direction-finding instrument performed the calculation in a few seconds, with five simple operations. This instrument is certainly a compass although it has not been recognised as such by the archaeologists who found it. For want of a better description, they refer to it, and other examples found at various other sites, as "portable sundials."

First of all let us look at the calculation described by the Roman architect and engineer, Vitruvius. He tells us that in order to find north: describe a circle on the ground and push a stick vertically into the centre. The stick's height must be such that the end of its shadow in the early morning and late afternoon lies outside the circumference of the circle, but inside, at midday. Once in the morning and again in the afternoon, the end of the shadow will just touch the circumference. Vitruvius tells us to join these points thus obtaining a chord. Then from the centre of the circle draw a line which bisects this chord, and this line is true north. The Roman instrument mentioned previously, called a "portable sundial" by the finders, performs this calculation if one knows how to operate it. As soon as I saw the device, I realised its purpose because of the significant figures on its dials. In transport aircraft, I had used an instrument which was inscribed with the same figures: in polar regions, magnetic compasses are unreliable because the Earth's magnetic lines of force are almost vertical, and compasses are very sluggish and hardly know which way to point. An instrument called an "astro-compass" (nothing to do with sextants) is used to determine true north and the aircraft's true heading, from a bearing taken of the Sun, Moon, planet or star. The Roman device works only with the Sun but surprisingly, it can be operated with the Royal Air Force/British Overseas Airways Corporation check-list!

At the point where all the straight roads converge on the River Tees at Barnard Castle, a search was made in the boulder-strewn river bed.
A well-worn Roman altar was found at NZ 047 167. This is 300 yards upstream from the A688 bridge. It is likely to prove to be the site of the Roman bridge.

At the Roman fort of Greta Bridge (NZ 086 129), it was thought that the Roman road was underneath the road past the farm, top left. This aerial photograph shows that the Roman road crosses the field above centre. A ground inspection shows the last remains of a possible bridge abutment at (A). On the opposite bank, there is a raised earthwork at (E).

The photograph opposite, of Binchester (Vinovia) Roman fort, County Durham, was taken by an unidentified pilot c1925. It has lain in a museum file, unrecognised for seventy years, but it solves a problem that has led archaeologists on a wild goose chase for years. The Roman road "Dere Street" can be seen from bottom left, up through the farm (just left of a black barn), through the fort and then along a hedge around the large loop of the River Wear.

An old plantation boundary which curves towards the river was incorrectly identified as the Roman road, and this led to futile searches. One school of thought was that the Romans had crossed the river loop twice. Another was that the river bend had moved 500 yards to the east since Roman times. Both were wrong; the river has not moved one yard and the Roman road went around the outside of the bend.

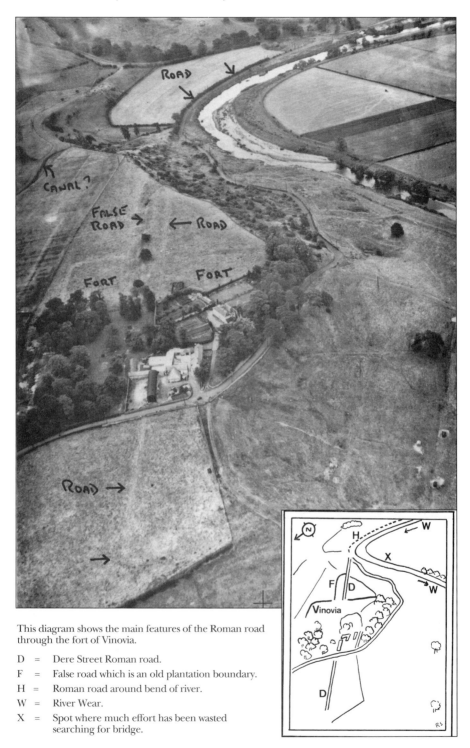

This diagram shows the main features of the Roman road through the fort of Vinovia.

D = Dere Street Roman road.

F = False road which is an old plantation boundary.

H = Roman road around bend of river.

W = River Wear.

X = Spot where much effort has been wasted searching for bridge.

To explain the function simply, let us look at an ordinary garden sundial. This consists of a circular horizontal plate, engraved around the edge with the hours of the day. Sticking up in the middle of the plate is a triangular piece called a *gnomon*. If this *gnomon* is lined up accurately on true north, its shadow cast by the Sun will indicate the correct time on the scale at the circumference of the horizontal plate. The device can be used backwards: if the instrument has been disturbed and is no longer lined up on true north, this can be remedied: note the time from a watch and rotate the sundial until the shadow of the *gnomon* coincides with the corresponding time on the circumference of the brass circle. The *gnomon* is now back on true north and the instrument has been used not as a sundial, but as a sun-compass. Simple devices like this were used by the Long Range Desert Group during the 39-45 War, and avoided possible fatal navigational errors which could have resulted from deviations of a magnetic compass needle due to the proximity of armour plate, machine-gun mounts and the like.

The Roman sun-compass is not complex. It consists of two concentric circular bronze plates, one slightly smaller than the other. The larger one has an eye obviously meant for the suspension of the whole instrument. Both are mounted on a common pivot, and on the same pivot, free to rotate is a peculiar-shaped *gnomon*. The edge of the larger plate is marked in tens of degrees, and these figures obviously represent latitude. The inner plate has four segments of $23\frac{1}{2}$ degrees which can only represent the declination of the Sun. This varies from $23\frac{1}{2}$ degrees South (in midwinter) to $23\frac{1}{2}$ degrees North (in midsummer). At the equinoxes, declination of the Sun is zero. The *gnomon* has a shadow-bar on one end and pointers at both ends. The curved surface of the *gnomon* is etched with lateral marks, obviously hour marks. To operate the instrument suspend it from a tree-branch making sure it is not in shadow; take the time (the Romans would have done this with an hour-glass); set a raised marker on the inner disc against the latitude on the outer plate; align the the point on the shadow-bar end of the *gnomon* against the declination of the Sun scale. This is easily worked out from the date but is usually written down and kept in a handy table. Then rotate the whole instrument around a vertical axis (the axis of the suspension string) until the the shadow of the shadow-bar lies along the hour mark on the *gnomon* which corresponds to the time indicated by the hour-glass (or the modern observer's watch). The instrument is now lined up exactly on true north; not magnetic north, but the meridian and the geographical North Pole. This is how the Romans surveyed their roads so accurately. The instrument would also have been of great assistance with the navigation of a ship.*

The Roman road constructors

When the road construction gangs came along later, following the surveyors' lines, they were allowed to make deviations to avoid obstacles or bad ground but they invariably regained the surveyed line at some distance beyond the obstruction. Little notice was taken of gradients which would horrify a modern car-driver. The roads pitched up and down hills, with deviations to ease the gradients at only the most awful places. At an extremely steep-sided ravine, or deep valley, the builders would turn to one side and angle down the slope to the river where a bridge would be built. On the other

* See Chapter 7 for illustrations and checklist.

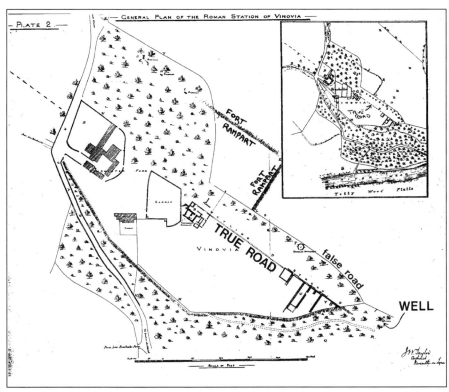

The excavation plan drawn by Hooppell and Taylor c1870, clearly shows the true Roman road. This was drawn before aeroplanes were invented. Why has it been ignored by modern archaeologists?

side of the water, the road would angle back with a mirror-image deviation, to the sighted line. These mirror-image deviations will be excellent identification features when we come to our searches for unknown Roman roads. If the gorge was deep and had almost vertical cliffs, zig-zags would be resorted-to on both sides. The gradients of the Roman deviations and zig-zags would challenge a present-day tank. In the Alps, a modern road makes fourteen hairpin-bends to reach a pass where the Roman predecessor made it in three!

The Roman zig-zags also provide the road-searching archaeologist with clues. A thousand years after the Romans departed, mediaeval people attempted to follow some of the ruinous Roman roads. Although the horse-collar had been developed by this time and was much more efficient than the Roman ox-yoke; the mediaeval horse-drawn wagons could not manage the Roman gradients, even where the Romans had lessened these with their mirror-image deviations or zig-zags. The frustrated mediaeval carters had to take large circuitous routes with very gentle gradients, around the Roman ravine crossings. These meandering mediaeval deviations are often followed by modern roads and provide further clues in our search for Roman roads. We often get the situation where a modern road is on top of a mediaeval track which itself is on a Roman road. Everything is fine as we drive along in a

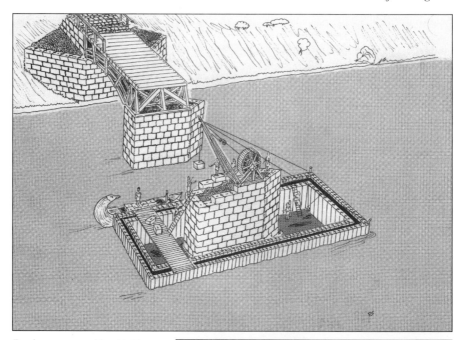

Roads are no use without bridges
and the Romans were skilled
bridge builders. They had excellent
cranes, pile-drivers, pumps,
architects, engineers, surveyors and
divers. Roman bridge piers always
had independent foundations on
the river bed and were constructed
inside coffer-dams.

A Roman crane depicted on the
"Funerary monument of the
Haterii" (Lateran Museum of
Rome), showing the man-powered
drum.

straight line, noting the blind summits as the Roman line switchbacked up and down, as on Dere Street north of Corbridge, Northumberland. Further evidence is obtained as the car has to alter course suddenly by ten degrees at a high point. When a steep valley is reached, the road completely alters in character, and the modern road follows the circuitous mediaeval deviation before regaining the straight Roman road, quarter of a mile or so further on. Stop the car, go back to the mediaeval bend and very often, a little searching will reveal the overgrown Roman road plunging down the side of the ravine.

On the Roman road "Dere Street" to the West of Hallington Reservoir at NY 940 760, the modern road makes a wide deviation to the east to avoid the Roman gradients down to the Swin Burn. If one drives up Dere Street from the south, as the swing to the right is approached, the *agger* of the Roman road will be seen carrying-on straight ahead right over the top of an isolated peak where an easy track could pass either side of it. Only a crazy engineer would lay a road for an ox-wagon in this manner.

The usual Roman road was constructed by digging a deep trench across country and filling the bottom with very large rough stones. Glacial boulders each weighing several tons, which had been dropped by the melting ice several thousand years previously, were ideal for this, and explains why so few are left around the English countryside; they are all in the Roman roads. Work in a Roman road-construction gang must have been extremely gruelling. On top of these large rocks, were placed smaller stones, and above ground level, the surface was cambered into what the Romans called an *agger*. This was for efficient drainage. The top was covered with rammed gravel.

Where necessary, slab-covered rectangular drainage culverts passed under the roads, usually at right-angles to the line. On both sides of the road, deep parallel drainage ditches were dug. Where the road ran along the side of a hill, the lower ditch was often dispensed with.

In addition to glacial boulders and any obvious stone which may have been lying about, small quarries were dug at the road sides. From an aircraft, these resemble lines of random bomb-craters. Most of them are now grass-covered.

At the sides of most Roman roads, two or three very large boulders lie at irregular intervals of several hundred yards. Could these be spare parts for road repairs? It is difficult to think of any other purpose for them.

Infilled Roman road ditches produce excellent crop marks which show up as parallel lines across cornfields. On many occasions the farmers have quarried the top stones from the Roman roads for their dry-stone walls and farm buildings but they have seldom been able to shift the heavy foundation stones very far. Nevertheless, Roman roads often show up from the air as three deeper green or darker gold lines instead of two, with the central robber-trench showing up as a positive crop mark instead of the usual stunted negative mark produced above metalling.

A field-walker may be able to detect the spread of gravel from a Roman road showing as a lighter band across a field where ploughing has disturbed the *agger*.

With modern deep-ploughing, farmers are hitting more of the Roman roads' foundation stones, and they often drag these very large boulders to the field boundaries where they remain. It is possible to find the line of a suspected Roman road across country merely by following these dumps of huge stones, too big for the dry-stone wallers to use, and too heavy for the farmer to shift very far.

The main Roman roads also had grass tracks for unshod animals, outside the drainage ditches. Most of these outer tracks have been lost under mediaeval and modern agriculture but here and there they survive. On the outer edges of the grass strips, there were lesser ditches, probably road markers rather than for drainage.

The raised *aggers* were often huge, and sometimes still exist for considerable distances. They resemble causeways or old railway embankments. In other places, especially at approaches to rivers, the roads survive as hollow-ways.

The top stones of the *agger* occasionally had a raised central spine, probably intended to assist with the retention of surface gravel. Large kerbstones, sometimes squared, but often left rough, retained the edges of the top stones and gravel. There is a vast amount of archaeological evidence for the gravel-surfacing of Roman roads in Britain. The gravel must have brought even more problems for wheeled transport. The following modern table compares the friction of wheels on various surfaces:

Friction: force required to carry 1 ton on level ground

Railroad	8 lbs	per ton
Macadam road	44 – 67 lbs	per ton
Gravelled road	320 lbs	per ton
Loose, sandy soil	457 lbs	per ton

The gravel surfaces of Roman arterial roads had six times the friction of their paved-stone town roads. At Ebchester, Co Durham, at NZ 103 553 the modern B6309 road attempts to follow the dive of the Roman Dere Street down to the fort in the valley of the Derwent, but has had to make deviations to ease the gradient. Nevertheless, emergency gravelled turn-offs have been provided to arrest juggernauts with brake failures. Gravel does not like wheels but it is excellent for marching feet. How many dozens of oxen would it have taken to get a Roman wagon up the same road if a gravel surface stops a runaway fifty ton lorry on its downward plunge?

Clues under our noses

Hints of the answer to the Roman supply problems are right under our noses if we can only see them. At the foot of the terrible Ebchester Roman bank lies the fort of Vindomora (NZ 102 555). In front of the fort in the River Derwent is an old mill-dam. The mediaeval and later mills have long gone but a dried mill-leat of very large size runs right by the Roman fort wall. Is it possible that this river was an inland supply route? A very small Roman barge as depicted on tombstones all over the Empire would have carried a cargo of at least ten tons, or the equivalent of twenty ox-wagons. Also in front of the fort and below the mill-dam is a very long artificial, stone-built linear island in the centre of the river. This looks just like the type used in flash-lock systems but there is no known history of navigation on the tiny Durham Derwent. It is widely held that nothing has moved along our minor rivers

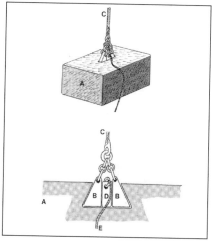

Roman cranes often lifted heavy stones with "lewis devices."

Two triangular iron wedges (B) and a spacer (D) fitted in a dove-tailed hole in the top surface of the stone (A). After the stone had been lowered into place, which could be underwater, the spacer was withdrawn with the lanyard (E). The crane-hoist (C) then lifted the lewis away and the process was repeated with another stone.

The Romans often cut horse-shoe-shaped grooves in large stones, for haulage ropes. This stone lies in a Roman quarry (NY 884 859) to the west of Risingham (Habitancum) fort, West Woodburn, Northumberland.

except ducks, water-hens, trout and salmon but a closer look may reveal much. At the down-stream end of the mill-leat was a postick mill. When this was dismantled some years ago, three Roman coins, *dupondii* of Antoninus Pius, were found in the foundations suggesting a Roman use of the building and its associated leat. The manoeuvring of flat-bottomed cargo-carrying punts up the shallow Derwent would have been an easy job compared with hoisting an ox-wagon up the Ebchester bank.

Steerable axles and mountain roads

This is an opportune place to discuss yet another problem. It has long been argued that the front axle of a Roman four-wheeled wagon would not pivot. The reasoning for this has been that on Roman reliefs, the front wheels of a wagon are depicted as the same size as the rear ones, therefore, it has been said: "they would not have been able to move under the main frame as the axle turned." However, if the wheels were quite wide of the cart's body, this problem would not have arisen. The answer has at last been found: in the Balkans, a fairly intact Roman-period wagon has been excavated. The front wheels were mounted on a turntable which allowed them to pivot. Let us hope there will be no more stories of Roman wagons being physically dragged sideways to get them around corners. (Venedikov 1960, *Trakijskate Kolesniza Sofia. Thracian Vehicle*). The "dragging sideways" argument should never have arisen, as it was known that pre-Roman Celtic four-wheeled wagons had steerable front axles. It was also well known that the *Edictum de pretiis* of AD 301 listed spare parts of wagons. In the list is a *columella* (vertical pillar). The same word was used for the pivot on which an upper mill-stone turned. The only place such a part could have been used in a wagon was on the turntable of a swivelling front axle.

In France, Spain and elsewhere, some Roman mountain roads were surfaced with rutted stones, like tram-lines. Sometimes these grooves were cut into solid rock. It is thought that they were purposely cut and not worn, as the ruts usually lie over the centres of the large stones. It is said that the ruts stopped the heavy Roman wagons from falling over the cliffs. The roads are far from straight and follow the twists and turns of the cliffs into which they are cut. Now that we know that Roman wagons were easily steerable, it would seem that the problem was solved but have you ever driven your car around a corner in snow and observed that the rear wheels do not follow the tracks of the front wheels? They take a short-cut. Therefore four-wheeled Roman wagons could not have negotiated the rutted cliff roads; the wheels would have jammed. The ruts are deep so even the wheels of a two-wheeled cart would have had difficulty. If so, what was the purpose of the grooves? It has been suggested that on the cliff roads, the Roman animals dragged "A-frames" behind them in North American Indian fashion. This would have provided braking action, stability, safety, and guidance.

There are vehicles other than those with wheels; a sledge for example. In France, in Roman quarries, steeply paved inclines have been found and these are known as *glissages*. They have deep ruts cut into them. A French archaeologist depicts a Roman sledge loaded with a large stone, making a controlled descent down the grooves, its progress restrained by a system of arrester-ropes. A few miles from the City of Durham, a similar grooved *glissage* descends from an old quarry at Malleygill, to the River Wear (NZ 307 460). It certainly looks like the Gallo-Roman *glissages* but it may be of Norman origin as stones for Durham Cathedral were quarried in the vicinity. Indeed, in another old and overgrown quarry close-by, a column-drum, obviously a reject, still lies unused. This brings up another interesting point: the Normans transported the stone up-river to Durham in barges and to deepen the river, they narrowed the channel with a long line of piles. The latter survive in the river bed.

Model of Roman bridge pier showing construction inside a coffer-dam. The coffer-dam's double wall of piles had the space between packed with watertight clay. When the pier was completed, the coffer-dam was flooded, and the space inside was often packed with rubble as an extra protection (as on Bridge No. 1 at Trier, Germany). Roman piers were massive so that each one could act as an independent abutment in case of an arch collapse. The pier depicted here would contain between 600 and 1,000 tons of stone.

River crossings

An all-weather military road system is of no use without bridges. Fords may be of use during dry periods but native uprisings do not always coincide with periods of good weather. First class bridges formed an essential part of the Roman road network.

It looks as if the Roman civil engineers were instructed by an army manual on bridge building and this makes their handiwork easy to identify. For medium and wide river crossings, the Roman bridges fall under three categories: all-timber construction; stone piers with a timber superstructure; and all-stone structures. They did not search about for the easiest crossing point and then deviate the road to it. The bridges were built on the survey lines and it seems that the engineers could handle extremely difficult river conditions. The all-timber bridges were probably built during campaigns and the most common type of permanent bridge in Britain was one with masonry piers and a timber superstructure. The abutments in the banksides were massive and often contained tens of thousands of tons of stone. The stone piers were also huge and the average would contain a thousand tons. If an arch, or a section of bridge fell, or was washed away, the whole bridge would not have gone down like a row of dominoes because each pier was solid enough to act as a temporary abutment and take the terrific sideways stresses. According to surviving records, Roman piers were always constructed with independent foundations on the river bed. The later practice, often used in

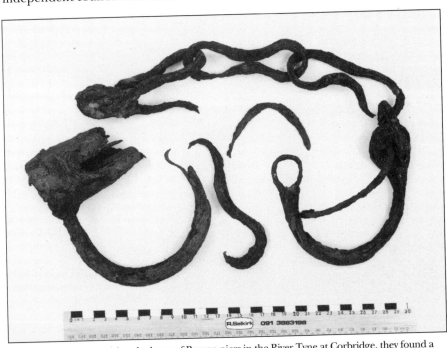

While divers were inspecting the bases of Roman piers in the River Tyne at Corbridge, they found a Roman slave-chain, complete with barrel-lock. This chain is almost identical to those found at Bigberry, near Canterbury. The main identification feature of Roman slave-chains is the figure-of-eight link which was not connected in the centre.

Top:
Reused Roman stone, with lewis hole, in the tower of St Andrew's Saxon Church, Bywell, NZ 048 615.

Bottom:
Reused Roman stone, with lewis hole, in the west wall of St Andrew's Saxon Church, Corbridge, NY 988 644

Reused Roman stone in the
tower of St Andrew's Saxon
Church, Corbridge.

the mediaeval period, of building solid causeways across a river, and then
placing piers on the barrier, was never used by the Romans. The Romans
regarded rivers as public property and a Roman law forbade the erection of
barriers across a river unless the barrier was for navigation or other essential
purposes. Some mediaeval bridges look as if they are standing on waterfalls.
Indeed the ramp *is* an artificial waterfall. Roman bridges *never* used this
system.

On the site of the planned bridge-pier, the engineers built a coffer-dam
which is a watertight enclosure around the construction area. This took the
form of a rectangular or lozenge-shaped fence of oak piles driven into the
river bed. The fence consisted of a double perimeter of piles, one within the
other. The space between was packed with watertight clay. Two types of
pumps were available to the builders; double-acting pumps, similar to those
in use by modern fire services until the 1920's and Archimedean screws which
were large hollowed logs with another log free to rotate, fitting neatly inside.
The internal log had a spiral groove cut into it. One end of the device was
lowered at an angle into the water inside the flooded coffer-dam with the
other end over the watertight fence. When the internal drum was rotated,
water was forced up the spiral groove and out into the river. Buckets removed
the last few gallons and kept abreast of seepage and leakage.

Inside the coffer-dam, a great many oaken timber piles about a foot square
and several feet in length, with iron-shod points at the lower end, were driven
vertically into the river bed. When firm resistance was met, the piles were

sawn-off level with the river bed. On the tops of these sawn-off piles was fixed a platform of extremely large oaken timbers. On this platform, the pier construction commenced, consisting of stone blocks or a three-dimensional trellis of massive timbers. The bridge-timbers were never less than a foot square in cross-section and usually much bigger.

When the bridge-pier was completed, the coffer-dam was often left in place and the gap between pier and fence filled with rubble to form an extra protection. Examples of this practice are still visible at Trier, Germany, on the first of the two Roman bridges (immediately downstream from the bridge number two, which has a modern superstructure on Roman piers, lie the bases of the piers of the earlier Roman bridge). These submerged pier-bases still have their coffer-dams in place.

The great bridge across the Danube at Turnu-Severin, built by civil engineer Apollodorus on the orders of Emperor Trajan. also had its gigantic piers built inside coffer-dams. This bridge was almost three-quarters of a mile long and is depicted on a relief on Trajan's column in Rome. The bridge according to Dio Cassius who wrote about a hundred years after its construction, had twenty stone-built piers, each 150 feet high, 60 feet long, and 50 feet thick. The openings between the piers were 110 feet wide and were spanned by timber arches. That is the type of bridge construction the Romans were able to achieve.

If the river bed was of solid rock, this was a bonus for the bridge constructors as piles were not necessary. An earthen coffer-dam was constructed from the river bank half way into the river and curved back to the same bank. The pound thus formed was evacuated as before and construction of the piers began directly on the bed-rock.

Where there was an island in the river, construction was simple; one channel was dammed and half of the bridge was built in the dry bed and the process repeated with the other channel.

The Romans had both cement and concrete. Sometimes one, or both were used; often neither, with neat stonework fitting tightly together without mortar. Several types of iron cramps were used to tie the stones together in the bridge sections where flood-water pressure was expected to be highest. Some of these were staple-shaped with the ends sealed with molten lead into adjacent stones. Another type was a "butterfly" which fitted into wedge-shaped recesses cut opposite each other. Iron tie-bars lying in grooves across many stones was another method of resisting sideways forces. Vertical ties were sometimes used such as iron dowels projecting from the top surface of one stone into the base of the one above.

Roman piers always had pointed cutwaters upstream and the downstream ends were either pointed, square or semi-circular. In tidal waters, there were always points at both ends.

The Romans had a guild of divers and could do repair work without coffer-dams. They also had "hydraulic-cement" (*pozzuolana*) which would actually harden underwater. This was made by mixing volcanic ash with their normal cement. The Roman concrete is easily recognisable because of the size of the aggregate. Nowadays building regulations recommend sizes no larger than a "bean" but the pebbles in Roman concrete often exceed the size of eggs. The dome of the Pantheon in Rome was constructed of concrete and done with a single "pour." The advantage of using dry-stone construction was in earthquake zones. During an earth-tremor, dry stonework would jiggle around slightly, whereas a solid structure would crack. On some of the large "arcades" (arched aqueduct bridges) in Italy, France, Spain and elsewhere, it has been noticed that the arch spans are not quite equal. The gaps progressively increase by small amounts. The end result is that during earthquake tremors, the whole structure does not have a single resonant frequency which could result in the whole structure shaking itself to pieces. It is not known if the Roman use of this technique was intentional or accidental.

For small river crossings, Roman bridges were much simpler. Two parallel lines of vertical timbers, usually about a foot in cross-section, were driven into the river bed or placed in square holes cut into the bed-rock. At Hartburn, in Northumberland, the post holes of a Roman bridge on the Devil's Causeway Roman road were recently found in the rock bed of the Hart Burn at NZ 088 865. When the sand and pebbles were removed from the holes very carefully by excavators, lying in the shallow water, using face-masks and breathing apparatus, a Roman bronze votive pin was found at the bottom of almost every hole. Roman bridge sites are rich in artefacts. In addition to all kinds of junk thrown into the river by the Romans, coins and other offerings lie jammed between boulders and under sediment. As will be desribed in full later, over a thousand artefacts were recovered from among the boulders on the river bed at Piercebridge by divers, along the line of the Dere Street Roman bridge.

After the Roman withdrawal from Britain, the next invaders, the illiterate and pagan Saxons, thought that the Romans must have been giants because of the size of the stones they had used in their buildings. The Saxons knew nothing of cranes or pile-drivers, which were essential to the Roman engineers. Even modern civil engineers are impressed by Roman constructions.

We know that the Romans had excellent cranes because written descriptions of them survive and they are also pictured on stone reliefs. Further evidence of cranes can be seen even today on most Roman sites, especially those where very large stones were used. The stones were not lifted by crane-hooks but by a device which had to have a specially shaped hole cut into the top surface of the stone. First of all let us study the crane itself.

The superstructure of the crane was a bipod derrick and its configuration could be adjusted by guy-ropes. The motive power was supplied by slaves working inside a cylindrical treadmill which turned the drum for the lifting ropes. Surviving stone reliefs show fixed cranes but there were also floating and wheeled varieties. It is likely that the floating cranes used a catamaran-type hull. The catamaran design was well known to the Romans and a large wine-transporting vessel on the River Moselle used this arrangement (stone relief in Landesmuseum, Trier).

When the Roman crane was used to lift stones, a hook could be used with slings but to prevent the ropes jamming under the block once it was in place, "U-shaped" grooves to take the ropes, were cut into the sides of the stone.

Pincers, which gripped into holes cut into the sides of the stone were also used but, by far the most common method of lifting, was with the "lewis." This device consisted of two triangular irons and a rectangular spacing piece which fitted into a dove-tailed hole cut into the top surface of the stone. When the stone was lowered into position which could be underwater, the spacing piece was withdrawn by a lanyard and the two triangular pieces were then free to be pulled out by the crane hoist and the process repeated with another stone. Unfortunately the lewis device was re-invented in the 14th century so a lewis-hole in a stone is not firm evidence of a Roman origin. However, as has been mentioned previously, the Saxons of the 6th and 7th centuries who were converting to Christianity, had been encouraged to build their new churches on the pagan sites and many of the latter were ex-Roman temples and *principia* of forts which 5th century Saxons had adapted for the worship of their tribal deities.

The early Saxon churches were of timber, but once the Saxons got the knack of building in stone with a bit of French and Flemish help, the ex-Roman stones came in very handy. Early Saxon churches are full of Roman stones, especially the towers which seem to predate the remaining parts of the buildings. The Saxons had no idea what the lewis-hole was for and in the reused positions of the stones, this can be on any surface of the stone. Saxon churches with reused lewis-holed stones tell us that there is very likely to be a Roman site very close by, and in many cases, right underneath the church.

Roman bricks and tiles are also found in reused positions in Saxon churches and are quite easy to identify. The most common Roman brick was about a foot square and $1\frac{1}{2}$ inches thick and most of the ones found in Britain are red in colour. The craft of brickmaking seems to have been forgotten after the Roman military departure c406 and hardly a brick was made in Britain for seven hundred years but there was a great demand by the Saxons from the seventh century onwards, for second-hand Roman bricks, salvaged from Roman buildings. The Normans also made use of them. The Saxon tower of Holy Trinity church in Colchester is built of Roman bricks and St Albans Cathedral has a profusion of them in its west front.

Norman and later churches were built on the sites of Saxon churches, so searchers for the Romans should look at church histories very closely.

We shall be looking at Saxon churches time and time again when we come to our search for "lost Roman roads."

Whenever historians are confronted with unexplained reused Roman stones in later buildings, the first explanations are usually: "The stones were robbed from the Roman Wall," or: "The stones were found in the river after being washed down from the Wall." Other common excuses are: "The stones were brought from the Roman fort at South Shields," or: "The stones were robbed from Binchester." The truth always seems to be missed and that truth usually proves to be: "The Romans were up to something right here."

In mediaeval times, roads were extremely poor and the principal transporter was the pack-horse which carried three hundredweights (152 kg). Salzman, in *Building in England* (Oxford 1952), quotes: "...repairs to Tutbury Castle in 1314, where the cost of transport over five or six miles came to nearly twice the cost of the quarried stone." There are exceptions of course

Abutment of small Roman bridge on the Cong Burn (NZ 260 517), before and after excavation. Nine Roman coins were recovered from the stonework. The bridge is on the direct line between the Ebchester and Chester-le-Street Roman forts. The stream is only ten feet wide and a few inches deep.

A Roman paved ford in a stream near Brancepeth, County Durham (NZ 219 379) on a branch of the Dere Street Roman road.

but where very large Roman stones are found, they are usually very close to home.

A lot of time has been spent on lewis-holes, but as will be seen, they can provide some excellent clues in our search. Now let us look at Roman pile-drivers. The iron-tipped wooden piles were about a foot square and as long as necessary for the job in hand.

Julius Caesar built a temporary bridge a quarter of a mile long across the Rhine. The construction was mainly of long piles driven into the river bed, sloping inwards, with a timber roadway fixed to the tops. The construction took ten days, after which Caesar's army crossed the bridge and fought a campaign against the German tribes. After the campaign, he returned across the bridge and dismantled it.

This type of task was not completed by soldiers hammering away at piles with mallets as depicted in some of our history books. The most common mistake made by both historians and archaeologists is to underestimate the capabilities of the Romans.

The Roman engineers must have had some kind of pile-driving machine that lifted and dropped a heavy weight fairly rapidly or they couldn't have built the Rhine bridge in ten days. It has been suggested to me how they did it; in the River Tiber, the Romans had floating corn-mills. These were ships which contained rotating milling machinery. The vessels were anchored against the river flow and paddle-wheels on the ship's sides were driven by the current. These paddle-wheels were connected to the mill-gears. An easy adaptation of this would have been a floating pile-driver which would have been ideal for bridge-building.

Fords

In addition to bridges, the Roman roads used fords, but mainly to cross minor streams. The bed of the stream was usually paved with very large stones. An excellent example has been located on the newly discovered length of the Stanegate Roman road between Bywell and Corbridge, Northumberland, in the bed of the Clockey Burn (full details in Chapter 6).

As well as fords across minor streams, the Romans have, on occasion, forded quite large rivers. On the River North Tyne, just upstream from the confluence of the North and South Tynes, the previously missing length of the Stanegate, crossed the river at Howford at NY 917 663. The Saxon church at Warden, a few hundred yards away contains many reused Roman stones. Does this church hide an unknown Roman site associated with the river crossing?

The Roman road *agger* is still *in situ* in the west bank of the river and extends right down to the water's edge. The reason the search for the missing Stanegate has taken so long is that everybody thought that it must have left Corbridge and headed for the Roman bridge at Chollerford on the North Tyne. It has actually gone to a ford two miles to the south of the bridge so this branch of the famous "Stanegate" was a summer road only. This, and more evidence to be produced later, casts doubt on its role as the frontier before the Wall was built. We will return to this subject when frontiers are discussed in Chapter 10.

Birds foot patterns

So much for river crossings; now let us get back to the roads which crossed these bridges and fords. Most maps of Roman sites show a single Roman road crossing a bridge but this is hardly likely. The French archaeologist Raymond Chevalier in his *Roman Roads* (1976), is confident that whole networks of roads met at the bridges. He calls these "bird's foot patterns." We are finding confirmation of this in Britain and in the last five years, over 250 miles of unknown Roman roads have been discovered in Northumberland, Durham and Cumbria (details later) and there are indications that many more remain to be found. Similar unknown networks must exist all over Britain.

Summary

It looks as if the Roman roads were built first and foremost for swift military movements at all times of the year and in all but the most severe winter weather conditions. Pack-animals would have been able to use them without much difficulty but wagons could have made it up (and down) the gradients only with the help of hundreds of soldiers. In mediaeval times, and the later stage-coach era, teams of oxen were kept at farms near inclines to assist vehicles up gradients which were quite gentle in comparison with the Roman ascents. There is no evidence whatsoever for accommodation for extra teams of animals at either the tops or bottoms of Roman hill roads.

The *Cursus Publicus*

As well as the army and pack animals, the roads were used by the government postal service, the *cursus publicus.* The system did not operate with relays; each messenger travelled the whole distance himself. In Italy on such smoothly paved roads as the "Via Appia," he probably rode in a light vehicle but on Britain's gravelled switchbacks, the courier must have travelled on horse-back. The couriers were usually drawn from the army and held a warrant to use the *cursus publicus.* This warrant was called a *diploma* and was a very precious document which could be signed only by the emperor, his authorised agent, or governors of provinces. They were strictly rationed as they entitled the holder to free transport and free food and accommodation. Along the routes of the service were inns called *mansiones* or *stationes.* They provided food and quarters and if necessary a change of animals or vehicles. They were usually between twenty-five and thirty-five miles apart as this was an average day's fast travel. Less important stopping places were called *mutationes* (changing places) and only supplied the very basic needs. Only in emergencies did the couriers travel by night and day and then the speed was trebled. Typical times taken for government couriers were:

Rome – Brindisi	7 days
Rome – London	13 days
Rome – Byzantium	25 days
Rome – Antioch	40 days
Rome – Alexandria	55 days

A record was set by a courier when the legions mutinied at Mainz (on the Rhine) in AD 69. News reached Rome in eight days. This was about 150 miles per day, or an overall average speed of just over 6 mph.

The unidentified rutted road (NZ 307 461) in a ravine which leads down to the River Wear near Durham, compared with a drawing of a known rutted Roman road in France. The road may be of Norman origin as the Normans transported stone upriver from here for the building of Durham Cathedral.

A normal day's travel by the courier was about thirty miles and this gives an overall average speed of just over 1 mph, or an average speed of 3 mph while actually travelling. If 3 mph was *fast* road travel, then what was the speed of the slow movers? It is obvious that road travel in Roman times was much slower than most historians (who write in the age of motorways) would have us believe. A better speed was made by couriers who travelled by sea as a Roman merchant ship sailed for weeks on end, around the twenty-four hours and averaged about 4 knots (4.5 mph). When Claudius travelled from Rome to Britain to take part in the final victories over the southern British tribes, he travelled by a combination of sea, river and roads. First of all, he sailed down the Tiber to Ostia and then to Massilia (Marseilles). He crossed Gaul partly by river and partly by road. Which rivers he used is not known. Dio Cassius tells us that: "Claudius joined his legions at the Thames and led them across the river to engage the Britons who had assembled there. Having defeated them, he took Camulodunum" (Colchester). Therefore, when we consider long distance travel in Roman times, we must include ships and river boats as well as road transport.

Contrary to popular belief, it seems that the Roman roads in Britain were not the equivalent of motorways at all. Proof of this comes from the Roman fort of Vindolanda which is situated on the Roman Stanegate road just to the south of Hadrian's Wall. The wet soil conditions there have preserved many Roman letters. One of these letters was written by one Octavius in AD 115 from an unknown address. The writer complains that he is still awaiting delivery of grain and hides for which he has already paid, from Cataractonia (Catterick) and laments the bad state of the roads. He goes on to say that if he does not get the supplies, he will be financially embarrassed. He adds that the roads are bad and are completely unfit for wheeled traffic and that mules are the best means of transport.

That is a shattering piece of evidence for all those who have imagined long convoys of ox-wagons plying their way up Ermine Street and Dere Street with supplies for the north.

The North-East correspondent of *The Times*, Chris Tighe, in an article on 30.9.88 tells of an interview with an academic from Durham University. This gentleman says that perhaps the roads in the north were not completed as the Romans had conquered the area only some twenty years previously. Here we have an eminent scholar saying that the Romans had been unable to provide roads suitable for wheeled transport in twenty years, whereas most of our history books tell us that as the Romans army advanced, so did the brilliant engineers provide instant cross-country all-weather "motorways" behind it. Our historians cannot have it both ways. If the Roman roads in the north of England couldn't handle Octavius' hides and grain, they couldn't supply the Roman military frontier which stretches from the Tyne to the Solway. Perhaps these last words contain the answers for which we search: The River Eden runs into the Irish Sea via the Solway, and the River Irthing is a tributary of the Eden. Both rivers pass through areas of intense Roman military occupation as do the Rivers South Tyne and North Tyne which combine as the Tyne, and enter the North sea beside the huge Roman supply base of South Shields with its twenty-plus granaries. A unit called the *Barcarii*

Tigrisenses (Bargemen of the River Tigris) was stationed here.

The River South Tyne and the Irthing come within four miles of each other in the Birdoswald/Carvoran area which is the central area of the Stanegate Roman road and the later Hadrian's Wall complex. If the Tipalt Burn and an unnamed drainage channel near Gilsland are included, the distance between the waters is reduced to a few yards in the same field at NY 646 668. Are we looking at a North Sea to Irish Sea water link? Dr Martin Eckoldt, a German archaeologist whose work will be discussed at length in Chapter 7, has found that the Romans navigated waterways in Germany which were, until recently, thought to be merely farm drainage ditches.

Preparing for the search

By now it is hoped that the reader will be acquiring an insight into the Roman road system and a sympathy for the surveyors and engineers who built it. We must now prepare ourselves for the fieldwork which I hope will produce a vast amount of new evidence right throughout England, Scotland and Wales (the Romans didn't invade Ireland although they contemplated it and reckoned they could do it with two legions).

Some research is essential and to simplify this, four subjects sum it up:

1 Place-names
2 Maps
3 Documents
4 False trails

Place-names

Let us start with place-names. The odd name here and there might originate from Celtic times, but most of them are from the Saxon, Viking and Norman periods. Many rivers though, have retained their Celtic names with some Latinisation from the Roman occupiers. The River Tyne was the Roman "Tinea Fluvius," the Thames, the "Tamesis Fl" and the Tay, the "Tava Fl" Readers should try to obtain the Ordnance Survey map of Roman Britain, now available as a single sheet printed on both sides. Most of the Latin names are marked.

Those who would go into the subject of place-names deeply, should consult *The Place-Names of Roman Britain* by A L F Rivet & C Smith, (1982), or various other works.

Old English (Saxon) contains only a few dozen words of the Celtic language such as *crag, tor* (high rock) and *combe* (deep valley). The Celtic name for a river is *avon* so *River Avon* means River River! *Cheet* is Celtic for "wood" so Cheetwood in Lancashire means "Wood-wood." It seems that the Saxons did not even bother to understand the few Celtic words that they borrowed. The Celtic word "eccles" (*eglos* in Cornwall and *eglwys* in Wales) however, is of great significance because it means "church." As previously explained, early churches were often placed on pagan sites and there are examples of them actually on top of pre-historic burial mounds. No doubt Celtic churches would be in the vicinity of Roman sites during the last hundred years of Roman occupation, when Christianity was tolerated by the Roman masters. After the Roman military departure c406, the incoming pagan Saxons would need a couple of hundred years to be Christianised by missionaries from two directions, Scotland in the north-west and Rome in the south-east. Once again, their churches would be placed on pagan sites which were often ex-Roman forts and shrines. As Saxon churches were associated with Saxon settlements, both should be identified where possible. A good example is *"Aldeburgh."* (Old Town) where a Saxon settlement was built on the ruins of Roman Isurium. A mediaeval town followed in turn but kept the Saxon name.

Place-names can furnish useful clues to the existence of Roman roads and settlements. This book is being written in a town called "Chester-le-Street," where there was a Roman fort at the tidal limit of the River Wear (Vedra Fl) and its junction with a small river, the Cone (Con Fl). A Roman road, not mentioned in any Roman documents, passed through here on its way from Brough on Humber (Petuaria) to Newcastle upon Tyne (Pons Aelius).

The Latin name for the Roman fort at Chester-le-Street was "Concangis" and it looks as if the Romans had Latinised the Celtic name of the River "Con." Later, Saxon monks who were fleeing from the Vikings built a church right on top of the Roman headquarters building and called their new town "Conceastre," retaining the Romanised Celtic name of the river plus their word for "castle." The Normans shortened the Saxon name to "Ceastre" and later to "Chester" and in the seventeenth century, it became "Chester-le-Street (fort-on-the-road).

The word *stane, stain,* or *stan* is Saxon for "stone" and *gate,* a derivative of the Old Norse *gata,* means "road." Thus, the Saxon/Viking name for the Roman road "Stanegate" means "Stone-road."

Clues for Roman roads are obvious names like Low Gate, Stony Gate, Green Gate, Street Houses, Stane Street etc, but for reasons unknown, "Mount Pleasants" and "Cold Harbours" are frequent indicators of Roman roads or sites. The Saxon word *burgh* (fortification) is also often used to describe former Roman fort sites as well as their own defended earthworks. The name "Causey" tells us that there was a Roman "causeway" in the vicinity.

Maps

Map-reading is by far the most important skill for Roman road hunters. A map is like a giant aerial photograph presented in a form of code. Once one learns to read it properly, much information is revealed. With the Ordnance Survey 1:50,000 map, it is like looking at the countryside from a U2 high altitude spy-plane, and to the practised eye, settlement patterns and communication systems emerge. The straight road with an obvious kink in it is where a mediaeval road couldn't take a Roman gradient. Where a road runs first on one edge of a straight alignment, and then on the other, is where a modern road has "frozen" the earlier road where stage-coaches switched from one side to the other trying to avoid bad patches of a Roman road which had received no maintenance for over a thousand years.

The place where the rivers' edges change from black ink to blue are the tidal limits. Does the road pattern hint at a Roman origin? If so we may have an unknown Roman harbour. If the tidal limit is fairly near the river mouth, there may be an artificial barrier in the river invariably described by chair-borne historians as a "fish-trap." According to some academic gentlemen, the mediaeval fishermen must have been multi-millionaires judging by the monumental stone barriers they are supposed to have placed in the rivers to provide their "fish suppers." Of course the stone barriers *were* used as fish-traps but that was not their original purpose. An ordinary fish-trap is a row of stakes in the water with baskets between, and would probably have cost a month's wages to erect, and not the equivalent cost of a modern airfield runway.

If the first edition (c1850) O S six inch to the mile maps are used, it is like flying low level over the countryside but seeing it as it was a hundred and fifty years ago. There is the added advantage of written information about antiquities found, or still visible at the time the map was drawn.

Mapping of Britain did not commence with the Ordnance Survey, and older maps, such as estate plans, are often inaccurate but can reveal much information. Tithe Maps can tell us the names of individual fields, and with field names like "Chesters Flatt," "The Streets," and "High Camp," it is obvious that a Roman road has crossed these fields. As will be seen in Chapter 6, these same field names revealed an unknown branch of the "Devil's Causeway" in Northumberland. On Tithe maps, all the fields are numbered and each map is accompanied by a book which gives details of the numbered fields. Most county record offices keep the six inch early edition Ordnance Survey maps and Tithe maps available for public inspection.

This is an appropriate place to mention very long distance Roman road alignments. It appears that the Roman surveyors sometimes lined-up their roads on distant forts or towns even though the road itself did not continue as far as that place. A typical example is the long straight stretch of Roman road under the A66(T) which runs south-east from Greta Bridge to Scotch Corner to join the north-bound road "Dere Street" under the A1(T). If a ruler is placed on the Greta Bridge – Scotch Corner road, it will be seen that a continuation passes right through the Malton Roman fort some forty-two miles distant. No Roman road has been found on this line. Also, the very straight stretch of Roman Dere Street in Northumberland is also lined up on Malton, seventy-eight miles away in Yorkshire, once again with no known road along the extended line beyond Ebchester.

The straight stretch of Ermine Street, north-bound through Lincoln, is lined up on Whitby Abbey seventy-five miles to the north on the other side of the Humber estuary, across the Yorkshire Wolds and the North York Moors. A Roman site has long been postulated under Whitby Abbey, but there is no sign of a Roman road along the above line. Similar long-distance alignments can be observed all over Britain. Much research remains to be done into Roman surveying methods.

Documents

I do not propose to bore readers with a long dialogue of how to research old documents, because, in Chapter 6, which is a case-study of an intense search in the county of Northumberland, it will become evident to the investigator, the type of information necessary to back-up fieldwork. The availability of old documents varies from place to place but most counties have excellent record offices with all the various documents available for that particular area. Historical societies and university libraries usually hold all the old books with references going back two hundred years or more. The antiquarians of the eighteenth and nineteenth century were very observant people and there was a lot more archaeological evidence visible in those days.

No maps of Roman Britain survive, but a road map of some of the main Roman roads can be reconstructed from the British section of a road book called the *Itinerarium Provinciarum Antonini Augusti* (Antonine Itinerary). Many well known Roman roads, such as the Devil's Causeway in Northumberland, are not even mentioned so we are unlikely to find any evidence of unknown Roman roads. By and large, the Itinerary distances between Roman forts agree with the surviving evidence but here and there, the archaeological authorities have got it hopelessly wrong and have twisted the evidence to fit their own interpretations. From High Rochester (Bremenium) in Northumberland to York (Eburacum), the following table shows a comparison with the distances quoted by the Romans and those measured by modern surveyors.

1 Roman mile = 1,620 yards (1,481 metres)

Roman fort/town		Itinerary distance *(Roman miles)*	Actual distance *(Roman miles)*
Bremenium	(High Rochester)		
Corstopitum	(Corbridge)	20	25
Vindomora	(Ebchester)	9	10
Vinovia	(Binchester)	19	20
Cataractonium	(Catterick)	22	22
Isurium	(Aldeburgh)	24	25
Eburacum	(York)	17	17

Then things go horribly wrong:

Our authorities have placed Roman Derventio at Malton and the distance between York and Malton is twenty Roman miles but the Itinerary said it was only seven.

The authorities are not at all sure where Roman Delgovicia was but the Itinerary said that Derventio to Delgovicia was thirteen miles.

As the authorities see it		Itinerary distance	Actual distance
Eburacum	(York)		
Derventio	(Malton)	7	20
Delgovicia	(unknown)	13	?
Praetorio	(Brough on Humber)	25	?

Roman Praetorio was placed at Brough on Humber by the authorities, but epigraphic evidence has proved that the Roman name of Brough was Petuaria. The Itinerary distance given between Delgovicia and Praetorio is twenty-five miles. In addition, in order to fiddle these distances, the archaeological authorities have had to make the Roman road make a right turn of one hundred degrees.

What has been ignored, is the suspected Roman site at Stamford Bridge where four and possibly five Roman roads meet. Let us now place Derventio at Stamford Bridge, Delgovicia at Malton and Praetorio at Whitby and see how the distances agree:

This makes more sense		Itinerary distance	Actual distance
Eburacum	(York)		
Derventio	(Stamford Bridge)	7	7
Delgovicia	(Malton)	13	13
Praetorio	(Whitby)	25	25
	[Roman site postulated here under site of abbey]		
or possibly	(Bridlington)	25	25
	[many recent finds here and a Roman road heads this way]		

The distances all agree. Derventio is still on the River Derwent and what is more, a Roman site has just been confirmed at Stamford Bridge by metal detectorists of the Consett Club of County Durham. An alternative to Whitby for Roman Praetorio is Bridlington where much new evidence has come to light of late.

Clearly, our history books are obsolete. Other mistakes elsewhere in Britain, in our interpretation of the Antonine Itinerary should be corrected.

Identification and misidentification

There were roads in Britain long before the Romans invaded. Quite often they followed ridges and they never used straight sections. Now and again the Roman engineers incorporated some of these native tracks into their system. After the Roman military departure, the new masters of England were the Saxon invaders who had little use for the Roman roads. Once the Roman bridges collapsed, the roads lost their importance except for local needs. The Saxons did find a use for them, and that was as territorial boundary markers where there were no suitable natural features such as streams or rivers. These land boundaries became parish boundaries and if a road, path or track follows a parish boundary, it is a good indication of its antiquity. Near my home, the recently discovered aqueduct-channel (*specus*) to the Chester-le-Street Roman fort has survived as a parish boundary for half a mile.

The next invaders, the Vikings who fought the Saxons for many generations before they intermarried and merged their languages, likewise had little use for roads which by this time were in a terrible state.

There are thousands of deserted mediaeval villages in Britain and the reasons for the abandonment for such reasons as plagues, and change of land use, are beyond the scope of this work. It has been noticed however that, time and time again, newly discovered Roman roads and quite a few known ones, transit these "DMV's." The villagers were still using the old Roman roads even if they were in a ruinous state. A recently discovered straight length of Roman road in Northumberland has three DMV's on it. The DMV's may be hiding unknown Roman features. Conversely, one should plot all the DMV's on a map in red ink and then juggle a ruler around on them to see if this produces any obvious alignments. The technique has proved successful in the north of England.

By far the best method of finding Roman roads is the search for alignments of various features. If the researcher finds, with a combination of fieldwalking and map interpretation, a length of parish boundary, a public footpath, a hedge-line, a cart track and a piece of modern road, all forming a greater alignment, then it is highly likely that this is an unknown Roman road. The finder should then go through a check-list to see if the suspected Roman road obeys some of the rules:

Check-list for suspected Roman roads

1   Does the suspected road have straight stretches?
2   Do these straight stretches run up and down hill without any attempt to ease the gradient?
3   Does the line have small corrections to heading at high points?
4   Are these changes of direction sudden?
5   Is the alignment on a distant peak?
6   Are there "mirror-image" deviations at ravines?
7   Are there zig-zags at descents of cliffs?
8   If a mediaeval or later road has followed the suspected Roman line, has the later road been forced to make a wide detour because it couldn't take the Roman gradient at the descents and climbs?
9   Are there small grass-covered quarries beside the line?
10 Is there an indication of a marked *agger*?
11 Are there any signs of drainage ditches at the road sides?
12 Have any large boulders been dragged out and dumped by the farmer?
13 Do field boundaries contain stones too large to have been used by dry-stone wallers?
14 Do the names *stane, stone, stan, gate, chester, castor, caistor, street, strat, causeway, causey, burgh, brough, Mount Pleasant, Cold Harbour,* or *arbour* occur?
15 Is there a Saxon church on the line?
16 Is there a post-Saxon church on the line? If so check the records for the history or tradition of a previous Saxon church.
17 Are there any Deserted Mediaeval Villages on the line?
18 Are there signs of a scatter of small stones across ploughed fields?
19 Are there signs of outlying grass tracks for unshod animals? (most of these have been ploughed away)
20 Are there any spare-parts in the form of large boulders at the road sides?
21 Does the road line cross streams or rivers beside mediaeval water-mills? (the reason for this question will become apparent later).
22 Are there any culverts of rectangular cross-section at right angles to the road direction?
23 At crossings of small streams, is the ford constructed with extremely large stones?
24 Are there double tree-lines or double hedgerows marking the line because the farmer has been unable to plough out the great amount of Roman stone?
25 If the road is along a ridge, does it follow the "military crest?" i.e. is it slightly below the skyline so that an enemy on the other side will not see troop movements? This applies particularly to frontier zones.

If the answers to some of these questions are positive, then suspected fords should be searched and trial trenching across the road line carried out.

Quite often, only a relatively short length of Roman road is found. If this contains a straight stretch, this might have been surveyed with a destination in mind. Often, it is merely lined up on a distant hill where there would probably have been an alteration of heading and the planned destination eludes us. With a bit of luck, the straight piece is lined up on the final destination. If the projected line coincides with a village at a river crossing, and the village has an existing, or a tradition of a Saxon church, then there is a good chance that the researcher's ruler laid along the Ordnance Survey map, has revealed an unknown Roman settlement.

False clues

There are other roads and features in our landscape which often resemble Roman roads and a lot of time can be wasted. Let us look at some of the features which can lead us on a wild goose chase.

Old roads other than Roman

The prehistoric trackways are usually winding "green lanes" but have been paved and used here and there by the Romans.

We need not worry too much about the Dark Age Saxons or the Vikings as neither showed any inclination towards civil engineering. The first real interest in roads since the Roman military departure was in the English monastic period, when money and technical assistance was supplied by the monks and the religious houses. The techniques of arch-building in the

Boy Scouts built this bridge over the Devil's Water at Dilston.
The construction is very similar to that of temporary Roman bridges. The Roman structures were of course, many times larger.

The Roman road south of Chester-le-Street at NZ 274 496, descends a slope as a hollow-way.

abbeys lent itself to bridge-building. Some excellent bridges survive but in no way can they be mistaken for Roman bridges although they may often be on sites of Roman bridges and contain reused Roman stones. Mostly, the mediaeval travellers used what was left of the old Roman roads, but deviated at the steep Roman inclines. Quite often, the disused stretch of Roman road up the hill is marked by a double hedgerow for reasons explained previously. Often, a single hedge followed by a steep footpath short-cuts the mediaeval deviation. This footpath follows the line of the old Roman road.

Mediaeval pack-horse trails are paved here and there but are extremely narrow. The distinctive hump-backed bridges are also narrow and have low parapets to allow the horse's panniers to overhang them. Some pack-horse routes were dedicated to one commodity such as salt or lead. Many ex-Roman roads were used, so salters' roads and lead roads together with roads with names like "Pilgrims' Way" and "Pedlars' Way" should be examined against the check-list for Roman roads.

Cattle Roads and Drove Roads

Cattle roads provide access to grazing lands. Often, short straight branch roads lead down to river-side meadows. Long distance cattle roads are known as "Drove Roads." They had wide verges to accommodate all kinds of animals on the move to markets around the country. Even geese had their feet encased in tar for the journey. Drove roads were often known as "Driftways" and can sometimes be identified by names such as "Bullock Road." Inns were located on them, and a marker, which often signalled a night-stopping place to the drover, was a clump of fir trees. Now and again, drove roads followed Roman roads.

When some roads were "turnpiked" after 1663, drove roads tried to avoid tolls and ran parallel to them, thus also avoiding traffic and at the same time retaining access to wide grass verges for grazing.

The turnpike roads were usually improved existing roads, but now and again, new stretches were built. They are all well documented so should cause no confusion in searches for Roman evidence.

Enclosure roads

Enclosure roads were made as a result of parliamentary enclosure awards in the period c1750-1850 and are easily identified from contemporary plans and maps held in the county record offices. They can be a trap for the unwary Roman road hunter.

Estate diversions

Diversions of roads around gentlemens' parks can also lead the field-walker to think that he has found an old Roman road when it turns out to be a discontinued road across private land. Estate records can help with the elimination of these false trails.

Obviously the best way to learn how to find Roman roads is to go out and do it. There are hundreds of miles of unknown Roman roads awaiting discovery in every county of England, Wales and southern Scotland. Aeroplanes are very useful tools but not essential. Keen observation, good map-reading and a feeling for the Roman road builders, are what counts.

To end this chapter and to try to create the correct atmosphere for a road search, I will quote excerpts from a delightful article by an anonymous author.

Along the Portway

"I should have been rather glad if someone at Silchester had asked me why I was walking in a perfectly straight line across a trackless field. It would have been a simple pleasure to reply that I was actually going along a Roman main road, the Portway, which was invisible just there but of which I hoped to see something farther on...

...Over the dark blanket of Pamber Forest, pale sunshine touched a distant lift of land. I thought that must be White Hill above Kingsclere where the line of the Portway goes. The first Roman surveyor must have stood just here when planning his road...

...The slope down was too rough to show any clear trace but I had my first sight of the Portway in the grass near the edge of the forest. A stream runs shallow there as at a ford...

...Just there I saw the the road again and a reassuring 'Portway Cottage' on a white gate.

...Crossing A340, I first noticed some ridges in the field beyond. Then past Skate's Farm, I saw a strip of grass of a lighter shade. It was like a low causeway...

...Then beyond the Ramsdell road I saw the Portway suddenly and quite clearly. It ran as a stony ridge across ploughland. I had not even hoped to see anything as fine as this...

At the junction of Cade's Roman road, between Chester-le-Street and Newcastle upon Tyne, and the Wrekendyke from South Shields, at NZ 269 591, there is a suspected Roman fort platform on the Wrekenton Golf Course. When the wagonway in the foreground was constructed, a hoard of gold and silver coins was found.

...After a mile or so, I saw the Portway again above Foscot Farm. It climbs steeply there to A339 from Basingstoke...

...Under the trees the Portway was so plain that I put my compass away. Elsewhere I had been grateful enough for a mere hint of a ditch or a ridge. Here I had a clear view of the road for about a mile, and in spite of the thick carpet of fallen leaves...

...Under Quarley Hill there is a slight change in direction. The Roman surveyor must have climbed that juniper dotted slope and fixed his new line...

...I also noticed a scoop hole from which the Romans would have taken the material for making their road...

...The mass of Old Sarum loomed darkly ahead like a sea cliff...

...The long past seemed very close and the cold wind full of history."

The next chapter describes an intensive search for Roman roads in the county of Northumberland. Obviously, I have neither the time nor the facilities to search the whole of Britain but I hope that readers will search their own areas and I shall be delighted to hear of any successes.

Chapter 6

The Lost Roman Roads of Northumberland

THE LOST ROMAN ROAD
by Bernard Berry
Some luck is needed
You may walk that way a hundred times
And then –
In a certain light
And at the right season
Say, when the smallest shoots
Best show the shaping of the soil
Like some close-fitting coat
Then you may see the line
Across that lonely field
And looking where their road once went
You see the Roman might
Just like a blaze of distant light
And brighter still for all the dark between.

This story begins in the closing stages of World War II when in 1945, I was an Air Training Corps cadet, eagerly awaiting a flight at the RAF aerodrome Ouston, near Heddon on the Wall, Northumberland. I did not realise that after a lifetime of airline flying and other aviation duties, I would become an archaeologist and return to this very same area, searching for traces of the handiwork of the Roman legions and auxiliaries.

My introduction to the Roman Wall was in an old Avro Anson aircraft. I was allowed to sit in the co-pilot's seat, and immediately after take-off, it was my job to wind up the undercarriage with 120 turns of a hand crank. The pilot flew low along the Roman Wall, over Housesteads and Crag Lough and I realised what a wonderful tool the aeroplane was for observing the history of our countryside.

On another occasion at the same airfield, a Free-French pilot took me up in a De Havilland Dragon Rapide, a twin engined biplane. There was no co-pilot's seat, but I sat in the radio operator's position just behind the pilot. He pointed out, in a plantation, the result of a German air-raid. A row of bomb craters were just a bit wide of the aerodrome. Forty years later, while looking for a Roman road in this same plantation, by this time a mature wood, I came across these craters. One of the bombs had scored a direct hit on the Roman road, saving me the trouble of an excavation.

My entry into professional archaeology came late in life when I was home on leave from my airline and became involved as a part-time air survey pilot for a university professor. My interest in the subject led me to become a fully qualified archaeologist and my favourite pursuit was, and still is, the search for long-lost Roman roads.

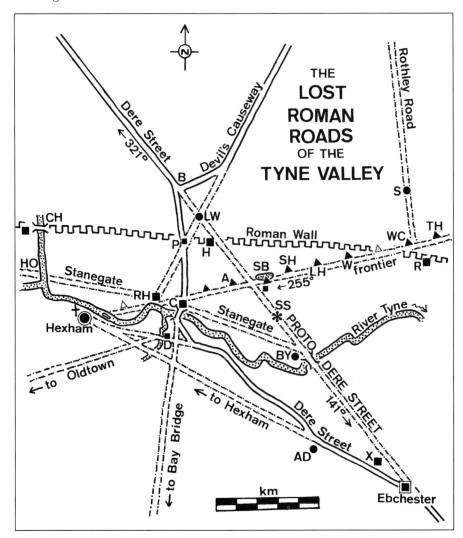

The Lost Roman Roads of the Tyne Valley.
A whole network has been found in the central Tyne Valley and some of these roads were quite easy to predict. Others had received vague mentions in old documents. The most important clue was the tradition, ignored by modern historians, that there had been a Roman bridge at Bywell.

PROTO DERE STREET

E = Ebchester (Vindomora) Roman fort.

X = Newly discovered suspected early Roman fort.

BY = Bywell, tradition of Roman bridge, Saxon church etc.

SS = Suspected signal station at NZ 032 647 (earthworks in wood).

SB = Shildon Bog, crossing with newly discovered frontier road.

H = Halton (Onnum) Roman Wall fort.

LW = Little Whittington DMV, crossing of Proto Devil's Causeway.

B = Beukley, junction with Dere Street.

STANEGATE

BY = Bywell, Stanegate excavated here.

C = Corbridge (Corstopitum) Roman fort and town.

RH = Red House early Roman fort (lost under A69(T).

HO = Howford (site of, to east of Warden Saxon Church)

ORIGINAL DEVIL'S CAUSEWAY

LW = Little Whittington DMV.

P = Portgate.

RH = Red House.

EBCHESTER - HEXHAM ROAD

E = Ebchester.

AD = Apperley Dene, (site of RB farm). Roman road divides here.

DILSTON NETWORK

D = Dilston, Roman crossroads and suspected fortlet.

FRONTIER ROAD

TH = Turpin's Hill.
WC = Whitchester.
W = Welton Hall and Welton DMV.
LH = Laker Hall.
SH = Shildon Hill Iron Age hillfort.
SB = Shildon Bog (Lake in Roman times).
A = Aydon.

ROTHLEY ROAD

S = Street Houses.

ROMAN WALL FORTS

CH = Chesters (Cilurnum).
H = Halton (Onnum).
R = Rudchester (Vindovala).

The Rothley Road

The Roman road which the German aircraft had inadvertently bombed was not initially found by aerial reconnaissance. I happened to be driving down the long straight stretch of road south from Grangemoor Farm (NY 046 866) near Scots Gap, to the River Wansbeck crossing at the deserted mediaeval village of South Middleton (NY 053 841) when I noticed in my driving mirror that the road behind me was lined-up exactly on the folly on the top of Rothley Crags (NY 044 887). As explained previously, this was a typical Roman surveyor's trick so a full-scale search was initiated.

The road was indeed Roman. The survey line had gone right across the top of Rothley Crags, but the Roman road constructors, who were allowed to bypass obstructions, had laid their road around the western base of the precipitous outcrop before regaining the original line. Just to the north of Rothley Crag, a Roman paved ford was found in the bed of a small stream (NY 041 896) and fourth century coins of Constantine the Great and Valentinian 1 were found by the field-walker who operated the expedition's metal detector. Combined aerial and ground searches located the Roman road all the way from the Iron Age fort at Great Tosson (NU 023 005) in the Coquet valley to Whitchester (NZ 099 683) a mile north-west of the Roman Wall fort of Rudchester.

According to J C Hodgson in his *History of Northumberland,* (1827) Vol 4, there was a Roman fortlet at Turpin's Hill, just east of Whitchester (NZ 109 685) and in 1766, an urn full of gold and silver coins was found there. The site gets a further mention in Sykes' *Local Records,* (1866) Vol 1: "In 1795, at a cairn on Turpin's Hill, a stone chest was found, it contained two urns and coins of Domitian, Antoninus Pius and Faustina." The reports of this fortlet have been ignored by archaeologists, presumably because it is off the line of the Wall and therefore difficult to understand, but more of this site later. Just for now there follows a table which indicates the important points of the Simonside Hills to Whitchester road hereafter called "The Rothley Road."

Points of interest on the Rothley Road

General alignment: 165/345 degrees

NU 024 004	Square earthwork (possible Roman fortlet or signal station) just to south of Great Tosson Iron Age hillfort on north side of Simonside Hills.
NZ 023 993	Imitation paving cut into solid rock. Possible niche for altar cut into cliff to west. Apart from this spot, road very rough, reused by public footpath.
NZ 022 975	Prominent *agger* across heather to west of Selby's Cove. Ruined shieling between road and cove contains reused stones.
NZ 025 965	Coquet Cairn: suspected Roman survey point.
NZ 033 922	Spot height, 284 metres: suspected Roman survey point.
NZ 035 909	Rothley West Shield Farm. Many small roadside quarries. Roman road under cart track.
NZ 038 902	*Agger* cut by old railway line.
NZ 039 900	Old culvert removed by farmer and rebuilt.
NZ 041 894	Roman coins found in paved ford: Constantine the Great (AD 307-337) and Valentinian 1 (AD 364-375)
NZ 042 885	Suspected Roman road around west base of crag.
NZ 043 888	Folly probably hides remains of Roman signal station.
NZ 043 881	Rothley DMV.
NZ 045 875	Roman road suspected underneath straight cart track.
NZ 045 871	Remains of Roman bridge abutment a few yards upstream from modern ford. Wade up river edge to observe stone. Just upstream from bridge, natural rock sill has post-hole cut into stone at south end.
NZ 045 869	Cross-section of Roman road visible in north bank of small stream just to west of farm road, 300 yards north of Grangemoor Farm.
NZ 046 866	Possible Roman columns reused in farm buildings of Grangemoor Farm. Farm on top of Roman road.
NZ 052 844	*Tumulus* in field to west of public road.
NZ 054 841	Crossing of River Wansbeck: South Middleton DMV.
NZ 059 822	Artificial cutting through small cliff near east end of reservoir. Two large burial mounds further east.
NZ 061 813	Crossing point with Devil's Causeway known Roman road.

NZ 062 810	Ford or bridge across small stream 150 yards east of Devil's Causeway crossing of same stream. Public footpath uses Devil's Causeway crossing.
NZ 064 802	Crossing point with modern A696(T) road.
NZ 064 798	*Agger* in strip wood to east of, and parallel to farm road.
NZ 066 796	Square earthwork of Roman shape inside South Bradford DMV.
NZ 069 786	Circular earthwork in Cuddy's View Plantation
NZ 070 785	Prominent road-paving in pasture down east side of Cuddy's View Plantation.
NZ 075 773	Square earthwork, suspected Roman fortlet, at south edge of wood, ("Cut Plantation") 300 yards north of isolated circular copse.
NZ 074 768	Circular copse: *tumulus* just to east.
NZ 077 751	Known Roman remains marked on O S map. Reason for presence not understood until discovery of Rothley Road.
NZ 079 751	Stony ford in Blackheddon Burn.
NZ 083 732	Heugh: quarry and unidentified earthworks.
NZ 089 716	Crossing of River Pont. Old mill-dam probably reused stones of Roman bridge.
NZ 092 708	Street Houses. Much stone behind copse 400 yards north of village, west side of road.
NZ 092 704	Hilltop Plantation, much stone.
NZ 097 695	Ford across Med Burn.
NZ 099 690	Loudside: large stones to west of farm.
NZ 099 683	Suspected pre-Wall Roman fort under farm.

Horsley's Blakehope "east road"

It is obvious that Rothley Crag was an important Roman survey point, and likely that the folly on the top hides the remains of a Roman signal station. In addition to the Great Tosson to Whitchester road, the modern road past Winter's Gibbet at Steng Cross (NY 963 908) is also lined up on Rothley Crag (to the east) and the Blakehope Roman fort (NY 859 946) on the known Roman road "Dere Street," to the west. It is possible that the Steng Cross road is on top of an unknown Roman road. Horsley in his *Britannia Romana* (1731) tells us of such a Roman road leaving the Blakehope fort area and heading east:

> "A branch of a military way seems to have gone from Elsdon through Greenchesters to Watling Street passing by Elishaw and falling near Blaikhope on Watling Street, at a large angle, not much short of a right one."

This road remains to be identified but at Hillhead (NY 940 918) to the west of Steng Cross, where the main road turns northwards to Elsdon, an *agger* continues straight ahead towards Greenchesters (NY 870 941) and Blakehope. There is a small unidentified square site seen from the air on the same line at NY 923 921 on the south side of a public bridleway.

Roman remains at Elsdon (NY 937 935) were reported by Hodgson in his *History of Northumberland,* Vol 2: "Strong Roman masonry, an urn, boar tusks and two Roman tablets were found here."

The Driftway

Although its name suggests a drove road, "The Driftway" which runs north-west from Elsdon should be checked to see if it obeys some of the rules for Roman roads. Extreme care should be taken as it runs through a military firing-range. This has also delayed attempts to investigate it from the air.

A lost Roman road network in the Central Tyne Valley

Before our surveys, only three Roman roads were known in Northumberland – Dere Street, the Devil's Causeway and the High Rochester to Learchild road. The most significant new evidence has been the discovery of a complete network in the Central Tyne Valley, an area which has seen more archaeologists at work than even the Valley of the Kings in Egypt. Nevertheless, until now, that major complex had remained undiscovered, so how many more miles lie hidden?

The first clue to its presence was the tradition, long ignored by archaeologists, that there had been a Roman bridge at Bywell. Old woodcuts show the remains of two ancient piers sticking out of the river there. On August 10th, 1836, these piers were blown up by gunpowder and work started on a new bridge further downstream on the same day. Reused Roman stones can be identified here and there in the new bridge, and about thirty, complete with lewis-holes, presumably surplus to requirements, lie on the river bed and are visible in low water conditions.

Experts denied any Roman presence whatsoever at Bywell but a little research showed that in 1750, a Roman silver cup was recovered from the Tyne there by an angler. It was inscribed *Desideri Vivas.* Surprisingly, for such a small hamlet, Bywell has two churches, very close to each other. St Andrew's is the older of the two and the tower and west wall of the nave are Saxon. The nearby St Peter's used to stand on a prominent platform before the levels of the surrounding fields were raised during landscaping. In January 1902, in St Peter's churchyard, part of a Roman altar was found at a depth of six feet. An inspection of the tower of St Andrew's revealed many ex-Roman lewis-holed stones identical in size and appearance to those lying on the river bed under the 1836 bridge. The bell-sounding holes at the top of St Andrew's tower looked peculiar: the holes were not always in the centre of the stones and these had obviously served another purpose in some other building. The pear-shaped holes looked remarkably like Roman lavatory seats. Clearly, in spite of official disinterest, a major investigation was called for at Bywell.

First of all, we had to find the position of the two suspected Roman bridge piers in order to give us a line on a possible Roman road. Our two expert divers, Rolfe Mitchinson and Bob Middlemass very quickly found the remains of the 1836 gunpowder explosions. Roman stones and large pieces of typical Roman concrete with its oversize aggregate, lay scattered on the river bed about a hundred yards upstream from the 1836 bridge. On the spacing, there should have been a third pier near the north bank. This would have placed it on a rock shelf and easily accessible to stone robbers. The third Roman pier was probably the source of the Roman stones in St Andrew's Church.

While the divers were in the water, a peculiar incident occurred. It has been widely claimed that the Tyne is un-navigable above the Tidal limit at Wylam but up the centre of the river walked a gentleman in waders, towing a fairly large rowing boat across some shallows. He introduced himself as an eel-man and enquired of the divers the state of his eel-traps in the deep pools. He had several hundredweight of eels on board his boat and he informed us that he was bound for Hexham to inspect more traps before returning to Wylam where a road tanker would take his cargo to a destination in Germany. The eel-man had never heard of the "experts" who said the upper Tyne was un-navigable, so he proceeded on his way and manned his oars when he regained deeper water. Had we just witnessed how the Romans transported their heavy cargoes?

From the Ordnance Survey map, it is very obvious that the very straight stretch of Roman Dere Street which heads south-east across southern Northumberland towards Beukley (NY 983 707) on a heading of 141 degrees is bound for a destination other than Corbridge. The known Roman road however bends off towards Corbridge at Beukley but a projection of the 141 degree line crosses the Tyne exactly at our Roman bridge position at Bywell. Furthermore, a continuation of the same line goes right in through the front gate of the Ebchester Roman fort (NZ 104 555). These surprising observations could not be discarded as coincidences. Permission to investigate at Bywell was kindly given by the landowners and a trial trench was opened along the top of the cliff on the north bank of the river in line with the river-bed ruins of the Roman piers. The bridge must have crossed the river at a slight angle because we could find no trace of a road. It was obvious that we were close, because our two expert metal detectorists, Dr Irene Robinson, and Liz Robinson (of the BBC) scanned all the spoil coming out of the trench, and many Roman coins, missed by trowellers, were recovered. Without this detector-derived information, we may have lost heart and given up. As it happened, our failure to find the road on the cliff top was fortunate because I moved away from the river into the woods to a point where I thought the line of the road must have crossed a small stream. In thick scrub, a large fir tree had fallen and its up-ended roots grasped large stones. The disc of surface soil removed by the fallen tree revealed a cobbled surface. A new excavation commenced and this involved heavy work removing jungle-type undergrowth and fallen trees but it was well worth the effort. A junction of three Roman roads was uncovered. One was the expected 141 degree line; a second was the long lost "Stanegate," postulated east of Corbridge but never found until now, and a third road headed off towards the Bywell churches. The excavation produced dozens of Roman coins and sherds of Roman pottery and a bonus-find was an excellent culvert-type bridge which had crossed the tiny stream just to the east of the road junction (NZ 048 623). Archaeologists made the journey from Oxford to view the evidence and went away very excited with this new piece for the jig-saw puzzle.

The second road which proved to be part of the missing "Stanegate" left the junction on a heading of 287 degrees, exactly on track for Roman Corbridge. A compass course was followed on the 287 heading and the

Clockey Burn was intercepted 900 yards to the west-north-west. Massive stone blocks lay *in-situ* in the bed of the burn at NZ 042 625. The detectorist was summoned and within minutes, found a Roman disc brooch between two of the stones. The same burn runs down to join the River Tyne just to the east of Bywell Castle. Before it reaches the river, it disappears into an underground channel and emerges from the Bywell cliffs via an arch which looks just like a miniature version of the discharge tunnel of Rome's main sewer, the *Cloaca Maxima. Cloaca* is Latin for "sewer." Is it a coincidence that Bywell's *cloaca* is called the "Clockey" Burn?

An aerial search of the newly-discovered Stanegate-line revealed a legionary-size temporary Roman camp straddling the road at NZ 001 639 in the parkland to the south of the Howden Dene country house. The Roman line subsequently joined Spoutwell Lane which heads exactly for the known section of Stanegate in the Corbridge Roman site.

The third road which left the Bywell excavation headed towards the churches where St Andrew's tower is built largely of Roman stones. The mound (now camouflaged by landscaping) on which St Peter's stands may well turn out to be the platform of a missing Roman fort.

Once we had an exact line on the Roman 141/321 degree road, now called "Proto Dere Street," we moved back to the cliff top and dug another trench some twenty yards to the west of our earlier failure. The cobbled surface and heavy foundation stones of a typical Roman road were exposed very quickly.

Proto Dere Street was followed both to the north and the south and a vast amount of information obtained. Further strange evidence was found in the river which seems to indicate that a possible Roman fort at Bywell may have been river-supplied by the ancestors of our eel-man but that is discussed in Chapter 8.

Points of interest on Proto Dere Street

Alignment: 321/141 degrees

NZ 103 555	Ebchester Roman fort
NZ 083 571	Suspected early Roman fort in angle between Dere Street and newly discovered Proto Dere Street.
NZ 083 579	Terraceway down hillside to south-east of Spring House.
NZ 078 585	Green road runs down hill from Hedley Grange.
NZ 068 597	Prominent *agger* in hedge line.
NZ 054 618	*Agger* through grounds of Stocksfield Hall.
NZ 051 619	Site of Bywell Roman bridge. Piers blown up 1836.
NZ 048 623	Junction of three Roman roads excavated, coins and pottery found.
NZ 032 648	Suspected Roman signal station in east corner of wood at spot height of 163 metres. Earthworks visible.
NZ 030 650	Causeway across linear quarry in strip wood.
NZ 020 658	Crop mark of Roman fortlet seen from air. Roman coins and pottery found while inspecting site on ground.
NZ 020 662	Crossing with suspected Roman frontier road (more of this later). Shildon Bog was a lake in Roman times and thought to have been a reservoir for Corbridge.

NZ 016 667   Roman road visible for 300 yards. Then passes along west edge of Fox Covert Plantation.

NZ 009 674   Suspected Roman culvert conducts stream under road.

NZ 003 683   Corner of fortlet projects from underneath field wall, directly below high tension power lines.

NY 999 684   Map of 1779 shows a road lined-up north-west/south-east, just clipping north-east corner of Halton Chesters Roman Wall fort.

NY 991 695   Little Whittington DMV. Crossing with early line of Devil's Causeway. Stanegate at Vindolanda is also lined up on this DMV. What else does it hide?

NY 983 707   Proto Dere Street joins known Dere Street at Beukley near Stagshaw BBC radio mast.

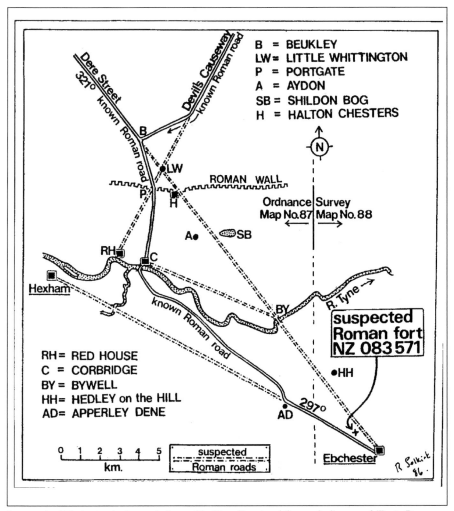

Just north of Ebchester, in the angle formed by Dere Street and the newly discovered "Proto Dere Street," a suspected Roman fort was seen from the air at NZ 083 571.

Ebchester to Hexham Roman road

The known Roman road "Dere Street" leaves Ebchester for Corbridge and for the first 3.7 miles (6 km), except for a very slight dog-leg is straight and approaches Apperley Dene on a heading of 297 degrees. At Apperley Dene there is a native British farm, at one time thought to be a Roman fortlet until its excavation some years ago. Just to the north-west of this Romano-British site, the Roman road leaves its 297 degree direction and makes a turn to the north after which it follows a winding and most un-Roman course to Corbridge. If one ignores this turn and places a ruler on the map on the 297 degree line, it will be seen that the extended line goes right through Hexham Abbey. Old antiquarians thought that Hexham had been a Roman town and there are hundreds of tons of reused Roman stones in the abbey and other buildings but current archaeological opinions, without the slightest proof, declare these stones to have originated from the Roman fort at Corbridge.

In his *Comprehensive Guide to Northumberland,* W W Tomlinson reports on Hexham:

"Dr Bruce ascribed a Roman origin to Hexham. There is a large number of tooled stones that comprise the crypt beneath the Abbey Church with many others that have been found with inscriptions upon them built into old houses.

A Mr Fairless discovered a connected chain of earthenware pipes, of manifest Roman workmanship, lying *in situ,* and intended to all appearance for the conveyance of water...

...two Roman altars of large size, of which only one bears an inscription; a sculptured slab, of Roman workmanship, discovered on 19th Sept. 1881 by Mr Charles Clement Hodges, when making an excavation under the floor of the slype, with a view to finding a crypt which was said to exist there. It represents a well armed cavalry soldier, with a standard in his hand and plumes on his helmet, riding over the crouching rude body of a repulsive-looking barbarian. In a sunken panel below is an inscription, rendered as follows by Dr Bruce: 'To the Gods the shades, Flavinus, a horse soldier of the cavalry regiment of Petriana, standard-bearer of the troop of Candidus, twenty-five years of age, having served seven years in the army, is laid here."

In Hodgson's *History of Northumberland,* Vol 4, he says: "Below the floors of St Wilfred's Church, a chapel was discovered built out of the ruins of a Roman town, Severus and Caracalla." The Ordnance Survey map of 1862 shows the graveyard in the north-west quadrant of Hexham Abbey grounds, named "Campey Hill." This is very suggestive of a Roman fort.

Now let us return to Apperley Dene (NZ 055 581) where the Roman road swings off towards Corbridge, obviously following a native track. Another road has continued straight ahead on a heading of 297 degrees and at NZ 051 584, a zig-zag containing hundreds of tons of stone descends to the Stocksfield Burn where a modern bridge carries a private road to Wheelbirks Farm. Older stone-cut abutments on a slightly different line can be seen under this bridge. On the north side, the farm road makes a zig-zag up the steep slope but the suspected Roman road short-circuits this zig-zag as a grass-covered angled terraceway.

Points of interest on the Ebchester to Hexham Roman road
Alignment: 297/117 degrees

NZ 104 555	Ebchester Roman fort.
NZ 085 564	Slight alteration of heading of Dere Street.
NZ 083 571	Suspected early Roman fort. Complete perimeter visible from air. Ditches visible at ground level. Two prominent gateways visible. Infilled Roman well intact, incorrectly labelled "coal-shaft" on 1850 O S map. Tithe Map calls this "Water Pit Field." Stream just to north-west of Wood House farm cottage has been used as Roman drain. Follow this to south-east corner of fort. Site is under threat from open-cast mining.
NZ 055 580	Apperley Dene native farmstead. Roman road junction here. Newly found road goes straight on to Hexham, known Dere Street bends away to Corbridge.
NZ 051 584	Zig-zag down to Stocksfield Burn. Hundreds of tons of stone visible.
NZ 049 584	Angled terraceway short-cuts farm road hairpin bend.
NZ 037 590	A small stream is crossed by a ford just upstream from overhead high-tension cables and a buried gas pipeline. This pipeline is marked by the usual orange markers to assist helicopter inspections.
NZ 035 593	A small stream flows through a culvert but no modern track, road or path use this bridge.
NZ 029 595	In a small pasture just to the south of Gallaw Hill Farm, suspected Roman road foundation stones seem to have been dragged out of the ground by the farmer, who has then given up and left them.
NY 999 609	An angled terraceway climbs up steep slope in wood on north side of March Burn.
NY 968 627	Remains of a modern timber footbridge on same spot as an old stone abutment at crossing of Devil's Water.
NY 959 632	Cottage named "Five Gates." Other Roman roads in vicinity; crossing with "Forster's Roman road," (more of this later).
NY 935 642	Hexham Abbey on site of suspected Roman town, possibly lost Roman town of "Epiacum." Other contender for this identity is Bywell.

There are more Roman roads arriving at Hexham from other directions but these will be dealt with in turn.

The Stanegate: further evidence

The Roman "Stanegate" has been mentioned several times so far, so this will be the next Roman road to be dealt with in detail. It has been widely held that this road was the Roman frontier across Britain prior to Hadrian's Wall being built. Excavations show however, that the Stanegate, unlike frontier roads in Germany and elsewhere, had neither a palisade nor a defensive

The suspected Roman fort at
Whittonstall Hall Farm, NZ
083 571

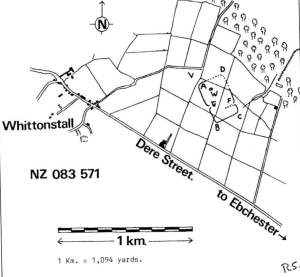

Location of Whittonstall Hall
Farm suspected Roman fort.
A,B,C,D, = rounded
              corners of fort.
E,F,   = entrances.
W   = infilled well.
V   = suspected *vicus.*

Old prints which show the Roman bridge piers at Bywell.
These were blown up by gunpowder in 1836.

BYWELL CHURCHES
c. 1800 A.D.

Top: The Bywell churches.
Left, St Peter's which used to stand on
a mound until landscaping raised fields
around, and right, St Andrew's, tower
which is built of Roman stones.
(from an old woodcut)

Bottom: Fragment of Roman altar
found in St Peter's churchyard in 1902.

ditch. The line of the road has been known for many years between Carlisle
and Chollerford on the North Tyne; also an isolated piece in the vicinity of
the Corbridge Roman fort. Many attempts have been made over the years to
trace the missing section between the North Tyne and Corbridge. An
extension east of Corbridge had been widely postulated but never discovered

until recently. The speculated routes of this missing road went to all kinds of weird and wonderful places.

The first solid evidence was our lucky excavation at Bywell and the subsequent discovery of the line all the way to Corbridge. The following table covers this length after which we will progress to further unknown sections:

Points of interest on the Stanegate between Bywell and Corbridge

Alignment: 287/107 degrees

NZ 048 623	Roman road junction in the Bywell Woods.
NZ 042 624	Paved ford in Clockey Burn, extremely large stones still *in situ*. Roman disc brooch found between stones.
NZ 029 629	Crossing of Stoneyverge Burn east side of A68. Very large stones in stream bank. Roman crossbow brooch and scatter of Roman coins found.
NZ 023 631	Roman road crosses neck of wood east of High Barnes Farm.
NZ 001 639	Legionary-size temporary camp seen from aircraft in park to south of Howden Dene country house. This camp straddles Stanegate. Gallow Hill is contained inside rounded corner of prominent earthwork. Further earthworks just to west. Roman brooch found. Cultivation terraces in steep wood to south of camp.
NY 997 640	Stanegate joins modern private road.
NY 994 641	Stanegate under private road joins Spoutwell Lane which is lined up exactly on Corbridge Roman site.
NY 993 640	Findspot of famous "Corbridge Lanx" (large silver plate).
NY 979 648	Known crossing of Stanegate over Cor Burn just to west of Corbridge Roman town.
NY 970 651	Last known position (until now) of Stanegate as it passed early Roman fort of Red House which predated Corstopitum.

An unusual Roman road

Before the search is described, just a few more words in general about the Stanegate: observations from aircraft show that it differs from most Roman roads in that it does actually select easy gradients in places. At Boothby, a kilometre south of Lanercost Priory and just to the north-west of Naworth Castle, at NY 553 627, the road bends back on itself as it runs south up a gully into West Park. What unusual behaviour for a supposed Roman frontier! About a mile south of Roman Wall Turret 52A, it does the same thing again at NY 575 633, this time deviating to the north. The Roman Military Way, the service road immediately behind Hadrian's Wall was not built until many years after the Wall's completion, so I am inclined to believe that the Stanegate served as the supply road for the Wall and was one of the very few Roman roads which the famous ox-wagons could actually have negotiated. The very straight length of Stanegate to the west of Vindolanda at NY 765 663 is lined up on the spot height of 279 metres on the crag to the east of the fort and also on Little Whittington DMV, thirteen miles to the east at NY 991 695, north-east of Portgate. The actual road does not follow the sighting line until it gets back to Newbrough (NY 873 678) and Fourstones (NY 893 680).

An obvious Roman road leaves Fourstones and routes to the north of Warden Hill which overlooks the junction of the two Tynes and is capped by a large Iron Age hillfort (NY 903 678). The road divides and the northern branch goes to the Roman fort and bridge at Chesters (Cilurnum) near Chollerford and the other branch was shown by E Sockett to transit the north side of Warden Hill and then turn south parallel to the North Tyne.

A little research however tells us more. At Fourstones, according to Hodgson in his *History of Northumberland*, Vol 4, "Carel Street" (Carlisle Street), [another name for the Roman road in this area] divided even before the fork on Warden Hill. Thus we have two divisions of the road very close together. At Fourstones, the first division took place. Hodgson was convinced that the southern branch went around the south of Warden Hill bound for Howford on the North Tyne very close to the confluence of the two rivers. Hodgson was absolutely correct. The Roman road is in perfect condition at NY 902 668 where it is a terraceway along the hillside north of Warden paper mill and some hundred yards east of the railway line and the public road. Park your car at the level-crossing beside the paper mill and the Roman road will be seen on the hillside. A couple of hundred yards further south, the Roman road is visible again but ends abruptly where the farmer has taken it out leaving about 250 tons of stone in a pile in the field. Past generations of farmers have also dumped stone into the railway cutting. The road heads for the Saxon church at Warden. As has been mentioned previously, this church contains reused Roman stones and although the usual excuses have been used to explain the stones away (they were "stolen from Chollerford," or were "washed down the river"), it is most likely that they came from a Roman building which was associated with the river crossing at Howford. In the west bank of the River North Tyne at NY 917 663, the Roman road surface is perfectly preserved and runs right down to the water's edge. Very large stones lie in the river and the rapids thus formed are an easy marker for the Roman ford which continued in use right through the mediaeval period and later.

According to the *Newcastle Journal* of May 25th, 1927, an interesting Roman stone was found here:

"A well-known local gentleman who was angling on the north side of the river, immediately opposite the Saxon Church of St Michael and All Angels, observed a stone some 3 feet long, which had long been lying there, but which has recently been turned over. On examination it was found that this stone had been a Roman altar... ...The find gives added interest to this historic part of Northumberland, for it was made immediately adjoining the Saxon village of Warden, which has now disappeared, but which stood in the fork of the meeting of the rivers, and where many Roman stones have already been discovered."

The Saxon village of Warden was probably placed on the promontory between the two Tynes because in addition to the ex-Roman ford over the North Tyne at Howford, the South Tyne was also easily fordable at the confluence of the rivers. The North Tyne is the dominant river and when it floods, it retards the South Tyne which has dropped a shingle bar over its mouth. This ridge of stones is easily fordable thus the Saxons and the Romans before them, had fords in close proximity over both the River Tynes.

Roman road excavated in
Bywell Wood.
Five hundred yards north of
the Roman Bywell bridge, a
Roman road junction was
excavated at NZ 048 623.
The above photograph shows
Proto Dere Street where it
crossed a small stream.
The long lost Stanegate
branches off to Corbridge
just to the left of the culvert.
A third Roman road headed
in the direction of the Bywell
churches.

Proto Dere Street emerges
from the ground in the
Bywell Woods.

A paved ford takes the long lost Stanegate across the Clockey Burn at NZ 042 625

The *agger* of the Stanegate at NY 904 665, to the east of Warden Paper Mill.

The *agger* of the Stanegate at NY 903 668, north of Warden Paper Mill, running along the hillside towards Fourstones.

At NY 905 665, the farmer is busy removing the Stanegate.

The Roman road from Ebchester to Hexham angles up a steep slope at NZ 050 584, on the west side of the Stocksfield Burn.

Forster's Roman road
at Dilston.

Top: The farm track at NY970
635, between Dilston Mill and
Dilston Park, is on top of the
Roman road.

Bottom: In a strip wood at NY
965 633, just to the south-west
of Dilston Park Farm, a farmer
has tried to move a Roman
road foundation stone, and
given up.

On the east side of the River North Tyne, exactly in line with the Roman ford, during the construction of the North British Railway, several cists (burials) of Bronze Age date were discovered but according to a letter published in the *Hexham Herald* in 1877, a "patera" was found and this was: "exactly similar in shape and size to those found in the sarcophagus discovered at Harpenden in Hertfordshire in 1844." (the Harpenden patera was samian DR33).

In the 1960's, Professor St Joseph of Cambridge University took aerial photographs (Numbers D001, D002 and D003) which indicated a Roman marching camp at the same position on the east side of the river at Howford.

Once again, I refer to Hodgson in his *History of Northumberland* Vol 4, where he continues with his prediction of the route of Carel Street (the Stanegate) towards Corbridge and Newcastle:

> "...and that it passed from Howford by Acomb and Anick to Corbridge, and thence by the Ald-he-way to Newcastle. It is still used each way from Howford as a drift-way for the fairs of Stagshaw-bank, and partly as a cart-way; and at Wardon is still known by the name of the *Warded-road*. I have also heard it said, or rather conjectured, that it went from Howford, under Earn's-how banks, by Hermitage to Corbridge."

If we stand on the old North British Railway embankment at Howford and look east in the direction indicated by Hodgson, a prominent feature straight ahead is the spire of the Church of St John Lee (NY 933 656) on the escarpment known as Eagle's Mount, one mile distant.

A very straight road leaves the church and is lined up exactly on Corbridge and Anick, as mentioned by Hodgson. Although the church is not Saxon, it had a Saxon predecessor, and just inside the door of the church is a Roman altar which was used as a font in the Saxon church. There is another Roman altar in the garden of the rectory.

A close inspection of the whole site shows that the graveyard and adjacent field are on a square promontory with rounded corners. It is a possible Roman site and adjacent to an almost certain Roman road.

The straight road carries on east-south-east for two thirds of a mile and passes a significant place-name, Peasley Gates on the way, and after West Oakwood continues in the same direction as a prominent stone-filled hedge-line. At Anick, a public footpath crosses this line and the construction of the Roman road can easily be identified at NY 953 653, just south of Anick Grange Farm. A typical Roman culvert passes under the Roman road which is a hedge-line at this point. Here, the observer is in sight of Red House and Corbridge and the Roman road is on the correct alignment. We now have the "long lost Stanegate" all the way from Carlisle to Bywell.

Checklist on Stanegate between Fourstones and Corbridge

Alignment between Fourstones and Howford: various

NY 884 679   Fork of Roman roads at Fourstones. Northern branch further divides at NY 894 683 with one branch going to Chesters Roman fort and the other across the north of Warden Hill before turning south near river.

NY 900 673	Southern branch passes springs at this position.
NY 902 668	*Agger* very prominent as hedge-line along hillside to east of railway line and public road.
NY 904 666	*Agger* very prominent over field. Farmer busy removing road at time of writing. Pile of several hundred tons of stone in field above railway cutting.
NY 906 664	Junction with another possible Roman road coming down from Warden Hill.
NY 910 665	Unrecorded suspected Neolithic long barrow to west of Warden's massive earthwork *motte* (NY 912 665).
NY 914 665	Warden Saxon church contains many reused Roman stones. Saxon village (Howford) used to occupy promontory to south-east of church. Saxon word *hoh*, (pronounced "how") means "promontory."
NY 917 664	Surface of Roman road descends west bank of North Tyne to ford. Many large stones in river. Roman altar found by angler, 1927.
NY 917 660	Although not on the "Stanegate" a shingle bar over the mouth of the South Tyne should be taken into consideration in the study of Roman roads in the area.
NY 921 665	Roman patera found, 1877. Marching camp found by Cambridge University, c1960.
NY 933 656	St John Lee Church on site of Saxon church. Roman altar in church. Possible Roman fort earthworks.
NY 936 656	Place-name "Peasley Gates" on straight road from St John Lee church aligned 100 degrees on Corbridge Roman site. Stone-filled hedge-lines continue on same alignment.
NY 953 653	Culvert under suspected Roman road beside public footpath south of Anick Grange Farm.
NY 970 651	Site of Red House Roman fort (pre-dated Corstopitum)
NY 979 648	Known crossing of Stanegate over Cor Burn.

The Stanegate is now known all the way from Carlisle to Bywell. In river flood conditions, the Romans have travelled via the bridge across the North Tyne at Chesters and at low water levels they have taken the short-cut across the ford at Howford.

Stanegate: The last missing section

The only major unknown section of the Stanegate is now between Bywell and Newcastle upon Tyne. It would be good practise for readers to use the search for this as an archaeological exercise and put the last piece of information in place.

To the east of Bywell, it looks as if the Stanegate runs east along the hillside above the north bank of the River Tyne, and heads for Ovingham (NZ 085 637) where there is yet another Saxon church with reused Roman stones in its tower. Between Bywell and Ovingham, the suspected Stanegate can be seen as an *agger* at NZ 053 623, a public footpath at NZ 060 627 and a possible Roman culvert-type bridge over a small stream at the south-east end of a strip wood at NZ 066 634, south of Ovington village.

To the east of Ovingham, a Roman period farmstead is visible from the air at NZ 095 646 in a field aptly called "Camp Hill." There are ancient bell-pits in Horsley Wood (NZ 104 650) and in the 1750's General Wade had trouble dragging his cannons along an old riverside road to the east of Wylam where later the famous George Stephenson was born. The significant name "Street Houses" occurs on this line. These clues may assist with the positive identification of the last missing piece of the elusive Stanegate.

The 255 degree suspected Frontier Road

Let us return to Turpin's Hill (NZ 108 685) just north of the Wall, where the hoard of Roman coins was found in 1766. JC Hodgson said that six *castella* were placed equally apart in a line along the Heddon ridge. I managed to locate four of these sites from the air, and when I came to plot them on the map, I was astonished to find that they were all 1,620 yards apart – a Roman mile. Not only was this a Roman road – it was some sort of defence line, or even part of a frontier system.

Before Hadrian built the Roman Wall in AD 122-26, there must have been an earlier frontier and until now it was thought that this was the Stanegate Roman road. Because of the road's lack of a palisade and defensive ditch, its meandering character and poor selection of a military line, this is unlikely. Hodgson's *castella* are on a line which if extended, would intercept the east coast at St Mary's Island and the west coast at Maryport. The line crosses the Roman Wall at NZ 086 681, just south of Albemarle Barracks, the former RAF Ouston aerodrome.

I plotted search areas across Northumberland at Roman mile intervals. Most of the sites appeared within a few yards of the predicted positions. Quite a few were located at significant places, the names of which crop up time and time again in our searches for the Romans. One was the Red House Roman fort (NY 970 651) which pre-dated Corstopitum. Another is the site of Hexham Abbey and a third, the Roman fort of Wreay.

The suspected early defence line will be discussed in greater detail in Chapter 10.

The network south of Corbridge

The main Roman road from Edinburgh to York is known by its Saxon name "Dere Street" because its Latin name is lost. The places it passed however are recorded in the *Antonine Itinerary* so its course is fairly certain.

On its way south, it crossed the Roman bridge at Corbridge, and then headed south-east to Broomhaugh (NZ 018 615), Ebchester, Lanchester, Binchester, Piercebridge, Catterick, Aldborough, and York.

Forster's Road

What is not so well known is that another Roman road left the southern end of the Roman bridge at Corbridge and headed 1½ miles due south to Dilston where it made a turn to the west. Robert Forster says in his *History of Corbridge*, (1881):

"Another Roman road commenced at the south end of the bridge, and proceeded in a straight line direct south, passing near the east side of the old toll bar at Dilston, continuing further south for about three hundred yards, then at right angles westward and onward through Hexhamshire, passing Alston on the north and still westward towards Penrith. When the new road was made in 1829, betwixt Corbridge bridge and Dilston, this ancient road was unexpectedly come upon and cut through, and was found to consist mostly of paving stones firmly bedded and united together; the discovery attracted at the time considerable attention."

Forster makes a further reference to the road:

"Besides the grand Roman way which proceeded from Dover in Kent and crossed the Tyne here (Corbridge), there was another military road, which passed from this place south-west through Dilston Park, over Hexham Fell to Old Town in Allendale, and meets with the Maiden Way at Whitley Castle."

Eric Birley in his *Corbridge Roman Station,* has this to say:

"Down Dere Street from the north came many a Scottish army, such as that of King David 1, which stayed at Corbridge for a time in 1138; and it was the Roman road system, still in use for all its ruinous state, that led the army of Henry VI's Queen Margaret to its disastrous defeat at Hexham, by the side of the branch- road to Whitley Castle, in 1464."

Dilston (NY 975 635) is a small hamlet on the modern A695 road between Corbridge and Hexham but it is a complex little place. A hall is built on the site of a mediaeval castle and a later castle survives in a ruinous state close by. There is also a mediaeval chapel with a Roman gravestone built into the east wall and a stone with a lewis-hole in the top of the tower, a watermill, two farms, the site of an old toll-bar and a disused mediaeval road. This hamlet presented several problems which had to be solved before we could concentrate on the search for Roman roads. There were obvious reused Roman stones in the Dilston watermill but records show that these were taken from the ruins of the Corbridge Roman bridge c1810 and used in the construction of the new mill-race.

The main problem was to find the Roman crossing point of the Devil's Water. About two hundred yards upstream from the A695 modern bridge, a ruinous mediaeval bridge pier stands close to the water-mill. Hodgson in his *History of Northumberland* says: "the bridge had ribbed arches." The springers of these can be seen on the ruined pier. The situation was confused by Frank Graham's *Bridges of Northumberland and Durham* (1975), which shows a drawing by Carmichael c1820. In this drawing, the artist depicts a bridge with vertical piers and a flat wooden superstructure. Graham took this to mean that the same bridge had been reconstructed but a little research solved the problem. The six inch O S first edition map shows that the flat-topped bridge was several yards further upstream from the mediaeval bridge. Hodgson tells us that it was an aqueduct which carried water from the water-mill to an hydraulic threshing machine at the farm on the opposite bank. A close inspection of old woodcuts of this aqueduct shows water dripping from the horizontal superstructure.

We still had to find the Roman crossing, but suspected Roman bridge-stones were found in the bed of the river downstream from the mediaeval

Dilston from the air. Bottom centre, with tractor marks bisecting it, is the faint trace of a Romano-British farmstead. Right centre is a field with a typical "envelope pattern" caused by the plough turning. Top right on the hill behind the farm is the slight earthwork of a suspected Roman fortlet. At 11 o'clock to same farm is mediaeval road curving down hill. A695 crosses Devil's Water beside farm. This view to south-east.

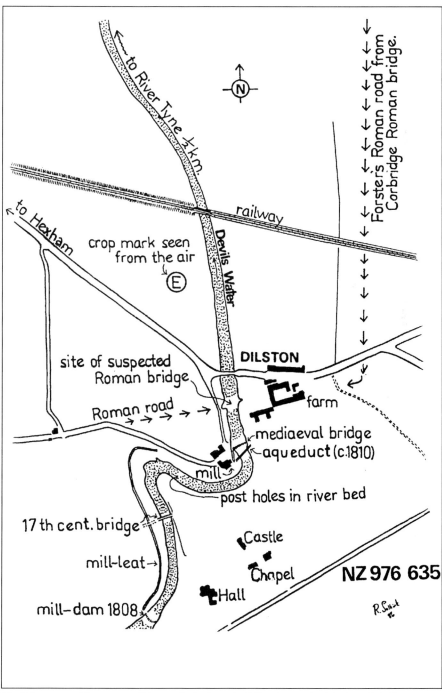

to River Tyne ½km.

to Hexham

railway

Devils Water

Forster's Roman road from Corbridge Roman bridge.

crop mark seen from the air Ⓔ

site of suspected Roman bridge

Roman road → → →

DILSTON

farm

mediaeval bridge
aqueduct (c.1810)

mill

post holes in river bed

17th cent. bridge

mill-leat→

mill-dam 1808

Castle

Chapel

Hall

NZ 976 635

R. Selkirk

The Dilston area. The suspected Roman fortlet is on the hill to the south of the farm. The Roman crossroads, with eastern and southern arms missing, is to east of farm.

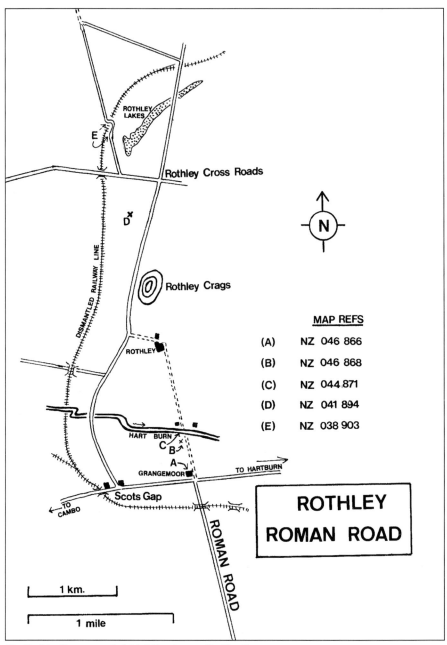

MAP REFS

(A)	NZ	046 866
(B)	NZ	046 868
(C)	NZ	044.871
(D)	NZ	041 894
(E)	NZ	038 903

ROTHLEY
ROMAN ROAD

1 km.

1 mile

The Rothley Roman road which is lined up on Rothley Crags.
A = Grangemoor Farm.
B = Exposed section of Roman road in bank of small stream.
C = Roman ford and slight remains of bridge a few yards upstream from modern ford.
D = Roman paved ford across small stream. Roman coins found here.
E = Farm road on top of Roman road deviates from Roman *agger* to
        cross railway bridge.

pier. One stone had a channel for a tie-bar, very similar to the stones in the Chollerford Roman bridge abutment. An aerial search located shadow marks of an earthworks on the hillock just to the south of Dilston Farm (NY 976 634) and this looks like a Roman fortlet. The aerial search also showed that a branch of Dere Street had continued due west to Dilston from the bend where the known road turned towards the Corbridge Roman bridge. Another unidentified suspected fortlet or signal station was observed close by this link-road at NY 985 629, in the field above a bungalow with a red roof. The earthwork has a single gate in the north side whereas native RB sites had their gates on the east. This site is in full view of the Corbridge Roman fort and could be a repeater signal station to relay messages to the Wall system which is out of sight of the Corbridge fort.

We now have an unknown Roman road heading for Dilston from the east. It is likely that Forster's right-angled turn of a Roman road at Dilston was actually a Roman crossroads with two arms not visible in Forster's day. The link with Dere Street is the third arm. A fourth arm went due south and I quote from the *Proceedings of the Society of Antiquaries of Newcastle upon Tyne,* Vol 6, c1839:

> "They would travel along the ancient Roman road from Corbridge to Stanhope still partly in use which is mentioned in ancient documents and which crosses the valley of the Derwent at Bay Bridge, a mile west from Blanchland."

This leaves only the westbound arm of the Roman crossroads on the west side of the Devil's Water at Dilston mill. Forster already mentioned it passing Dilston Park (NY 968 635), and a very straight farm track runs from Dilston mill to this position. The suspected Roman road gets a mention by Henry Maclauchlan in his *Survey of the Watling Street,* 1852, when he quotes the evidence of Thomas Harle, a drainer, for the existence of an ancient road which ran south-westwards from Corstopitum crossing the Devil's Water at Dilston mill and running onwards for about sixty yards on the south side of Park South Farm, and thence by a bend towards the wood.

There is a double hedge-line in exactly this position and a central *agger* is crammed with large stones. The bend is still there and the road heads for "Five Gates Cottage," mentioned previously in connection with the Roman road from Ebchester direct to Hexham.

The road from Dilston to the west is surely the long lost Roman road to Old Town in Allendale, mentioned by all the old antiquarians but ignored by present-day students.

Checklist for network south of Corbridge

North to South road from Corbridge Roman bridge

NY 980 647	South end of Corbridge Roman bridge (abutment can be seen in river at low water conditions).
NY 977 635	Site of Dilston toll-bar.
NY 976 634	Suspected Roman crossroads beside possible fortlet on hillock to south of Dilston Farm.
NY 974 628	Suspected Roman road joins modern B6307.
NY 955 555	Suspected Roman road through Slaley Forest.

NY 950 518   Pennypie House, on line of suspected Roman road.

NY 959 499   Bay Bridge. Reports of remains of old bridge.

Westward extension of Dere Street

NY 987 633   Dere Street forks. One branch goes to Corbridge Roman bridge. The other continues westwards to Dilston. Ignore obvious mediaeval road which runs down bank just east of Dilston towards position of old toll.

NY 976 634   Crossroads (invisible at ground level) beside hillock and suspected fortlet.

NY 975 635   Suspected site of Roman bridge across Devil's Water.

NY 970 635   Roman road under straight cart track to Dilston Park.

NY 968 635   Dilston Park Farm. Roman road just to south.

NY 965 633   *Agger* up strip wood. Many large stones.

NY 959 632   Five Gates Cottage.

NY 930 610   Diptonmill. Natural rock ford 150 yards upstream of public house and modern road bridge.

NY 814 582   Supposed site of Roman fort at Old Town reported by many antiquarians but now mostly disregarded.

NY 745 515   Suspected Roman road underneath modern A688.

NY 699 493   Roman bridge abutment, now high and dry in west bank of South Tyne, directly opposite Underbank Farm. To east of Underbank Farm, Roman road can be seen zig-zagging up steep slope. Inscribed Roman stones in byres of Underbank Farm. Whitley Castle Roman fort just to west.

South of Hexham

There is another network to the south of Hexham. One evening a couple of years ago, a gentleman knocked on my door and enquired if I was interested in the findspot of a few dozen Roman coins in the Hexham area. He had found the scatter of coins close to the deserted mediaeval village of Dotland (NY 923 595).

Many times from the air, I had looked at the long straight road which heads north-north-west from this place and I wondered if once again, there had been a continuity of occupation of an ex-Roman site. Now I was sure. Because of the excellent metal detector-derived information, the aircraft could be left in its hangar and an immediate start made with a ground search.

The straight road NNW from Dotland makes a switch to the east to avoid a steep descent at Channel Well Farm (NY 921 603) and the very name of the farm hints at a possible spring-fed Roman well with a leat of aqueduct-type stones. A quick search failed to reveal the well and a return would have to be made later.

Forster's Road coming in from the north-east on its way from Corbridge, Dilston and Diptonmill to Old Town, is also lined up on Channel Well Farm so there could well have been a Roman cross-roads here. Back on our northbound road, zig-zags across the Dipton Burn ravine may be ex-Roman but modern paths and foot-bridges have confused the issue. Beyond the ravine, a compass course was followed to the north over the Hexham racecourse towards the junction of the two Tynes. On the descent towards the

The Rothley Roman road peeps out of the bank of a small stream at NZ 045 869, north of Grangemoor Farm.

Romans have cut small cliff away at NZ 059 823, at east end of small lake, north of East Shaftoe Hall.

The Rothley Road crosses the Simonside Hills and it is little more than a pack-horse trail, but at one point (NZ 023 994), a natural rock outcrop has been carved into imitation road paving. This was puzzling. The road runs along a cliff here, and a search located a niche for an altar in the face of the cliff, underneath the Roman road. This was a holy spot.

Cockshaw Burn, a hedgerow full of large stones co-incided with our search-line and made a steep dive into the ravine at Summerrods. At this point there was a paved ford on the bed of the burn (NY 911 636) and the six inch O S map of 1850 marks "old walls" on the bank to the north of the stream. [The Red House Roman fort near Corbridge was excavated by a rescue excavation a few years ago, just before the A69(T) was constructed. The map of 1850 also marks "old walls" on this site and if an observant archaeologist had noticed this, the new road could have been routed around the Red House site and the Roman fort saved.]

As our suspected Dotland/Channel-Well/Summerrods road progresses north, it crosses a very prominent east-west Roman-looking *agger* with large stones sticking out here and there, at NY 906 650. The latter follows the northern edge of High Wood at this point and seems to be lined up on

Hexham Abbey. To the south-west of Highwood Farm the *agger* is flanked by small quarries. Also in the field south-west of the farm, at NY 906 652, two Romano-British farmsteads were observed from the air a few years ago. They were well camouflaged by the later rig and furrow agriculture. Nearer the river, the line of our north-bound road descends a bank called "Gateless Field" (NY 905 657) and ends up at the South Tyne at Burnfoot (NY 904 659) where "stepping stones" are marked across the river on the 1850 map. On the other side of the river is the "Stanegate" on its way from Fourstones to Howford.

This network of previously unknown Roman roads in the Tyne Valley was reported to Professor Sheppard Frere, the leading Roman period archaeologist in Britain. He remarked in his *Oxford Lecture,* entitled *Since Haverfield and Richmond,* delivered in All Souls College on 23.10.87, that the evidence was exciting but should have been predicted long ago. He also called for the publication of the information. This is it.

THE DEVIL'S NETWORK

The Devil's Causeway

In addition to Dere Street which ran the length of Northumberland en route from York to Edinburgh, and which is mentioned by the Romans in their Antonine Itinerary, another major Roman road left the Corbridge area but diverged from Dere Street on a north-easterly heading on its way to the mouth of the River Tweed. No mention is made of it by the Romans. Like many other Roman massive works, it was attributed by later inhabitants to the work of the Devil and this resulted in the name, "The Devil's Causeway." The historian Hodgson made these remarks:

> "...for generations this road has been regarded as a freak; its persistence in ascending heavy and almost impracticable gradients and in traversing vast wastes, leading nowhere, seems incomprehensible, and may sufficiently explain the belief in supernatural origin."

It presented problems for historians and archaeologists because it didn't seem to have a single military site on its whole length between the Wall and the Tweed. What was believed to have been a Roman fortlet at Hartburn to the west of Morpeth, proved to be a Romano-British farmstead when it was excavated (NZ 084 866).

For a time, the military sites eluded even aerial searches, but what was immediately obvious from the aircraft was that the Roman road at Hartburn did not follow the route shown on the Ordnance Survey map. Just to the south-west of the village, the north-bound Roman road which could be seen under the crops, made a sharp turn to the east and a ground inspection of the wooded gorge of the Hart Burn showed that the turn was lined-up with an overgrown hollow-way some two hundred yards east of the supposed track, and at the other end of the village.

The hollow-way was followed down to the stream and a search of the river bed carried out. When water-weeds were cleared, a double line of square post-holes appeared. These were each about a foot square and had been cut into the bed-rock. Without doubt these holes marked the site of a timber

Top: The last remnants of the Devil's Causeway Roman bridge across the Wansbeck at NZ 077 844, south of Marlish Farm.
Bottom: The Roman bridge over the Hart Burn. The Devil's Causeway crossed the Hart Burn at Hartburn at NZ 088 866, which is two hundred yards downstream from the crossing marked on the OS map. When the stream bed was cleared of weeds, two lines of post- holes were revealed. Although the stream is only a foot deep at this point, divers, wearing breathing apparatus, excavated the Roman post-holes with small spoons. Bronze Roman votive pins were found in almost every hole. In the hollow-way at the south end of the bridge site, the Devil's Causeway was excavated and the construction was seen to follow the normal Roman pattern of large foundation stones, rough kerbs, and a cobble and gravel *agger*.

A few yards upstream from the Devil's Causeway bridge site at Hartburn is Hartburn Grotto. This is a natural cave in the cliff on the south side of the stream. It has been enlarged by the hand of man. In the 18th century, Archdeacon Sharpe converted it into a chapel, with internal walls, Gothic arches and a fireplace.

The walls of the entrance however, are carved to simulate Roman ashlar with feathered toolmarks, quite out of keeping with the Archdeacon's handiwork. The cave was probably a Roman Mithraic temple. Two niches above the entrance once held statues of Adam and Eve, but it is likely that they originally housed the Mithraic torchbearers, Cautes and Cautopates.

Roman bridge at NZ 087 865. Although the stream was only a couple of feet deep, the holes which were full of sand and gravel, were excavated slowly and meticulously by divers lying in the water, taking out one spoonful at a time. In the bottom of almost every hole, a bronze Roman votive pin was found.

An excavation of the suspected road in the hollow-way was carried out and a typical cobbled Roman *agger* was found. Close by the Roman bridge site is the famous "Hartburn Grotto" which is a cave in the riverside cliffs. This was converted into a chapel, complete with Gothic-arched internal walls and a fireplace, during the eighteenth century by an enthusiastic clergyman, Archdeacon Sharpe. The archdeacon was a keen folly-builder and his various other works can be seen around the woodlands. He was very fond of Gothic arches. It is my opinion though, that the cave beside the Roman bridge was originally a Roman Mithraic temple. Above the cave's entrance are two niches cut into the rock face. In later times they contained statues of Adam and Eve but it is likely that the original occupants were images of the Mithraic torch-bearers, Cautes and Cautopates. The roof of the cave has had its natural dome cut to resemble corbelling, surmounted by a large flat oval-shaped capping stone. I have seen similar roof designs on Mithraic caves elsewhere. The natural rock walls of the cave are carved to look like massive Roman ashlar with feathered toolmarks, quite different in character to the masonry of the archdeacon's improvements.

From the cave's entrance, a passage leads under the riverside path to the water's edge and it is said that this was to allow ladies in the archdeacon's bathing parties to proceed to the river out of view of the local village louts. How the same layabouts were prevented from looking at the river scene once the ladies had emerged from the passage is not explained. It is more likely that the tunnel was connected with the mystical rites of the Mithraic religion. Identical niches to those above the Hartburn cave can be seen in the Roman quarry at Aldborough, Yorkshire, SE 403 663.

It is extremely likely that the Roman fort or fortlet at Hartburn is underneath the church. There is a cliff to the north, a steep slope to the south, an artifical cutting through solid rock to the east and the remains of a slight earthwork to the west. The famous historian, the Rev Hodgson who was rector here is buried in the churchyard so it is hoped that he can see the few secrets which eluded him in his very active life.

While looking for the Devil's Causeway crossing of the River Wansbeck (the next river to the south) at the position marked on the Ordnance Survey map at NZ 077 844, a suspected Roman fortlet was spotted in the field immediately to the south-east of Marlish Farm at NZ 078 848. The remains of the Roman bridge, just a few stumps of vertical timbers, were also found exactly at the position marked on the O S map.

When the Causeway approaches the Roman Wall from the north on a straight alignment of about 210 degrees, it suddenly makes an unusually large turn of forty degrees to the west and joins the known Dere Street near Beukley. If the road had continued straight ahead, it would have traversed the mysterious deserted mediaeval village of Little Whittington (NY 991 695) upon which several other Roman roads are aligned. A further continuation of the same line takes it to the Red House Roman fort site (NY 969 651) which predated Corstopitum but is now lost under the A69(T) road. An aerial search shows the possibility that the Devil's Causeway may have crossed the River Tyne at NY 966 648, just to the south-west of Prior Thorns and three-quarters of a mile upstream from the Dere Street Roman bridge at Corbridge. Two grass-covered roads, as if from both ends of the early period Red House fort, converge at one point on the river's north bank at this point. Investigations continue.

The uncharacteristic turn which takes the Causeway to Beukley, off its 210 degree heading, is lined up on a distinct *agger* to the west of Dere Street, so this bend may have been a road junction and not the original road. Old antiquarians said that a "military way" proceeded from this area to Chesters on the North Tyne. They might well have been right.

Both Dere Street and "Proto Devil's Causeway" cross the Roman Wall at "Portgate" (NY 987 687) which is now under a traffic roundabout at the crossing of the A68 and B6318, but which was thought to have been a gateway expressly constructed for Dere Street. This may not have been the case. The road construction sequence was probably as follows.

1 At Beukley, Dere Street originally continued straight ahead to Little Whittington, Bywell and Ebchester (141 degrees). 2 The Devil's Causeway went straight ahead to Red House (210 degrees). 3 When the Wall was built, a hole was left in it at Portgate for the existing Devil's Causeway on its direct track to Red House. 4 When the later Dere Street was built, it utilised the existing hole in the Wall at Portgate, hence the un-Roman type bend towards the gateway. 5 The bend of the Devil's Causeway towards Beukley was a branch road bound for Chesters, and the original road to Red House has been lost under rig and furrow. The suspected branch road can be traced to the west of Dere Street and passes a pre-historic settlement at NY 971 705 and Keepwick Fell Farm (NY 951 699) on its way to Chollerford Roman bridge.

The Devil's Coast Road

We have not finished with the Devil's Causeway. As we trace it northwards beyond the Wansbeck, the Hart Burn and the Font another unusually large alteration of heading takes place at NZ 122 923, 3½ miles south-west of Longhorsley. The Roman road alters course suddenly from 029 degrees to due north. There is no sign near the turn, of a continuation of the 029 heading but nevertheless it is there, or has been at one time because there is evidence further on. This turn, for reference purposes will be known as the "Devil's Corner." The turn from 029 to 360 degrees is a branch road and the original went straight ahead to Howick Haven (NZ 262 168) on the Northumberland coast two miles north of the RAF helicopter base at Boulmer. It was difficult to find the Roman road at first, even from the air, but clues came from research of field names.

The following names were found and plotted on graph paper. They were all on, or very near, the 029 degree line:

1	NZ 151 974	Field name	"Coolgate Head"
2	NZ 165 998	Field name	"The Streets"
3	NU 180 023	DMV	"Old Felton"
4	NU 189 039	Field name	"High Camp"

5	NU 192 040	Field name	"Low Camp"
6	NU 191 038	Field name	"Low South Camp"
7	NU 191 042	Field name	"Nell's Walls"
8	NU 193 045	DMV	"Hazon"
9	NU 202 061	DMV	"Hartlaw"
10	NU 21? 08?	Field name	"Chesters Flatt"

The first signs of the road are in the south side of a wood just west of the spot height of 155m (NZ 125 932). The *agger* goes into the wood but the farmer has cut a ditch through it and dumped the large stones at the fence slightly to the west. It is prominent to the south-west of Highmoor (NZ 150 973) and at Hazon where it is a marked *agger* in the wood on the north side of the Hazon Burn at NU 193 044. The farmer at Hazon, Mr Bell, reported that he had hit the road several times while ploughing in the vicinity of NU 197 052, and he drove us in his landrover to view a square earthwork on the hilltop at NU 193 053, on the western side of the buried Roman road, four hundred yards south of High Hazon Farm. For reference purposes, this branch of the Devil's Causeway from the Devil's Corner to Howick Haven will be known as the "Devil's Coast Road."

At Howick Haven, there is an Iron Age hillfort (NU 255 163) and there have been several Roman finds in the area. Another suspected Roman road coming in from the direction of the High Rochester fort, from the south-west is suspected underneath the modern B6341 road to the west-south-west of Alnwick at NU 140 110. This road is also lined up on the Howick Haven Iron Age fort. The signs are that there is an unidentified Roman harbour at Howick Haven. The B6341 road is also lined up on Holystone on the River Coquet to the south-west (NT 955 025) where there have been Roman finds and from where a known Roman road leads to High Rochester. A Roman site is suspected under the Holystone Church and the adjacent farm over the road to the west. This may be the long lost Roman site of Coccuveda which is thought might lie on the River Coquet.

The Devil's Crossroad

Just north of the Devil's Corner is yet another previously unknown Roman road which runs east-south-east to west-north-west, and forms a triangle with the northbound Devil's Causeway and the north-eastbound Devil's Coast Road. In places this road still has its original three lanes intact. Outside the central *agger* there are grass tracks for unshod animals. The road can best be picked up at NZ 138 931, on the south side of a triangular wood on the west side of a public road, four hundred yards south of Muckley Farm, south-west of Longhorsley. The Roman road which has been named the "Devil's Crossroad" is lined up on 285/105 degrees and is followed by a public footpath. At the south-west corner of the triangular wood, a farmer has cut a large drainage culvert through the road and removed a hundred tons of massive road-stones which at time of writing are still lying there. At NZ 126 934 where a small stream is crossed, there is the crossing with the Devil's Coast Road. Seven hundred and fifty yards further west at NZ 123 935 is the crossing of the known Devil's Causeway and there is a possible turret at the junction. This is a gorse-covered mound. The Roman road continues beyond

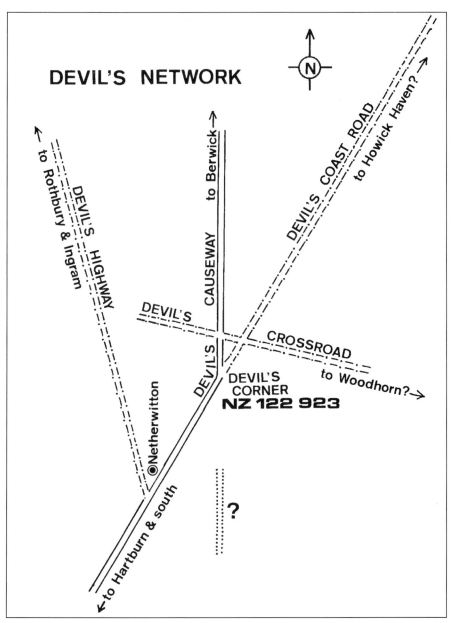

A network of Roman roads, associated with the Devil's Causeway, has been found in Northumberland. They have all been given names beginning with "Devil." The Devil's Causeway has a peculiar bend (Devil's Corner) and a road straight ahead was identified initially from field names. The Devil's Highway is a major road and it is astonishing how it has remained undiscovered for so long.

Southward Edge Farm and there is an obvious Romano-British farm at NZ 103 942 at the point where a public footpath crosses a public road. Ditches can be seen on the north side of the modern road and large stones stick out of the ground on the south side. The road is lined-up on Coquet Cairn (NZ 025 965) which is also a suspected survey point on the Rothley Roman road mentioned very early in this chapter. Roman surveyors have carried out some very precise work in this area. If we proceed in a reciprocal direction on a heading of 105 degrees to attempt to find where the road originated, we will come to the Northumberland coast and pass right through the Saxon church of Woodhorn at NZ 301 888, just north-west of Newbiggin-by-the-Sea. As we would expect, there are many strange and unexplained earthworks around this church.

While searching this road, I happened to be chatting to a farmer who said that he had always suspected a Roman road across his land because of the tremendous stones he kept hitting with his plough. During this conversation, I pointed out that one of his farm trailers seemed to have aircraft wheels on it, upon which he showed me more wheels in his barn. He had bought them at a sale on an airfield forty years before. The wheels were all from Spitfires and are extremley valuable as a rebuilt Spitfire in flying condition is now worth about half a million pounds. This information and the address of an aircraft manufacturer which specialises in rebuilding antique aircraft, was passed on to the farmer.

The Devil's Highway

There is more to come. Yet another Roman road associated with the Devil's Causeway was recently found in the area. The known Devil's Causeway passes through the village of Hartburn where we found the post-holes in the rock bed of the stream. If the known Roman road is followed for one mile to the north, one comes to Thornton Moor Farm (NZ 097 879) just over a mile south of the village of Netherwitton. Another Roman road has either crossed or branched off from just south of Thornton Moor Farm and can be seen to the north-west where the public road makes a double-right-angled turn one mile south-west of Netherwitton. The Roman road's heading is 338 degrees and emerges from a swamp at NZ 093 886 and approaches the zig-zag of the modern road via the strip of trees to the south-east of the spot height marked 154m. The *agger* can be seen up this tree-line and it continues underneath the zig-zag, emerging again where the public road turns on its second right-angle towards Netherwitton. At NZ 090 890, a rough farm track, which is also a public footpath continues straight ahead down the right-hand edge of a strip wood on a heading of 340 degrees. The cart track and footpath are on the grass-covered *agger* of a very recently discovered Roman road, the "Devil's Highway", so-named because of its association with the known Devil's Causeway.

The road is a three-lane type and the grass strips outside the drainage ditches are in excellent condition. At the bottom of the hill at NZ 089 893, the road crosses a small stream. Roman stone bridge abutments are intact but are almost hidden by a farmer's plank bridge which has replaced very large original Roman lintel-type stones. These lie a few yards away beside a field wall. Each must weigh over a ton.

The agger of the Devil's Coast Road at Hazon, Northumberland (NZ 192 044).

On the north side of the stream, the rammed gravel and cobble Roman road surface is exposed where it coincides with a farm gate. To the right of the road is an area of waste land which contains many robber-trenches. There is a possible Roman site here (NZ 090 893) three hundred yards west of Longlea Farm. The road continues on the same alignment towards Bellion, and before the next stream, the three grass-covered lanes are easily visible. There are lots of "spare parts" at the road's edges. A stream is crossed just south of Bellion and on the north side of the stream and the west side of the road is a possible Roman turret. A tree-covered square-shaped mound has a possible gateway facing the road. There is a grass-covered quarry on the opposite side of the road.

A cart track joins the Roman road and overlies it as far as Bellion (NZ 087 899). At Bellion, a very straight footpath is lined up on the much-discussed Rothley Crag Roman survey-point to the west. The Devil's Highway continues down the east side of a strip wood. The *agger* is prominent and spare parts lie around but the outlying tracks are lost under the wood on the west side and modern agriculture on the east. There is a paved ford in the stream at NZ 084 904 and the *agger* can be followed as far as the next stream at NZ 083 907. At this point there is a "mirror image" deviation, the Roman road angling to the west and after crossing the stream, to the east, back to the surveyed line. The road becomes difficult to follow over rough pasture but can be picked up again on the north side of the Ewesley Burn at NZ 082 911. The Roman road

A Roman bridge at NZ 089 893 crosses a small stream. The Roman abutments are intact but are almost hidden by a farmer's plank bridge. The road is a three-lane type, with grass strips for unshod animals, flanking the drainage ditches of the central paved *agger*.

South of the Roman Wall fort of Halton (Onnum), a cart track heads east from the Castle and hamlet of Halton. An unlisted Roman road crosses this track, south of the fort, heading south, at NZ 000 679. In Halton churchyard, a Roman altar has been reused as a modern gravestone.

is underneath a cart track on its run north to South Healey Farm and due north of the farm, to the east of the public footpath, is the playing card shape of a typical Roman fortlet. This overlooks the crossing of the River Font where there are the vestiges of a mill-dam slightly upstream from the suspected Roman crossing point. Permission has not yet been obtained to search the lands to the north of the River Font, but the Roman *agger* is almost definitely under a field boundary which runs northwards to a wood at NZ 084 923. Just to the north-west is Nunnykirk, where Hodgson in his Vol 2 mentions "underground Roman remains." Right on the line of our suspected road, across a gully in a wood at NZ 083 929, is an old bridge with no road, path or track anywhere near it. This will be inspected as soon as permission is obtained.

The road heads for Forestburn Gate (NZ 067 963) and the name almost certainly confirms the position of the Roman road's crossing of the Forest Burn. To the north, the Roman road is underneath the modern B6342 and the 1850 map marks a house, "Street Gate" at NZ 063 972. The B6342 swings off the Roman road at NZ 060 977 but the latter continues straight ahead under the farm track past Lordenshaws Farm. Where the farm road bends to the west, the Roman road continues straight ahead over the rough ground and right past the west side of the magnificent Iron Age hillfort of Lordenshaws. The Devil's Highway is very prominent down the steep slope to the north but after the stream crossing, is lost in modern farmland.

The route to the north of Rothbury is still under investigation but its general line will be included in the check-list which follows:

Check-list of important points on the Devil's Network. Devil's Causeway

Alignment: 029 to Devil's Corner, then 360 degrees.

NY 970 649	Red House Roman fort. Suspected original departure point of Devil's Causeway.
NY 987 687	Portgate, where original Devil's Causeway is thought to have passed through Wall.
NY 991 695	Little Whittington DMV, upon which many Roman roads are aligned.
NZ 077 844	Crossing of River Wansbeck. Remains of bridge timbers visible in water.
NZ 078 848	Possible fortlet to south-west of Marlish Farm.
NZ 088 866	Roman bridge over Hart Burn at Hartburn.
NZ 122 923	Devil's Corner (where Devil's Causeway turns north)
NZ 119 984	Brinkheugh crossing of River Coquet by branch of Devil's Causeway. Roman road excavated on south bank.

Devil's Coast Road

Alignment: 029 degrees.

NZ 125 932	*Agger* of Devil's Coast Road cut by farmer.
NZ 193 044	*Agger* visible in wood south-west of Hazon Farm.
NZ 193 053	Square earthwork on hill

NZ 197 053   Roman road hit by farmer while ploughing.
NZ 255 163   Iron Age hillfort near Howick Haven. Several Roman artefacts
               found here. No Roman site found to-date.

Devil's Crossroad

   Alignment: 285/105 degrees

NZ 301 888   Woodhorn Saxon church. Unidentified earthworks.
NZ 138 931   Roman three-lane road on south side of triangular wood.
               Culvert cut through road by farmer. Much stone.
NZ 126 934   Crossing with Devil's Coast Road.
NZ 123 935   Crossing with Devil's Causeway. Possible Roman turret at
                 junction.
NZ 103 942   Romano-British farm under modern road.
NZ 025 965   Coquet Cairn, suspected Roman survey point. Junction with
                 Rothley Roman Road.

Devil's Highway

General alignment: 340 degrees.

NZ 097 878   Devil's Highway leaves Devil's Causeway at Thornton Moor
               Farm.
NZ 093 886   Roman road emerges from swamp.
NZ 092 887   Roman *agger* in hedge-line.
NZ 091 888   Roman road underneath zig-zag of modern road.
NZ 090 890   Three-lane Roman road runs down strip wood.
NZ 089 893   Suspected Roman bridge over small stream.
NZ 088 898   Suspected Roman turret beside stream.
NZ 087 900   Roman road passes Bellion under cart track. Straight footpath
               to west lined up on Rothley Crags suspected Roman survey
               point.
NZ 085 903   Roman road down east side of strip wood.
NZ 084 904   Paved ford.
NZ 083 907   Mirror-image deviation across ravine.
NZ 083 914   Roman road under cart track to South Healey Farm.
NZ 084 919   Suspected Roman fortlet north of South Healey Farm on high
               bank above River Font.
NZ 083 926   Hodgson reported Roman remains here. Saxon cross removed
               from school grounds to Newcastle University.
NZ 082 929   Report of unidentified old bridge. Not yet inspected.
NZ 067 963   Forestburn Gate. Typical place-name indication.
NZ 062 972   1850 O S marks "Street House." Typical place-name.
NZ 053 993   Roman road clearly visible to west of Lordenshaws Iron Age
               hillfort.
NU 044 046   Roman road under field wall to east of Cartington Castle.
NU 036 060   *Agger* down hedge-line towards Lorbottle.
NU 035 065   Unidentified earthworks at Lorbottle. Road thought to divide
               here with one branch leaving to north-west to NU 010 084,
               then to Alnham via NU 000 101.   After Alnham, possibly
               under Salters' Road to Ewartley Shank, NT 961 134. Main

Roman road thought to transit, Yetlington, Little Ryle, Great Ryle, and Ingram.

NU 019 163   Murray reports in his *Handbook for Travellers in Durham and Northumberland* that the church at Ingram was built on the site of an earlier building and that the piers of a Roman bridge were found in the River Breamish to the north of the church.

NU 018 205   Crossing of Roddam Burn. Very obvious Roman road up hill to north of crossing. Roman road then thought to pass to east of Ilderton Moor, through South Middleton and Caldgate Mill (NT 998 248) and then through ravine to south-west of Wooler at NT 986 272. After that, possibly to Ford and then to Norham on the River Tweed where there have been considerable Roman finds.

Heighley Gate

To finish off, I will mention a piece of newly-discovered Roman road which throws a bit of light on the mysterious Roman fortlet of Longshaws, on the cliff above the River Font at NZ 135 885. The road leaves the A697 at NZ 175 894 on a heading of 250 degrees and passes through Benridge Moor, north of Maidens Hall, down the wood at NZ 137 885, over a ford and up the cliff to the fortlet. It then probably went to Thornton House (NZ 097 867) where Hodgson (Vol 2) placed a "Roman town" and then to Hartburn.

There is more to find in Northumberland but that will have to do for now. Every county should produce a similar amount of evidence so it is up to the readers. We can now move on to the search for the heavy goods supply lines which everyone will have realised were the sea routes and the rivers, even the tiny ones.

Craft with rectangular sail, on a vase from Naqada, Egypt, dated c3100 BC.

A Roman warship being manoeuvred. Note *corvus* in the raised position.

Chapter 7

The Roman Navy and Merchant Marine
(and other mariners, ancient and modern)

Whosoever commands the sea commands the trade; Whosoever commands the trade of the world commands the riches of the world, and consequently the world itself

Sir Walter Raleigh

So many are the merchant vessels that arrive here that Rome has practically become a common workshop for the whole world...
There are always ships putting into or sailing out of the harbour.

Aristides

Although the Roman road network was a magnificent all-weather grid for the deployment of troops, we have seen that it had severe limitations for the movement of heavy items and for large logistical operations. The very design of the road system shows that little thought was given to problems of wheeled vehicles except around the towns and farms. Water transport was the obvious answer but several factors were involved. First of all, a fleet of merchant ships was required for both overseas and coastal traffic, and warships were necessary to escort these vessels in waters frequented by enemies and pirates. If possible, it was better to operate a large navy and clear the seas completely of hostile vessels thus allowing merchant ships a freedom of navigation.

Once merchant ships have arrived in the river as close as possible to their cargoes' destinations, they may be able to proceed upstream for a considerable distance and in lots of cases discharge the freight directly onto the riverside quay of the addressee without any need for trans-shipment into lighters thus saving much expense. The Thames, Severn, Humber, Rhine, Seine, Danube, Nile, Tigris and Euphrates are typical examples of large rivers, navigable for considerable distances inland. An exception was the River Tiber where Roman records (Pliny the Elder) tell us that at the port of Ostia, cargoes were transferred into river barges for onward towage up the Tiber to Rome. These lighters of a hundred tons or more were pulled upstream by teams of oxen. The use of the River Tiber as a goods route did not stop at Rome. Both Pliny the Elder and Strabo tell us that some of the upper reaches of the Tiber and its tributaries were navigable and used for the transportation of foodstuffs, building stone and timber. Some of the stretches were difficult and used only by rafts. Pliny has this to say:

> "The Tiber, the former name of which was Thybris, and before that Albula, rises in about the middle of the Apennine chain in the territory of Arezzo. At first it is a narrow stream, only navigable when its water is dammed by sluices and then discharged, in the same way as its tributaries, the Tinia and the Chiana, the waters of which must be so collected for nine days, unless augmented by showers of rain."

The inference from this is: that it was better to sit around for nine days waiting for water to collect than to transport the goods by road. We will return to specific Roman problems many times but just for now let us examine water transport in general.

Why is water transport so cheap compared with all forms of land transport? If a large horse is harnessed to a modern cart with well-oiled wheels, it can pull a two-ton load along a smooth and level road. If we hitch the same horse to a canal barge, it can pull a hundred tons.

It costs more to go by car or bus to the local supermarket than to ship a bag of apples from New Zealand. It was also cheaper to bring open-cast coal from Australia than to dig deep coal from the mines of County Durham.

The following table has been prepared, to show the comparative costs of operating various forms of ancient and modern transport. It tabulates the distance which each vessel, vehicle or animal could move a ton of cargo on one gallon of fuel or the equivalent weight of fodder:

Vehicle/Animal/Vessel	Fuel type	Distance able to carry 1 ton on 1 gallon
Large modern cargo ship	heavy oil	4,600 miles
Modern coaster	heavy oil	600 miles
Modern freight train	diesel oil	250 miles
Modern lorry	diesel oil	50 miles
1944 Lancaster bomber	aviation gasoline	1 mile
Camel	fodder	2.4 miles
Roman merchant ship	food/cooking fuel	1,280 miles
Roman *codicaria*	food/cooking fuel	32 miles
Mule	fodder	2.4 miles
Roman ox-wagon	fodder	0.8 miles

The efficiency of water transport was brought home to me at a very early age because my ambition to fly military aircraft was shattered when World War II ended. The Navy and RAF had a glut of highly experienced flyers and the mushrooming civil airlines could also pick and choose their war-experienced crews, most of whom did not want to return to their pre-war mundane professions. An airline would not train an Air Training Corps cadet who could only fly gliders, when ex-lieutenant-commanders and squadron leaders with DSO's and DFC's were available. Rather reluctantly, I became an ordinary ship's officer with a resolve to change to flying as soon as an opportunity arose. The nautical training was to prove extremely useful because, by the time I got into the pilot's seat of an aeroplane a few years later, I was an experienced navigator, radio operator and meteorologist, all skills which help a pilot to reach old age.

An added bonus was that I gained a working knowledge of the transportation of massive amounts of material around the world.

The Suez Canal never failed to impress me. I admired the French engineer Ferdinand de Lesseps, who had cut this eighty-five mile sea-level ditch between the Mediterranean and the Red Sea, thus shortening the journey from the English Channel to Bombay by five thousand miles. The canal was opened in 1869 and the Khedive of Egypt commissioned the Italian composer Verdi, to write the opera "Aida" for the occasion.

The French lost the controlling interest in the canal company when the bankrupt Khedive sold his shares. The British prime minister, Disraeli snapped them up.

I had been amazed to learn from my geography master at school that, thousands of years before de Lesseps cut his canal, ships sailed between the two seas. This ancient route was first up the River Nile and then along a canal between the Nile and the Red Sea. The canal is reputed to have been built by Pharaoh Sesostris of the Twelfth Dynasty. It fell into disuse but was repaired by various later rulers; by Necho in 600 BC, Darius in 521 BC, Ptolemy Philadelphus in the third century BC, and finally by the Roman emperor Trajan in AD 98. From then it remained navigable until the third century AD. The canal length was over 60 miles and it was evidently deep enough and wide enough to take the largest sea-going vessels of the period.

De Lesseps' canal had no problems with level changes as the Mediterranean and Red Seas are the same height although the usual prophets of doom had argued otherwise. There *was*, however, a difference of level between the River Nile and the Red Sea and two ancient writers, Strabo, and Diodorus both refer to a device which overcame this problem. Strabo says:

"The Ptolemaic kings cut their canal and made it so that it could be closed so that, when desired, they could sail into the sea without difficulty and also sail back."

Diodorus Siculus also refers to the device in the canal:

"At a later time, the Second Ptolemy completed it, and in the most suitable spot, constructed an ingenious kind of lock. This he opened whenever he wished to pass through, and quickly closed again, a contrivance whose usage proved to be highly successful."

We are not sure whether this device was a pound-lock or a flash-lock but both of these devices will be discussed in due course. Before we move away from Egypt navigations, there is another item of interest mentioned by

Strabo: he tells us of a canal between the River Nile and Lake Moaris. Strabo refers to the difference in levels between the river and the lake and says:

> "While these conditions are the work of nature, yet locks have been placed at both mouths of the canal, by which the engineers regulate both the inflow and outflow of water."

Clearly, the ancient engineers could accommodate changes of levels of water.

A third of the way round the world from the Suez Canal, another artificial navigation astonished me even more – the Panama Canal. The Spanish explorers of the early sixteenth century realised that only a relatively narrow strip of land separated the Atlantic and Pacific Oceans but the isthmus, although only fifty miles wide, did not encourage canal builders. It consisted of a range of hills covered with tropical rain-forest and was infested with all kinds of diseases and dangerous wildlife.

After de Lesseps' success with the Suez Canal, his fame as an engineer encouraged him to attempt a repeat performance at Panama. He elected to cut a sea-level canal between the two oceans and work began in 1881. Before his army of excavators had gone very far into the jungle, fever mowed down their ranks. It was not known at the time that malaria and yellow fever were spread by mosquitoes.

From the port of Cristobal, at the Atlantic end of the modern canal, the unfinished cut of de Lesseps can be seen curving away into the rain forest and then stopping abruptly.

In 1903, the United States took over the task and bought a strip of land ten miles wide from the infant Republic of Panama which had declared itself independent from Columbia just fifteen days before. By now the cause of the spread of the fevers had been discovered within the test-tubes and microscopes of the doctors' laboratories. The mosquitoes had to be controlled before work on the canal could start. The diseases were not cured – the sources were exterminated.

In 1904 all was ready, but a sea-level canal was ruled out by the American engineers. What they did, was build a mighty dam with an integral spillway which harnessed the previously wild and uncontrollable Chagres River. The dam ponded the river back into a giant lake in the hills, eighty-five feet above sea-level. The spillway in the dam's rim allowed excess flood-water to escape to the sea and kept the lake at a constant level. The engineers also had to provide a method of lifting the ocean-going ships from the Atlantic to the artificial lake and then lower them into the Pacific after the transit of the lake. The lifting and lowering device is known as a "pound-lock" and it uses nature's forces to do most of the work. The only man-produced energy necessary is for the operation of sluices, to open and shut lock-gates and for locomotives which tow the ships from one lock to another.

The system works as follows. A flight of three giant interconnected rectangular lock-chambers climbs up the hillside from the Caribbean Sea to the Gatun Lake. The construction of these locks was completed of course, before the lake was flooded. Double lock-gates are fitted at both the sea and lake ends of the staircase and also between each individual lock, so there are four sets of gates for an ascending or descending ship to pass.

By means of sluices, which are very large diameter pipes under the floors of the locks, and opening and shutting valves inside them, the level of the water in each lock can be controlled.

As a ship waiting to ascend sits at sea-level outside the bottom lock facing the closed outer gates, the lock-keeper makes sure that the inner gates at the other end of the lock are closed and then opens the valve in a sluice between the bottom of the lock and the sea. The water leaves the lock like a bath emptying when the plug is pulled, and the level inside, falls to that of the sea outside. With the water-level in the lock equal to that outside, the bottom gates are opened and the ship moves into the chamber. In case of an accident caused by ramming lock-gates, ships are not allowed to use their own engines in the locks; towage and braking is provided by three pairs of locomotives (called "mules") which run on lines along both sides of the lock.

With the ship inside the first lock, the outer gates are closed behind it. Another underground sluice connects the middle lock and the lower one and, after checking that the upper doors of the middle lock are shut, the sluice-valve is opened. Water floods via the sluice from the middle lock into the lower lock and after a short interval, the levels of water in middle and lower locks are equal. The level has fallen in the middle lock but the ship has been raised some thirty feet in the lower one. The ship is now one third of the way up to Lake Gatun. The gates between the middle lock and the lower are now opened and the process repeated. As each ship ascends the flight of locks, the controlled release of water from the lake to the sea via the sluices and locks, totals 52 million gallons. Thus the lifting of each ship involves a loss from the lake of enough fresh water to supply a city with a population of 350,000 people for one day. As long as the tropical rains keep the level of the Gatun Lake, fed by the Chagres River, at the dam's spillway level, no harm is done. When it was built, the dam was the largest in the world and in order to keep the lake at the same level during varying amounts of rainfall, the spillway is equipped with dozens of lifting-type gates *(cataractae)*. Some of these can be closed in dry spells but all are open in times of flood.

The flights of locks are doubled-up in a side by side arrangement like a dual carriageway but this is to speed up operations by allowing opposite direction ships to climb and descend at the same time. It also allows locks to be closed for maintenance during which time, one-way operations only are possible.

At the Pacific end of the lake, a cut through high ground conducts ships to another flight of three double locks. The arrangement is slightly different from the Atlantic locks but the principle is the same. The isolated Pedro Miguel Lock drops the Pacific bound ships to the Miraflores Lake and then a flight of two locks, the Miraflores Locks, connects the small Miraflores Lake to a sea level inlet which leads to the Pacific Ocean.

Although the canal was opened in 1914, the foresight of American engineers allowed for the increase in size of ships, and supertankers can get through. Some US Navy aircraft carriers have to be given a one-degree list so that their projecting offset bridges do not scrape the lock-side control buildings.

Thousands of pound-locks are in use all over the world. Some are in tiny canals and can handle only pleasure-craft and small barges, but the main principle of operation is the same. The invention is attributed, by some, to the Dutch in 1373 at Vreeswijk, and by others to the Chinese in AD 983 at Huai-yin. It is possible that the Romans used them but positive proof of this has yet to be found. That discovery may not be far away. In our search for Roman navigations, there will be mentions of dams, weirs, spillways, *cataractae*, water channels, basins, staunches, paddles, sluices and many other technical terms and it is hoped that these will soon become familiar to readers to whom this is all new. It may be some consolation to know that most of our archaeologists have little knowledge of the subject and in Britain every single feature found on a river-bed is automatically identified as a bridge or a fish-trap.

Before we examine the rivers, we must first look at the seaward end of the logistical chain; the Roman merchant ships and the warships which made peaceful navigation possible.

Warships and merchant ships

Throughout history, two basic groups of ships have existed; warships and merchant ships. Warships are government-owned and are crewed by personnel who are members of the nation's fighting forces. Merchant ships are commercial vessels and are usually owned by shipping companies and crewed by civilians. The modern British merchant marine is called the "Merchant Navy" and this tends to obscure the fact that it is a fleet of commercial ships which belong to various shipping companies. The fact that the merchant sailors wear a similar uniform to that of the war fleet, the Royal Navy, also clouds the difference. Also in wartime, merchant ships may be defensively-armed, but this does not make them warships. Some Roman merchant ships carried catapults for defence and, in later history, merchant ships were armed with cannon for defence against pirates. A pirate ship can be defined as a private warship, operated illegally by waterborne thieves.

In 1939, the borderline between merchant ships and warships became harder to detect when the British merchant marine was taken over and operated by the Ministry of War Transport. All merchant ships were armed for defence against submarines and aircraft. It was decreed that such ships, defensively armed, would still be classed as merchantmen, but some fast ships were taken over by the Royal Navy and were more heavily armed as auxiliary warships which, under international law, in wartime, were liable to be attacked without warning.

Much has been written about the Battle of Britain in 1940, when Adolf Hitler's *Luftwaffe* attempted to gain control of the air over England; a pre-requisite for an invasion. Britain came much closer to losing the war in 1942 when the "Battle of the Atlantic" reached a critical phase. Britain, which was not self-supporting in food, fuel or munitions, was attempting to bring convoys of merchant ships, loaded with essential war material, across the North Atlantic from Canada and the USA.

The *Kriegsmarine* had been no match for the Royal Navy's surface ships, so switched to the building of a submarine fleet. The highly efficient "wolf-packs" of German U-boats were sinking British merchant ships at an unacceptable rate. The convoys were thinly protected by inadequate numbers and outdated warships and the U-boats were concentrating their attacks in mid-Atlantic outside the range of the submarine's worst enemy, the depth-charge equipped patrol aircraft. In 1942, Britain was down to a few weeks' supplies of food and fuel. With a brand new fleet of submarines, the German army-orientated nation almost defeated the greatest naval power since Carthage, and who had it been that defeated the Carthaginian navy? It was that other great army-orientated power, the Romans, widely held by many of our historians, to have been incompetent at sea. We will consider Rome and Carthage shortly.

In the crisis of the North Atlantic in 1942, the German U-boats and their scouts, the extra-long-range Focke-Wulf Condor reconnaissance aircraft, were defeated by unorthodox methods. Aircraft carriers should have been the answer, but the allies had only a limited number of these and they were thinly spread around the world. The first move was to equip selected merchant ships with aircraft catapults and a single Hurricane fighter plane for each ship so equipped. When the U-boats' spy in the sky, the Focke-Wulf arrived, the Hurricane was catapulted off and shot down or drove off the German aircraft, after which the fighter pilot either baled out or, if the sea was relatively calm, ditched alongside a ship.

The next step was to provide stop-gap aircraft carriers. It was decided to convert selected merchant ships by cutting off their superstructures and fitting flight-decks. The first was a captured German banana boat, the *Hannover,* and, in a shipyard in Blyth, Northumberland, not far north of the Roman Wall, the ex-enemy merchant ship became HMS Audacity. Many more were to follow. Not only did the Royal Navy convoy escorts now have the power to shoot down the long Range Focke-Wulfs; they could also operate anti-submarine bombers equipped with depth charges. Britain's life-lines were secured but she had almost lost the war due to a logistical failure. With unconventional methods, Britain had been saved from a similar fate to that which befell Carthage.

An unorthodox Roman invention helped the Roman navy to overcome the Carthaginians at sea in 260 BC off the coast of Sicily. The usual tactics up to this time, had been to ram an enemy ship but every large Roman warship carried, in addition to its seamen and oarsmen, forty marines and eighty legionaires. The new device was known as a *corvus* (raven) and this was a long gangway suspended from a pivoting derrick in the bows of the ship. The gangway had a large beak-shaped spike on the underside of the outer end, and the idea was, to drop the *corvus* so that the spike penetrated an enemy deck and so hold the ships together. Across the gangway poured the experienced Roman marines and land troops. Some historians have suggested that, as a *corvus* swung out, it would overturn the ship. These gentlemen should have seen the modest list our ship used to take in the Kenyan port of Mombasa when we swung a locomotive for East African Railways, out over the quay on our jumbo-derrick. In any case, when the *corvus* went down, it would have been stabilised by the enemy ship. No doubt, at the end of the engagement, or, if the fighting had gone against the Romans, the *corvus* would have been jettisoned.

With their "secret weapon," the Romans had brought organised land

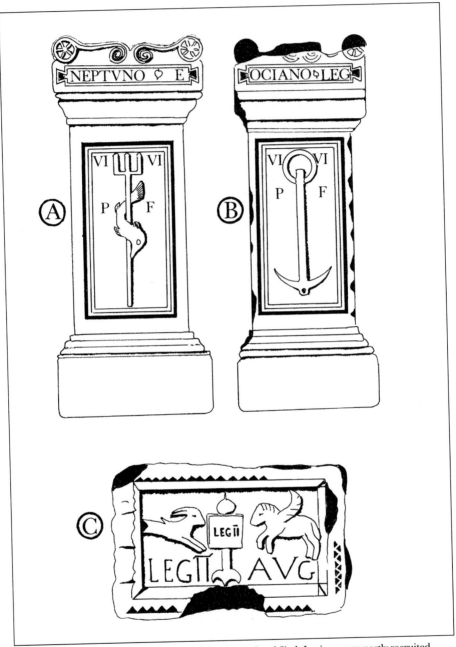

Were the Roman soldiers such landlubbers? The Second and Sixth Legions were partly recruited from merchant seamen. Insignia on their altars reflect this:
A Sixth Legion. Sea creature curled around staff of trident.
B Sixth Legion. Anchor.
C Second Legion. Does the Capricorn (fish-tailed goat) signify that the legion spent half its time on land and half at sea?
Also, does the winged horse imply the legion's ability to strike behind enemy lines?

warfare to the high seas. Like modern Germany though, the Romans had started off as a land power, so we must examine the developments which brought about the change.

Long before Rome's wars with Carthage, other Mediterranean countries had vied for control of the seas, the resultant trade, and opportunities for colonisation. Rock carvings in southern Egypt, dated to c3000 BC, portray ships with simple rigging and sails, and we have a record of the wreck of an Egyptian ship which was on a voyage c2000 BC, to pick up a cargo of copper ore in Sinai. This ship was 180 ft long with a beam of 60 ft and carried a crew of 120. The sole survivor describes a sudden storm which blew the ship onto the rocks.

By c2000 BC, the Minoans who lived on the island of Crete, seem to have taken over as the major sea power in the area but they were overrun c1450 BC by a warlike tribe from southern Greece, the Achaeans, who absorbed them. These Achaeans went in for piracy in a big way, and Egypt is recorded as inflicting defeats on them in the Nile Delta. While Egypt was the supreme naval power of the area, another tribe called the Phoenicians, settled on the coast of Syria and became extremely successful traders and colonists. One of these colonies was Carthage.

King Solomon c960 BC used Phoenician ships to carry cargoes to and from India, and the Phoenician circumnavigation of Africa c600 BC on the orders of Pharaoh Necho has already been described in Chapter 1.

A major factor which helped Phoenician expansion, was the defeat of the Achaeans in southern Greece, when invading tribes from the north settled there. The newcomers were the Greeks and they eventually became the masters of the eastern Mediterranean Sea. Only in the west, could the Phoenician colony of Carthage compete with them.

By 490 BC, another power to the east, Persia, was rivalling the Greek expansion. The Persian Empire extended from India to the Mediterranean and included Egypt, Phoenicia and some former Greek colonies in Asia Minor.

Just about this time, a small nation to the west was flexing its muscles. This nation had developed a very efficient army which had marched forth from the original settlements on the banks of the Tiber, and was busy conquering its neighbours in central Italy. The Roman expansion had begun.

The first Persian monarch to attack Greece was Darius (521- 485 BC) but the expedition failed when many of the ships were wrecked trying to round the rocky promontory of Mt Athos on the Macedonian coast.

A second expedition was sent in 490 BC and this time it arrived safely in Greece and prepared for battle on the plain of Marathon, just north-east of Athens. The result was, that a small army from Athens and Plataea, using superior tactics, defeated the Persian army, killing 6,400 for the loss of only 192 men. Darius 1 began preparations for a third expedition but before this was ready, he had to put down an insurrection in Egypt and the year after, he died. His successor was Xerxes.

Xerxes prepared to attack the Greeks again, and his mobilisation was on a stupendous scale. He built a bridge of boats across the Hellespont to connect Asia with Europe, and when this bridge was wrecked, he built two more. The second two bridges were constructed by anchoring hundreds of 120 ft ships side by side across the mile wide channel. Across these ships, wooden causeways were laid, and it took his army a week to cross. He cut a canal through the isthmus of Mt Athos and thus by-passed the dangerous cape which had wrecked a previous expedition. On his way to Athens, he found the pass at Thermopylae guarded by a small force of Spartans and this delayed his army for two days. When he reached Athens, the Athenians had abandoned the city and he set fire to it. The Athenian warships had drawn up in the narrow strait between the island of Salamis and the coast of Attica. Xerxes took up a position on the heights overlooking the scene to witness his expected victory but the battle went against him and two hundred Persian ships were sunk and many more captured. Xerxes left his forces under the command of a general and hastened back to Persia. Shortly afterwards, the Persian army was defeated at Plataea and no Persian force ever again set foot in Greece.

During the Battle of Salamis, the warships of both sides were *triremes,* and these were a development of the *bireme,* but had three banks of oars instead of two. This type of vessel, with a few modifications, was to be the standard warship of the Mediterranean for the next seven hundred years.

The Greek *trireme,* as used at Salamis, was 120 ft long and had a beam of 12 ft at the main deck. Just above the main deck, outriggers down both sides of the ship carried the seats for the upper bank of oarsmen, and these outriggers brought the total width of the ship to 16 ft. The ship was strongly built as its main function was to ram enemy ships, and a multi-pronged ram extended from the bow at water level. The bow was low and the stern swept up and curved forward over the after deck. A *trireme* would carry up to 170 rowers but the total crew could be far in excess of that number, with seamen, spearmen, archers and marines.

Other types of warships mentioned are, *quinqueremes* which at one time were thought to have had five banks of oars even though commonsense told us that the upper tiers of oars would have been impossibly long. It is now widely held that the maximum number of oar banks was three, and the classification of the ship was not decided by the banks of oars but by the number of rowers in a vertical line. For example, a *hepteres* which would have been translated years ago as a ship with six tiers of rowers, is now thought to have been a vessel with three banks only, two men at each oar. The warships had a single mast with a square-rigged sail which served for positioning voyages, but in action only the oars were used for propulsion.

After the Battle of Salamis, pressure on the Greeks from the Persian Empire decreased, and Greek commerce, culture and ideas spread throughout the known world. Athens was the leading Greek state, and its port of Piraeus became extremely busy and wealthy. The thousands of merchant ships which plied around the Mediterranean were not at all like the *trireme* warships. The merchantmen were fat and rounded and had square sails but usually no oars, although there were exceptions. They could carry between 100 and 500 tons at a speed of 4 knots.

They sailed for journeys lasting several weeks and definitely did not hug the coasts for navigational purposes. Various records tell us that warship crews went ashore each night but this was probably for the feeding and entertainment of its large crew. In peacetime, there is usually no tight schedule for warships but a merchant ship must get its cargo to a very distant destination in the shortest possible time for economic reasons. The merchant ship with a minimum crew, ploughs on for weeks on end and has always taken the shortest possible route. What a lot of nonsense has been written about the inability of the ancients to navigate out of the sight of land. A couple of years ago, I served as navigator on the sailing vessel *Golden Hinde*, a replica of Sir Francis Drake's galleon. We always took direct tracks if the wind allowed, because sticking to the coasts would have meant all hands on deck to trim sails at every one of the dozens of alterations of course. Contrary to landsmens' beliefs, a sailor breathes a sigh of relief when the land is left behind because the main dangers have gone and a routine can be established. A steady course means that sail-trimming and yard-work need only be undertaken when the wind speed or direction changes. We will return to the handling and navigation of ancient type ships shortly, but for now, let us take up again developments in the Mediterranean after Salamis.

The next trouble for the Greek states came from the north. A powerful and ambitious ruler of Macedonia, Philip II, looked enviously at the Greek states to the south, especially Athens. Philip's army used new and deadly tactics. The infantry fought with a new type of formation called a *phalanx*. This was a solid square of 256 men consisting of sixteen ranks, each containing sixteen men, and all armed with very long spears. This well-drilled formation would have looked like a hedgehog as it advanced.

Philip managed to overcome some of the Greek states by diplomacy, but he had to use force against Athens and by 338 BC, all of Greece was under his rule. His next project was the conquest of the Persian Empire, but he was assassinated in 336 BC and succeeded by his son, Alexander. This was the king who became known as Alexander the Great. Along to the west, the Romans were still busy with their campaigns in Italy, and had not yet entered the naval scene.

Alexander was twenty when he ascended the throne, and proved to be a brilliant general. He liberated the Greek colonial cities of Asia Minor and, after several battles, met the Persian king, Darius III and defeated him at the battle of Issus in 333 BC. He swept on and conquered Egypt and founded the city of Alexandria. He then struck at Persia itself, and met Darius again in 331 BC at the Batle of Arbela, near the River Tigris. The Persian was defeated and Darius III was killed by his own men.

Alexander entered Babylon in triumph, and went on to conquer the Scythians. He then turned south and planned to conquer India but his soldiers were weary after eight years of campaigning and refused to go further, so he was forced to turn back.

Alexander founded new cities, erected public buildings and carried out scientific research. Even during his campaigns, he collected natural history specimens and sent them back to his old tutor Aristotle, in Athens. He sent an expedition up the Nile to try to discover the cause of the river's annual floods. He also ordered the restoration of the canal system in Babylonia and built the famous city of Alexandria in Egypt. This ancient city was on the island of Pharos which was connected with the mainland by a mole almost a mile long. This mole has silted up since ancient times and the new strip of land forms part of the modern city. Alexander contracted fever and died in 323 BC at the age of thirty-three.

Shortly after this, the Romans built the beginnings of a merchant fleet and in 311 BC, they commissioned twenty war galleys for the protection of their ships against pirates.

In 264 BC Rome attacked the Carthaginian colony on the island of Sicily. The Roman troops crossed the Straits of Messina in troop transports, and this war, known as the First Punic War, (the Latin word for Phoenicians is *Punicas*) lasted twenty-three years. A land power had attacked a sea power.

The Romans realised that, in order to defeat the Carthaginians, they too would have to become a sea power and in 260 BC, the Senate ordered the immediate building of a hundred *quinqueremes* and twenty *triremes*. The choice of *quinqueremes* was because this was the main type of warship in the Carthaginian navy, and it was fortunate for the Romans that a Carthaginian *quinquereme* fell into their hands. We have a record from the Greek historian Polybius who reported that, when Carthaginian *quinqueremes* attacked the Roman troop transports, one of them ran aground and was captured. This vessel was copied by the Romans. The Romans needed 32,000 oarsmen and 3,600 seamen for their ships and it is very likely that the Greek colonies in southern Italy, defeated by the Roman army, provided trained seamen, willing or otherwise. The rowers were not slaves as is commonly thought in some circles. As previously mentioned, the Roman ships carried marines and were fitted with their secret weapon, the *corvus*.

The Roman and Carthaginian fleets met in 260 BC, off the coast of Sicily. The Carthaginians had 130 warships and the Romans slightly more, but this did not worry the Carthaginians as they prepared to attack these newcomers to naval warfare. The Carthaginians must have wondered at the peculiar devices dangling from the bows of the Roman ships, and it may have been obvious that the Roman decks were crammed with troops. Nevertheless the Carthaginians, expecting an easy victory, attacked without even forming a battle order, and used their normal tactics of attempting to ram. Instead of trying to avoid the enemy ships, the Romans steered towards them and, when at close quarters, the ravens dropped and the spikes stuck firmly in the enemy decks. The Roman legionnaires and marines then swarmed down the gangways and cut the opposing crews to pieces. The Romans had brought infantry warfare to the high seas. The Carthaginians lost seventy-four ships captured or sunk including the flagship, and the admiral made an escape in a small boat. The commander of the Roman fleet was Consul Caius Duilius, an experienced infantry commander, and this soldier had won Rome's first naval victory. A column was erected in Rome to commemorate this, and the monument is decorated with anchors. From the sides, protrude six stone replicas, in miniature, of the bows of the Carthaginian warships. The Roman wars against Carthage were long and bitter and we will pick them up again soon, but a mention must be made here of what happened to Alexander's empire after his death as this has a bearing on a later major Roman sea battle.

After the death of Alexander in 323 BC, his generals quarrelled and the empire was torn into three parts: Seleucus took Syria and Asia Minor, Antigonus became ruler of Greece and Macedonia, and Ptolemy appropriated Egypt together with most of Alexander's warships. Antigonus was determined not to let Ptolemy become master of the seas and began building up his own fleet, and Antigonus' son, Demetrius, became commander of the Greek fleet.

The Greek and Egyptian fleets clashed several times, and each attempted to overcome the other by building bigger ships. The ships of both sides got larger and finally Ptolemy had a giant warship of catamaran design with a huge square deck joining the two hulls. Each hull had 2,000 rowers and three tiers of oars. The inside tiers operated underneath the deck, between the hulls and there were twenty men to each vertical row of three oars. This gave a total of 4,000 oarsmen manning 600 oars. A likely arrangement might have been eight men to each top oar, seven to a central, and five to the lower oar. The ship was unwieldy and a gradual return to the *trireme* seems to have been made over many years.

Several victories were won by both sides, but Demetrius was the more successful admiral, and obtained naval supremacy in the eastern Mediterranean for about twenty years. Then political trouble at home removed him and the Egyptians gained supremacy. The Ptolemies capitalised on this and Alexandria became the largest trading port in the Mediterranean. The harbour could accommodate over a thousand ships and the famous lighthouse, the "Pharos," completed by Ptolemy II c260 BC, was five hundred feet high.

By this time, merchant ships had increased in size and some were huge. All these Mediterranean merchant fleets, together with the shipyards and operating technology, were to fall into the hands of the Romans, but not just yet as the Romans were still occupied with their Punic Wars.

After the Roman victory at sea against Carthage, assisted by their new techniques with the "ravens," they could not occupy all of Sicily because of the heavily defended Carthaginian cities on the island, but they did manage to defeat a Carthaginian fleet which was attempting to supply Sardinia. The Carthaginian sailors in their defeat, nailed their own admiral to a cross.

In 256 BC, the Romans attempted a seaborne assault on the Carthaginian mainland in North Africa. The Romans had 330 *quinqueremes* and eighty *trireme* horse transports while the Carthaginian fleet numbered 350 *quinqueremes* under the command of their highly experienced admiral, Hamilcar. Possibly by good luck, the Romans managed to avoid a Carthaginian attempt to encircle them, and the end result was a loss of twenty-four ships by the Romans and a hundred by Carthage. The Romans landed and captured the coastal town of Aspis and the Roman fleet returned home for a refit. Then the Romans made a fatal mistake; they attacked the Carthaginians in the spring of 255 before the fleet had returned. It was to cost them dearly. The Carthaginian cavalry and elephants shattered the Roman lines, and seaborne reinforcements, which could have saved the day, were not available. The Romans lost 23,000 dead and 500 captured and 2,000 survivors retreated to Aspis.

When the Roman fleet arrived to rescue the survivors, it met the

Carthaginian navy and won a victory. The Romans sunk sixteen ships and captured 114 and were returning to Sicily when a storm hit them. Only eighty ships survived. They built a new fleet during the winter of 255 BC and these new ships were used to mount successful attacks against Carthaginian towns in Sicily. During the return, another storm struck them and over three-quarters of the fleet of two hundred ships were lost with most of the crews.

The Romans were slower to recover from this disaster, but by 250 BC they had yet another fleet and 120 Roman warships blockaded the Carthaginian port of Lilybaeum in that year. The Carthaginian navy broke this blockade, and the Romans made another mistake. They tried to make their ships faster and copied the design of the more successful enemy ships. In their new type, the Romans dispensed with their raven boarding bridges. The price was heavy. At the next battle, at Drepanum, the Carthaginians used ramming tactics and the Roman soldiers were unable to get onto the enemy decks. They lost ninety-three ships and 20,000 men. They were certainly learning the hard way. This was not the end of the disasters; the remainder of the fleet sailed to reinforce the blockade of Lilybaeum and another storm struck them. Only two ships survived. The Roman navy had ceased to exist and once again Carthage ruled the central Mediterranean.

One must just look at the archaeological reconstruction of the naval harbour at Carthage to realise what a formidable fleet was based there. The base was a horseshoe-shaped lagoon with 200 ship-sheds arranged around it and also on an island in the centre of the horse-shoe. Each covered shed contained a ramp and the resident warships were winched out of the water up these inclines. There was also a lozenge-shaped commercial harbour in addition to the naval base.

The ancient Greek historian Appius tells us of these harbours but the late French expert on Carthage, Pierre Cintas, in his *Manuel d'Archéologie Punique* poured scorn on both Appian's description and modern suggestions that two ponds marked the harbour sites. Even before the book went to press, the British archaeologist, Dr Henry Hurst excavated one of the ponds and discovered the naval harbour just as Appian had described it. The admiral's headquarters was also found on the island in the centre of the horse-shoe.

It took the Romans seven years to gather finances, build new ships and train the crews for them. This time they had fast manoeuvrable ships and well-trained men. They used the Carthaginians' own tactics of ramming and inflicted a total defeat on them. They had fought as proper sailors and did not rely on marines fighting on enemy decks. They had completed their apprenticeship as a proper naval power. This ended the First Punic War and the whole of Sicily became part of the Roman Empire. How is it that we still read books which tell us that the Romans were useless at sea?

All navies make mistakes. Britain withdrew its large aircraft carrier, *Ark Royal* from service just before the Falklands War, and lost the navy's capacity to position fixed-wing Gannet early-warning radar planes ahead of the fleet. Single surface ships, vulnerable to air attack, had to be used as radar-pickets and suffered losses from Argentinian low-level bombers.

The admiralty, in its wisdom, made ships faster and lighter by constructing the superstructures of aluminium alloys. Although aluminium does not burn until it reaches its gaseous state at about 2,000 degrees C, it transfers heat extremely efficiently and even at 250 degrees C will collapse into molten heaps. Everybody realises that war is a dangerous business and new weapons and innovations do not always work but nobody has called the Royal Navy incompetent.

After the First Punic War, two more wars followed in the next 105 years. The second Punic War was won by the mere existence of a superior Roman navy. The famous Hannibal could not attack Rome by sea because of this Roman sea power so he landed in Spain and crossed the Alps complete with his elephants. After several victories, long supply lines, lack of reinforcements and inhospitable terrain weakened his army, he returned to Carthage. Rome's naval power had been the decisive factor but few historians seem to realise this.

The last Punic war was a combined effort by the Roman navy and army. The fleet blockaded the city of Carthage in North Africa and a Roman army landed and inflicted a final defeat on the enemy. The Romans were the masters of the Mediterranean after their perfection of naval skills. The year was 146 BC and the first fleet of Roman warships had left the mouth of the Tiber in 260 BC. The course of instruction had lasted 114 years but the Romans had added a few ideas of their own to the curriculum.

While the main occupation of the Roman navy had been the wars against Carthage, smaller fleets had been busy in the eastern Mediterranean. The two major parts of Alexander's former empire, Macedonia and Egypt, were still at war. An independent nation, Rhodes, became worried because Macedonia threatened to take over the whole area and asked Rome for assistance. Fifty *quinqueremes* were provided; the Macedonians were defeated and sued for peace and the Roman ships returned home.

The Romans had acquired a taste for the eastern Mediterranean and established a trading base on the island of Delos. The Rhodians who had asked the Romans for aid went into decline because of the loss of trade to their allies. One of the main functions of the Rhodian navy had been to control piracy and with the decline of Rhodes, the pirates grew bolder. In 69 BC, these pirates made the mistake of attacking the Roman base at Delos and the Roman administrator, Pompey was given the job of putting matters right. He created several fleets and on a specified date, attacked and eliminated all the pirates' nests around the whole Mediterranean. Organised "D-day-type" attacks were not invented by modern war departments.

Rome's next troubles did not come from the sea; they came from within, in the form of internal quarrels. Julius Caesar and Pompey were rivals for power and both were assassinated. In the power struggle which followed, the ambitious Octavian, Caesar's grand-nephew, managed to eliminate, by one means or another, all the rivals except the tough soldier, Mark Antony. These two survivors divided the Roman possessions between them; Octavian took Italy and territories to the west, Antony the remainder of the Empire to the east. Antony joined forces with Cleopatra of Egypt. She was a Greek Ptolemy and Antony married her in 37 BC. It was not long before Octavian attempted to take over all the Roman territories and in 31 BC, Antony and Cleopatra defended the western coast of Greece with a vast army and navy. This force was supplied by merchant ships which brought grain and other supplies from Egypt.

Octavian's commander-in-chief, Agrippa, made a seaborne assault on southern Greece and captured Antony's base at Methone, and from there attacked the supply ships *en-route* from Egypt.

During World War II, the main reason for the German *Afrika Korps'* defeat in North Africa, was the sinking of Axis supply ships by British aircraft from the isolated outpost of Malta. Nothing changes in warfare and most of the successes and failures are tied up with logistics.

Octavian sent a task force to Greece, landed an army and then trapped Antony's fleet in a land-locked gulf. Octavian's blockading fleet consisted of all types of ships including *liburnae* – fast galleys with two banks of oars and the equivalent of modern destroyers. They had been copied from the ships of the successful pirates of the Adriatic. Agrippa's fleet was equipped for boarding as well as ramming and, in addition to the ravens, had catapult-fired grapnels.

Antony and Cleopatra's ships, after a long siege, broke out and this resulted in the Battle of Actium. This ended in a crushing defeat for Antony and Cleopatra and they were lucky to escape to Egypt with a third of their fleet. In 30 BC, Octavian made a combined land and sea assault on Egypt. The land forces marched by way of Syria. Antony's soldiers either deserted or were defeated and his fleet surrendered. Antony committed suicide and, after unsuccessful negotians with Octavian, Cleopatra did so too.

All the lands surrounding the Mediterranean were now Roman, and the Mediterranean itself became a Roman lake. All the fleets of merchant ships from the various trading nations fell under Roman control and the resultant merchant marine was the largest the world had ever seen. Crews could be found who had experienced trading voyages to all parts of the known world. Some had sailed to northern Europe, others to India. The navigators were competent and had a far greater knowledge of astronomical navigation than some modern historians give them credit for.

This then, was the vast merchant marine which supplied the Roman world. These were the ships which entered the hundreds of rivers, large and small, and transferred their cargoes, where necessary, to the barges of the military lightermen and the guilds of watermen. When Claudius' fleet invaded Britain, it was not entering the unknown; there were probably pilots who knew all of the estuaries and who could calculate the local tides.

The Roman navy was divided into several fleets which would police the various parts of the Empire, and assist land forces in further campaigns. For two hundred years, a traveller would be able to make his way from the Euphrates to Scotland without crossing a single hostile frontier. Two languages only, Latin and Greek, could take a traveller anywhere in the vast area under Roman domination and only one currency was needed. After centuries of bloodshed, the whole Mediterranean area, and surrounds, were for the first and last time in history, politically and culturally united and this had been made possible by Roman seapower.

Some time has been spent on the story behind the growth of Roman naval and merchant seapower, and we must now look at some of the technical problems in greater detail, i.e. the operation of the deep-sea ships and the final distribution of cargoes to inland destinations beyond the reach of merchantmen.

The captain of a Roman warship ship was called a *trierarchus,* a squadron was commanded by a *navarchus* and a fleet by a *praefectus.* A warship also carried a centurion who was presumably in command of the marines and other troops on board.

The Roman navy was organised as auxiliaries because of the high percentage of foreigners and non-Roman citizens. The foreign naval personnel had to serve twenty-six years in order to qualify for Roman citizenship, whereas the auxiliary soldiers of the army needed to serve twenty-five. Clearly, the Roman navy was regarded as the junior service, as was the Royal Air Force, the United States Air Force, the German *Luftwaffe* and the German *Kriegsmarine.* A famous British field marshal declared in 1914 that:

"The aeroplane will never replace the horse as a means of reconnaissance."

In the 1930's, General Billy Mitchell of the United States Army Air Corps was forced to resign, when he demonstrated that an aircraft could sink a battleship. An ex-German warship, captured in 1918 served as a target. The admirals were horrified when the ship was sunk, and accused Mitchell of cheating by using bombs of a large size and dropping them from too low an altitude. The Americans had to learn the hard way at Pearl Harbor. In Germany c1936, the men of the new *Luftwaffe* were nicknamed: "the collar and tie soldiers."

Even if the Roman navy lacked the traditions and glamour of the Legions, thousands of young Phoenicians, Greeks, Syrians, Egyptians and others flocked to the Roman bases at Misenum and Ravenna to enlist. There they swore an oath of allegiance to the Emperor and received seamanship and weapons training. All sailors were also soldiers, and, from time to time, were impressed as land troops. A seaman on a Roman warship was called a *miles* (soldier). The name *nauta* (sailor) was reserved for merchant seamen. *I* and *II Adiutrix* were both raised from marines of the Roman fleet, I by Nero and II by Vespasian. *Legio II Adiutrix* was stationed at Lincoln and between 76 and 79 moved to Chester. Hadrian also brought *Leg X Fretensis* up to strength from the Misenum fleet.

The Roman navy was formed at Forum Iulii (Fréjus, near Marseilles) but two Italian harbours, Misenum and Ravenna, became the main bases. Detached squadrons from these bases policed the central Mediterranean, but the Romans operated several fleets in other parts of the Empire and those which receive mention are as follows.

Name of fleet	Operating areas
Classis Augusta Alexandrina	Egypt
Classis Britannica	North Sea, Channel, Irish Sea.
Classis Flaviae	Associated with Danube area?
Classis Germanica	River Rhine
Classis Moesica	Lower River Danube
Classis Pannonica	Upper River Danube
Classsis Perinthia	Thrace
Classis Pontica	Black Sea
Classis Syriaca	Eastern Mediterranean

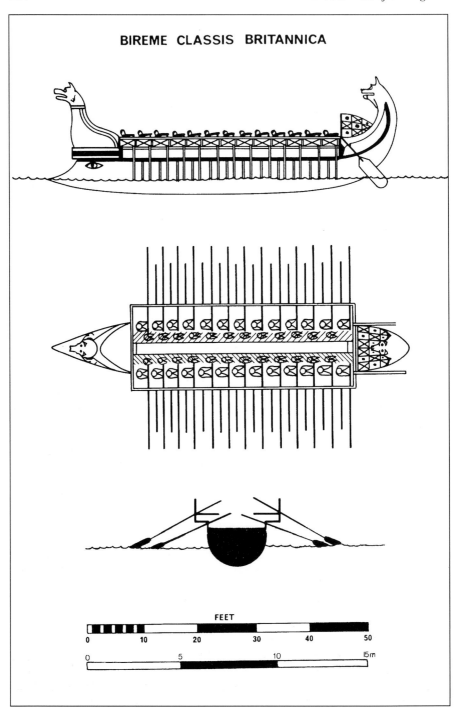

Bireme of the *Classis Britannica.*

The *Classis Britannica* had two major bases; at Dover and Boulogne. We have a record of at least one ship operated by this fleet – a *bireme* called *Sabrina* (Latin name for the Severn).

The *biremes* and *triremes* operated by the Roman British fleet were designed specially for service in northern waters – they had higher sides and bows than their counterparts elsewhere. We are told that the ships were camouflaged blue-green and, that even the sails, ropes and sailors' uniforms were the same colour. The seamen dyed their faces green and were nicknamed "Picts" because of this. All warships were designed for speed and resembled the shape of the Oxford and Cambridge "eights" whereas merchant ships needed to carry as much cargo as possible and were known as "round ships."

When a warship was used as a horse-transport, we are told that its rowers were reduced from 230 to sixty to make way for the horses. Such transports lost their fighting ability and had to be escorted. Roman warships flew flags and the admiral's insignia was a red banner. The flagship also displayed three lights at night. The insignia of a merchant ship was a basket displayed at a mast-head or on a pole. Merchant ships had their names carved or painted on the bows in the same place as on modern ships. Both warships and merchant ships had figureheads on or near the bows and the sterns were also decorated.

We know that the Second Legion was brought up to strength by impressing sailors from the Roman fleet, and it is therefore no coincidence that the insignia on the altars of this legion is usually a capricorn, i.e. a goat with the tail of a fish. It is highly likely that the Sixth Legion also had naval connections as their altars were always decorated with tridents, fishes and anchors. Here are two Roman legions, the soldiers of which can hardly be dubbed "landlubbers." The Second Legion also used as an insignia, the winged horse "Pegasus." This was the shoulder badge of the British Airborne Division during the 39-45 War and I hasten to assure critics that I am not suggesting that the Romans had a parachute regiment! I think the use of this insignia by *Leg II* demonstrates that they could attack behind enemy lines, or supply an army which had pressed on through trackless enemy territory without ponderous and vulnerable stores columns. The advantages of forward logistical support (the ancient equivalent of para-drops) over base-line support (the massive wedge of animals moving from the rear) was well known to the Romans.

In the fourth century, the Roman British fleet came under pressure from Saxon pirates, and special coastal defences were built, but for over three hundred years, the Romans were masters of the northern seas and this created suitable conditions for the operation of large numbers of merchant ships around the British coast. Let us now consider the Roman merchant marine.

The portly Roman merchant ships which had beams of about a third of their length, were usually between 250 and 500 tons and, with odd exceptions, were propelled at sea entirely by sails. The ship towed a boat behind it and this was a general purpose workboat but could be used as a harbour tug if necessary. Usually, dozens of oar-powered tugboats plied for trade at the harbour mouths.

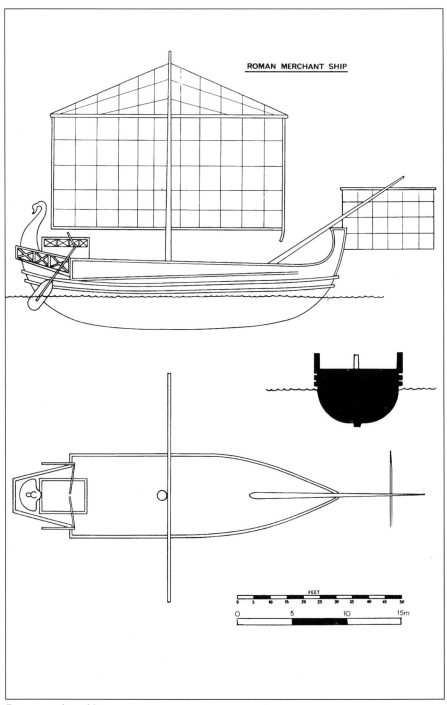

Roman merchant ship.

We have a description of one of the larger Roman merchant ships, the *Isis,* which was on the grain run from Alexandria to Ostia but was blown off course and ended up at Piraeus, the port of Athens. The homeward journey from Egypt, which involved tacking against contrary winds, always took longer than the outward journey. The *Isis* had encountered some of these adverse winds. The description is by one "Lucian" who travelled from Athens down to Piraeus to view the vessel:

> "What a size the ship was! 180 ft in length, the ship's carpenter told me, the beam more than a quarter of that, and 44 ft from the deck to the lowest point in the hold, and the height of the mast, and what a yard it carried, and what a forestay held it up; and the way the stern rose up in a gradual curve ending in a gilded goose head, matched at the other end by the forward, more flattened sweep of the prow with its figures of Isis, the goddess the ship was named after, on each side. Everything was incredible; the rest of the decorations, the paintings, the red topsail, even more, the anchors with their capstans and winches, the cabins aft. The crew was like an army. They told me she carried enough grain to feed every mouth in Athens for a year, and it all depended for its safety on one little old man who turns those great steering oars with a tiller that is no more than a stick! They pointed him out to me; woolly-haired little fellow, half bald. Heron was his name, I think."

Roman merchant ship. Note "basket insignia" above stern. (from a relief on a Pompeian tomb)

This ship was of unusual size, but the description clearly demonstrates the ability of the Romans to construct and operate very large sea-going ships. Various writers have estimated the cargo capacity of the *Isis*. Let us use the figures given by Lucian.

If the depth of the hold was 44 ft from deck level, a safe draught would be about 30 ft, which would give the ship a freeboard of 14 ft, that is, the distance from the deck down to the water with the ship fully loaded. This gives the figures in Roman feet of: waterline length (about 20 ft less than overall length) 160 ft, beam 45 ft, draught 30 ft. Convert these figures into English feet and use the standard naval formula to find the capacity of a boat or ship, which is *length x beam x draught x 0.6* (the 0.6 takes care of the pointed and rounded ends of the vessel):

$$155 \times 43.6 \times 29 \quad = \quad 195{,}982 \text{ cu ft}$$
$$195{,}982 \times 0.6 \quad = \quad 117{,}589 \text{ cu ft}$$
$$= \quad \text{vol of water displaced by loaded ship.}$$

By Archimedes' Principle, a floating object displaces a weight of water equal to its own weight, and this volume of water weighs 7,349,325 lb = 3,281 tons. This is the total weight of the ship plus cargo. If one third of this is the weight of the empty ship, then the weight of cargo is 2,187 tons.

On Lucian's figures, on arrival at Ostia, the onward journey of the cargo up the Tiber to Rome would have needed 109 twenty-ton barges or 218 ten-ton barges. If the cargo had to be moved by road, it would have taken 4,896 ox-carts between 20,000 and 50,000 oxen and 9,792 drivers and bridle-leaders. The wagon train would have been 83 miles long. If pack-mules had been used, 18,135 animals would have been needed. If hundred-ton barges were available, only twenty-two would have been necessary. The port handled half a million tons of grain per year.

In order to ship a 500 ton obelisk from Alexandria to Rome, the Emperor Caligula ordered the construction of a giant vessel. Pliny the Elder, in his *Natural History,* tells us that the main-mast could only be spanned by four men linking arms. He also tells us that, in addition to the obelisk, the ship carried 800 tons of lentils as ballast. The huge transport was later filled with rocks and concrete and sunk to form the base for a breakwater at the harbour of Portus, just north of Ostia. The outer harbour was built by Claudius and an inner hexagonal-shaped one by Trajan. The latter was linked to the Tiber by a canal. The port was the largest man-made haven in the ancient world and the two breakwaters were each over 2,500 ft long. A very large lighthouse stood on the southern arm and the Romans had scores of similar lighthouses around the coasts of the Empire, some of which are depicted on coins and mosaics. Most of them seem to have followed the "wedding cake" design of the famous Pharos at Alexandria. The Portus tower consisted of three square stories of diminishing size, topped by a cylindrical tower and fire-beacon. Historians thought that Pliny had exaggerated the size of the ship which carried the obelisk to Portus, but excavations have proved that he was right. Due to siltation, both the Claudian and Trajanic harbours are now inland and when the new airport was constructed, O. Testaguzza siezed the opportunity to excavate. In his "Port of Rome" in *Archaeology,* Vol 17, No 3

(Sept 1964), he describes the stone and concrete-filled blockship found underneath the lighthouse and gives the dimensions as 94.8m (311 ft) x 21m (69 ft). The ship had six decks and the capacity has been calculated at 7,400 tonnes.

There were two Roman lighthouses at Dover. One still survives at two-thirds the original height and has been used in the mediaeval period as a spire for the church in the grounds of Dover Castle. Only the foundations of the other remain and these are engulfed and preserved in the remains of an abandoned Victorian fort called the "Drop Redoubt" on the western side of the town. Caligula built a lighthouse at Boulogne and this was an octagonal tower of twelve diminishing stories. It fell into the sea c1640, but can be seen on an engraving of 1549. There is a strong tradition that the "Tower of Hercules" at La Coruña, is Roman; it is still in operation. There is also a tradition that the Phoenicians built a lighthouse at Cadiz and it is known that the famous "Colossus" at Rhodes, a giant statue of the sun god Helios, erected 280 BC, guided ships into the harbour. An earthquake overthrew it in 224 BC. An early lighthouse existed at Aegea, in Eastern Cicilia on what is now the Gulf of Iskenderum. It is represented on a coin of Antiochus IV of Syria, 175-164 BC. A sixteenth century translater quotes Pliny's comments of the first century AD on the Pharos at Alexandria:

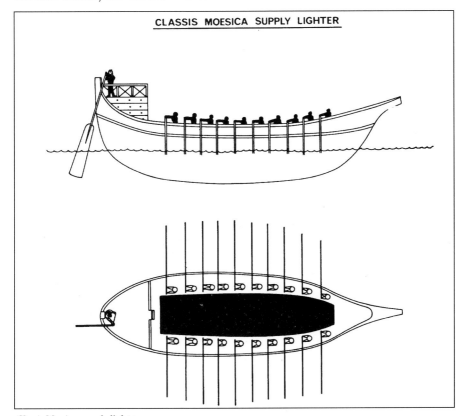

Classis Moesica supply lighter.

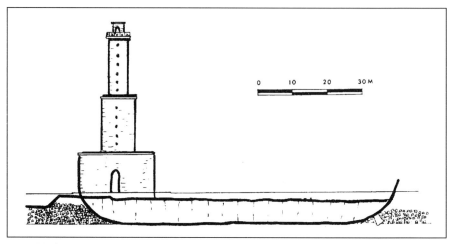

Caligula's giant ship, which was purpose-built to bring an obelisk from Egypt, was later filled with rocks and concrete and sunk to form the base for a breakwater at the harbour of Portus, just north of Ostia. Pliny had described the tremendous size of the ship but he was not believed by later historians. An ancient ship of such dimensions seemed impossible, but excavations by O. Testaguzza have established that the dimensions of the ship were: 300 ft, x 70 ft. It had six decks and the capacity has been calculated at a phenomenal 7,400 tonnes.

The Roman lighthouse at Boulogne built by Caligula cAD 40. It was repaired by Charlemagne and fell to pieces c1644. It was 200 ft high and had twelve stepped stages. The diameter of the base was 64 ft. It was built of white and yellow stone and red brick. This sketch is based on one drawn by Chatillon, cartographer to Henry IV.

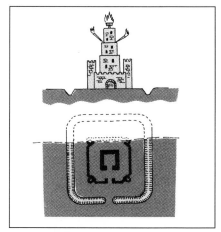

The Roman signal station on the cliff top at Scarborough (TA 052 892) may have served also as a lighthouse. Note from the plan view that a third of the site has fallen down the cliff.

Lighthouses as depicted in Roman mosaics.

"the use of this watch tower is to shew light as a lanthorne and give direction in the night season to ships for to enter the haven and where they shall avoid barrs and shelves; like to which there be many beacons burning to the same purpose, and namely at Puteoli and Ravenna."

Roman lighthouses must not be confused with ship to shore and point to point signal stations. These will be mentioned in due course.

Most Roman sea travel was done in the months between April and September. In Greek and Roman times, what was a rule of prudence became in the Middle Ages a rule of law. The *Pisan Constitutum Usus* declared that, if a ship were in port after the calends of November, the shipowners were forbidden to leave before the calends of March without the consent of the merchants who owned the cargo. These rules do not reflect the ability of sailors in ancient times. The sailors of the Classical period were every bit as skilled – probably more so – than modern seamen. Troop movements and voyages to alleviate food shortages were exempt from sailing season rules.

Here are some typical average times taken for voyages by Roman merchant ships:

Byzantium	–	Alexandria	9 days
Byzantium	–	Rhodes	5 days
Gibraltar	–	Carthage	7 days
Ostia	–	Alexandria	10 days
(this journey by road took two months)			
Ostia	–	Cadiz	7 days
Ostia	–	Corinth	5 days
Ostia	–	Narbonne	3 days
Ostia	–	NE Spain	4 days
(this journey by road took one month)			
Straits of Messina	–	Alexandria	7 days

Trade was also carried on between Egypt and India. In 120 BC, Eudoxus, a native of Cyzicus, was working as a ship's captain for Ptolemy VIII. At that time, the Indian spices were transported to Egypt by Indian and Arab ships. Indian ships carried the cargoes as far as the Red Sea, and Arab ships the rest of the way. The secret of the seasonal monsoon winds was not known to the Greeks at the time.

Eudoxus happened to be in Alexandria when a half-drowned Indian sailor was brought to the court. The sailor was nursed back to health and given lessons in Greek. He was taken home by Eudoxus who learned that from May to September, in the Gulf of Aden and the Arabian Sea, the monsoon blew from the south-west and a ship could proceed direct from the Red Sea to India, keeping clear of the coast and its pirates. He also learned that between November and March, the wind shifted 180 degrees and the north-east monsoon enabled a ship to make a quick passage direct from India back to the Red Sea. This information subsequently became available to the Romans when they took over Egypt and its merchant marine. The Romans also traded with China, but Roman ships did not make through-voyages; cargoes were trans-shipped between Graeco-Roman freighters and Indian and Malaysian ships in southern India and Ceylon (Sri Lanka). Chinese ships took no part in the trade.

It is now time to look at ancient sea navigation. The general consensus of opinion is that the Romans did not possess magnetic compasses but these, although extremely useful, are not essential. There are direction-finders other than those which use the Earth's magnetism. The Sun is the best example. Almost as long as man has lived on Earth, he has known that the Sun rises in the east, is south (in the northern hemisphere) at midday, and sets in the west. The alignments of Neolithic henge monuments tell us that the Stone Age people had an excellent knowledge of the movements of the Sun and other heavenly bodies.

The Roman-period native farmsteads all had their entrances facing east. The Sun therefore is an excellent compass. It can also be used as a time check because at midday, as well as being due south (in the northern hemisphere) it is at its highest point in the sky and timepieces such as hour-glasses can be set.

The Vikings who navigated between Norway and Iceland and between Ireland and Iceland could see the Sun even in fog and when the sky was overcast. They used a "sunstone" which was a calcite mineral crystal named cordierite, found in Iceland and Scandinavia. When a crystal of this material is held at right angles to the plane of the Sun's polarised light, the crystal changes instantly from yellow to dark blue. The crystal also worked with the Sun up to seven degrees below the horizon so Viking navigators continued to take sun-bearings after sunset. A reference to the use of the sunstone is made in *Raudúlfs Páttr ok Sonum Hans*:

> "the weather was thick and stormy. The King (St Olaf d1030) looked
> about and saw no blue sky;...then the King took the Sunstone and held
> it up, and then saw where (the Sun) beamed from the stone..."

An airman's navigation aid called a "Kollsman's Sky Compass" uses the same principle.

The RAF Astro Compass. This is not a sextant. The sextant measures altitudes and other angles. The astro-compass measures directions but uses heavenly bodies instead of the Earth's magnetism. The device is particularly useful in polar regions where magnetic compasses are unreliable.

ROYAL AIR FORCE

Checklist for operation of Astro Compass

1,2 Set levelling screws and observe spirit levels (3).

4 Set latitude on scale via knob (5).

6 Set gnomon at Sun's declination on scale (7).

8 Set Greenwich Hour Angle of Sun (from tables) (Scale 9 is for use in southern hemisphere).

10 Twist body of instrument until shadow bar of gnomon falls on etched line on gnomon screen.

11 Read off aircraft's true heading against lubber-line.

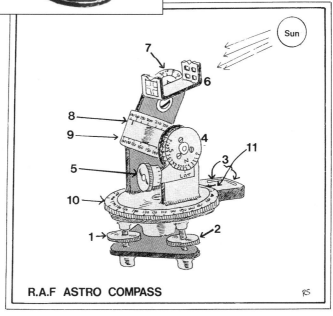

R.A.F ASTRO COMPASS

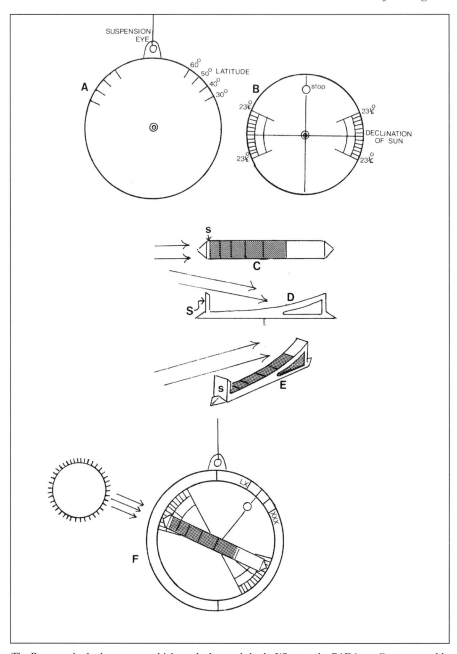

The Romans also had a compass which used a heavenly body. Whereas the RAF Astro Compass could be used with the Sun, Moon, stars and planets, the Roman device used only the Sun.

A = Brass disc with latitude scale.
B = Smaller brass disc with declination-of-Sun scale.
C = Double ended needle.

D = Side view of needle showing shadow-bar at (S).
E = Oblique view of needle and shadow bar.
F = The assembled Sun Compass.

ROMAN ARMY

Possible checklist for Sun Compass

1,2,3   As instrument is supended, no levelling needed.

4   Set latitude on outer scale via knob (5) on inner scale.

6   Set gnomon to declination of Sun. (this is marked as a date on the Roman instrument [7]).

8   Note the time from hour glass or other device.

10   Twist body of instrument on its suspension string until shadow of gnomon bar coincides with hour-line (as noted from hour glass) on gnomon scale.

11   The instrument is now lined up exactly north-south.
The Roman instrument can be set up with the RAF checklist.

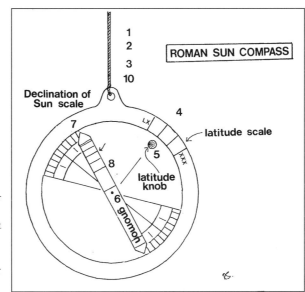

The relationship of the altitude (angle above horizon) of Polaris (Pole Star) to the observer's latitude.

P	=	North Pole
P2	=	South Pole
EQ	=	Equator
C	=	Centre of Earth
X	=	Direction of Polaris
O	=	Observer
Z	=	Observer's Zenith (overhead)
YH	=	Observer's horizon
OCQ	=	Observer's latitude
YOS	=	Altitude of Polaris
OCQ	=	YOS

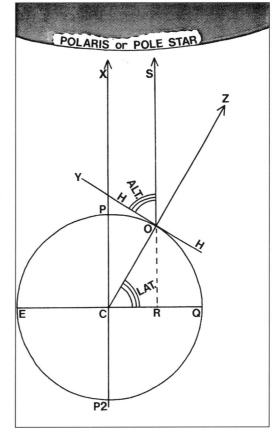

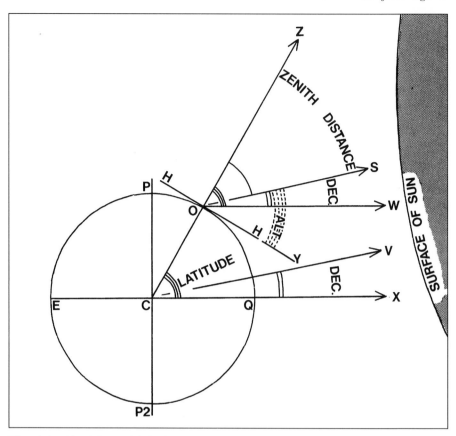

The relationship of observer's latitude to the altitude of the Sun at its meridian crossing.
With Zero declination (at the equinoxes) the Noon Zenith Distance
(90 degrees minus Sun's meridian altitude) is equal to the observer's latitude.
At other times, to obtain latitude from the meridian altidude of the sun, the Sun's declination must
be taken from the tables and added to or subtracted from the Noon Zenith Distance depending upon
whether the declination is North or South.
A sextant measures altitudes but the ancient navigators had cruder but still effective instruments.

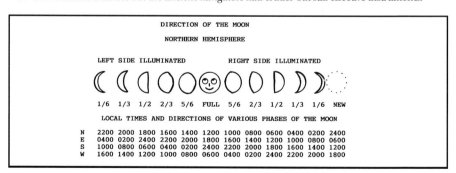

The practised navigator can establish the direction of the moon with the phase and the local time.
This is most useful during thin overcast when the stars are obscured but the moon still visible. With
thicker cloud, a quick glimpse of the moon through a gap in the clouds will suffice.

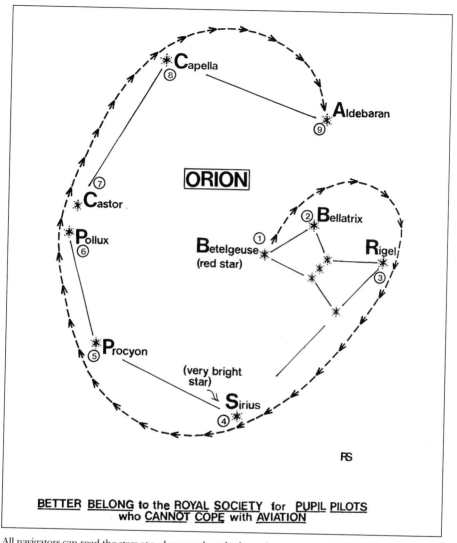

All navigators can read the stars at a glance and no doubt ancient navigators could do the same.
The RAF taught aircrew cadets the positions of all the Stars in the constellation of Orion by starting in the centre and chanting:
Better Belong to the Royal Society for Pupil Pilots who Cannot Cope with Aviation.
Betelgeuse, Bellatrix, Rigel, Sirius, Procyon, Pollux, Castor, Capella, Aldebaran.

It is highly likely that the Romans could also take bearings on an obscured Sun because Pliny the Elder in his *Natural History* also makes a reference to a "sunstone." He describes it as: "*solis gemma,* a white stone which casts rays of the Sun."

During an archaeological investigation, would a sunstone be recognised, or merely consigned to the spoil-heap as a translucent pebble?

At night, if the stars are visible, course-keeping is easy. In hazy conditions with stars obscured, the Moon is often still visible even though surrounded by a halo, and the Earth's satellite is far more useful to the sea navigator than the landsman may appreciate. Julius Caesar tells us that the Celts had a good working knowledge of astronomy with particular emphasis on the Moon, but more of this shortly.

Courses can be held for considerable periods by helmsmen who are not navigators, merely by reference to the wind, sea or swell direction.

For those readers to whom navigation is a new subject, the explanation of a few basic principles may assist with the appreciation of methods available to the ancient navigators.

The Earth is a large spinning ball and the axis about which it rotates remains in exactly the same place, just as if a giant nail had been driven throught it. One end of the nail is called the North Pole and the other the South Pole. These geographic poles have nothing to do with magnetic poles which are caused by the Earth's magnetism and wander all over the place and will be mentioned later. The Geographic North Pole is the end of the nail which, when viewed from above, is the centre of the Earth's anticlockwise rotation. The end of the nail at the South Pole would have a clockwise rotation around it. Because of the spin, the Earth is also a gyroscope and therefore tries to keeps its axis pointed in a fixed direction in space.

As well as spinning on its own axis once a day, the Earth also orbits the Sun, taking one year to get round. When viewed from above the North Pole, this elliptical, almost circular flight-path of the Earth around the Sun, is also anti-clockwise. The Earth flies around the Sun at 19 miles per second and if it were not for the Sun's gravity tethering it as if on a giant elastic band, it would fly off across the galaxy. The Earth's axis of daily spin is inclined at $23\frac{1}{2}$ degrees to the plane of the annual flight-path around the Sun. This tilt among other things causes our seasons.

The stars are all giant glowing suns at tremendous distances from us. Some are so big that a large part of our own solar system could fit inside one. As far as the humble navigator on Earth is concerned, the stars are merely points of light which traverse our sky in an easily predictable manner. The Earth-based navigator uses them just as if they were lights on the tops of very tall flag-poles. Unfortunately, as the Earth spins, the bases of the flag-poles race around the terrestial globe at 1,000 mph at the Equator and over 500 mph across Britain.

As the Earth completes a yearly orbit of the Sun, less than half of the stars are visible at a time. The stars are still there even in daytime but it has to be dark to see them and even then, some of them are below the horizon. In winter, the Earth's dark half at night-time is under the opposite side of the sky to that of the summer nights therefore different stars are seen, except those above the polar regions which are visible all the year round. The polar stars merely appear to rotate around a central point in the sky as the Earth performs its 24-hourly spin. This central point in the sky of the northern hemisphere is directly above the Earth's North Pole.

A stroke of luck for navigators is, that the central spot about which the northern stars appear to rotate, is marked by a star and this star is called the Pole Star or Polaris, not because of its brightness (it is rather dim) but because of its unique position in the heavens above the north end of the Earth's axis. The star is therefore always True North so, if it can be seen, a compass is not necessary. Polaris only appears to be a dim star because of its distance from Earth. It is actually 6,000 times brighter than our own Sun but it is 680 light years away; that means that the light arriving here as this is being written (1994), left the star about the time of the Battle of Bannockburn (1314) and light travels at 186,000 miles per second or 669.6 million miles per hour.

In the southern hemisphere, no handy star marks the Celestial South Pole so the direction of True South has to be judged from the stars which complete their 24-hourly clockwise rotation of that part of the sky. A useful constellation from which to estimate the elevated South Pole is the famous "Southern Cross", depicted on the flags of Australia and New Zealand.

The stars, sitting on top of their very tall flag-poles, follow the same tracks all the time, the bases of the poles tracing out parallels of latitude. Other heavenly bodies such as the Sun, Moon and planets, can also be likened to sitting on flag-poles except as well as racing westerly around the Earth, the bases of the flag-poles wander north and south due to other factors which will be mentioned in due course. The Sun, Moon, brighter planets, and about 180 prominent stars can be used for navigation.

Heavenly bodies are used in two distinct ways, first to provide directional information, i.e. the navigator finds in which direction the base of the flag-pole lies at the time of observation, and second, the angle of the heavenly body above the horizon (altitude), found with a sextant or ancient equivalent, can be used in calculations to determine the position of the observer.

The unique position of Polaris in the northern polar sky presents another advantage in addition to that of indicating True North. The altitude of this particular star is equal to the observer's latitude. Unfortunately, Polaris is not exactly over the North Pole but almost one degree offset; 58 minutes, or 58 sixtieths of a degree to be exact. This can cause an error of up to 58 nautical miles with an observed latitude and a correction has to be made. The error varies and depends on whether Polaris is above or below the observer's celestial pole, to one side, or points in between. Merely for a course check, a one degree error can be disregarded.

In Classical times, it was known that the world was round. This information was lost in mediaeval times. The Greek geographer, Strabo tells us of the work of Eratosthenes, who was born in 276 BC at Cyrene (now Shahat in Libya). At the age of 30, Eratosthenes spent most of his time in Alexandria and in 235 BC, Ptolemy III appointed him chief librarian. Eratosthenes constructed a map of the known world and his principal meridian (central north-south line) ran through Alexandria. He knew that the world was round but wondered how big it was and worked out a method of measuring the circumference. He knew that at the summer solstice (the longest day) at Syene (Aswan), the midday Sun was directly overhead because it shone down a deep well and illuminated the water perfectly with no shadow whatsoever. At the summer soltice of the following year, he had positioned himself at Alexandria, which he thought to be due north of Syene, and measured the angle between the midday Sun and his vertical. This angle, is equal to the angle at the centre of the earth between the extended sunshine line down the Syene well to the Earth's centre and the line from this centre up to Alexandria.

Eratosthenes found that the angle at Alexandria between the midday Sun and his vertical, was 7 degrees 14 minutes therefore the angle at the centre of the Earth between Syene and Alexandria was the same. This angle subtended the arc of the Earth's surface between Syene and Alexandria. From travellers he learned that camels needed 50 days to cover the journey and a camel travelled 100 stadia in a day, thus the distance from Syene to Alexandria was 5,000 stadia (1 stadia was 600 Greek feet, 607 English feet). So, if the angle of 7 degrees 14 minutes at the Earth's centre subtended 5,000 stadia at the surface, then 360 degrees at the Earth's centre must subtend 250,000 stadia which works out at 28,700 English statute miles; about 15% too high but not bad for c230 BC.

Because the Earth is a gyroscope, the direction of its spinning axis should remain fixed in space but this does not happen in practice due to centrifugal force slightly swelling Earth's radius at the Equator by about 40 miles. The tilt of the Earth's axis of $23\frac{1}{2}$ degrees means that, except at the equinoxes, the swollen girth of Earth is off the gravitational line between the Sun's centre and Earth's centre. This causes a gyroscopic wobble of Earth's axis but one wobble takes 25,800 years to complete. The end result is that the north end of the "nail" of Earth's axis describes a circle of $23\frac{1}{2}$ degrees radius in the polar sky but takes 25,800 years to do it. Polaris therefore has not always been the North Pole Star. It will be again though in 25,800 years time. This wobble of the Earth's axis is like the slow superimposed oscillation of a child's rapidly spinning top. In astronomy and navigation, the wobble of the Earth's axis is known by the rather frightening term, "The Precession of the Equinoxes." This was discovered by the Greek astronomer Hipparchus of Nicaea c140 BC. He also catalogued 1,000 stars and pioneered the reference grid of lines of latitude and longitude.

In classical times, mathematicians had long been using 360 degrees to a circle and 60 minutes to a degree. The origin of these figures is obscure. Hipparchus, the Greek astronomer (c165 -c127 BC), was the first to use a grid of lines of latitude and longitude to cover the Earth. We still use them today. The lines of longitude (meridians) run from the North Pole to the South Pole and are like the lines dividing the segments of an orange. The Equator is the zero-degree line of latitude and all the other lines of latitude are parallel to it; each one a slightly smaller circle until the North Pole is merely a point at 90 degrees North and the South Pole a similar point at 90 degrees South. Latitude is defined as the angle at the centre of the Earth between the Plane of the Equator and the line to the Earth's surface at the position of the observer. Athens is 38 degrees North, Rome 41 degrees 55 minutes North and London 51 degrees 30 minutes North. A degree of latitude at the Earth's centre subtends an arc of one degree at the Earth's surface and to make navigation easy, this arc has been divided into sixty and the divisions called "nautical miles" so that sixty nautical miles is subtended by one degree of latitude. Therefore it is 360 x 60 nautical miles from the North Pole down to the South Pole and, up the other side, back to the North Pole = 21,600. To convert to statute miles (which is never done by navigators as statute miles are useless at sea and in the air), divide by 66 and multiply by 76. Newcastle upon Tyne is at latitude 55 degrees North, therefore from the equator to Newcastle upon Tyne is 55 x 60 = 3,300 nautical miles. The North Pole's latitude is 90 degrees North so it is 90 – 55 = 35 x 60 = 2,100 nautical miles from Newcastle to the North Pole. The South Pole is 90 degrees South, so Newcastle is 55 + 90 = 145 x 60 = 8,700 nautical miles from the South Pole. The Nautical Mile and its easy conversion to arc and *vice-versa* makes navigation simple.

The unit of speed both at sea and in the air is the *knot* which means one nautical mile per hour so saying "knots per hour" is landlubberly and is repeating "per hour" twice.

The present international zero-degree longitude line (Prime Meridian) is through the Greenwich Naval College in London but various nations have tried Prime Meridians through their own capitals. Eratosthenes' principal meridian passed through Alexandria. Ptolemy placed his, two degrees west of the Fortunate Islands (Canary Islands) which he thought were the farthermost westerly points of land in the world.

Although Polaris is the pole star at the moment, in 2,700 BC it was Thuban and in Roman times Kochab was the nearest star to the elevated pole. However, north on our planet is the direction of the "nail" sticking out of the North Pole and this does not alter. It just so happens that the direction of the nail describes a circle in the sky over a 25,800 year period. There has been much confusion over this and an atlas of astronomy gets it wrong. The Pyramids which are squared-up almost exactly on north-south, were lined up on Thuban when they were built. This meant they were also orientated on Earth's North Pole and they retain this alignment no matter where Earth's axis points in space. The atlas in question implies that the Pyramids are still lined up on Thuban and this would only be the case if they swivelled on their giant bases as Earth's axis precesssed away from Thuban.

Quite recently, there has been a magnificent breakthrough by two amateur Egyptologists, who have discovered the purpose of the Pyramids. The layout of the Pyramids in the desert corresponds to a star-map of the constellation of Orion. The three major Pyramids at Giza represent the slightly crooked line of the three stars of Orion's belt. Other pyramids represent the positions of the stars Betelgeuse and Rigel. Orion receives many hieroglyphic mentions concerning the after-life, and the ancient Egyptians thought that the souls of the departed proceeded there. Shafts cut between the burial chambers and southern faces of the Pyramids have long been incorrectly identified as air-shafts. They are now recognised as "long range gun barrels" up which the spirits of the dead were projected to Orion as the constellation passed the "gun nozzles." Due to the precession of the Earth's axis, the gun barrels no longer line up on Orion as the star group crosses the meridian of the Pyramids but calculations show that they did so at the time of the Pyramids' construction. The new interpretation of the Pyramids has met with little enthusiasm from the establishment but that is to be expected. All the facts fit perfectly.

One does not have to be at sea very long to appreciate that every night, Polaris is due north and, as the night wears on, the other stars apparently rotate around it in an anticlockwise direction. It is also easy to see, that, as a ship travels north, the Pole Star is higher in the sky every night and this angle above the horizon is equal to the latitude of the ship. As a ship sails south, the Pole Star gets lower and as the Equator is approached, it dips into the haze on the horizon.

It has been mentioned earlier that due to the Precession of the Equinoxes, the Pole Star in Roman times was Kochab in the constellation of *Ursa Minor* (The Lesser Bear). The Greek poet Aratus writing c275 BC mentions Phoenician navigators' use of the Lesser Bear:–

"By her [the Little Bear's] guidance, the men of Sidon steer the straightest course."

The Roman poet Lucan (AD 39-65) mentions the Pole Star and the circumpolar stars which revolved around it:

"We do not follow any of the restless stars which move in the sky, for they deceive poor sailors. We follow no stars but one, that does not dip into the waves, the never-setting Axis, brightest star in the twin Bears. This it is that guides our ships."

The Sun can also be used both as a direction-finder and a source of finding latitude. The Sun is near enough due south at midday (it can be a few minutes late or early due to the slightly elliptical orbit of the Earth) and at midday it is at its highest point in the sky. As the Earth rotates once in 24 hours relative to the Sun, the Sun apparently moves 15 degrees in an hour. Therefore if the local time is known, the Sun's direction can be found. At 1000 hours, the Sun has 2 x 15 degrees to go to be due south, therefore its bearing is due south (180 degrees) minus 2 x 15 degrees = 180 − 30 = 150 degrees. The Roman Sun-compass and the modern astro-compass do this for us.

The angle between the midday Sun and the zenith (observer's vertical), with a correction for Sun's declination, can be used to determine the ship's latitude and this is easiest seen in the diagrams on navigation.

Although the Romans probably did not possess magnetic compasses, a mention must be made of them, even if just to avoid confusion between geographic and magnetic poles of the Earth. As has been mentioned, the geographic poles are the ends of the axis of the Earth's rotation and remain fixed, except for tiny oscillations of a few metres which do not affect navigation.

The Earth acts as a generator and produces a magnetic field and the poles of this magnetic field only approximate to the geographic poles. In fact, the Magnetic North Pole is now in Arctic Canada, and is 840 nautical miles (967 statute miles) from the Geographic North Pole. The Magnetic South Pole is in Victoria Land on the Antarctic continent, and is 1,080 nautical miles (1,244 statute miles) from the Geographic South Pole. It will be seen that, if an aircraft is between the Geographical North Pole and the Magnetic North Pole, the aircraft compass will try to point south instead of north. In practice, the lines of force in this area are almost vertical and the compass hardly knows which way to point. At one time, an astro-compass was used in these regions, but modern electronic-satellite systems have made polar navigation quite simple. In addition to this, the Canadian civil aviation authorities have placed a special type of radio beacon on the Magnetic Pole and where the compass needle becomes sluggish and confused, the radio needle takes over. It would be nice to have a powerful radio beacon on the Geographic North Pole but there is no land there and the sea ice is in constant movement due to the currents of the Arctic Ocean.

It will be seen also that, unless the navigator is in line with both the Geographic and Magnetic Poles, the direction of Magnetic North will differ from True North. The difference is called *Variation* and must be allowed for. The magnetic poles move and during the 39-45 War, *Variation* was ten degrees West in northern England but it has reduced to seven degrees West in 1994. It becomes thirteen degrees West in Ireland, twenty degrees West in Iceland and fifty degrees West in southern Greenland. In Arctic Canada, the magnetic needle becomes confused and unreliable.

Away from the magnetic poles, the magnetic compass is extremely useful but it is never believed implicitly by modern sailors. More than once per day, it is checked for error by comparing its reading with the bearing of an astronomical body. The errors are caused by the distance of the Magnetic Pole away from the Geographic Pole (Variation), and the magnetism of the ship's structure and cargo (Deviation). The latter varies from one cargo to another and from one compass course to another. A more accurate type of compass is the modern gyroscopic compass which does not depend on magnetism but senses the Earth's rotation and points to the axis of rotation. By altering the direction of spin of the gyroscope, it could be made to seek out either the North or South Geographic Poles, but international convention decrees that True Geographic *North* is the zero line for all charts. Had ancient civilisations evolved in the southern hemisphere, no doubt True South would have been the zero degree line.

Few modern aircraft carry sextants, astro-compasses or other astronomical observation equipment, but when electronic navigation devices blow their fuses or pop-out the circuit-breakers, the experienced aviator can still steer an approximate course to civilisation if he just glimpses the Sun, Moon, or stars from the cockpit window. The ancient navigators also had rule-of-thumb astronomical formulae and they had no fuses to worry about.

For those readers who wish to gain a clearer insight into old methods of navigation, the movement of the Earth and other bodies must be examined more closely.

During one Earth-orbit of the Sun, which is called a "year," the Earth spins on its own axis once a day and although we count 365 days in our calendar year, the Earth completes 365.242199 spins (almost an extra quarter of a spin) by the time it crosses the finishing post in space at the end of the calendar year. To keep the seasons in the right place, every four years an extra day has to be included in our calendar. Unfortunately the .242199 of a spin is not quite a quarter of a day, and at 5 hours, 48 minutes and 46 seconds, is 11 minutes and 14 seconds short, so three times every 400 years, a leap year has to be omitted even though the date is divisible by four. This is achieved by discounting the years ending in double zeros, such as 1700, 1800, 1900, as leap years, and only counting such whole numbers of hundreds if the date is divisible by 400. Thus, the year 1900 was not a leap year but 2000 will be.

For the purposes of navigation, the stars can be regarded as fixed points of light on an enormous glass sphere, and this sphere appears to rotate, but of course it is Earth that is spinning. It is easier for the navigator to assume that the glass bowl rotates and as it does, the stars' sub-stellar points (the bases of the flag-poles mentioned earlier) trace out lines of latitude on Earth's surface. As each star crosses the observer's meridian, the altitude (angular distance above the horizon) bears a direct relationship to the observer's latitude.

Our own Sun has eight other *planets* in orbit around it in addition to Earth. They are: Mercury, Venus, Mars, Jupiter, Saturn, Uranus, Neptune and Pluto, They all orbit in the same direction as Earth and in a fairly flat disc; Mercury and Venus closer to the Sun than Earth, and the remainder with orbits outside that of Earth. The outer two, Neptune and Pluto, are invisible to the naked eye and Uranus is just visible when at its brightest. The others look like stars but are not fixed points of light on our large glass bowl; because of their orbits around the Sun, they wander across the sky and that is why the ancient Greeks called them *planetes* (wanderers). Their wanderings are tabulated in navigational almanacs and they can be used to check compass bearings, for meridian-crossing derived latitudes and for other position-fixing calculations. Venus is so bright that it can often be seen in day-time if the navigator presets his sextant telescope to the approximate altitude and then searches the sky on the expected azimuth (direction).

From altitudes of the Pole Star, and meridian crossings of the Sun and stars, it would have been quite easy for ancient navigators to estimate their approximate latitudes without accurate determination of time. Longitude is more difficult and a very accurate timepiece is needed. However, if latitude can be determined by astronomical methods, that is half the battle. The longitude can be estimated from distance (time x speed) and directions sailed. Exact determination of longitude at sea was not achieved until 1762 when a timepiece constructed by Mr John Harrison of Yorkshire was accepted by the British Admiralty. Captain Cook used one of Mr Harrison's chronometers during his expedition to the Antarctic and South Pacific, 1772-75.

Ptolemy of Alexandria (c. AD 130) calculated latitudes of towns and other positions quite easily, with the use of gnomons which gave him the angles of the Sun's rays. He also managed to establish longitudes by simultaneous observations of eclipses of the Moon from different places. Sea navigators cannot wait for eclipses, nor can they observe them simultaneously from two locations, but this technique shows that the ancients had a highly developed knowledge of astronomy.

To recap, we have seen that True North can always be obtained from the Pole Star and, with a slight correction, also the observer's latitude. In addition, with only approximate knowledge of time, latitude can be found from the altitude of the Sun's meridian crossing which occurs at noon. Latitudes can also be derived easily from meridian crossings of prominent stars, but from a ship the observations must be taken at twilight when both the star and sea horizon are visible. An aircraft sextant has a spirit level incorporated in its telescope (artificial horizon) and altitudes of stars, planets and Moon can be taken all through the night. The motion of a ship upsets the bubble and makes this type of sextant difficult to use at sea. Slightly more astronomical information is necessary for the use of planets but they can also be used for both compass checks, latitudes from meridian crossings and other position-finding calculations. Briefly, this position-finding from two astronomical bodies works as follows: instead of the star, Sun or planet being on top of a flag-pole, replace the flag-pole with a maypole with lots of ropes hanging down. One must note the exact time of observation and this effectively "freezes" the foot of the maypole in position at the time of the observation. Note the angle of the rope between horizontal and the top of the pole and let us say that this is 70 degrees. If the observer keeps the rope at the same angle and starts walking, he will describe a circle of 1,200 nautical miles radius around the base of the pole $(90 - 70) \times 60 = 1,200$. A second observation is taken of another body and a another circle of position obtained around a second maypole. Let us say that the angle of elevation of the top of the second pole is 50 degrees. The radius of the second circle will be 2,400 nautical miles $(90 - 50) \times 60 = 2,400$. The two circles cross at two points on the Earth's surface many thousands of miles apart. The observer is at one of these positions. Very accurate chronometers are necessary, and the ancients could not have used this technique. In practice, the huge circles are not plotted on charts. An estimated position is plotted and the altitudes and azimuths of the two astronomical bodies calculated for that position using tables. These calculated altitudes are compared with the actual observations and the estimated position moved accordingly. Thus, all the plotting can be done on a local chart. If the Earth did not spin, navigation would be simplified as a star over the observer's home town could be recognised and a course set towards it. When the star was overhead, the observer was home. The disadvantage of no Earth-spin is that there would be six months' day and six months' night.

This brings us to the use of the Moon as an aid to navigation. At a distance of 240,000 miles from the Earth, the Moon is Earth's companion in orbit around the Sun. In addition, both rotate around each other; actually about a common centre of gravity, but due to the Earth's larger size (49 x volume and 81 x mass of Moon), this centre is inside the Earth's crust. The time taken for one orbit of the Moon around the Earth is 29 days and many ancient peoples used this as a calendar. We still use the old word *moonth* but our month no longer coincides with the Moon's phases.

As the Moon makes an orbit of the Earth in 29 days, it also rotates on its own axis in exactly the same period, so that it always keeps the same face towards Earth. Thus the length of a day on the Moon is also a month.

In the pre-electronic navigation period, observations of the Moon were of great use to a navigator using sextants, chronometers and astronomical tables. If the Sun and Moon were visible at the same time, an excellent fix by a cross of astro-position-lines could usually be obtained.

Without any navigation instruments, the Moon can be used for north-finding, though these rule-of-thumb methods seem to be lost to modern electronic-navigators, historians, archaeologists and most of the general public. They were obvious to my generation of navigators and would have been of even more use to the ancients. Let us look at the Moon as a direction finder.

The Moon orbits the Earth approximately around Earth's equator, although it wanders from 29 degrees North to 29 degrees South. When the Moon is on the opposite side of the Earth from the Sun, the side of the Moon towards Earth is fully illuminated. This is a Full Moon. When the Moon is on the same side as the Sun, the Moon's illuminated side is away from the Earth and the Moon is invisible but soon shows as a thin crescent line as the Moon swings in its orbit off the Sun-Earth line. This is a "New Moon." On occasion, the Earth, Moon and Sun are *exactly* in line and this is when an eclipse occurs. If the Earth is between the Sun and the Moon, the shadow of the Earth falls on the Moon (Eclipse of the Moon) and if the Moon is between Earth and Sun, the Moon blots out the Sun's light for a short while (Eclipse of the Sun). Eclipses are very useful for astronomers and geographers but too infrequent for navigators.

Once a month, the Moon is full, and to be full, it has to be on the opposite side of the Earth from the Sun; we know that the Sun is due south at midday (in the northern hemisphere) therefore although below the horizon, it must be due north at midnight. As the Full Moon is opposite the Sun, this Full Moon must therefore be due south at midnight. If the time is known, we have a "Moon-compass." The Earth's daily spin is at 15 degrees per hour and the Moon is orbiting in the same direction at half a degree per hour. Let us ignore the half degree, as this is merely a rule-of-thumb system. If it is 10 pm, the Full Moon has 2 x 15 degrees to go to be due south, so its bearing is 180 – 30 = 150 degrees. At 7 pm, it will be five hours before the Full Moon is due south (crosses the meridian) so the bearing of the Moon will be 180 – (5 x 15) = 105 degrees or if we wish to be more accurate, 180 – (5 x 14½) = 107 degrees. The Full Moon therefore makes an easy-to-read compass as long as we have some idea of the local time. The Full Moon is half way round its monthly orbit from New Moon so the New Moon, although unseen, will be due south at midday. The first hint of a crescent on the right hand side of the New Moon makes it visible, and this crescent Moon will be due south at about 1 pm and due west at 7 pm. When the Moon has the right half (in the northern hemisphere) illuminated, it has gone a quarter way round its monthly orbit, so it will be six hours late at due south and be there at 6 pm and west at midnight. When the left hand half of the Moon is illuminated, the Moon is three-quarters of the way around its monthly orbit, so it will be eighteen hours late at due south which is 6 am and west at midday. The experienced eye can estimate directions at all phases of the Moon: new crescent, right half, right-gibbous (gibbous means more than half from Latin *gibbus* = "hump"), full, left-gibbous, left half, left crescent.

With a little practice, the observer can obtain north from the Moon without knowing the time at all, and even from a quick glimpse in bad weather through a rift in the storm clouds. In order to appreciate this method, we must look at the Moon's orbit around the Earth and this approximates to the Earth's equator but swings between 29 degrees North declination and 29 degrees South. The line on the Moon which divides the illuminated half from the dark half, therefore runs near enough from the Moon's North Pole to its South Pole. As we have now established where the Moon's poles are, and we also know that the Moon is circling our equator, we can estimate (in the northern hemisphere) the direction of our own North Pole. The procedure is as follows.

Note the points of the Moon's crescent, half, or gibbous shape and imagine a ruler stretching from the horizon below the Moon and crossing these horns or points on the Moon. Then following the line of the ruler, sweep one's hand right across the celestial dome to the farthermost horizon. That point on the farthest horizon is approximately north. This system is most accurate when the dividing line between day and night on the Moon is straight up and down. If the Moon is on its back, or the daylight line otherwise away from the vertical, as one sweeps through the Moon's horns, imagine that the hand sweeping across the sky is holding a weighted fishing line. Where the weighted hook hits the far horizon is approximately north.

If the navigator has the advantage of a watch or other device showing local time, and the Moon is visible, he can use his watch as a Sun-compass even though the Sun is below the horizon. Take the local time and express it in the 24 hour system; divide by two, point the answer on the dial in the direction in space from which the Sun's rays must be coming to illuminate the Moon's globe in crescent, half, or gibbous shape. The figure 12 on the dial of the watch will indicate True North. In the southern hemisphere, the figure 12 indicates True South.

All the other methods described above can be easily adapted for the southern hemisphere but have not been mentioned as we are investigating the Romans whose Empire was in the northern hemisphere.

We can now examine the account of the explorations of Pytheas in greater detail. About 300 BC, he explored Britain and Ireland and then sailed to the island of "Thule" which Pytheas said was six days sailing from Britain and one day south of the "Frozen Sea."

Historians have identified Pytheas' Thule as either Norway (which is *not* an island), or the Shetlands which are 90 nautical miles north of Scotland and less than one day's sail at 4 knots. The only place which fits the description is Iceland. It is 400 nautical miles from Scotland to Iceland and at 4 knots, would have taken Pytheas just over four days to cover the distance. At three knots, it would have taken him 5 days. Pytheas said six.

The North Cape of Norway is 1,050 miles from Scotland and would have taken Pytheas 11 days at 4 knots and 15 days at 3 knots. He also said that Thule was one day south of the ice and this is correct for Iceland, even though there is no part of mainland Iceland inside the Arctic Circle. Tourists in Iceland, who wish to claim their "Blue-nose certificates" for crossing the Arctic Circle, have to be taken in a light aircraft around a rock called Grimsey. As Iceland is completely south of the Arctic Circle, the Midnight Sun is never visible, though it is only just below the northern horizon at midsummer.

Pytheas said that at Thule, the Sun was below the horizon for two to three hours each night. Pytheus was aware of the phenomenon of the Midnight Sun but does not mention it in his references to Thule. We can safely assume therefore that Thule was south of the Arctic Circle.

Even though the latitude of the North Cape of Norway is 287 miles further north than the north coast of Iceland, the cape is kept clear of the Arctic ice by the Gulf Stream and the drift-ice seldom gets south of Bear Island which is yet another 260 miles to the north.

Pytheas mentions the "Frozen Sea" which is at its greatest southerly limit in March/April and within 100 miles of the northern coast of Iceland, say 68 degrees North. He said that the Sun was below the horizon for two to three hours per day. At 68 degrees North, the Sun is below the horizon for only two hours on May 22nd and July 22nd. At the same latitude, the Sun is below the horizon for three hours on May 17th and July 25th. The Midnight Sun becomes visible at that latitude from 25th May until July 17th and the Sun does not set at all betweeen those dates. It looks therefore as if Pytheas was in the Iceland area in late July and this ties in with his exploration of Britain before he sailed north to Iceland.

If our historians who identify Pytheas' Thule with northern Norway are correct, then at the drift-ice limit of about 75 degrees North, near Bear Island, the Midnight Sun would have been visible from April 30th to August 12th – the whole of the Mediterranean sailing season. If he was up at Bear Island before April or after August, he was lucky to survive. Ask anyone who served on the convoys to Russia during the 39-45 War.

We must now look at methods of navigation other than those which involve astronomy, which were available two thousand years ago. The most obvious is coastal navigation where the sailor recognises features on the shore. In thick weather, he is aided by the lead line. When the water becomes shallow, the line tells the depth and, in addition to that, a cavity on the bottom of the weight can be armed with grease so that a sample of the sea bed can be inspected when the line is brought up. Sounding poles can be used in very shallow water. A sounding or depth pole was found with the Cheops ship of the 3rd millenium BC and lead lines were known to Herodotus.

Much of the time, the presence of a distant coastline can be detected hundreds of miles away long before the land is visible. As the wind rises up over the land, it carries up moist air which condenses in the cooler air at altitude. These "orographic" clouds mark the land. Other tell-tale clouds which give away the presence of land are those caused by convection, where the Sun's differential heating of various types of terrain causes thermals to rise. When these reach a certain height, the water vapour condenses forming the fluffy white "cumulus" clouds. These are the clouds which tell the circling seagulls and other soaring birds where "free lift" is available. They are also sought by sporting glider pilots. A hot-air balloon is merely an artificial thermal wrapped-up in a plastic bag.

On many occasions, I have approached the British Isles from the Atlantic in high-flying aircraft and although the land was obscured, the exact shape of the coastline was revealed by the cloud above it. This phenomenon although not so obvious from the deck of a Roman merchant ship, would not have been lost on observant navigators.

In addition to their very clever sunstones, tradition has it that the Vikings used a primitive form of radar in thick weather. As they closed the coast in bad visibility, a horn was sounded and unseen cliffs betrayed their presence with echoes.

At dusk, shoreward flying seabirds tell the observant seaman the direction of land. In my own experience, on ships bound from Gibraltar to the English Channel, I have always known when I would sight the magnificent gannets of which a large colony is based at Cape Finisterre at the north-western corner of Spain. Another air escort of the same type of bird greets the ship as it approaches Ushant on the corresponding "Lands End" of France.

In the South Atlantic, on the long and tedious month's voyage (at 10 knots) from Capetown, South Africa to New York, USA, just south of the Equator, the track passes by Ascension Island. Even at night, the presence of the island is revealed by the screaming "Wideawake birds" which circle the ship in large numbers. We used to put the ship's searchlight on the clouds of noisy night-fliers. This bird has given its name to the military air base on the island, "Wideawake Field." The runway is cut through the side of a volcano and the surface of the island resembles a moonscape. In 1982, for a few weeks this lonely outpost was to become the busiest airfield in the world as it happened to be halfway along the 8,000 miles from UK to the Falkland Islands. A massive logistical support for the British task force was organised at this island. In my semi-retirement from thirty years in aviation, I found myself as a temporary ship's officer and emerged from an RAF transport aircraft at Wideawake Field, and once again heard the screaming of the Wideawake birds which I recognised from my memories of those voyages of long ago.

Many coastal locations have their own particular aerial residents which give early warning of the proximity of their home rocks, islands and peninsulas.

By a very early date, probably in the later prehistoric period in Europe, seamen had learned how to navigate the seas. What they most certainly did not do was hug the coastlines in sailing ships which is a most dangerous practice. Oared warships were a different kettle of fish and could manoeuvre against wind and tide. No doubt, the very large crews of these fighting vessels also liked to wine and dine ashore. Warships could "show the flag" here and there and did not rely on the delivery of cargoes for their upkeep. Merchant ships, then as now, ploughed on for weeks on end.

Now we must switch from the navigation of the ancient ships, to the ships themselves. Another myth, which is rapidly being dispelled, is the theory that ancient ships could only run before the wind because of their square-rigged sails. If that were the case, the Romans could never have completed the grain-runs from Alexandria to Ostia. Year after year, Roman square-rigged

Sir Francis Drake's warship
Golden Hinde had many similar
features to Roman merchant
ships. It was tubby, square-
rigged, had an
artemon sail for'd and a
lateen aft. Many Roman
merchant ships were far
larger than the 300 tons
displacement of the
Golden Hinde.

The replica *Golden Hinde* in
which the author sailed as
navigator.

merchant ships made the passage from the Nile to Roman ports during the summer months against the north-westerly prevailing winds. It is true that the homeward journey took longer than the outward, but even modern sailing vessels have to "tack" when their destination lies to windward. It was on one of these deviations from the direct track that the *Isis* ended up in Piraeus.

There is proof that both the Greeks and Romans had fore-and-aft sails of the types known as sprit-sails and lateen sails. Fore-and-aft rigged ships can certainly sail closer to the wind than square riggers but the latter can also make progress to windward. On square-riggers, the truss-ropes which fasten the yard to the mast can be eased and the yard swung round so that it lies almost fore-and-aft. Also, quite a few Roman reliefs show ships with a combination of square-rig and fore-and-aft sails.

Not so long ago, I had the pleasure of sailing as navigator in the replica of Sir Francis Drake's ship, *Golden Hinde*. Although the original was a warship, by Tudor times, the fighting ships had lost the racing-boat shapes of the *biremes and triremes* and the tubby shape of the *Golden Hinde's* hull and the sail arrangement closely resemble the reliefs of Roman merchant ships. The Roman ship *Isis* was much larger than the *Golden Hinde*. The latter sailed round the world during the voyage of 1577-80 and the replica has also circumnavigated the globe but took advantage of the Panama and Suez Canals which were not available to Sir Francis Drake. If the Romans had guessed at the existence of an unknown continent on the other side of the Atlantic, there is little doubt that ships like the *Isis* could have made the crossing.

While serving in the *Golden Hinde*, I could not help noticing the similarity of rig to that of Roman ships. In particular, our steeply angled bowsprit closely resembled the raked foremast of Roman merchant ships. I was also puzzled by the strange circular holes of about two feet in diameter at the bottom corners of the *artemon* sail which was spread below our bowsprit. Our captain, Dennis Ord, one of Britain's leading sailing ship experts, told me that the holes were to drain water from the sail if the ship dipped her bows. In fine weather, our seamen used to lie in the belly of this sail, sunning themselves. The captain informed me that our bowsprit was not a true one and was rigged like a mast and was indeed a descendant of the Roman angled foremast. Our conventional foremast and mainmast carried square-rigged sails but the mizzen-mast had a fore-and-aft lateen sail.

Another criticism historians make of ancient ships is their use of steering oars instead of stern rudders. Far from being inefficient, the steering oar, which rotated on its near-vertical shaft, worked like the balanced rudder of an aircraft. The steering oar would have been easy to repair or replace at sea.

It is now time to leave the open seas and see what happened to the Roman cargoes once they arrived in British harbours and rivers.

A Tyne keelboat c1820. Roman barges
would have been of similar design and
capacity.

This modern Dutch canal barge carries the same
cargo as eighty freight-wagons.

During the keelmens' strike of 1822, William Hedley's early locomotive, the *Wylam Dilly,* was mounted
on a Tyne keelboat and with its railway wheels replaced with paddles, it became one of the river's first
steam tugs. After the strike, the locomotive was returned to colliery railway service. It is now preserved
in the Royal Scottish Museum, Edinburgh.

Chapter 8

The Roman Supply Lines

"Ob periculum cataractarum derivato flumine tutam Danuvi navigationem fecit."
(On account of the danger of the waterfall, he diverted the river and made a safe passage of the Danube.)
[Trajanic inscription found near the Roman canal which was cut through the cliffs of the Danube in order to bypass the Iron Gates waterfall.]

During my aerial and ground archaeological searches in northern England, I continued to be puzzled by the severity of the Roman road gradients. I was also confused by some authors' repetitive descriptions of Roman forts being built on well defended sites. It was clear from the air that, unlike Iron Age hillforts, Roman fort sites were *not* selected for their ease of defence. With the exception of the frontier forts of Hadrian's Wall and the Antonine Wall, the favourite Roman site seemed to be on a river bank, often in a large bend and usually at the confluence of a river with a smaller stream. When this was pointed out to lecturers, the answer was invariably the same: "Roman sites were located on rivers in order to protect bridges." This was even more puzzling. Why did the Romans have only sixteen forts on the Tyne/Solway Wall facing the semi-hostile tribes in Northumberland, and for a period, about twenty-five on the Antonine frontier and environs, to hold in check the whole beligerent Caledonian nation, but over three hundred to protect bridges in the friendly territory between the Tyne and the south coast?

When Hitler's army occupied France, the German soldiers did not build military bases to protect bridges. A couple of sentries for each important bridge was considered sufficient for the task. The severe penalties inflicted by the Germans upon resistance fighters and hostages was a great deterrent. I am sure that likewise, the Roman army was not inclined to behave in a benevolent manner towards saboteurs.

The selection of Roman sites was obviously for purposes other than the provision of bridge sentries. Judging by the vast sizes of timbers and stones in the remains of Roman frontier-zone bridges, the very casting-down of such structures would have needed a small army of vandals. What then was the reason for the choice of poor strategic riverside sites?

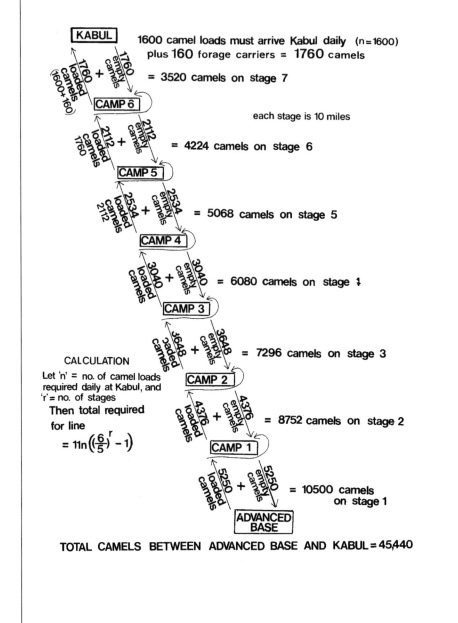

KABUL
1600 camel loads must arrive Kabul daily (n=1600)
plus 160 forage carriers = 1760 camels
= 3520 camels on stage 7

1760 loaded camels (1600+160) + 1760 empty camels

CAMP 6

each stage is 10 miles

2112 loaded camels 1760 + 2112 empty camels   = 4224 camels on stage 6

CAMP 5

2534 loaded camels 2112 + 2534 empty camels   = 5068 camels on stage 5

CAMP 4

3040 loaded camels + 3040 empty camels   = 6080 camels on stage 4

CAMP 3

3648 loaded camels + 3648 empty camels   = 7296 camels on stage 3

CALCULATION

Let 'n' = no. of camel loads required daily at Kabul, and 'r' = no. of stages

Then total required for line

$$= 11n\left(\left(\frac{6}{5}\right)^r - 1\right)$$

CAMP 2

4376 loaded camels + 4376 empty camels   = 8752 camels on stage 2

CAMP 1

5250 loaded camels + 5250 empty camels   = 10500 camels on stage 1

ADVANCED BASE

TOTAL CAMELS BETWEEN ADVANCED BASE AND KABUL = 45,440

The calculation by the Royal Engineers to establish the number of pack-animals necessary for an invasion of friendly territory in Afghanistan. Even though the supply lines did not need to be defended, 45,440 camels were required, which was an impossible number.

The famous Roman ox-wagon has always been regarded as the standard Roman method of heavy goods transport but simple calculations and an inspection of the road system show that this could not have been the case.

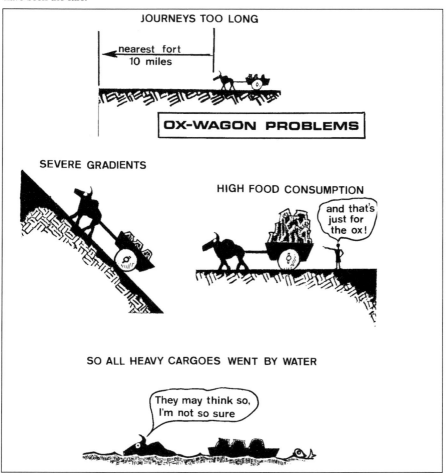

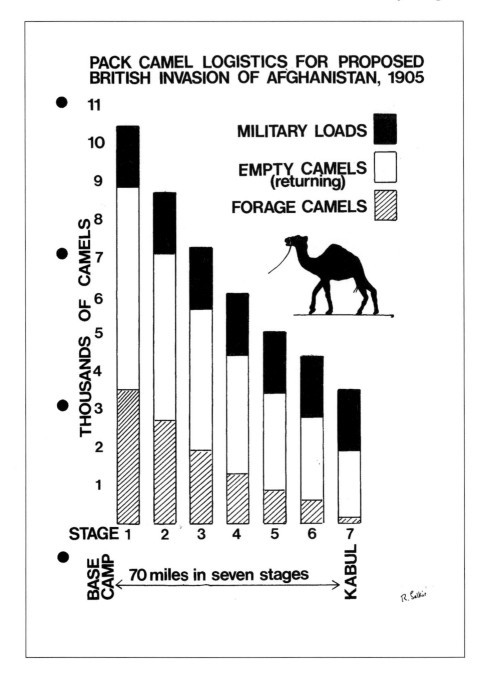

PACK CAMEL LOGISTICS FOR PROPOSED
BRITISH INVASION OF AFGHANISTAN, 1905

The only way an ox-wagon could have negotiated Dere Street in Northumberland, with its impossibly steep switchbacks, would have been for the Romans to load all the oxen and themselves onto the wagon and try to achieve 100 mph on the dive, in the hope that the impetus would get them up the other side.

I had long wondered how far Roman ships or barges had penetrated our smaller British rivers, but the slightest suggestion of Roman river navigation was resisted by the establishment, even though the famous historian Joan Liversidge said that she thought most Roman inland forts had barge basins. Reliefs on Trajan's column in Rome also show Roman riverside forts complete with harbours. The attitude of the British establishment is surprising, as what the Roman army did in one part of their Empire, they did in all parts, just as bridges built by our own Royal Engineers in Scotland were identical to those built by them in India.

The more I flew, the more puzzling became the evidence. The Roman fort-sites certainly followed a distinct pattern. It was obvious that the Roman fort of Vinovia at Binchester, County Durham, NZ 210 314, thirty-seven miles from the sea, had been entirely surrounded by water at one time, with the River Wear to the west and south and a strange dried-up channel to the east and north. This channel has been described by various historians as: "an old course of the River Gaunless" but the dry channel is too high above the river. From the air, it is also obvious that the old channel does not follow natural bends but consists of straight sections with sharp corners, very similar to Roman road layouts. A map of 1772, found in the Bishop's Palace at Bishop Auckland, shows the canal in its entirety, leaving the River Wear to the south of the fort and rejoining it to the north. The map is entitled: A PLAN OF THE PARK AND DEMESNES AT AUCKLAND CASTLE BELONGING TO THE RIGHT REVEREND FATHER IN GOD, JOHN LORD, BISHOP OF

DURHAM, TAKEN IN 1772 BY JEREMIAH DIXON. The canal traverses
fields called: "Low Park, Low Bishop Mead, Stone Horse Field, Low Car and
Low Wood Field."

The answer to the whole problem came to me in a flash one night as I
studied an old map of my home town, Chester-le-Street, one time Saxon
settlement of Conceastre, and before that, Roman Concangis.

The map marked a dried-up loop of the River Wear and another old
course of the smaller River Cone which joined the Wear near the Roman fort.
As a small boy, I had sledged down the hill below the Roman fort and
bumped in and out of the so-called old channel of the Cone. This dry
channel led to a duck pond right underneath the north-eastern corner of the
Roman fort. Even as a schoolboy, I could see that the channel was too far up
the bank-side to have been part of a river bed. Now as I looked at the map of
1850, I saw in the old loop of the main river, a feature marked as: "ruins of a
stone pier." This structure was at right-angles to the former river flow and
could not have been a bridge-pier. It must have been a dam or a weir. It was
also the findspot of a Roman inscription which told us about the engineering
abilities of the Roman prefect.

In a flash, I knew how the Romans had supplied their forts. They had
deepened the rivers artificially with barriers at intervals. This was why the
Roman roads had severe gradients; the Romans were not worried about
difficulties for ox-wagons because the wagons didn't use the roads. The heavy
goods, as on the Thames, Tiber, Rhine, Moselle, Seine, Rhône, Tagus, etc,

A Roman general purpose *codicaria* could be rowed, sailed, towed or poled. The smallest carried a
cargo of 10 tons and was operated by four hauliers and one steersman. The same cargo by road,
assuming the oxen could have managed the gradients, would have needed 20 ox-wagons and 40 men.
The problem did not stop there as, after a day's journey of little more than 5 miles, the ox-teams
would have needed much of their own cargo as fodder.

had also come up our minor rivers. The wagons were used only between jetties and forts where strangely, the *vici* roads *did* seek out easy gradients. Unfortunately, in 1930, the site selected for the town sewage works was the dry course of the River Wear and the suspected Roman structure was destroyed. Also, a few years ago, the suspected canal along the bank-side was landscaped over to provide foundations for a youth club and a municipal swimming bath.

A little research told me that, in addition to being magnificent constructors of roads, forts, houses, palaces, temples, monuments, baths and aqueducts, the Romans had also built large numbers of dams or barrages across rivers. One that dammed a branch of the mighty Rhine, gets a mention only because it was destroyed in an uprising (Tacitus, *Hist*). Nero had a cascade of three dams in the garden of his villa on the River Anio. They were evidently for ornamental purposes and the middle one was 120 feet high. This dam was later used as a source for Rome's "Anio Novus" aqueduct (Frontinus, *The Strategems and Aqueducts of Rome*). How strange it is that the only Roman dam I have seen mentioned in Britain is the small earth one (NZ 106 474) which deflected water into the Roman aqueduct to Lanchester, County Durham (Steer 1938). If the Romans built large barrages in the rest of their Empire, surely they must have also built some in Britain. Unfortunately, all structures found in British rivers are immediately classified as remains of bridges, paved fords or fish-traps. However, if one studies the descriptions of Roman bridge-remains found in Britain, there are some very funny structures indeed, but more of this later.

In addition to the Roman forts being located at riverside sites, other common factors were noticed; more often than not, a mediaeval water-mill reused the old Roman site. The standard excuse for this is: "the millers were attracted to the place because of the free stone in the Roman ruins." Was it not also because of dam structures and associated bypass channels already in existence? A miller would be saved tremendous expense if there was already a barrier across the river and an associated channel in which to place his wheel. All dams in British rivers are classified as either mediaeval or of Industrial Revolution date. The recorded mediaeval use of a dam or the addition of modern Portland cement on the top does not eliminate an unseen Roman base. Using the same arguments put forward by some archaeologists, the local castle near where this is being written cannot be Norman because the great hall contains modern man-made-fibre carpets.

Before we proceed further, I must differentiate between the construction of artificial canals and the improvement of rivers for navigation. The Romans did both. Canals are artificial ditches, dug for transport, drainage or both and in dry climates also for irrigation. When a river, difficult to navigate, is improved, the river itself is the navigable route, but here and there, rapids and waterfalls have to be overcome. Large bends are often short-circuited and shallows are deepened. Much more will be said about dams and the conflict in mediaeval and later times between bargees who had to negotiate the barriers, which involved the release of water, and millers who attempted to delay these operations because they wished to retain a head of water essential for the supply of power to their water-wheels. The various methods of raising barges across barriers will also be discussed in detail. For now, let us go half-way back to the Roman period and look at the navigation of minor British rivers in the mediaeval period long before the canal-building mania of the Industrial Revolution. The mediaeval road system was in an appalling state, but it is surprising what tremendous use was made of very small rivers, streams and ditches, where nowadays there is hardly enough water for ducks to paddle.

Thomas Baines' *Yorkshire Past and Present,* Vol 1, c1870 tells us of some of the river journeys by passengers:

> "At the time when the *Domesday Book* was drawn up in the reign of William the Conqueror, travellers on their way from London to the north, took boat at Nottingham, and were floated down the Trent into the Humber, whence the tides carried them up the River Ouse to Acaster Malbis, a few miles below York. This great line of internal navigation was, at a very early age, connected with another, by the Foss Dyke, cut from the Trent in Lincolnshire, at Torksey, to the Witham at Lincoln; from which there was a water communication down the River Witham to Boston in Lincolnshire, which was then one of the principal ports of the eastern coast of England, and greatly frequented by Flemish and German merchants."

Thomas Baines also tells us that the City of York was returned amongst the free boroughs on the sea, being easily accessible by vessels. He quotes a rise of tide of 10 ft 11 inches at Naburn just upstream from Acaster Malbis, 16 ft 9 inches at Goole and 27.92 ft at Hull.

Professor W G Hoskins in his *Fieldwork in Local History* reveals some astonishing limits of navigation in the mediaeval period:

> "In mediaeval and later times, a large proportion of inland trade went by river, far more than has ever been generally realized. Thus the major river systems - and some of the minor ones - developed numerous little river-ports, many of them scarcely recognizable today unless one is led to them by some clue from a document. The only book on the subject covers a late period (T S Willan, *River Navigation in England 1600-1750*) and, admirable as it is, fails to reveal the full extent of river navigation in pre-industrial England."

Hoskins tells us that, although the head of navigation on the Parrett in Somerset is shown as Bridgewater in 1600-60, previously, there was regular barge traffic as far as Langport, and occasionally up the tributary Yeo, as far as Ilchester.

Hoskins also mentions rivers in East Anglia, the Yare, Bure and Waveney. Norwich was the head of Yare navigation and the Bure was navigable right up to Aylsham in the late sixteenth century for lighters of thirty tons, and the Waveney up to Beccles for barges of twenty tons. On the Severn, river traffic could get up as far as Welshpool.

Already mentioned in Chapter 5 was the reference to sixteenth century barges reaching Wye on the River Stour in Kent.

It comes as no surprise to me to learn that on, or near all of these mediaeval heads of navigation, there was a Roman site. Let us take them in

A Roman *codicaria* under tow. (from a relief in the Musée Calvet, Avignon). The bargemen had independent tow-ropes and are usually depicted with walking sticks. According to Roman writers, they chanted as they progressed along the river and canal banks.

The insignia of the *Utricularii* (civilian boatmen) was an inflated animal skin. To negotiate shallows, dozens of pairs of skins were tied under the hull, thus greatly reducing the already shallow draught.

This painting is of a cargo canoe in northern Canada. The heavy craft is being towed up rapids by four hauliers. Rivers like this in Britain are assessed as having been un-navigable to the Romans.

turn.

Near Nottingham, on the Trent (Roman Trisantona) where the Norman period passengers embarked for their river voyage to York, there is the Roman town of Marigidunum at Castle Hill. Downstream is the Roman town and fort of Ad Pontem (East Stoke) and the Roman vexillation fortress and two temporary camps at Newton on Trent. Torksey is the entrance to the Roman Foss Dyke Canal which leads to the Roman legionary fortress and town of Lindum (Lincoln), and back on the main Trent, lies the Roman fort at Marton and the major Roman settlement of Segelocum (Littleborough).

Across the Humber (Roman Abus) and into the Ouse (Roman name unknown) the very name Acaster Malbis, near York tells us that there was a Roman site there. In the Roman legionary fortress of Eburacum (York) there was stationed a river pilot called Minucius Audens. He was from neither the Roman navy nor the merchant marine, but from the Sixth Legion. The Roman army was obviously involved in river transport, as of course are all armies. Above York, it is highly likely that the River Ouse was navigated by Roman supply barges, but we will return to the evidence for this later.

Professor Hoskins refers to Ilchester as the sixteenth century navigation limit of the Parrett (Roman Uxela) and its tributary the Yeo (Roman name unknown). Ilchester was the Roman town of Lindinis and five major Roman roads met there. At the mouth of the Parrett is the known Roman port of Combwich.

In addition to Professor Hoskins' information, civil engineer P Myall, of Yeovil, in "Roman Rivers of the South-west" in *Narrow Boat, Jan 85,* tells us that the layout of the Roman port at Ilchester can still be seen. He is also of the opinion that the Romans navigated the Whitelake River, the Brue, the Carg and Welham's Brook. He also mentions that Mr Rodney Legg, writing in *Dorset Magazine,* speculated that a Roman canal in Dorchester extended from a man-made arm of the River Frome at the foot of High Street West.

Next we will look at the Severn (Roman Sabrina) with its sixteenth century navigation limit at Welshpool. On the river below Welshpool, we find the Roman town and legionary fortress of Virroconnium (Wroxeter), the vexillation fortress at Leighton, the Roman town at Worcester, and the Roman town and legionary fortress of Glevum (Gloucester).

The sixteenth century limit of the Yare (Roman Gariannus) is given as Norwich. Close by is the Roman town of Venta (Caistor St Edmund) and near the mouth of the river is the Roman Saxon Shore fort of Gariannonum (Burgh Castle). Aylsham is Hoskins' quoted limit for the Bure (Roman name unknown) and just downstream is the Roman settlement at Brampton.

In the sixteenth century, twenty-ton barges proceeded up the Waveney (Roman name unknown) as far as Beccles. The Waveney joins the Yare at the Burgh Castle Roman fort. Quite recently, on the River Waveney, a Roman site was excavated at Scole on the Norfolk - Suffolk border, ahead of the A140 Scole Trunk Road construction works. A twenty-foot-wide Roman canal was found short-circuiting a loop of the river. As will be seen later, this is exactly the type of evidence that is being found elsewhere. It is to be hoped that the Scole canal will not be interpreted as another mill-leat and any associated weir as a fish-trap. It is of interest to note that the River Waveney has its source only one field away from that of the Little Ouse, which flows in the other direction and which joined up with the known river network which connected with the Nene in Roman times. There are some unexplained artificial stretches on the Little Ouse and the Nene has many suspected Roman short-circuiting canals cutting off its meanders. It is now time to look at the technology used for a water-supplied logistical system, all the way from the sea to the very limits of navigation in the hills. The Tiber is not a big river and we have Roman references to large ships transferring their cargoes at Ostia to barges for the journey up to Rome. We also know that the Romans navigated the upper Tiber and tributaries, with some difficulty, at least as far as Citta di Castella in the Appenines, 180 miles inland and about 1,050 feet above sea level. We will look at the whole problem of river navigation and the best place to start is with a merchant ship approaching harbour.

The Roman harbours in Britain would not have rivalled the sophistication of Ostia, Alexandria, Leptis Magna and the like but essentials such as beacons (cairns or poles) marking dangers would have been provided. An advantage Britain possessed was the large tides. A 250 ton Roman merchant ship with a draught of eight feet, approaching the River Wear (Vedra) on a High Spring tide would have had an extra seventeen feet of water above the lowest tidal level (Spring tides occur twice per month when the Sun, Earth and Moon are in line). Neap tides occur when the Sun-Earth-Moon line makes a right angle one week after spring tides, and provide minimum high tides. A High Neap would have given the Roman ship an extra twelve feet of water in addition to the natural depth of the river. The river was extremely shallow at the mouth, therefore our Roman ships relied on the depth of tide for entry into Sunderland.

Eight miles to the north of Sunderland is South Shields, where the Roman fort of Arbeia sits at the mouth of the Tyne which is a major river. According to the *Notitia Dignitatum,* a list of officials, officers and units of the Roman Empire, a unit of the River Tigris lightermen was stationed there, so there is not much doubt about Roman navigation of that river. We will come to navigation of the Tyne in due course, but I have selected the Wear for consideration first because it is a minor river and presented difficulties. If the Romans used the Wear for transport, then they could have done the same in nearly every other British river.

Imagine the arrival of our Roman supply ship at the mouth of the River Wear, inbound from the Rhine with a general cargo. Deep in the hold were heavy millstones under thousands of other items such as crates of pottery. Wine figured largely on the cargo manifest and row upon row of *amphorae* sat with their pointed bases firmly seated in holes in specially designed racks.

The initial approach to the harbour had been made with a beam wind from the south-west and to cope with this, the trusses had been eased and the yard of the main-sail swung round. When the shallow-water markers on the bar were just a few cables away, the main-sail had been furled and the ship crept slowly ahead with steerage-way provided by the trimmed artemon for'd balanced by a lateen sail aft. As the helsman steered the ship along the deepest approach-channel by keeping two markers on shore in line, the leadsman called out the decreasing soundings. In case things went wrong

Codicaria being loaded (from a fresco in the Vatican Museum).

A Roman warship transporting a cargo of barrels on the River Moselle. (stone relief found at Neumagen, Germany, now in the Landesmuseum, Trier).

A 1,500 lb, 50 ft riverboat with a five-man crew being poled against fast water in the rapids of the Seneca Bypass of George Washington's Patowmack Canal. The boat is a replica built by the Virginia Canals and Navigations Society. One crewman handles the steering sweep while another stands in the bow, fending off rocks. The other three propel the boat by jamming their poles against the bottom and walking the planks that run on both sides from bow to stern. The Seneca Bypass avoids a seven foot waterfall in the main river and does so without any kind of lock.

The subject of Constable's painting entitled *Boat-Building near Flatford Mill*, is a barge under construction in a simple riverside dry-dock. The Romans describe exactly the same method of construction. Constable's dry-dock has a gate through which water will enter when the barge is completed. The dry-dock would become a pound lock if it were situated in a river loop, and had gates at both ends.

before the oar-powered harbour-tugs got their tow-ropes aboard, the anchor was ready to let go. The clanking of a double-acting bilge pump could be heard from below decks and regular jets of water, keeping time with the sailor's strokes of the pump handle, spurted from a discharge pipe in the ship's side.

The high tide was more than enough to keep the ship's keel well clear of the bar and as the ship crossed into calm water, the tugs got their lines aboard and the ship's artemon and lateen sails were taken in.

Not only does the High Spring tide provide the maximum depth of water; 6 hours later the sea drops to its minumum level at the Low Spring which provided only a foot of water above the normal river depth at the mouth of the Wear. As the river itself was only a foot deep at the bar (until modern dredging), the Roman ship would have had to anchor off for a few hours if it had arrived at Low Spring tide.

As the tugs eased the ship towards the jetty, light heaving-lines snaked across the narrowing gap between ship and wharf, to be caught by waiting hands. These lines were then used to drag heavy mooring ropes ashore, and

This strange structure in the River Eden was used as a fish-trap by the monks of Wetheral Priory. It looks however, as if it was designed originally as a flashlock for navigation. Three stone piers span a channel between the river bank and an artificial stone island of considerable length. Beyond the island, the river tumbles down a series of rapids. To operate as a flash lock, an opening gate would have been provided in the widest gap and there is a winch pit in the central pier. This winch would have been used to pull barges through the gap against the current. Winch pits in the other piers may have housed winches for operating movable weirs which could have been planks, gates or a system of movable timbers called rimers and paddles. When movable weirs are lowered or opened, the level of the river above the flash lock drops. When the level decreases sufficiently, the navigation gate is opened and a barge is winched upstream. A downstream bound craft shoots the fast flow. The upstream bound craft has the gate closed behind it so that a depth of water builds up for navigation to the next barrier. The types of barriers were many and varied and had different names from place to place, but the principle was always the same: open the weir, let most of the water out, open the gate, pull a barge up through the gap or let one ride down it.

soon the ship was tied up with head, breast and stern ropes plus a couple of springs (angled ropes to prevent the ship ranging along the quay wall). Mooring ropes would have been slackened frequently as the tide ebbed; this was not a Mediterranean harbour. Perhaps the Romans overcame this problem by bringing the ship though a gate in a wall into an inner harbour. If so, after the ship's entry at high tide, the gate would have been closed, and as the tide dropped and the outer harbour emptied, the ship sat safely in its sanctuary (called a non-tidal basin) with the water level inside the wall and closed gate, equal to that of high tide. In practice, this level is usually slightly lower than high tide to allow ships time to negotiate the gate for a period before and after high water.

Many modern yacht marinas have gated-basins because deep-keeled yachts cannot sit on mud when a harbour dries out. Modern ships need large non-tidal docks as they can break their backs if allowed to ground, and the sheathing of hulls of ancient ships could have been holed by rocks and stones on the harbour or river beds. A simplified version of the non-tidal basin dispenses with the gate and has a permanent cill across the entrance at a level of about half tide. Thus, small craft can enter at high tide with their keels clear of the cill. On the ebb, the level of water in the basin never drops below that of the top of the cill and the boats are prevented from grounding. The ability to construct non-tidal basins long predates the Roman period and excavations have unearthed one dating from the Bronze Age, at Lothal on the River Indus, in Pakistan. The dock was modified c2300 BC which places its original construction earlier.

It was built by the Harappans, and was the largest baked-brick structure ever built by those people. The dock is trapezoidal in plan with brick-built walls enclosing an excavated basin. This basin was fed with water through an inlet channel, and the excess water was allowed to escape over a spillway. The inlet was 40 ft wide and over 65 ft long. At high tide when the gate was opened, two ships could be sluiced through at once. The main dock was 705 ft x 121 ft.

Native ships on the Arabian, Indian and Pakistan coasts have not changed much in the last few thousand years, and the ships which docked at Lothal would have closely resembled modern Arab dhows. At the port of Gogha, an early historical port on the Kathiawar coast, sailing vessels of the dhow type still dock. There is no water-locking arrangement at this port and the dhows

This photograph of an unidentified creek, possibly in Lincolnshire, shows the amount of traffic handled by even tiny rivers.

sit ignominiously at low tide on the mud bottom of the harbour, whereas 4,000 years ago, their Bronze Age predecessors floated proudly and professionally in the non-tidal basin at Lothal.

Roman period British harbours may have contained other structures which depended on water-level differentials for their operation. These were dry-docks. The Romans made extensive use of them in the Mediterranean for ship repair, and occasionally a ship was built inside such a dock. Modern ships could be built inside dry-docks, but that system is expensive as the dock relies on ship repairs for its income. Ships are usually built on a slipway and slide into the water at an advanced state of construction. Small ships such as trawlers can be winched up slipways on wheeled cradles for repairs. Phoenician and Greek warships, when not in use, were drawn out of the water up greased ramps into their ship-sheds.

In antiquity, the simplest way to repair or replace underwater parts of a ship was to beach the vessel and wait until the tide went out. This was difficult in the Mediterranean where the tides are very small so the Romans constructed floodable, gated chambers into which a ship was moved, the gate closed and the water pumped out.

Athenaeus of Naucritus writing c200 BC wrote about the invention of dry-docks:

"A Phoenician conceived the method of launching by digging a trench under the ship near the harbour, equal in length to the ship. He constructed for this trench, foundations of solid stone 7½ ft in depth,

Fish-traps were simple and inexpensive devices like this one on the River Severn. This technique has been used for thousands of years. Expensive barriers such as weirs have naturally been used as fish-traps and this has confused the original purpose of the structures.

and from one end of these foundations to the other he fixed a row of skids, which ran transversely to the stones across the width of the trench, leaving a space below them 6 ft deep, and having dug a sluice from the sea, he let the sea into all the excavated space, filling it full."

Obviously, this explains the launching of the ship. He then goes on to describe what must have been the entry into the same dock, of a ship for repair:

"Into this space he easily brought the vessel, with the help of unskilled men, and when they had barred the entrance which had been opened up at the beginning, they again pumped out the seawater with engines, and when this had been done, the ship rested securely on the skids beforementioned."

Cicero mentions a man called Hermodorus of Salamis: "who flourished in Rome, and was a builder of dry-docks (*navalia*)"

Boats were built in simple riverside dry-docks in Britain in the early nineteenth century, and one of Constable's paintings entitled *Boat-building near Flatford Mill* (1814), shows a barge nearing completion in a dry-dock which is merely an excavated hole in the bank of the Suffolk River Stour. The barge rests on transverse timbers across the bottom of the dock, and a wooden gate in the closed position in the painting will allow the dock to be flooded for the launching of the completed barge.

If Athenaeus of Naucritus had built his dry-dock in Britain, he wouldn't have needed a pump to drain it. He could have moved the ship in at high tide and merely left the gate open, closing it at low tide.

It will be seen that a

Aviation fuel on its 750 mile river journey up the River Tocantins to the Brazilian airfield at Carolina. This river is dangerous and riddled with rapids. Progress was slow and time after time, the big drums had to be unloaded to make the river boats light enough to be hand-hauled through the swirling waters.

On the first leg of the trip, from Belem to Maraba, five trans-shipments had to be made. Each time, the drums had to be heaved up the bank and hand-rolled around the rapids. At one spot, the job was made easier by a little wood-burning railway. At another, a truck was used. At a third spot, the undergrowth was too dense for the drums to be carried overland so they were dragged through the water. At Maraba, the drums were transferred to smaller, more agile craft, but the endless unloading-hauling-loading sequence continued. The author thinks that the Brazilian hauliers of the River Tocantin would regard minor British rivers as easy transport routes. No doubt the Romans thought so too.

dry-dock is a very similar device to a pound-lock, the invention of which is attributed to Chiao Wei-Yo, assistant commissioner for transport, on a section of the Grand Canal of China in the year AD 983. This was 250 ft long and was built on the West River near Huai-yin. It had a guillotine gate of the type to be seen on modern locks on the River Nene.

In Europe, the first recorded use of the pound-lock is AD 1373 at Vreeswijk, in Holland. This also had a vertically-rising gate. It looks as if the Romans may have used pound-locks long before either the Chinese or Dutch. As yet there is no firm evidence, but there are many Roman riverside sites and Roman canals just waiting to be excavated.

The main difference between a dry-dock and a pound-lock is that the dry-dock has a gate, or gates, at one end whereas the pound-lock has gates at both ends. The function of a dry-dock is for ship repair or shipbuilding and the pound-lock for raising or lowering vessels from one level in a canal or river to another. Before we consider the use of pound-locks, we must look at more primitive methods of rendering waterways navigable but for now let us return to Sunderland and the mouth of the River Wear.

A Roman fort has long been suspected at Sunderland but never confirmed. In 1873, Mr John Moore inspected foundations of an ancient building at the north end of Castle Street. The walls were four feet thick and Mr Moore was of the opinion that the workmanship was Roman. Some years ago, an inscribed stone and many Roman coins were found when old houses were demolished in the same Castle Street and a Roman road was uncovered during modern road improvements at Low Row. A Roman ford is suspected in line with this road, in the river at Deptford. The Castle Street site is quite close to the gill which would have made an ideal inner harbour. In 1849, when the river entrance to Sunderland dock was being dug, the remains of a Roman pottery were found. Specimens of pottery were presented by Mr Meik to the Newcastle Antiquarian Society and to Sunderland Museum.

An unlocated Roman fort called "Dicti" is mentioned in the *Ravenna Cosmography"* (which was compiled in the seventh century and based on Roman sources) and the entry appears between "Arbeia" (South Shields) and Concangis (Chester-le-Street) so it looks as if it is in County Durham. Further mention will be made of this later; meanwhile we must consider the navigation of the River Wear inland from Sunderland.

To help understand the problems of the use of the River Wear for transport in Roman times, we can be assisted by later navigators of the river who have left facts and figures. These were the keelboatmen who provided the link between inland riverside coal staithes and sea-going colliers waiting to load at Sunderland. At one period, 250 keels were in operation on the river.

Before we go into the details of the seventeenth, eighteenth and nineteenth-century coal trade, a local fable may throw a chink of light on Dark Age navigators of the river. Tradition has it that a sea-monster dwelt in the River Wear in the vicinity of the Lambton Estate which is just downstream from Chester-le-Street (Saxon Conceastre). Children sing songs about the beast which is known as the "Lambton Worm."

The monster was supposed to devour cattle and slay riverside inhabitants.

It is interesting to note that the Saxon word *wurm* means "dragon." It is possible that the terrible monster was a Viking "dragon-ship" with its fearsome serpent's figure-head and snake-tail stern decoration. Conceastre had been founded by Saxon monks who fled from Lindisfarne because of Viking attacks. Fourteen miles from the sea, they thought they were safe, but had to flee again because of Norse raids into the Wear. According to legend, another similar monster, the "Sockburn Worm," frequented the River Tees. Were the "dragon-ships" raiding that river too? The Viking ships drew only about two feet of water and could penetrate well inland. If they came to un-navigable stretches, the raiders dragged their ships overland on logs.

In the seventeenth century the coalowners could not sink their pits more than five miles from navigable water because of the high cost of transport to the river. Packhorses are recorded as carrying 2 cwt (102 kg) and carts 8 cwt (407 kg). These modes of transport were abandoned very early for the "wain" which carried 17 cwt (864 kg). The wain was drawn by two horses and two oxen. In the mid-seventeenth century, horse-drawn wagons which ran on primitive wooden rails began to replace the wains, and these wagons (chaldrons) transported coal from the mines to the staithes where keels (coal barges; *cyul* = Saxon for "ship") were each loaded with 21 tons for the downstream run to Sunderland and the waiting colliers. Each wagon, pulled by only one horse, could make 2½ trips per day on a five mile run between mine and staithe whereas a wain, with four draught animals could complete only one return journey. The chaldron's load was 2½ tons.

The rule for the coal industry was that you used sea transport wherever possible, inland water where you couldn't, and land transport (prior to the development of iron rails and the invention of the steam engine) only for very short distances, otherwise the operation went bankrupt. The Elizabethan tycoon Thomas Sutton bought up Leicestershire coal for the London market in an attempt to undercut Tyneside's product. The River Trent should have allowed him to do this but his colliery at Coleorton was eight miles from the river and this short land journey increased his costs out of proportion and defeated his plans. He sold out very quickly.

In Bath, Tyne coal coming 400 miles by sea and canal undercut Mendip coal which travelled only twelve miles by road.

During a coal shortage in Bordeaux in the eighteenth century, the Marquis de Solage sent an experimental load six miles from Carmaux by road and 200 miles by inland water. A Tyne collier beat his cargo to Bordeaux and he made a very heavy loss on the operation. These examples demonstrate the high costs of the pre-railway era land transport. Historians often quote the Silk Road as an example of long distance road transport but commercial roads of that type were used only for luxuries of the very highest value. They could not have coped with vast quantities of heavy or bulky loads. Mail, diamonds and pharmaceutics go as air-cargo today; coal, oil, grain and ore go by ship.

I am grateful to Dr Eric Clavering, writing to me from Atherstone, for bringing my attention to the fact that, in addition to the likelihood of the River Wear being used for the supply of Roman forts, an even greater use by the Romans may have been for exports. He points out that imperial traffic is centripetal whether it be Red Indian furs or Aztec gold. He sees a function of the Chester-le-Street Roman fort as a gathering point for lead exports.

Next, we must look at the known navigation difficulties encountered by the keelmen of the coal trade, and then look for evidence of earlier attempts by the Romans to solve the same problems.

The Roman fort of Concangis at Chester-le-Street, fourteen miles upstream from Sunderland, is just above the present Spring tidal limit of the Wear. Due to isostasy, the Romans would have experienced tides very slightly higher, so the siting of the fort was probably because of the Spring tide limit and the juction with the River Cone or Cong Burn (Roman Con) which conveniently led from the main river right to the gate of the fort.

Over a thousand years after the Roman military departure from Britain, the coal industry began as a light-periodic trade but became a heavy-scheduled one. The first staithes on the Wear were at Picktree, which is a mile downstream from Chester-le-Street, and the coal was cleared by keels only on Spring tides. These special-purpose barges were equipped with sails, poles and sculling sweeps, but they relied on the flood-tide to bring them up to Picktree. On occasion they resorted to tows by horses.

Burleigh and Thompson's map of 1737 shows that between the fourteenth-century bridge just upstream from Picktree, and Biddick two miles downstream, there were three places where there was only one foot of water at Low Spring tide. The keelmen therefore, between Biddick and Picktree, could not negotiate the river without the help of tides.

In 1739, John Millett who owned Whitehill colliery just to the west of Chester-le-Street, explained his problems to a parliamentary committee. He had free access to the nearest point of the Wear 1½ miles away but that was

British army boats in the Falkland Islands in 1983. Until the Royal Engineers built the roads, everything went by helicopter or boat. The army had more boats than the navy and the waterborne soldiers were the modern equivalent of the *Barcarii Tigrisenses*.

above the head of the tide. Millett could not gain access to Biddick with a wagonway so he converted his coal to coke to lighten it. He could not compete with collieries further downstream, which were transporting their coal on wooden wagonways to Biddick which was navigable from the sea on all high tides.

There were further depth problems downstream. Although there was 14½ ft of water at low tide at Hylton Ferry, only four miles from the sea (the deepest point of the river), only 250 yards downstream, it rapidly shoaled to 2½ ft and to only one foot at Baron's Quay. From there to the modern Alexandra Bridge, there was only three feet of water at low tide. In 1760, sea-going colliers loaded only half of their cargo from keels in Sunderland harbour and then moved out over the bar into the roads to take on the rest.

In these days of sophisticated transport, the car driver tends to think that road transport was always easy. He does not see the vast logistical pyramid that has enabled him to switch on his engine and cruise effortlessly along a motorway. Neither does he think about the prospecting for, and the drilling of oil wells in the Middle East, nor the wars, military alignments, and political intrigues necessary to ensure a flow of oil. He does not visualise the fuel's six thousand mile voyage by tanker or De Lessep's Suez Canal which halved the journey, or the complex oil refinery in U.K.

The ancient peoples had to rely on animal transport which was very slow and cripplingly expensive.

During the Industrial Revolution coal industry of the Tyne area, collieries were divided into two classes; sea-coal and land-coal mines. Sea-coal came from mines with close access to the rivers and land-coal from pits further away from navigable water. In 1800, the land-coal mines were on seasonal work and each one employed only ten men or less. The sea-coal enterprises all employed more than a hundred men each.

Changes came about with new technology. Cast iron rails replaced the wooden ones c1767, thus friction for traction was further decreased. Steam engines made their appearance and were first used to pump water out of mines; then they replaced the horse-driven gin-mills for lifting the coal to the surface. After that, stationary steam engines pulled trains of wagons up inclines via cables to points where gravity allowed them to complete controlled descents to river-staithes. Finally, the steam engine itself became mobile and dragged the wagons along the lines. For the first time, land transport could compete with inland water. It was still more expensive, but lines between pit and sea-going collier-staithes bypassed the river keels and eliminated one trans-shipment. New ports like Seaham Harbour, not situated on rivers, sprang up in competition with the river-served harbours. The railway age had arrived. If it had not been for the development of iron rails and mobile steam engines, Britain's transport system would have developed into a vast network of canals and canalised rivers.

When Roman ships arrived in Sunderland, and it is highly likely that they did do, as Ptolemy refers to the mouth of the River Wear as "Vedra Fluvii Ostia," there remained the problem of moving supplies to forts in the hinterland and, if Dr Clavering is right, bringing out exports.

The Roman ship had several possible methods for the onward dispatch of its cargo: it could discharge into lighters either in a non-tidal basin or in the tidal estuary. The latter would have entailed the ship sitting on the river bed at low tides. A third option was open to the Roman captain; he could move up-river at high tide, over the shoal water and anchor in the deep reach at Hylton, where there was sufficient water to float the ship at all stages of all tides. Evidence points towards this last option.

When the keelmen were engaged in the Picktree-Sunderland coal trade, they relied on the flooding tide to carry them upstream and provide depth for loading at Picktree, which meant that they had to commence their journey as soon after low water as possible. At Hylton Ferry, there was an artificial barrier across the river which impeded their progress. The keels had to be manoeuvred through a gap at the southern end of a solid causeway, through which water poured in a torrent at low tide. The structure was finally dismantled at the insistence of the keelmen, in 1865 (*Proceedings of the Society of Antiquarians of Newcastle upon Tyne,* 1884). The local name for the structure was the "Brigstanes" and it was acknowledged by the antiquarians of the period that it was of Roman origin, but they were at a loss as to its function. Except for the rough gap at the southern end, the surviving remains formed a huge solid barrage across the river, lined up south-west to north-east at 45 degrees to the river flow. At a meeting attended by the Sunderland Antiquarians late in the 19th century (date lost from manuscript), the origin of the structure was discussed at great length. The secretary, Mr Blair, read out a letter from the historian, Mr F Haverfield, and in this letter, Haverfield made the following points: an inscribed lead plate (described in *Archaeological Journal,* XL, 1883) was found at a Roman bridge or causeway over the River Wear, and historians Mr Hodges and Mr Robinson had reported that the structure was not a bridge, but a causeway. After hearing the reading of Mr Haverfield's letter, another local historian, the Rev W Featherstonhaugh described how he had interviewed some old inhabitants of the area who remembered the structure before and during its removal. These witnesses described it as a causeway of solid stone masonry extending across the river and raised some feet above its bed. It had formed a substantial dam, over which at ebb tide, the water fell in a considerable cascade. A witness of the destruction said that initially, the masonry was broken into between the centre and the northern shore, and the stones were of massive size, of regular shape, and tied with iron cramps bedded in lead. These stones were laid on oaken piles driven into the bed of the river, and on the lower side, and outside the structure stood piles of greater height. There was a good deal of horizontally laid timber with morticed joints between the piles.

The witness had told Rev Featherstonhaugh that he understood the structure to be a Roman causeway to cross the river, and that it had always been known in his lifetime as the "Brigstuns" or "Brigstanes." The Rev Featherstonhaugh said that this name had caused people to think that this structure had been a Roman bridge, but he went on to point out that Roman bridges were not constructed in this manner - they were never built on level masonry extending across a river; each Roman bridge pier had an independent foundation on the river bed. He came to the conclusion that the structure was a built-ford, a level causeway of solid masonry, possibly protected on the lower side by a massive open rail or parapet.

The name "Brigstanes" does not necessarily imply a bridge. In County Durham the first railway bridge in the world, built in 1778 survives. It carried an early wooden wagonway over the Beamish Burn. The bridge is called the "Tanfield *arch*" whereas the solid earthen *embankment* close by which carried the later steam railway across the ravine is called the "Tanfield *bridge*."

A meeting in Newcastle upon Tyne in 1884 further discussed the Roman structure. Records were read which mentioned that the "Breakstones" were always dry at low water, leaving a steep channel from twelve to fourteen feet wide at the south side, through which the river rushed with great velocity. This gap had been made by keelmen at an earlier date. It is not known if an engineered spillway or channel already existed at this point.

Some of the lead plates connecting the cramps to the stones had curious markings; one circular metal plate out of one stone had Roman letters and figures raised on the margin. The letters were IM.D.AG.....AVG around the margin, and S.C. or S.G. in the body of the plate. Many stones had finely cut decorations of columns, vine leaves, and castellations. Also, the causeway did not lie straight across the river; it ran at an angle north-east to south-west.

An interesting point was raised at the meeting; if the structure was a ford, then it was a dangerous one. A Mr William Maude was drowned in 1753 when trying to ride over it, and Mr Rowland Burdon was so inconvenienced that it gave him the incentive to prospect the new Sunderland bridge. At the close of the meeting, the purpose of the causeway remained a mystery.

It does not seem to have been known to antiquarians of that period that the Romans had dammed a branch of the Rhine, and that they had built barrages for various purposes at many places in their Empire. The Hylton structure certainly wasn't a bridge; if the Romans could build a three-quarter-mile-long bridge with piers 150 ft high, across the Danube, they wouldn't build a causeway over the Wear with three times the amount of stone needed for a bridge. Also rivers were regarded as public property and blocking them to navigation was forbidden under Roman law; therefore any barrage must have been either *to assist* navigation or have had a bypass around it.

The site of the Hylton dam is at NZ 351 570 and lay between the present "Golden Lion" public house on the south bank of the river and the "Shipwrights" on the north. To the west of the Shipwrights inn is a very large old quarry cut into the cliffs. This is probably the source of the massive amount of stone for the Roman causeway.

The position of the barrage defeats the argument that it was a built-up ford. This is the deepest part of the river for miles and, just 250 yards dowstream, shallows with only one to three feet of water at low tide, extended to Sunderland.

The usual mention of fish-traps has been made, some unfortunately from people of academic standing. Do they really believe that salmon fishermen of old could afford the equivalent of multi-million pound structures? No doubt the dam *was used* as a fish-trap, as were all other barriers across rivers both natural and man-made. A purpose-built fish-trap usually consisted of a few wooden stakes with wicker baskets between.

Why build a fish-trap at a place where the river was over fourteen feet deep at low tide, when there were extensive shallows of one to three feet beginning only a few hundred yards away? The fourteenth-century bridge at Newbridge, above Picktree is built in the typical mediaeval manner with its piers standing on a massive sloping ramp which forms an artificial waterfall. This ramp is the present limit of Spring tides. As a small boy, I used to lift fish out of the river at the base of the ramp, and an excellent fish-trap it was and still is, but it was not built for that purpose.

Let us now visualise our Roman ship lying at Hylton in the deep water below the barrage. Originally, a gate may have been installed in the gap at the south end. If this gate were left open, the flooding tide would pour through and at High Spring tides perhaps go over the crest. If the gate were closed at High tide, the river would remain navigable to keel-sized barges all the way to Chester-le-Street, and remain navigable after the tide below the dam ebbed, thus obviating the need to stick to tide times for the run to Picktree. As the moon circles the earth once per month, the tides are fifty minutes later each day and can occurr at very unsocial hours. With a barrier turning the whole river upstream into an elongated non-tidal basin, regular daylight navigation routines could have been established by the lightermen.

A single gate in a river barrier is known as a flash-lock and is an ancient device. It was known to the Romans and used on the Tiber and elsewere. The disadvantage was that when the gate was opened, the river above the barrier drained away quite violently in a "flash-flood" for a while. A barge proceeding upstream could be winched through the gap against this flood and when through the barrier, the gate was closed. The river level above the gated-barrier would then rise and the barge could proceed upstream to the next "flash-lock." Bargemen coming downstream would open the gate and lower the river level before negotiating the aperture but some were tempted to shoot the artificial rapids and many lives were lost. Often, a barrage across a river, known as a dam or weir served the dual purpose of ponding back water for navigation and also providing a head of water for a mill-wheel. There was a conflict of interests between the bargemen and the millers. The lightermen had to transit the barriers and the miller needed to keep a head of water to power his wheel. Many quarrels ensued and in dry weather, bargees often had to wait several days before the miller would agree to open the gate.

If our Roman dam at Hylton had been equipped with two sets of gates, one at the upstream end of the gap and the other at the downstream end, the river above the barrier could have remained at a level equal to permanent high tide and barges could have negotiated the dam without lowering the river level upstream. According to the little information available, it is likely that any such gates would have been of the lifting "guillotine" type. The chamber enclosed by the gates is what is known today as a "pound-lock" and those in modern use are small versions of the massive engineering structures of the Panama canal, described earlier. Lifting gates do not need underground sluices or the controllable apertures of "mitre-gates."

If a barrage across a river is used for navigation, it is usually called a "weir." If impounded water is used to drive a water-mill, the head of water was originally called the "dam" but this now also refers to the masonry structure. The leat which takes water to a mill-wheel is called the head-race, and the channel which leads the spent water back to the river is called the tail-race. The operation of a postualted Roman pound-lock might have been as follows:

The Roman merchant ship is anchored in midstream, or tied to a jetty below the weir, and has discharged some of its cargo to barges. The first barge is ready to transit the lock in the weir. The bottom gate is lifted slightly so that any water inside the chamber from a previous operation, or from leakage of the upper gate, surges under the gate. When the water-level in the lock equals that of the river below the weir, the gate is lifted fully, the barge pulled into the chamber and the door closed behind it. The upper gate is then lifted slightly and water flooding underneath soon raises the level in the chamber to that of the river above the weir. The gate is then fully lifted and the barge proceeds upstream. The upper gate is now closed and the lock is ready for the operation to be repeated with a second barge. For downstream traffic the processes are reversed. The river surface above the weir is kept at a constant level by an overflow spillway let into the rim of the structure, and navigation upstream is possible at all times except in serious flood conditions.

If the simpler flash-lock was used, the single gate would have made the operation more tedious. The gate would have been opened and the head of water above the weir released downstream. When the torrent subsided, the barge could be winched or dragged through the lock and the gate closed behind it. The barge could then proceed upstream as the river level rose again. With a flash-lock, it is likely that several barges would have transitted the lock at one opening. At High Spring tide, the gate could have been left open for a while.

The Latin word *cataracta* has two meanings: "waterfall" and "portcullis." When used to describe a lifting water-gate, the word combines both meanings.

Two other methods of negotiating a river barrier were available to the Romans. They could have used an inclined plane, which is a dry ramp up which the barge could be dragged from the low river level below the weir to the high level above. I know of no Roman reference that even hints at the use of such a device. It is unlikely that such a system was used at places like Hylton where there was no shortage of water. The operation of a pound-lock requires no effort except the lifting of the gates, and in the case of the flash-lock, the opening of the gate plus the effort of dragging the barge against the current through the gap.

Perhaps the Roman weir had no lock or gate at all and the cargo was manhandled from the ship below the weir to barges above it. Such systems are still in use in Africa.

After the Hylton weir's removal in 1865, some of the stone was rumoured to have been dumped out at sea. This is difficult to believe as ashlar stone is very expensive. Some of the stones were deposited in Lister's shipyard and it is thought that several barge-loads went to Seaham Harbour for construction work at the new port. Before recent river bank improvements at Hylton, many ex-Roman stones could be seen in the old quay which served the Hylton ferry-boat. One Roman stone can still be seen on a gate-post at North Hylton Farm and more were reported in the *Sunderland Echo*, June 4th, 1992, to have been re-used in the old Blacken Factory in High Wood. Suspected

Roman stones from the weir can be seen on the beach in front of the pilot house which stands on the inner mole on the north side of the river in Sunderland harbour. The stones are massive and have lewis-holes and butterfly-cramp recesses.

The dredger *Hercules* removed further debris from the river bed at Hylton in 1881 and no doubt this was the spoil reported to have been dumped at sea.

On Penshaw Hill close to the River Wear, there stands a monument which is a near replica of the Doric temple of Theseus in Athens. Seemingly well-informed locals will tell you that it commemorates the slaying of the "Lambton Worm" monster, but it was built in 1844 in honour of John George Lambton, 1st Earl of Durham and the first Governor-General of Canada. Most of the stone for the monument came from a quarry on the east side of the hill but the building has a few possible ex-Roman stones complete with lewis-holes. These holes were not used by cranes during the monument's construction as some of the stones have been recut and the holes are not on the point of balance. It is possible that the stones came from the Hylton weir (by barge?) when the keelmen made, or enlarged, the first cut in the structure before the massive demolition of 1865.

An interesting feature of the hill is the helical track from base to top. A local legend tells us that this was the mark made by the giant monster as it curled around the hill but it is actually the easy-gradient road constructed so that stone-laden carts could get to the top. Unlike modern vehicles, carts had no gears but the equivalent was to provide an elongated incline and extend the time taken for an ascent, thus reducing the *rate* at which work was done. The *trekpads* of South Africa are a typical example. The Roman roads mostly ignored gradients, as on the terribly steep hill from the River Witham in Lincoln up to their fort, now under the cathedral.

Our Roman barge is still lying just above the weir at Hylton so we must now trace its probable progress to Chester-le-Street and beyond. There is sufficient water above the Hylton weir to get it to Picktree but there may have been an intermediate weir between. In the mediaeval period, a profuse number of barriers sprung up in rivers, many of them ramshackle fish-traps. *Summer's History of Sunderland,* Vol 1, refers to them as *Yares.* The book quotes: "These yares were not only a hindrance to the free passage of salmon and other fish up the river but also obstructed the passage of ships, vessels, boats and keels."

The yare on the Tyne near Whickham was destroyed c1300 by men of Prudhoe. Summer goes on to quote:

"In 1440, Bishop Neville ordered the reduction or removal of the following yares; Robert Jackson for Marle and Chestan yares, John Wessington (Prior of Durham) for Drilad and Eb yares, John Hedworth for Owen's yare, Lord Lumley for Outlaw yare, William Bowes, knight, for Rowden and Biddick yares, and Robert Hilton, knight, for Wediles and Synden yares."

Two of these yares may be reused Roman structures. On the river bed opposite Lambton Castle, the remains of a curved stone dam can be seen from the air. It is completely submerged at high tide. The other is Lord Lumley's yare which may be part of the suspected Chester-le-Street Roman navigation complex. We will come to that as we progress up the river.

If the ruinous structure abeam Lambton Castle had a Roman origin, then it may have served as an intermediate weir between Hylton and Chester-le-Street. Such a weir would have raised the river-level all the way to the suspected Roman basin below the Roman fort. The weir would have acted also as insurance if the Hylton structure contained a flash-lock, so that barges above the Lambton Castle weir would not have been affected by an opening of the Hylton gate. Further upstream as we approach Picktree, there is an intact keelboat jetty which consists of a large oak tree-trunk fixed in the eastern bank at NZ 287 526. The OS map of 1850 marks a gin-crane at this point. This is just a few hundred yards above the present limit of Ordinary tides.

Slightly further upstream, we come to Picktree Quay Wood, so-named because of the keelboat staithes and an old wagonway which served them. We are still two miles from the known Roman fort of Concangis which is situated under the Chester-le-Street parish church and its Saxon predecessors. The wooden Saxon cathedral was founded in 883 and the Bishop's seat was moved to Durham in 995 where the "White Church" was built. The Norman cathedral was later built on this site.

Concangis is dated by artefacts to c120, and an earlier Roman settlement has long been suspected in the vicinity. Such a suspected fort was spotted from the air at Picktree close to the river at NZ 280 530 and just above Picktree Quay Wood. It looks as if the builders of the early Roman fort may have come up with the same answers to transportation problems as the keelmen. The suspected Picktree fort would have been accessible to Roman barges on High Spring tides before weirs at Hylton and Lambton were built. Navigation improvements would have enabled the later fort to be located a mile further upstream where the confluence of the rivers provided excellent ingredients for a barge basin. Many Roman coins have been recovered at Picktree. A potato-picker in 1945 found a gold one on the surface of the field at NZ 283 523, just west of the fourteenth-century bridge, and when the A1(M) Motorway was constructed, a detector-equipped workman found a profusion in the copse on the east side of the A1(M) at NZ 281 527 and just a few yards south of the crop mark of the suspected Picktree fort.

On the west side of the A1(M), in a strip wood on a slope at NZ 276 530, a suspected Roman road, heading west, leads first down a hollow-way and then onto an artificial ramp constructed from the hollow-way spoil, to a stream crossing. Presumably this is a link road to the main Roman north-south road (Cade's Road) just to the west. The stream just mentioned may be on the line of the canal proposed in 1796 which was to link Durham City with the River Tyne, down the Wear to Picktree and then via a canal. The canal was never built, but dare I suggest that the Romans had already beaten the eighteenth century planners to it? I quote from R Dodd's *Report* of 1796:

"The fecond part of the line is from the River Wear, near Picktree, to Redheugh in the River Tyne, nearly oppofite to Newcastle, containing 7 miles 2 furlongs and 6 chains, and lies down the beautiful Vale of Team; the lower part of which, near the River Tyne is fo flat, that after locking up from the river fouthwards, one lock will carry us nearly 3 miles, as may be feen by the profile of levels on the plan. Still purfuing this vale fouthwards for the purpofes of navigation, I find it rifes to the height of 91 feet 7 inches above high water mark; but as the extreme height of this is but a few chains in length, I recommend a little deep cutting to reduce it to 80 feet, fo that 10 eight feet locks will enable us to afcend its height; with the like number to defcend; the principal part of this cutting will be, in croffing the road from Durham to Newcaftle, near Sir John Eden's waggon-way, the line then defcends through a deep hollow-way, part of it like a canal already cut, and abounding with fprings of water; it then curves a little to the eaftward, and enters the navigable part of the River Wear, near Picktree." Thus two great rivers are joined by only 7 miles 2 furlongs and 6 chains, canal navigation."

Is it a coincidence that we have found a Roman site on the same line? The Eighteenth-century proposed Durham-Tyne Canal was never built, but the stream to the west of the Picktree site and a massive unexplained dry ditch which descends the wood to the river on the east, should be investigated for signs of Roman artefacts or workmanship.

The crop mark site of the possible early Roman fort at Picktree still has to be proved by excavation, so let us continue with the suspected slightly later Roman navigation of the river up to the known fort of Concangis, in the centre of Chester-le-Street.

Above Picktree, the present limit of Spring tides is the barrier-ramp-waterfall upon which the fourteenth century bridge at Newbridge is built. Just below this bridge, in tidal water, is an ancient ford known as "Bruggeford." The paving, consisting of stones set on edge, can still be seen at the eastern side of the river. Tradition has it that there was a Saxon chapel here. Several reused Roman stones are built into field walls in the vicinity.

I have heard historians argue that you cannot have fords across tidal rivers. Nonsense: at Lindisfarne, off the Northumberland coast, the road to the offshore island, usable only at low tide, runs along the sea bed. There is even an airfield in Britain where scheduled aircraft have to wait for the tide to go out before they can land; at Barra, in the Hebrides, the runway is on the beach and pilots usually touchdown at Islay or Tiree Airports to wait for the Barra tide to ebb.

Above Newbridge, and beyond the new A1(M) motorway bridge, is the old loop of the river containing the town sewage works where the suspected Roman weir was destroyed in 1930. This weir, just below the confluence of the Wear and the Cone, could have ponded both rivers back into a barge basin below the fort, and a suspected canal (which I used to bump through on my sledge) headed onwards from the basin towards the river upstream to yet another river barrier at NZ 283 512. The latter is the site of the "Lumley Fish-Locks" and possibly one of the yares ordered by Bishop Neville in 1440, to be reduced in size. The structure was removed a few years ago and replaced by a concrete ridge to deepen the river upstream for a water inlet to a sewerage plant at Lumley.

The old barrier had been a curved weir just above the mouth of the Lumley Park Burn which joined the Wear from the east. On the west side of the river were the old fish-locks which served in the 1930's 40's and 50's as a childrens' paddling pool and, in more distant times, probably as locks for bigger water-travellers than salmon. They are now filled with rubble and concrete. Records also tell us that opposite the Lumley Park Burn, a water-channel left the locks on a westerly heading and terminated in a dead end. Fish were driven up this blind alley and then caught. This channel was on the line of the suspected canal which left the fort in the direction of the fish-locks. Close by, Roman cremation urns were found when the bowling-greens were made in the 1930's in the town park.

In 1771, much of the original dam was swept away by the great flood of that year, but the engineer John Smeaton who happened to be in the area, suggested methods of rebuilding it. The dam was further damaged in 1795 and again in 1814. In 1854, yet more damage encouraged fishermen from upstream to destroy it completely, making Lord Scarborough of Lumley Castle, very angry.

Old drawings show that the repaired weir was a very rough affair. In the western bank however, about a hundred yards upstream from the modern concrete ramp, a little digging in the bankside exposes some excellent sloping masonry which seems to be the end of the original curved dam. The workmanship is first class and could easily be Roman.

From here, the gradient of the river upstream is $7\frac{1}{2}$ feet per mile which is relatively gentle. Let me quote figures from the other side of the Atlantic. During George Washington's presidency of the United States of America, he championed the case for rendering the wild Potomac River navigable. In 1802, a series of five pound-locks allowed fifty-foot-long, 1,500 lb (682 kg) boats carrying 20-ton loads, to negotiate the 77 ft high Great Falls. At Little Falls, three locks were used to overcome a 38 ft drop, but elsewhere, obstacles were overcome without any locks at all. Rapids and waterfalls were skirted with bypass channels. Instead of building a lock to negotiate the 15 ft drop at Shenandoah Falls, a mile-long bypass sluice was dug which gave an acceptable gradient of 1:352. A very short bypass only 150 ft long at House Falls avoided a three foot waterfall with a gradient of 1:50. The boats were operated by crews of four men who controlled the craft with poles. (*National Geographic Magazine*, Vol 171 No. 6 June 1987).

Opponents of the theory of Roman river navigation of our minor rivers have postualted an impossible number of weirs necessary, but their calculations assume that a weir ponds a river upstream into a perfectly level surface. It does not. The river backs up into a long incline. The Romans would have needed weirs only at severe rapids, waterfalls and dried-out shallows and I estimate that four would have got them from Concangis to Durham. The first above Chester-le-Street must have been at the Lumley Mill rapids. At the bottom of these, the massive stub of the Lumley mill-dam can still be seen (NZ 286 479). Is it a coincidence that the old mill-dams are just in the right places to serve as navigation weirs? The next is at Finchale Priory (NZ 298 472) where twelve Roman utensils dated c140 to 350 were found in the 1920's (Jarrett & Edwards, *Archaeologia Aeliana*, Vol 39, 1961). An old woodcut by Samuel and Nathanial Buck, dated 1728, shows a massive dam just upstream from the priory. Not a stone of the dam remains but post-holes can be seen in conditions of drought. The next is at Rainton Park Wood, (NZ

302 462) where a ruinous curved weir still exists. Further upstream, evidence of Norman narrowing (and deepening) of the channel for stone-laden barges for the construction of Durham Cathedral, still survives. At Kepier (NZ 283 433), beside the mediaeval Leper Hospital, a mill-dam in the river may have had an earlier origin. The name is derived from *kep* (catch) so once again, a dam for some other purpose (recorded mill-dam in this case) has been used as a fish-trap.

The river in Durham City is navigable because of a weir of unknown age below Prebend's Bridge. This weir provides sufficient depth of water for the 40 ton, 150 passenger-steamer *Prince Bishop*, to operate on a two mile stretch between Prebend's Bridge and just below the Iron Age hill-fort at Maiden Castle. Dozens of pleasure boats and Durham University's racing boats also use the same reach.

Durham Cathedral sits on a high rock almost entirely surrounded by water. The Saxon White Church occupied the site before the cathedral and there may have been a Roman fort there before that, as Roman pottery has been found in the cathedral gardens. The old name for Durham is "*Dunholm.*" (*Dun* = rock, *holm* = island) There is a tradition that at one time, the neck of the peninsula was cut by a water-channel. This explains better the old name.

Beyond Durham, there are several possible ex-navigation weirs in the river, yet to be investigated. High on the list is a line of piles and an old by-pass channel at Spring Wood (NZ 363 245). The suspected Roman navigation complex at Binchester (Vinovia) has already been mentioned at length.

Before we look at any more suspected Roman waterways handiwork, let us examine some of their known systems right throughout their Empire.

A well-documented canal existed alongside the Appian Way near Tarracine. The Roman poet Horace has left us an amusing account of this canal during a journey from Rome to Brindisi:

"Next we reached the Forum of Appius, swarming with sailors and knavish tavern keepers. We felt lazy enough to cut this stretch in two, whereas travellers who gird up their loins take it in one go. The Appian Way is less tiring to those who are not in a hurry. There, by reason of the water, which was frightful, my stomach and I were on hostile terms and I waited with some impatience for my companions, who were dining.

Already the shadows of night were beginning to creep over the earth, and stars were pinpointing in the heavens. Then slaves bellowed at boatmen and boatmen at slaves - 'Heave to here, you've got three hundred in! Stop! That's enough.' After the fares had been collected and the mule harnessed, a whole hour went by. The cursed mosquitoes and the frogs of the marshland drove off sleep. Whereupon after their fill of poor wine, a boatmen and a passenger vied in singing of the girl each of them had left behind. At length, the weary passengers fell asleep and the lazy boatman unharnessed his mule and let it out to graze, tying its leading rein to a stone. Then he too started to snore away on his back, and it was already daylight when we found that the boat was not yet under way, so one of us, a hot-headed fellow, jumped ashore and, with a stick cut from a willow, belaboured head and back of both mule and boatman. At last, upon the fourth hour, no earlier, we came ashore.

We washed face and hands in thy waters, O Feronia."

Although Horace did not think much of the canal, it is interesting to note that the barge, towed by one mule, carried three hundred passengers. It would have taken between sixty and a hundred wheeled vehicles to carry them along the roads.

Roman historians Suetonius and Tacitus mention the "Fossa Druisiana," a military canal constructed by Drusus' troops. The canal linked the Rhine to the Yssel and was flooded by a dam across the Rhine's northern arm diverting water into it. An expedition of AD 15 under Drusus' son Germanicus used the canal. Tacitus gives an account:

"Germanicus himself put four legions on ship-board and conveyed them through the lakes, and the infantry, cavalry and fleet met simultaneously at the river already mentioned (Ems)."

Tacitus also describes Germanicus' campaign of AD 17 and mentions the canal again:

"By this time the fleet had arrived and Caesar, having sent on his supplies, and assigned vessels for the legions and the allied troops, entered the Fossa Drusiana, as it was called, and he arrived after a prosperous voyage through the lakes and the ocean as far as the River Amisia (Ems)."

The Roman historian Strabo refers to canals built in the second century BC across the plains to the south of the River Po. He remarks:

"Scaurus drained the plains by running navigable canals from the Padus (Po) as far as Parma, for near Placentia, the Padus is joined by the Trebia, as also before that by several other rivers, and is thus made excessively full."

Pliny the Elder identifies a number of canals by name: Fossa Flavia, Fossa Philistina, Fossa Clodia, Fossa Carbonaria and Fossa Augusta. The last-named linked the Padus to the Roman port of Ravenna, the home port of the Roman Adriatic fleet.

An inscription discovered at Este in 1907 refers to a Roman canal associated with the Adige near Ferrara and Padua, and describes the construction by a body of soldiers. It reads:

"The squad of Quintus Arruntius Sura, acting under the orders of Quintus Arruntius Sura and Gaius Sabellus and under contract to Titus Arrius, built a work, a total of 4,214 ft long each, of 98 men building 43 ft each."

In times of peace, it seems that, in order to keep the soldiers usefully occupied, they were employed in the construction of canals, for Tacitus says of Corbulo:

"To keep his soldiers free from sloth, he dug a canal of twenty-three miles in length between the Rhine and the Meuse, as a means of avoiding the uncertain perils of the ocean."

The rivers of Gaul were extremely important to the Romans for both military and civil transport, and Arles was a commercial centre where cargoes were trans-shipped from ships to barges. From Arles, the Fossa Mariana ran south-east to the Mediterranean. Another important water transport centre in Gaul was Narbonne, and many inscriptions refer to the *navicularii* (shipowners). Narbonne was an inland town and Roman inland ports were quite common.

Excellent pictorial evidence comes from Trajan's Column in Rome. This monument was designed and built by Roman engineer and architect, Apollodorus, to commemorate the Emperor Trajan's campaigns. It has a spiral frieze 656 ft long, carved into the marble. In 1874, Mr John Hungerford Pollen described the information displayed on this column, and he mentions the *Scaphae Onerariae*, a fleet of small boats for transport on the Danube, under the command of the *Classis Pannonica*, the Roman Danube fleet. Pollen vividly describes a scene from the column which leaves us in no doubt about the importance and vast scale of Roman river navigation:

"Immense activity is shown in the landing of stores and other preparations in this advance, probably for a second passage of the Danube by a separate portion of the Roman army. Convoys of large transport boats are seen bringing stores of all kinds, which are landed by soldiers of the garrison. Besides corn, the first vessel carries stores of arms, shields and armour. The boats are protected by *liburnae*, light vessels of war, carrying two or three banks of oars. Sacks of grain are seen corded carefully over. The vessel in front has two banks of oars. It carries a small poop covered by an awning for the commanding officer. It is steered by broad-bladed paddles on either quarter. The stern-post curves over the top of the poop awning and ends in an ornament composed of three curves, like three feathers, and a gallery defended by an open-latticed bulwark runs round the raised portion.

Two ranks of rowers pull the oars, the lower ranks with the upper. The upper row of oars are put through the latticed bulwark that protects a gallery running fore and aft the entire length of each side of the vessel. A man in the bows secures the rope by which she is moored.

This armed vessel has entered the port under an arch which stands apparently over the water joining the two ends of a mole, so as to span the entrance with some facility for closing it by means of a chain. The boats represented pass under it. It has one arch in the front, and the ends are pierced by smaller arches. It stands on a dado, has a shallow attic above the arch, on the top is a *quadriga*, a chariot drawn by four horses, intended probably to hold a statue of the conqueror. Outside the arch are other boats following the first one, and others rowing in the opposite direction carrying stores and ammunitions of war to a strong place represented in the next composition. Of those entering the arch, one conveys four horses. It is a smaller boat than the first described and is sculled by one rower. The stern of the boat rises high and turns over; it is square on the end, having bluff bows of the build still in use in Holland. One of the boats rowing away has two rowers and a steerer sitting in the stern, who manages a paddle on the boat's quarter. To this boat there is a flat platform or deck raised on four uprights high enough for the men to walk under. They appear to be soldiers, as two shields are on this platform overhead, and a soldier's knapsack and long-handled pot are hung on one of the uprights."

Mr Pollen goes on to describe a river harbour attached to a Roman fort on the Danube:

"In front, men are digging and preparing to fortify an outwork. The outwork, from the cavity in which they work and from which baskets of sand and shingle are being lifted, appears to be intended for a small basin or harbour, such as will be seen completed in other bas-reliefs representing river forts and towns. This basin is being surrounded by walls of hewn masonry which appear just above the ground, and it is separated from the river by only a narrow space of ground through which probably it is intended to cut an opening when the arch is completed."

To complete the picture, the writer describes a Roman dockyard on the Danube:

"A Roman naval building yard is in the further background. Great stores of wood are piled around it, and soldiers, artificers, are seen with mallets and chisels at work on the construction of a boat. They wear their helmets during this operation, and the place is perhaps dangerously open to attack."

Whilst on the subject of Roman navigation of the Danube, this is an appropriate place to mention the Roman solution to the navigation problems of the Djerdap (Iron Gates) where the river tumbles down rapids and waterfalls at the bottom of a deep gorge which has vertical cliffs dropping into the water.

The Romans cut a road into the face of the cliff on the west side of the river (the Roman frontier), just above the water, and widened it with an extension of planks supported on horizontal timbers which projected from holes cut into the cliff face. It was not understood why the Romans went to such great lengths to build a peculiar road like this until fairly recently when a Roman canal was found which had bypassed the dangerous rapids. The peculiar road was a towpath for the navigable sections of the gorge.

A recently discovered inscription of Trajan attests the construction of the canal in the Iron Gates (András Mócsy, *Pannonia and Upper Moesia*):

"ob periculum cataractarum derivato flumine tutam Danuvi navigationem fecit."

The 2½ mile canal was divided into sections and these were topped-up by streams via flood-gates. It is not known what type of locks the canal contained. The fort of Ducis Pratum lies at the eastern end of the canal, and a fort and signal-station of unknown name at the western end. There are further forts upstream and downstream and a second signal-station sits on an island 2 miles downstream from the bottom end of the canal.

Although we still do not know what type of locks the Romans have been using, they have demonstrated their ability to negotiate changes in levels of water. The next evidence is from the Roman province of Bithynia (northern Turkey) where cAD 112, the governor, Pliny the Younger, wished to construct a canal which was obviously not going to be a straightforward level ditch. The correspondence between Pliny and Emperor Trajan, survives:

[Pliny to Emperor Trajan]

"It seems to me as I survey the sublimity of your station and ambition, wholly appropriate to bring to your notice, works which are worthy of your immortal name no less than your glory: and likely to possess magnificence with utility.

There is a sizeable lake in the area of Nicomedia across which marble, farm produce, wood and timber are easily and cheaply conveyed by boats right up to the main road, from which, with great effort, and even greater expense, carts take them to the sea. To connect the lake with the sea would require a lot of labour, but there is no shortage of that in this area. There are many people in the countryside and even more in the town, and it seems that everyone would gladly help with such a scheme which would benefit them all.

It remains for you, if you agree, to send an architect or engineer to determine by an accurate survey whether the lake is higher than the sea. The local experts say that it is 40 cubits (60 ft) above sea-level. In the same place, I have looked at an old canal dug by a former King of Bithynia, but whether this was intended to drain the surrounding fields or to join the lake with the sea, is not clear, since it was left unfinished. It is also uncertain whether the work was abandoned because the king died, or because he despaired of finishing it. This however, encourages my desire and enthusiasm - you will bear with me my ambition for you the greater glory - for you to acomplish what kings could only attempt."

[Trajan to Pliny]

"This lake of yours interests me, and I should like to see it connected with the sea, but there must be an accurate survey to find out how much water the lake contains, and the quantity of water that flows in, and from what source, otherwise, once given an outlet, it may completely drain away to the sea. You may apply to Calpurnius Macer for a surveyor and I myself will send you someone with experience in this type of work."

[Pliny to Emperor Trajan]

"You very wisely express the fear sir, that the lake near Nicomedia might be drained away if connected to the river and the sea, but I think I have found a way of avoiding the danger of this. The lake can be brought right up to the river by means of a canal but without actually joining it. A dyke can be left between the two. It will be easy to transfer the cargoes across this narrow dyke."

[Author's note: This leaving of an uncut dyke between two sections of canal has been taken as proof in Britain that the Car Dyke Roman canal was not intended for navigation. On the contrary, an uncut dyke may have been a safety device at a point where accidental damage, sabotage, or a lock-keeper's mistake might have created havoc in the waterway.]

[Pliny's letter continues..]

"This would be one solution, but I hope that it will not be needed, for the lake is fairly deep, and has a river flowing out at the opposite side.

This river could be dammed and diverted wherever we like, so that it would carry off no more water than at present. There are also several more streams along the course of the proposed canal, and the water from these can be used to augment the supply from the lake. If we decide to cut a longer canal, and bring it down to sea level so that the water will flow direct into the sea, the counter pressure from the sea will check the outflow of the lake. Even if we had none of these natural advantages, we could regulate the flow of water by sluices."

[Emperor Trajan to Pliny]

"I can see, my dear Pliny, that you are applying all your energy and intelligence to your lake. You have worked out so many ways of avoiding the danger of its water draining, and making it useful to us in the future. You choose the way you think best and I am sure Calpurnius Macer will send you an engineer, and there is no lack of such experts in the provinces where you are."

Here the correspondence ends and the canal was not completed, very probably because Pliny the Younger died just about this time (AD 113). The correspondence shows however that the Romans were not worried about level changes in artificial watercourses. Unfortunately we do not know if Pliny's use of the word "sluice" referred to a pound-lock or flash-lock gates.

A proposed Roman project in Gaul, which would have needed large water-level changes, was the proposed linkage of the Rivers Moselle and Saône by a canal. The Roman general Lucius Vetus prepared to connect these rivers so that goods could route from the Mediterranean, up the Rivers Rhône and Saône, through the canal, into the Rivers Moselle and Rhine, and then down to the North Sea. When this canal was proposed, the Romans were already making full use of the above rivers for transport, and the linking canal would obviously simplify transport arrangements allowing the same barges to proceed over the watershed without the great expense of a road link and the double trans-shipment of cargoes from barge to wagon and back to barge.

It was the intention of Lucius Vetus to employ soldiers for the construction of this canal, but it was never built because the Legate of Belgica, Aelius Gracilis, owing to jealousy or other motives, persuaded Nero that the use of so many troops for public works in a civilian province would create political and economic problems. A canal over this water-shed was not built until the mid-twentieth century. The exact route of the projected Roman canal is not known but it is fairly certain that the route would have approximated to the modern one, the Canal de l'Est which rises 130 ft in two miles from a point on the Moselle near Epinal to the summit level. This summit level is eight miles long, and then falls 450 ft in thirty miles to the Saône at Corre. The modern canal contains a large number of pound-locks. If the Roman had used flash-locks, the barriers would have been so close together that they would have functioned as pound-locks. The modern definition of a pound-lock is a chamber with opening doors at each end, with walls at the sides linking the gate-posts. Two flash-locks close together still form an effective pound-lock even if the modern definition is not fulfilled exactly.

Next we must look at Roman and other ancient dams because technical details of Roman dam construction will become extremely important when we assess shortly some very strange Roman riverside remains in Britain. The correct identification of civil engineering structures will help to provide answers to the positioning of Roman sites in Britain and elsewhere.

Who built the first dams is not known, but German archaeologists discovered the ruins of one which had impounded a reservoir in the Wadi el-Garawi twenty miles south of Cairo. It was dated to the c2985 BC, in either the Third of Fourth Dynasty. An estimated 100,000 tons of material had been used in its construction.

Many other extremely old dams have been identified all over the Middle-East and by the Roman period, the technology of dam-building was already ancient. It is surprising therefore that the subject of dams in antiquity seems to be shunned by most archaeologists.

Dams serve several purposes and the earliest use was most likely to have been to feed irrigation-channels. Closely related are dams which fed aqueducts for the supply of towns. At some stage, ancient engineers found that a shallow canal could be led from a river-bank at a higher level than the river, across dry land and if the river were dammed just below the junction, water would be diverted into the artificial channel. The canal could be used for transport, to drive water-wheels, flood defensive ditches, and numerous other purposes.

Dams fall into three categories, defined by the methods of resisting the tremendous weight of water. The simplest is a "gravity dam" which is a straight barrier of earth, stone, rubble, concrete or combinations, and resists water pressure by its sheer weight. The second is an "arch dam" and this is curved with the convex side facing upstream. The horizontal arch takes the pressure of the water, just as an arch in a building supports the weight of masonry. The third type is the "arched dam." This is a curved gravity dam of very heavy construction but the curvature is not sufficient to act as an arch.

The collapse of a dam can be catastrophic and precautions must be taken to prevent this. Flooding is the number one enemy and in the case of an earth dam, if flood-water is allowed to spill over the crest, the dam soon crumbles and washes away. Such a dam will always have two outlets; the canal or aqueduct will be drawn off at one end of the dam at a safe level below the rim of the structure. In times of flood, the service channel cannot cope with excess water but this water must not be allowed to go over the crest. At a higher level than the aqueduct or canal outlet, but still a few feet below the top of the dam, a masonry spillway channel for unwanted surplus water is engineered into the dam's crest. The level of the river, lake or reservoir upstream from the dam can be controlled by installing gates (usually of the lifting type) in the spillway. A simpler method is merely to place planks in vertical slots prepared in the spillway side-walls. The overflow spillways are usually at the opposite end of a dam to the canal or aqueduct outlets. As a second precaution, an earth dam is usually revetted with stone. Masonry dams also use spillways but sometimes the crest is lower in the centre and this serves as a spillway. In order to run equipment such as mobile cranes and stone-laden carts, onto the dam for repairs, or merely to use the structure as a crossing point of the river or valley, a light timber bridge usually spanned the gap of the spillway channel. If an earth dam has been completely eroded away as on Roman dam-sites in Libya, the masonry spillway which at one time was at one end of the dam may survive incongruously high and dry up the side of the valley. This informs an archaeologist acquainted with civil engineering techniques that here was once a dam. As some spillway side-walls have angled cut-waters on the upstream ends, an untrained observer could be led to believe that the stream, now at the bottom of the valley after the dam's disappearance, once flowed up here, otherwise, why build a bridge in such a peculiar position? The next false deduction is that the stream has cut a deeper channel along the valley since the bridge was built. The valley or river may be huge, and the remains of the bridge over the old spillway tiny, but in archaeology, a bridge is a bridge unless it is a fish-trap.

In addition to floods, another problem, although not catastrophic, causes dams to lose efficiency and that is siltation. As a dam retards the flow of water, sediment is dropped and in time, the whole surface of the impounded lake or reservoir can be turned into a dry surface. This has happened behind Roman dams near Leptis Magna in North Africa.

At a suspected small Roman reservoir at NY 997 664 in Northumberland, which is thought to have served one of several of Corstopitum's aqueducts, an earth dam spans the small ravine to the south-west of Halton-Chesters (Hunnum) Roman Wall fort. An aqueduct leads from the eastern end and at the western end is a small masonry spillway through the lip of which the Stagshawbank Burn tumbles. The water surface of the old reservoir is now firm ground and the stream bed has been elevated to the level of the spillway. The air face of the spillway is stepped, but the water face is not visible due to the completely solid infill.

The description of a few known Roman dams around the Empire may help to appreciate evidence which will be presented in due course.

There are ruins of a Roman curved dam at Kasserine, in North Africa. This dam is 135 miles south-west of Tunis, and is thought to have held a reservoir for the Roman town of Cillium about the second century AD. The dam was discovered in 1886 by Henry Saladin, and fortunately he left drawings and a report because since then, floods and stone-robbing have removed much of the structure. According to Mr Saladin, the dam had a rubble core with mortared-masonry air and water faces. The dam was 164 yards long and its height was 33 ft. The base was 33 ft thick and the crest 16 ft wide. The water face was vertical and the air face stepped two-thirds of the way down and then vertical. The top of the dam was of stones set in mortar and the outlet tunnel was low down in the wall and was 6 ft wide.

Another Roman dam was discovered in Syria by Sir Aurel Stein in 1938 at Qasr Khubbaz on the Euphrates. It seems to be the standard type of Roman dam, and is 20 ft high, constructed of masonry blocks, and has a vertical water face and a stepped air face. There is another dam of this type at Harbaka, 45 miles south-east of Homs in Libya. It was built in 132 AD and is 656 ft long and 59 ft high.

Also near Homs, the Romans dammed the River Orontes to form a large reservoir, and this dam was just over a mile long. It was built by Emperor Diocletian in AD 284, and the construction was typically Roman with a rubble core bound together by mortar and masonry blocks on both air and water faces. The height was about 20 ft. The air face was stepped in the usual Roman manner and the water face sloped. A new dam was built on top of the original in 1934. A cross-section of this dam, drawn by M L Brossé in 1922, distinctly shows a canal.

Near Mérida, in western Spain, there are two dams, the Cornalvo and the Proserpina. Both are of basically Roman construction with a few repairs and additions of later dates. The Cornalvo dam is ten miles north-east of the town, and was built across the River Albarregas at a very suitable point between two outcrops of rock. It is 656 ft long and 66 ft high at the centre. It has a peculiar construction which is a mixture of earth and masonry. Vertical walls along the length of the dam, and across its width, divide it into boxes and these are filled with rubble, clay and earth. The water face has a masonry covering. The dam was considerably altered in 1936 and a Roman spillway channel in the rim of the dam near one end, was dispensed with. The main Roman outlet channel still survives and is interesting. It consists of a masonry tower standing at the foot of the sloping water face. In Roman times, it was connected to the crest of the dam by an arch, and the springers for the arch can still be seen on the tower. The latter is hollow and had steps inside. In Roman times, the tower had water openings at various levels, and the water which poured into the tower was taken away from the base by a culvert under the dam. This ingenious system meant that the Romans could tap water from the reservoir irrespective of the water level. Water was taken to Mérida in a contoured channel. The dam is still in use today for irrigation purposes.

The other dam, the Proserpina, is on a small river and was also built at a suitably narrow place. It is 467 yards long and 40 ft high at the centre. It has a concrete core faced and topped with stone blocks and there is a massive earth bank in front of the air face. The water face has masonry buttresses. Water from this dam was carried to Mérida via an aqueduct, and this aqueduct can still be seen where it crosses the River Albarregas on a bridge some 80 ft high.

It is now time to look further at ancient river traffic and some of the evidence that has come to light over the years.

The Roman military transport organisation, the *Barcarii Tigrisenses* gets only the briefest mention in our history books but together with the civilian organisation of lightermen, the *Utricularii,* they probably handled the bulk of all heavy Roman inland transport. The River Tigris boatmen were in operation three thousand years before the Romans recruited their skills and the men of this river had a much more difficult job than their counterparts on the Nile. The latter had a convenient prevailing wind to waft their craft upstream and sails could be lowered for the return journey on the current. The two Mesopotamiam rivers, the Tigris and Euphrates were more difficult: there was no convenient wind. The bargemen were natives of Armenia and when it was time to return upstream, a file of hauliers manned a towline attached to their craft. Similar scenes are depicted on many Roman stone reliefs, so obviously such well-tried systems expanded all over their Empire when the Mesopotamian rivermen were pressed into service. The expert watermen used rafts as well as boats, and according to Herodotus, each raft was buoyed by numerous inflated skins and had a live donkey on board. Some of the larger rafts carried several donkeys. After arriving at Babylon and disposing of the cargo, they auctioned the frames of the craft, loaded their now deflated goatskins onto the donkeys and walked back to Armenia.

Inflated animal skins were used by Roman lightermen to reduce the draught of their barges to negotiate very shallow water. Dozens of pairs of skins were strapped under the hull, almost lifting their craft out of the water. An inflated skin was the insignia of the *Utricularii*. Eighty strapped-pairs of inflated six-inch diameter bladders would raise a ten-ton barge eighteen inches out of the water and reduce its draught from two feet to six inches.

We have a record in cuneiform, from c2500 BC, of the crew list of a barge. This requests oil rations and gives the crew of the barge as: two boat-towing men at the outside rope, one man watching the depth, three able-bodied workers and one scribe.

Three flat-bottomed barges were recovered in 1958 from excavations of the harbour Claudius built at Ostia, and were similar to those depicted on the statue of Father Tiber in the Louvre. Three craft are shown on this relief. One is being hauled by four men and the tow-rope is attached to a low towing mast. A second craft is being poled away from a collision with a third. On one of these craft, cargo is being carried on board on the shoulders of a porter and another stevedore waits to stow it in the hold. A tally-clerk is recording the cargo coming on board and another crew-member is brewing-up some beverage in a pot over a fire.

Altogether, seven Roman river barges were found at the Portus of Rome and presumably these were used to carry the cargoes of grain to the City of Rome from the merchant ships which berthed at Ostia.

In 1958, the remains of two vessels of the Roman period were found in London, one in the River Thames in the mud under Blackfriars bridge, and the other at Guy's Hospital in Bermondsey when the foundations for a new surgical block were being excavated. The Blackfriars ship was flat-bottomed, constructed of oak with iron fastenings and had a cargo of Kentish ragstone on board. Pottery sherds on board dated the vessel to the second century AD. Only part of the Guy's Hospital vessel survived, but the construction was similar to the Blackfriars ship and, although both ships had been used by the Romans, they were of Celtic-type construction; Roman-built ships used planks edge-to-edge (carvel built) with mortise-and-tenon joints whereas Celtic types used caulking of hazel twigs in the seams. The "clinker" type of construction (overlapping planks) was developed in northern Germany and examples of this type found in Britain are usually from the later Saxon period.

In 1910, a Roman ship was found at County Hall in London and this vessel was of standard Roman mortise-and-tenon construction although the species of oak used was not native to the Mediterranean.

A craft estimated to have been fifteen metres in length was found in 1899 at a depth of five metres during the excavation of the Brugge-Zeebrugge canal. This craft had a step for a mast similar to that found in the Blackfriars ship. The remains which are stored in the Musée de la Marine at Antwerp have been recently radiocarbon-dated to AD 180.

The partial remains of a Roman river barge were found at Wanzenau in Alsace and this had a cargo of basalt-lava millstones. It is thought to have been a *lintre* of the third century AD.

In 1892, a craft believed to be Roman was found at Vechten near Utrecht in the Netherlands. From its description, it is similar to the County Hall ship. Another vessel similar to the County Hall ship was found in 1809 on the banks of the Somme and was surrounded by Roman weapons and pottery.

During the period 1968-71, the *Instituut voor Prae-en Protohistorie* of the University of Amsterdam excavated a Roman auxiliary fort called Nigrum Pullum (Black Chicken) on the south bank of the River Rhine. In 1971, a dugout boat was found and in 1974, a series of further excavations recovered three more dugouts, three barges and a steering oar. The three dugouts are all of oak and their length and beam measurements are: 6.99m x 1.05m; 5.48m x 0.76m; and 10.40m x 1.40m. These craft would have been capable of navigation into the very highest reaches of rivers and calculations show that two of them would have carried five tons each and the third, ten tons. This last cargo is equal to that of twenty ox-wagons.

The three barges found at the same site at Nigrum Pullum/Zwammerdam, have been dated to the second century AD. The first one is 22.75m in length with a beam of 2.80m. It has a mast-step too small for a sail-carrying mast so the mast must have been for tow-ropes. The second barge is 34m long with a beam of 4.40m. It has a step for a large mast and was therefore capable of being sailed. The third barge is 20.25m long and has a beam of 3.40m. Typical Roman mortise-and-tenon joints were used in its construction. The mast-step is a quarter of the length from the bow, and this is not on the point of balance necessary for a sailing mast, so this craft must also have been of the towed variety. The largest of the three barges would have carried over fifty tons of cargo which is equivalent to a hundred ox-wagon loads.

In 1975, a new canal was under construction near the small village of Pommeroeul in Belgium. This village is about half-way between the towns of Mons and Tournai and is close to the point where a Roman road leading from Bavai to the north crosses the small River Haine and a tributary. The canal constructors uncovered a completely unknown Roman settlement beside the junction of the rivers. Archaeologists found a Roman *vicus* in the silted-up bed of the River Haine, and also Roman timber quays which they were able to date to the second century AD. Five boats were also found in the silt of the river bed. One was too badly damaged to be identified, but of the remaining four craft, two were identified as dugouts and two as barges. The date of abandonment of the vessels has been estimated at either the second half of the first century AD or the first half of the second century. One barge is estimated to have been 18-20m long with a beam of 3m and including the gunwhale, 0.67m high. The construction was a large dugout split down the middle with extra planks inserted between the halves. On the poop was a transverse steering-platform fitted with anti-slip strips and there was a cabin 2.30m long near the stern.

Large amounts of Roman artefacts were recovered from the river silt, many of them pieces of nautical equipment. Several dozen pole-ferrules and boat-hooks were found as well as a stone sounding-weight with a groove for the string, and anchor-stones. Other finds indicated that the cargoes had been varied; leather, coal, peat, pottery and building stone.

Pommeroeul is on a very tiny river and is sixty-three miles from the sea. The Roman port has a layout which will be noticed time and time again as our search progresses. A bend in the river has been short-circuited by an artificial channel and the main river has been widened to form a basin with an island in the middle. This configuration provides ideal sites for weirs and locks. For want of a better term, for now, I will call them "funny rivers." A typical example is St Albans, (Verulamium). The River Ver divides into two branches north of the Roman town wall and there are tell-tale signs of a possible barge basin. In the eleventh century, the biographer of Abbot Ealdred of St Albans recorded that, when the holy man had stones for his new church dug from the Roman ruins of Verulamium, his men came across oak timbers smeared with pitch and with rivets in them, half-rusted anchors, and pine oars, down by the river bank. Presumably these were the remains of a Roman ship, and this is the earliest account of the digging-up of one. Just over two miles downstream at the Roman Park Street villa site, a Roman jetty was found. In 1630, the Benedictine monks at St Albans were using an old Roman "causeway" as a mill-dam.

Other Ex-Roman towns and forts with "funny rivers" are Canterbury (Durovernum), Dorchester (Durnovaria), Colchester (Camulodunum), Winchester (Venta), Lincoln (Lindum), Chester (Deva), Inchtuthil, Bertha, Glenlochar, and dozens more.

Mr J Gibbons-Partridge writing in *Popular Archaeology*, Feb 1985, refers to Irchester and a possible artificial Roman canal from the River Nene. A small inlet from the Nene leads to a wide suspected harbour and then to a ten-feet-wide waterway which extends for nearly four hundred yards and terminates below the north wall of the fort.

More definite evidence comes from Netherby (Castra Exploratorum) NY 397 716, on the River Esk, north of Carlisle. An account is left for us by the antiquarians Leland and Bainbrigg c. 1536:

> "Men alyve have sene rynges and staples yn the walles, as yt had bene stayes or holdes for shyppes...Ships' sides, anchors and iron rings, such as ships are tied up to, were found there, but the accumulation of sand had shut the sea out for a distance of several miles, blocking the port, and the ancient little city was now a corpse."

An aerial search showed that a stream passing the fort and joining the Esk at Scaurbank, may have been used as a canal. In the vicinity of the fort, a ground inspection showed that the bed of the stream is paved.

In the main river, upstream from the fort, is a broken weir and the stonework is of the "herring-bone" type so often seen in the cores of Roman buildings. The dam, now ruinous, has been impressed in more recent years to provide a head of water for an electric generator which supplied Netherby mansion house. The latter sits right on top of the fort and obscures all the Roman works.

Although nothing to do with navigation and away from the river, a curious auditorium-shaped, semicircular recess has been cut into a bank-side to the north of the fort. It may turn out to be a small unknown theatre.

Britain is not the only ex-Roman province to have "funny rivers" in the vicinity of its Roman towns and fort-sites: France is full of them. Professer

Albert Grenier's *Manuel D'Archaéologie Gallo-Romaine,* Paris, 1934, contains dozens of maps and plans of them. He also knew that the Romans had navigated the minor rivers and even the small streams of France, as he has this to say:

"In addition to the large rivers and principal streams, many moderate water-courses, which today seem unsuited to navigation, had been used by Gallo-Roman traffic. Here again, the works of the Middle Ages have provided useful indications to ancient archaeology. As with the study of the roads, where we must place the greatest regard on documents of the Middle Ages and place names, so also with research into water communications. The existence of navigation, until quite recent times, must lead us to research the documents and any remains in order to establish that waterways had been used by the Gauls and Romans. It must be conceded that river traffic in the Gallo-Roman era had been extremely developed and that even the smallest waterways had played the same part as the innumerate local roads of which traces have been found."

Professor Grenier also mentions *gués pavés* (paved fords). He writes about a most interesting one in Brittany:

"In Brittany, Count Devoir reported on an examination of a ford close to a bridge, the Pont-Crac'h, between Plouguerneau and Lannilis, at the back end of the estuary of Aber-Krac'h. It is a stone pavement 62m long and raised 3.5m to 4m above the bed of the river: four openings or arches give passage to water; the structure is submerged at high tide. Léon Maitre describes many examples in the Vilaine between Fegréac and Rieux and in the Loire opposite Ancenis, Mauves, and around Nantes. A good number of these fords have disappeared over the ages because they were an obstruction and a danger to navigation......

.....most of the examples traverse the river diagonally. The route to begin with is not at right-angles to the river-flow; it follows the river for a few metres before becoming oblique."

These so-called "paved fords" are most likely curved weirs and fit the description of the Hylton dam which caused so much confusion to the Sunderland antiquarians during the nineteenth century. Count Devoir's structure is four metres proud of the river bed and although it has four culverts, it cannot be a bridge as it is submerged at high tide. It fits the description of a barrier which could impound water in a non-tidal basin. It seems that obvious evidence for Roman river navigation survives in France. Count Devoir's report is dated 1922. Let us hope that the structure in Brittany is still intact (approx position estimated at 48 degs 34 mins North, 4 degs 35 mins West). Obviously there is great scope for investigations in France and if this book is read by French field-workers, I shall be extremely pleased to hear from them.

One of the "funny river" configurations drawn by Grenier is at Lyon where an ancient canal has been cut across the peninsula between the Rhône and the Saône just to the south of the amphitheatre.

Others shown in his book are at Arles, Basle, Bayonne, Beauvais,

Bescançon, Bordeaux, Chalons-sur-Saône, Cologne, Dax, Évreux, Fréjus, Geneva, Grenoble, Metz, Naix, Nantes, Narbonne, Neuchatel, Orleans, Paris, Poitiers, Rennes, Rouen, St Martory, Scarponne, Sens, Soissons, Strasbourg, Tournus, Tréves (Trier), and Vienne.

He also shows a very peculiar Roman bridge at Montignies-Saint-Christophe (Hainaut) on the River Hantes (Haine) in Belgium, which has twelve tiny culverts instead of two arches normal for this length of bridge. The structure looks like a major navigation barrage. This is on the same river and close to the Roman port found at Pommeroeul. Information from Belgium would be most welcome.

In the Midi area of France, the River Lot is joined by the Célé near Bouziés. Downstream is the Roman town of Cahors. Near the confluence of the rivers, on the Lot, is a towpath to St Cirq-Lapopie. It is carved out of the sheer cliff-face and looks remarkably like the Roman handiwork in the cliffs of the Danube gorge.

The next evidence comes from Germany where, unknown to me until recently, Dr Martin Eckoldt has been working on the same subject of Roman navigation of minor rivers. I have been in contact with Dr Eckoldt and I quote short excerpts from his paper: *Navigation on small rivers in Central Europe in Roman and mediaeval times*, 1984:

"It has long been accepted that, until the widespread adoption of the railway, man made use of waterways for transportation of himself and his goods wherever possible.....

It is generally accepted that the only way the Romans could have transported cut-stone from the quarries was by water, even if there was only a small river nearby. Votive reliefs belonging to the Shipmasters' Guilds provide evidence that even small tributaries were included in the Roman water transport system.....

Very often these sources refer to a river which today is not regarded as navigable. It seems to be impossible that these little rivers or brooks could ever have carried shipping. The view that the rivers had more water in those times is often advocated, but there is no proof. It is time that this problem be explored in every aspect....."

Dr Eckoldt describes various types of Roman rivercraft already mentioned previously. He then continues with a reference to a minor river:

"The Weschnitz was probably used by the Romans for the transport of granite columns (30t weight) from the Felsberg (Odenwald) to the Rhine. Such columns were transported, via Rhine and Mosel, to Trier, and there, used for Imperial palaces in the fourth century in the Constantinian period."

He shows a photograph of a stream which looks like little more than a farm ditch; the "Pfrimm," 6 km west of Worms/Rhine which was used for the transport of cereals according to a document of 893. Dr Eckoldt then discusses methods of deepening the watercourses:

"Gravel ploughs were used until 1875 for deepening the Weser. These were rake-shaped implements which were drawn over the gravel banks by means of horses or windlasses so that the gravel was pushed to the sides. On the other rivers it was necessary only to loosen the river bed, so that the current was sufficient. The current could be concentrated by rows of oars, driven vertically into the bottom, to form a narrow channel, thus generating a strong rush of water in its course which would remove the gravel.

Who would have carried out such maintenance work? The Romans set conscripts and tribal groups, often prisoners of war, to carry out such tasks to maintain communications, both by road and by river, for whose support, land was parcelled out.....

.....In some rivers, navigation would have been restricted to special flat-bottomed ships at times of full flow, or in conditions of particularly careful river bed conservancy. In a few cases, it indicates a waterflow too slight for navigation and where the cargo would have had to be lightened by dividing up the blocks of stone to be transported, or by making shallow rivers navigable with the aid of barrages.

The simplest artificial method of making shallow waters navigable is by means of constructing a reservoir up-stream which would be filled with water when water was high, which could be released as required. Such places were well known in antiquity; Pliny, for example, mentions in his *Natural History,* Book 3, such ponds (*piscinas*) on the upper Tiber. Whether such reservoirs were known in Central Europe during the Roman period has not been established. A second method is by navigable storage locks. They would be positioned at distances of between 5 and 20 km and would raise the water level 1 or 2 metres. Navigation could take place about every two or three days when the locks would be opened, and as soon as the water in the lock was level with the transom across the stern, the ship would go up on the rising swell below the lock and with less depth to the upper reaches of the river.....

.....Thirdly, the level of the water in the river can be raised over its whole length, so that a ship will always have sufficient water. So, a ship will go through the barrage, even when the water has been released and the sluice gates are open. The river thus acquires the character of a chain of locks. Another possibility is to raise gradually the permanent level of the river, but then the problem arises of having to raise or lower the ships over the flights, which have been erected from one level to another......

.....Our researches have shown that several of the small, shallow rivers could probably have been used for navigation in the Roman period and in the early Middle Ages, contrary to their appearance today....

.....In some cases it is clear that navigation can only have been accomplished through artificial means, possibly with the aid of dams.....

.....The purpose of this essay is not only to develop a tool for the solution of the question as to whether a small river could have served for navigation, but much more, to serve as a stimulus for those interested, particularly archaeologists and historians, to appreciate that in finds from river beds and documents, there is evidence, hitherto disregarded, which should be investigated to see whether it may not be connected with navigation....."

I applaud Dr Eckoldt's call for investigation into Roman river navigation. His observations agree with those of Professor Grenier. What the Romans did in France and Germany, they would have also done in Britain.

Critics of the river navigation theory often point out the apparent lack of tow-paths on many British rivers. For the answer to this we must go to China.

In 1930, an American engineer, John Hersey, who travelled into the upper reaches of the great Chinese river the Yangtze, transformed his experiences into the superb novel *Single Pebble*. While reading his account, I realised that here in China, history had been "frozen" and that the transport methods in use in the 1930's were exactly the same as four thousand years ago. The story of Hersey's voyage makes fascinating reading and some of the scenes match almost exactly those shown on Roman stone-reliefs of barges under tow.

Hersey travelled the first thousand miles up the Yangtze, from Shanghai to Ichang, in a British steam-gunboat. Just above Ichang, the Yangtze became un-navigable to steamboats and he transferred to a vessel of the *Ma-Yang-Tzu* type, which was an eighty-ton junk, 102 ft long, 19 ft in the beam and constructed of cypress wood. The hull was divided into fourteen cargo compartments; living quarters were on deck abaft the mast, and there was a cabin for the owner on the stern. A long steering-oar was operated by a helmsman who stood on a raised plank-bridge at the stern. This type of vessel was designed four thousand years ago. The cargo on this occasion was cotton bales and the destination was Wanhsien, two hundred miles upstream from Ichang.

For the first few miles, the vessel used a bamboo-stiffened lugsail to utilise a fine breeze. Ahead was mountainous country and after a while, a cleft in the massif became visible. Here the river narrowed to two-hundred yards.

On board the junk, in addition to the normal crew were thirty "trackers," or hauliers. As the vessel entered the Yellow Cat Gorge, there was too little wind to cope with the swift current and the junk was rowed to the left bank where they disembarked and prepared for a tow. In the gorges of the upper Yangtze, the winds are funnelled into either "upwinds" or "downwinds" but the upwinds are not sufficient to propel the vessel, they merely take a bit of weight off the trackers.

By evening, the vessel had completed ten miles under the tow of the trackers, all in a slow, strained step and keeping time with the leader at the head of the tow-rope, who was singing weird rhythmic melodies.[there is a Roman reference to: "the sad chant of the hauliers, which heralded the approach of a Roman barge under tow"]

On the first evening, the junk was moored securely in a little cove at the head of Yellow Cat Gorge. The next day saw the thirty trackers scrambling over the rough banks and splashing through the shallows. There was no tow-path whatsoever. A signalling-drum just forward of the mast provided a communication link between vessel and trackers. The tow-rope was attached to the mast [as in Roman reliefs] and this mast served the dual purpose of

内河船

(River Vessel)

An eighty ton Chinese junk being pulled up a "near waterfall" on the River Yangtze, in the 1930's. The normal complement of hauliers for the river journey was thirty, but an extra three hundred were engaged locally for the ascent of the rapids. The junk is of the *Ma-Yang-Tzu* type and was designed over four thousand years ago. Like the Roman *codicaria*, this type of vessel could be rowed, towed, poled or sailed.

sailing-mast and towing-mast [as did the mast of a Roman *codicaria*]. A third use of the mast will be mentioned shortly.

On the raised bridge aft, the helmsman stood, controlling the junk's long tiller-oar. On the up-river journey, his duties were easy, with the towing speed against the river-current providing ample steerage-way. The steering was assisted by a remarkable device which served the same purpose as a "bow-thruster" on a modern ship. A "bow-thruster" is a tranverse pipe below water-level, in a ship's bows. In this pipe is a small propeller and, depending on its direction of rotation, can push the ship's bow sideways to either port or starboard. For those readers who are not familiar with ships and the sea, a little explanation is necessary - With a single-screw ship, and no bow-thruster, it is difficult to leave a jetty, or come alongside without the assistance of tugs. It *can* be done though; let us assume that it is slack water with the ship about to depart, port-side to the jetty. All the mooring ropes are cast off except one which is known as a "for'd spring" and this runs from the fore part of the ship to a bollard on the jetty about half-way along the ship's side. The ship is thus restrained from moving ahead. The rudder is put over to port (left) and the engine given "slow ahead." As the vessel cannot move forward due to the "spring," the propeller-wash pushes against the deflected rudder and the ship's stern moves away from the jetty. The rudder is then centralised, the "spring" cast off and the engine given "slow astern." The ship moves backwards away from, and at an angle to, the jetty. At a safe distance, the engine is stopped, the rudder put over to starboard and the engine given "half-ahead." The ship is now under-way and clear of the quay and has managed its departure without the assistance of tugboats. Tides, winds and river-currents can complicate the issue and skill and experience is needed.

On modern ships with two engines and two screws, the manoeuvering is much simpler. Such a ship can turn on the spot with one engine going ahead and the other astern. An ancient oar-powered warship could do the same, with the rowers on one side "giving way" and the other side "back-watering."

With a twin-screw ship also equipped with a bow-thruster, tugs are seldom needed. Now let us return to our junk.

This vessel had a bow-thruster in the form of a huge oar pivotted on the bow and manned by twelve men. In the neutral position, it stuck out straight ahead of the vessel and was held clear of the water by a quick-release lashing on deck. When the junk, under tow, had to negotiate rapids, whirlpools etc, the bow was kept in exactly the correct direction through the turbulent water by swift strokes, one way or another, of this bow oar, according to the bow-steersman's hand signals to the twelve men who handled the oar.

As the junk moved slowly upstream, the American passenger described the trackers. Each one was bent forward, straining at his harness which was attached to the main tow-rope with a quick-release knot. The passenger describes how the trackers scrambled from rock to rock, sometimes crawling along a natural ledge, calling all the time "ayah, ayah" as in unison, they planted each step. Here and there, obstructing boulders which jutted out into the stream, had grooves worn into them, where, for centuries, tow-ropes had dragged across.

The head-tracker's formal title was "noise suppressor" as his song was

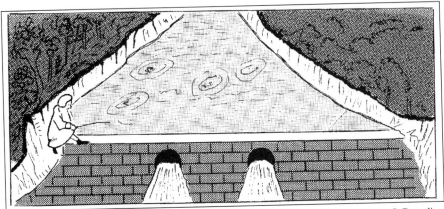

The Romans were extremely capable builders of dams, and this mediaeval painting shows St Benedict fishing from the crest of one on the River Anio. Note the design of the spillways. This dam was 120 ft high and was one of a cascade of three built for ornamental purposes beside Nero's villa. The dam depicted was later used to supply one of Rome's aqueducts. If the Romans could build 120 ft high scenic dams on the Anio, then ten foot high navigation weirs on our minor British rivers would have been easy jobs by comparison.

Ancient timbers on the bed of the River Tyne at Ovingham at NZ 084 634. These may be the remains of a Roman navigation dam.
It looks as if the structure has been timber boxes filled with rocks. It lies at an angle of thirty degrees to the river flow.
Ovingham Saxon Church close by uses ex-Roman stones in its tower.

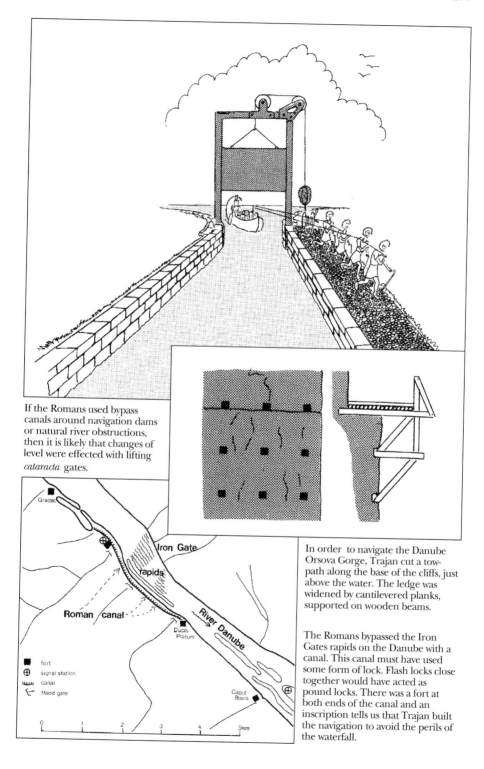

If the Romans used bypass canals around navigation dams or natural river obstructions, then it is likely that changes of level were effected with lifting *cataracta* gates.

In order to navigate the Danube Orsova Gorge, Trajan cut a tow-path along the base of the cliffs, just above the water. The ledge was widened by cantilevered planks, supported on wooden beams.

The Romans bypassed the Iron Gates rapids on the Danube with a canal. This canal must have used some form of lock. Flash locks close together would have acted as pound locks. There was a fort at both ends of the canal and an inscription tells us that Trajan built the navigation to avoid the perils of the waterfall.

Gradac

Iron Gate

rapids

Roman canal

River Danube

Ducis Pratum

fort

signal station

canal

flood gate

Caput Bovis

0   1   2   3   4   5km

supposed to suppress the groan-shouts that marked each step.

At one point, at an excited drum-signal, the trackers halted; the tow-rope was snagged on a submerged rock. The tracker-leader stripped off his clothes and disappeared under the horrible-looking brown water. After a while, the tow-rope broke the surface with a "swish" and lifted the head tracker clear out of the water. He then returned to the shore swinging hand-over-hand along the tow-rope and the tow was resumed.

This voyage was made just before the spring floods and the American passenger tells us that since records have been kept, the maximum recorded rise of flood-water in this gorge was 275 feet. Upper Yangtze navigation ceases for a few weeks in the flood season.

As the junk approached the bad rapids at Hsintan, the dull roar of water could be heard. There was a consultation between the head tracker and the owner as to which bank would be the safer for the ascent at this time of year, and at this level of water. They finally decided to use the right-hand (north) bank.

Moored below the rapids were several junks which had descended the rapids. The crews were ashore celebrating the event in reed-mat constructed wine houses, and the strains of singing and two-stringed Chinese fiddles could be heard faintly against the roar of the water.

The owner of the upstream-bound junk hired fifty porters and the entire cargo was discharged. Under the command of the ship's cook, these porters carried the cargo around the three sets of rapids.

Occasionally, a down-bound junk would shoot the rapids, and on the foredeck of each vessel stood a "rapids pilot," clad in a black gown, his arms outstretched, transmitting hand signals to the frantic oarsmen.

The lower and middle sets of rapids were classed as severe but not dangerous. Three hundred extra trackers had been hired locally for the ascent, and after an hour of straining, inch by inch, the 330 trackers hauled the eighty-ton junk into the smooth water between the middle and upper rapids.

The upper rapids presented an awesome picture. They were formed by a huge moraine across the river, forming a low natural dam. The water poured in torrents through several gaps and one of these gaps between rocks at the head of the steeply-inclined race of swiftly falling water was just wide enough to take the eighty-ton vessel's nineteen-foot beam.

Just before the three-hundred-odd trackers took the strain, the tow-rope attached to the mast, was fed through a notch in the gunwhale, thus biassing the tow, so that as the trackers moved forward, the vessel swung out into midstream (using the same principle as a naval mine-sweeping paravane, or the principle used by a small boy who attaches a string a third of the way along a kite's longitudinal spar. When the boy runs into wind, the biassed tow on the kite causes it to climb high into the air).

At first, the junk negotiated the violent eddies below the race, which was about seventy feet from the shore. Sidelines to the bank prevented the biassed tow moving more than the correct 70 ft distance from the bank. The main tow-rope was as taut as a piano-string as the junk passed from the tormented water onto the smooth but fast-moving incline. Inch by inch, to

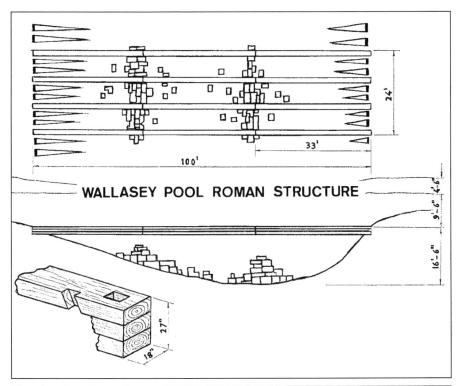

WALLASEY POOL ROMAN STRUCTURE

There have been Roman dams at many places in Britain but their remains have always been misidentified as bridges, or fish-traps. A typical example is the Roman Wallasey Pool structure which was discovered in 1850 and immediately labelled "Roman bridge," although it was entirely covered by water at high tide. In order to accommodate this theory, a massive sinking of the land was postulated, but engineer David Armstrong points out that the land there has actually risen since Roman times.

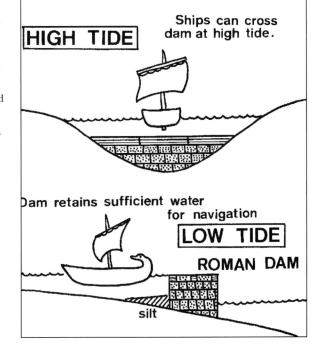

Engineer David Armstrong's drawing of the Wallasey Pool Roman structure.

the three hundred-plus cries of "ayah, ayah," the junk moved up the spout of water and finally slid into the quiet surface above the rapids.

The extra trackers were paid-off, the cargo reloaded and the vessel continued its voyage upstream.

The trackers continued to scramble over unprepared river banks, but quite often they came on board and used oars for several miles. Under oar-power, the junk was steered from one side of the river to the other to take advantage of occasional upstream eddies. At other times, the vessel was poled or manhandled along sheer cliff-faces with bare hands. A small sampan, its usual position in tow astern of the junk, was used to transport the trackers between shore and vessel at each change of mode of propulsion.

The mast was used for its third purpose before entering a ravine called "Wind Box Gorge." Here in addition to the owner's flags, two tiny bells on springy antennae were hoisted, their purpose to scare evil spirits away. In the gorge, a long uphill slope of water had to be negotiated, and to take advantage of an "upwind," the lugsail was hoisted. Even with this wind-assistance, the trackers often took a whole minute to gather up enough strength for a six-inch step. As sails and oars were unable to cope with the rapids, and the cliffs were vertical, a tow-path had been carved thousands of years earlier into the sheer cliff face, thirty feet above the river level. The tow-path was rectangular in section with the roof just high enough to clear the heads of the trackers in their leaning-forward attitudes.

The vessel finally arrived at Wanhsien, sometimes having covered twenty miles on a good day.

The American engineer speculated that one high dam across the Yangtze (with a series of locks to negotiate it) would make navigation easy. All the rapids would disappear into the depths below dam-deepened water.

Before we return to the search for Roman evidence in Britain, let us look at two examples of river navigation in more recent times.

For the Americans, the steamboat became, from the outset, an important means of internal transport. Development was rapid and by the 1840's, it is thought that there, the tonnage on American rivers exceeded that of the whole British Empire. These ships were powerful enough to counter the currents, and had very shallow drafts - it is said that: "they could sail up valleys only moistened by the morning dew."

We can judge the amount of river traffic from recorded accidents. Between 1816 and 1848, 233 steamboats blew up on the Mississippi, killing 2,563 people. The worst case was the *Louisiana* in which almost two hundred died when the boiler exploded.

With reference to steamboats negotiating "wet grass," this was brought home to me when I worked for West African Airways in the 1950's. I was in the co-pilot's seat of a de-Havilland Dove, and I can't remember exactly where it was, but it was somewhere to the south of the great Jos escarpment and an awful long way from the sea. The South-west monsoon had swollen a stream which I had hardly noticed on dozens of previous flights over the area. This time there was a stern-wheeler steamboat making good progress up a river where before only a brook had trickled through the valley.

It seems a long time since we left Aulius Plautius and his invasion of southern England, but this book is concerned with the little known subject of Roman logistics and space does not allow an account of the years of campaigning up the length and breadth of Britain. In any case, the reader has a choice of hundreds of books on the subject.

One campaign however which may provide evidence for our specialised subject is Agricola's invasion of Scotland in AD 82. Fortunately, Agricola's son-in-law was the Roman historian Tacitus who chronicled the campaign. We can look at some of his comments in his surviving book *Agricola*.

After waiting a year on the Clyde-Forth frontier, and exploring south-west Scotland, Agricola was ready to move forward again from his line of forts with an army of at least 21,000 men. Agricola's army was entering very hostile territory and this was no place for long strings of wagons and pack-animals straggling along for miles behind the army. Nor was it suitable territory for ill-protected engineers to be engaged in road-building activities in territory perfectly suitable for guerrilla-type warfare.

Agricola's answer to the supply problem was simple; he used his navy. Not only did the ships enter navigable rivers; it seems that he used them to attack behind enemy lines. Tacitus has this to say:

"In the summer in which his sixth year of office began (AD 83), Agricola overran the people living beyond the Forth. He was worried by a general unrest in the north and some ominous movements of an enemy force, and sent his fleet to reconnoitre the harbours. He was now for the first time employing the fleet (which had in the past merely transported the army) on offensive operations, with remarkable effect, since the war could be hurried on by land and sea simultaneously.

Often infantry, cavalry and marines, together in the same camp, shared their rations and their entertainment; they capped each other's stories of their deeds and adventures, and, with typical boastfulness, compared the dangers of storm and tide with the perils of the forests and mountains, the conquest of the seas with a victory over an enemy on land. Prisoners confirmed that the sight of the fleet dumbfounded the British too; they supposed that their last refuge in defeat was closed to them now that the secrets of their seas were disclosed."

The most obvious route for ship-borne supplies was up the magnificent River Tay which was navigable to Perth and beyond. The tidal limit in Roman times is estimated to have been at the confluence of the Tay and the Almond (NO 101 268, 2 miles upstream from Perth) and it just so happens that the Roman fort of Bertha sits right beside the junction. There is also a mysterious curved weir known as Derder's Ford just below the confluence. This would have served to deepen both rivers. Slightly upstream was a Roman timber bridge over the Tay. This was recorded by the meticulous engineer, General Roy, c1750. Up the River Almond is Fendoch Roman fort (NN 908 285) and to the south-west is the line of Roman watch-towers along the Gask Ridge (Parkneuk NN 916 184; Ardunie NN 946 187; Kirkhill NN 967 188; Muir O'Fauld NN 981 189; Gask House NN 990 191; Witch Knowe NN 991 195 and Thorney Hill NO 021 204). South-west of the ridge are the Roman forts of Strageath (NN 879 191) on the River Earn and Ardoch (NN 840 100) on the

Allan Water. In *The Piercebridge Formula* of 1983, I said that I thought the Pow Water to the north of the Gask Ridge looked like an artificial canal. Now more information is coming to light, but just for the moment let us get back to the main obvious Roman supply route, the River Tay.

Eleven miles upstream from Bertha is the Roman legionary fortress of Inchtuthil (NO 125 397). This fortress was built by Agricola during the Scottish campaign but it was left unfinished due to a complete change in Roman policy. Constructed largely of earth and timber, the buildings included sixty-four barracks, granaries, houses, headquarters building, hospital, workshop and storehouses. The turf rampart was fronted by a stone wall and there were four timber gates.

The change in policy which left the fortress unfinished was Agricola's withdrawal from Scotland because of the need for troops on the Danube frontier in AD 85 where there had been a serious invasion by the Dacians. About AD 87-88 the unfinished Inchtuthil fortress was systematically dismantled. Crockery and glassware were deliberately broken and as revealed by excavation, a million nails were buried, but that is leaping ahead a little.

It is obvious from the air that the fortress was at one time entirely surrounded by water by a very artificial-looking loop from the main river. Delvine Loch looks like a remnant of the suspected canal-cum-moat. To the east of the main fortress is a three-sided camp known as the "redoubt" with its open side protected by the old water-course. This is reminiscent of similar three-sided ship-beaching fortifications all the way up the Rhine.

The seven tons of hand-forged iron nails were supposedly buried to prevent them from falling into enemy hands. If so, why did the Romans not simply dump them into the River Tay just a few yards away? Did the Romans intend to return to Inchtuthil once their other military problems around the Empire had been resolved? Were nails a valuable commodity? Even if they were not valuable in themselves, the transportation of seven tons of iron, either in nail form or raw material to the hinterland of Scotland, must have been quite an expensive exercise. If the transportation had been by land, it would have involved over fifty pack-animals for the iron alone, plus fodder-carrying animals, plus escorts. The seven tons of nails get more expensive the longer we look at the problem.

The nails probably came as far as Bertha in one of the ships mentioned by Tacitus, where they may have been off-loaded into a *codicaria* general-purpose barge which could be rowed, sailed, towed or poled. Before we examine possible obstructions in the Tay between Bertha and Inchtuthil, let us look at the cost of nails in a later period of history. Hand-forged iron nails, almost identical to Roman types, were used in the American colonies where their manufacture was a cottage industry. Almost every farm had an anvil to shape them and, according to information provided by the Industrial Fastener Institute of Cleveland, Ohio, a colonial farmer, planning to build a new house, often burned down his old one in order to recover the nails from the ashes. Some communities offered vacating owners an ample supply of nails to discourage them from burning down their old houses before moving to new sites.

Did the Romans also burn down old buildings in order to recover valuable nails? Maybe this would explain some of the stratified layers of ash on Roman sites, often presented as evidence of attacks or rebellions. Whilst on the subject of nails, I may as well add a few more points of interest: nails had evolved from wedge-shaped wooden pins to more or less their modern shape by the beginning of the first century AD. The Romans also used rivets, but ancient goldsmiths used threaded screws as early as 250 BC. Archimedes went in for screws of a larger type and, in addition to his screw-pumps, he invented a screw-type winch which dragged ships up slipways.

Pointed screws were not invented until 1837, but great use was made of straight screws by mediaeval knights. On a French suit of armour dating from c1475, the flowing plume was fastened to the helmet with a metal nut and matching screw. Early fifteenth century clocks and firearms made extensive use of screws with slotted heads, but the first mention of a screwdriver was in an Italian treatise of 1588.

Now let us return to the possible navigation of the River Tay. I am extremely grateful to civil engineer John V Smith of Croxton Kerrial for information on his researches into Roman navigation of this river and its tributaries.

Mr Smith says that the official attitude is that the Tay was not navigated between Bertha and Inchtuthil because of falls at Stanley and at Campsie Linn. He reports that ninety per-cent of the river between the forts is navigable without improvements or diversions.

He commenced his search at Inchtuthil in 1992 when the Tay was at its lowest level for years. I quote excerpts from his report:

"Moving downstream for about three miles, we come to the junction of the River Tay with one of its larger tributaries, the Isla. It is also the point at which Strathmore joins the Tay Valley and was a place of high strategic importance to the Romans..."

[author's note: Up the Isla at NO 292 459, at the confluence of the Isla and the Dean Water is the Roman fort of Cardean. The River Isla has had several loops short-circuited by the hand of man; they are not ox-bow lakes. There is also a very strange and very long mill-leat all the way from Cardean down through Meigle, Arthurstone, and Coupar Angus. This should be investigated, as it is close to a suspected Roman road which approximates to the modern A94.]

"....The existing bridge (Cargill) is mentioned in the *Statistical Account of Scotland* (1799) as being under construction 'next to the site of the wooden Roman bridge.' The new bridge is built in an interesting variety of stones, some apparently cut for the job and some re-used from elsewhere. I did wonder whether any stone was recovered from Roman piers. The river is not particularly deep - four feet maybe. A mile below the Isla is the village of Cargill and directly above the village and about a mile on up the hillside is an identified Roman stone quarry (Frere). The road from the quarry comes straight down the hill, through the village and down to the river bank. I wonder why? .....Four miles further downstream, we come to Campsie Linn, a fascinating place. On the left (east) bank is St Adamanns Chapel, a mediaeval ruin on a small knoll overlooking the river. Behind it is a very extensive quarry........About a

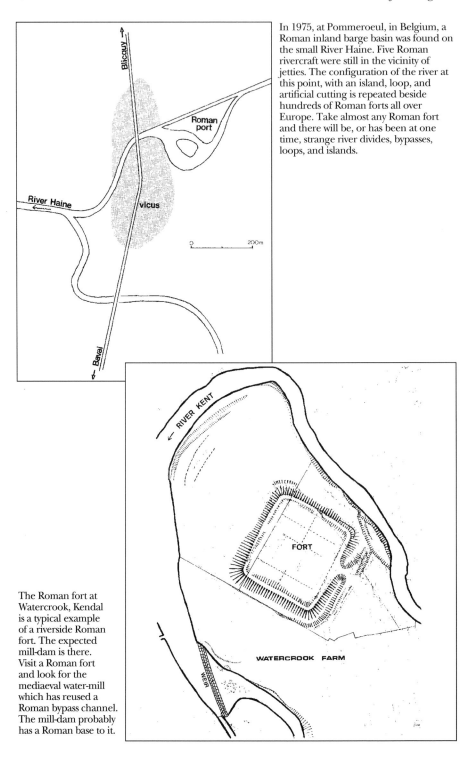

In 1975, at Pommeroeul, in Belgium, a Roman inland barge basin was found on the small River Haine. Five Roman rivercraft were still in the vicinity of jetties. The configuration of the river at this point, with an island, loop, and artificial cutting is repeated beside hundreds of Roman forts all over Europe. Take almost any Roman fort and there will be, or has been at one time, strange river divides, bypasses, loops, and islands.

The Roman fort at Watercrook, Kendal is a typical example of a riverside Roman fort. The expected mill-dam is there. Visit a Roman fort and look for the mediaeval water-mill which has reused a Roman bypass channel. The mill-dam probably has a Roman base to it.

The Roman fort at Chester-le-Street at
the tidal limit of the River Wear, is a
typical example of a river supplied site.

A = Concangis Roman fort.
K = Present tidal limit of river.
F = Present course of river.
G = Old loop as shown on O S
      1856 map.
H = Suspected Roman weir
      (destroyed by Sewage Works,
      1930. Roman inscription
      found here.)
C = Old channel, believed to have
      been Roman canal fed by Cone.
E = Present course of River Cone.
B = Canal ditch which author used
      to "bump" through on sledge
      as a schoolboy.
X = Second Roman weir, for
      navigation upstream.
J = Mediaeval ford, also suspected
      Roman crossing.
Z = Author's house where this is
      being written.

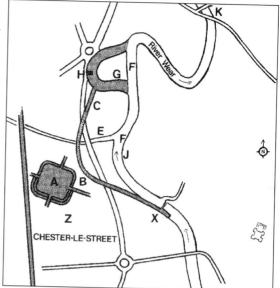

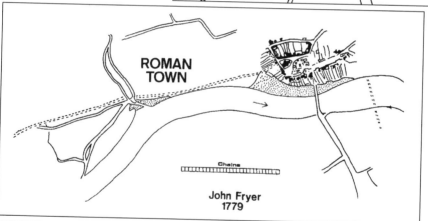

John Fryer
1779

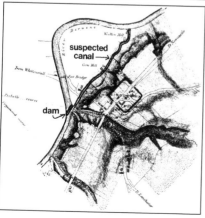

suspected
canal →

dam

John Fryer's map of 1779 shows that Corbridge once
had an unusual river loop and island beside the
Roman town.

Ebchester Roman fort has a canal-sized mill-leat in
close proximity and there have been finds of Roman
coins in the ruins of the mediaeval water-mill. The
dam in the river survives. Does it have a Roman
base?

quarter-mile upstream from this, also on the east side, a large dump of stones has been put into the river. On the downstream side, it is almost ten feet high and the whole pile must weigh four or five hundred tons. Its general effect is to reduce the width of the river and hence increase its depth proportionately. Campsie Linn falls is a narrowing of the river by a transverse outcrop of rock which forms a series of islands across the channel. On the right (west) side, the flood waters have formed a relief channel which bypasses the falls. At normal river levels, the water passes through a very narrow opening on the west side. This is not a fall as such but a steep slope down which the water rushes.....I have no doubt that a gang of men with ropes and pulley-blocks could haul a raft or small boat up it. Attempts have been made to improve both the water flow by additional gaps in the natural rock barrier, and by clearing the bypass channel. Some of this work must be fairly recent as there are two 4-inch shot-holes cut into the stone.....

The upstream side of the barrier has been extensively altered and there is no very evident reason for this so far as water control is concerned. The faces of the rock have been cut back to form straight and plumb faces from the river bed upward. This to my mind strongly suggests a navigation requirement. In addition to this, the bypass has been completely cleared of large boulders and stones and the line where this work stopped is very distinct..... .....Half a mile below Campsie is a more modern weir. This was put in between the wars to improve the water level at the end of the Hydro Tunnel to Stanley Mill.   Below this again and on the east side of the river, a channel seems to have been formed by removing all the larger stones and using them to form a longitudinal wall in the river. We saw this when the water was low....."

Mr Smith thinks that the part of the nineteenth century industrial leat from Cambusmichael church may have utilised a channel that was already there. Part of this leat is canal-sized and out of keeping with the remainder.

He then goes on to quote *Stat Acc Scot* with regard to the parishes north of Perth. According to this, the Tay was navigable to Bertha and ships of 100 tons used Perth town quay. The same source also says:

"A wall has been built across the Almond below Almondbank to provide a canal which runs for 4½ miles down between Kinnoul and Perth to join the Tay beside the old town. This canal was eighteen feet wide and three feet deep. It is mentioned in Abbey documents dated 1244 and was believed to be the work of the Romans."

This confirms my own views that the Pow Water was an artificial canal. It has typically Roman angled-straight lengths instead of bends, it is overlooked by the Gask Ridge watch-towers, leaves the River Almond at NO 068 256 and proceeds across country to join the River Earn at NN 897 186, exactly at a Roman bridge or ford site, and just opposite Strageath Roman fort. I would also like to bet that at NN 953 225, Inchaffray Abbey hides a Roman site.

According to Perth Library "pow" is the vernacular for a large ditch. At Pow Bridge, NO 050 245, the stream is in a cutting fifteen feet deep and crosses the same contour line on both sides of the hill, a sure sign of the

The base of a small Roman crane was found in a hole in the eastern abutment of the Chesters Roman bridge at Chollerford.

The crane was too small to have been used for the construction of the bridge so it is likely that the southern wing of the abutment served a secondary purpose as a jetty. The "jetty" is ten feet above the present river level, but a suspected Roman weir has been located downstream. There must have been another dam upstream to feed the now high and dry mill-leat in the abutment. It looks as if this structure was a combined bridge, wharf and mill.

The hole for a small crane in the Chesters Roman bridge abutment. The stub of the crane was recovered from the hole

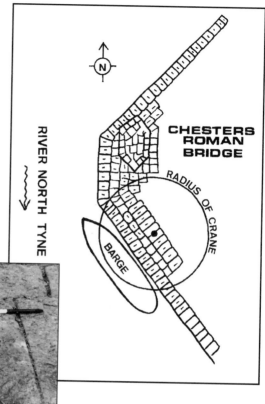

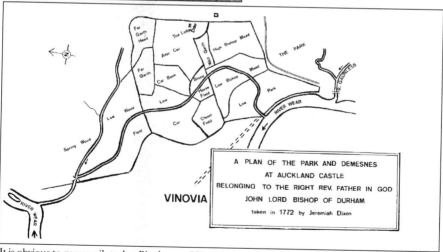

It is obvious to survey pilots that Binchester (Vinovia) fort was entirely surrounded by water at one time, with the loop of the River Wear to the north, west and south and a narrow channel (now dry) to the east. Suggestions that this eastern channel was a Roman canal, were pooh-poohed but now a map of 1772 has come to light and the canal is marked. The canal passes through "Stone Horse Field." What marvellous artefact was found here?

artificial.

A theory exists that the original course of the Almond ran down past Huntingtower and joined the Tay between Muirton and Perth. It is more likely that this old course was a branch of the Pow Water.

Agricola, with 21,000+ men operating in hostile territory, certainly had immense logistical problems which he seems to have solved with water transport, both sea-going and inland. Let us compare Agricola's supply requirements with those of a modern British colonial army for a possible invasion of Afghanistan in 1905.

It came to the notice of the British government in 1905, that Imperial Russia was planning an invasion of Afganistan and a contingency plan for a British counter-invasion was drawn up. An Indian division of 16,000 men was to march to Kabul and as the Afghans preferred the British and Indians to the Russians, the Indian division would have been treated as a friendly force, therefore no extra troops were necessary to protect the flanks of the supply lines. A memo by Sir G S Clarke, with suggestions for the calculation of the required transport for the expeditionary force, dated 7.7.1905, is explained as briefly as possible as follows.

The railway could be used to get supplies to within 70 miles of Kabul. After that it was to be pack-animals only, and no grain or forage was availabe on the line of march. The most suitable animal was the camel which could manage ten miles per day. The 70 miles would therefore be divided into 7 stages with relays of animals operating on each of the 7 stages of 10 miles.

For every 10 Indian soldiers at Kabul, 1 camel load had to arrive each day which amounted to 1,600 military loads per day. As no fodder was available over the 70 miles, all requirements had to be met from base-camp, so for every 10 camels with military loads, 1 fodder-carrying camel was necessary plus food for the drivers who each controlled 3 camels. Therefore 1,600 military load-carriers plus 160 fodder-carriers = 1,760 were needed to carry loads daily between Camp Six and Kabul, moving outwards on one day and returning unloaded the next. Therefore 2 x 1,760 = 3,520 camels were needed to operate the stage. As the 1,760 loaded camels were *en-route* each day between Camp Six and Kabul, they passed about half-way, 1,760 unloaded camels coming in the opposite direction on their return from Kabul to Camp Six. There was no food at Camp Six except that brought up by camel, therefore between Camp Five and Six, 2,112 loaded camels had to make the daily outward journey with military loads, fodder-loads for the military load-carriers, and further fodder-loads for the original fodder-carriers, and so on. These were passed by 2,112 unloaded camels returning from Camp Six to Camp 5. The calculation for the number of camels required on each stage and for the total operation, was worked out by the following formula.

Let n = number of camel loads required daily at Kabul, and r = number of stages. Then total number of camels required for the line will be:

$$11n[(6/5)r - 1]$$

which works out as follows:

Stages of 10 miles	Calculation	No. of Camels
Kabul - 6	2 x 1,760	= 3,520
Camp 6 - 5	2 x 1,760 x 1.2	= 4,224
Camp 5 - 4	2 x 2,112 x 1.2	= 5,068
Camp 4 - 3	2 x 2,534 x 1.2	= 6,080
Camp 3 - 2	2 x 3,040 x 1.2	= 7,296
Camp 2 - 1	2 x 3,648 x 1.2	= 8,752
Camp 1 - Base	2 x 4,376 x 1.2	= 10,500
Therefore total camels required on any one day		= 45,440

This does not include the transport of fuel for cooking, and it should be noted that the Indian division will require 20 tons of this per day, but it is assumed that this will be available locally.

As the operation is through friendly territory, neither has any provision been made for escorting troops nor troops guarding the camps or flanks.

Allowing 20 per cent for camels resting, and 100 per cent per annum for casualties, the total number required for the line for one year is:

109,956 camels

It was realised that the Russians could not mount their operation because of similar logistical problems, therefore the British/Indian invasion was not necessary. The Russians made it seventy-four years later with heavy transport aircraft, helicopters and military vehicles. Bulldozers and explosives were used for building and improving roads.

If Agricola had used pack-animals for his expedition into Scotland, how many would he have needed, taking into consideration the problems of operating in enemy territory? There just wouldn't have been enough animals in the whole of Britain.

An example of the logistical problems encountered by the Romans was shown when Antioch experienced a famine in AD 362. Despite the fact that grain in plenty was available fifty miles away across desert terrain, the people were allowed to starve. The British army formula can be used to explain the reason why.

Comparisons with British army techniques may help us to understand the time necessary for the Romans to build their campaign roads and the subsequent network of occupation roads for police action. We must now go down to the South Atlantic and look at the Falkland Islands. The Argentine invasion of 1982 was easy because there were only forty-four defending troops. The subsequent return of the British forces was a tremendous logistical exercise, assisted by the British-owned Ascension Island, about half-way along the eight-thousand mile sea supply line.

There were hardly any roads at all in the Falklands and farmers operated old motor-bikes along sheep tracks. The only half-decent roads were from Stanley to the airport, and from Stanley to Moody Brook, and even those were fit only for four-wheel-drive vehicles.

The Argentine occupation forces settled into two main defended areas, Stanley and Goose Green, and surrounded themselves with minefields. If the Romans had occupied similar islands, they would have set to work immediately building roads to all parts so that they could meet any military threats. The Argentine forces made no such efforts during the seventy-four days of occupation. The British landing was unopposed by the Argentine navy after the loss of its capital ship the *General Belgrano*. This modernised cruiser, armed with the deadly *Exocet* (flying-fish) missiles, was the ex-*USS Phoenix*, which had survived the Japanese attack on Pearl Harbor.

Only the Argentine air force opposed the British landings at San Carlos, and this was made possible only by the scrapping, before the conflict, of the angled-deck aircraft-carrier *Ark Royal* and the inability of the *Invincible* and *Hermes* to operate Gannet radar picket aircraft to give early warning of air attacks.

The Argentine forces did not expect the British to land forty miles from the capital and walk to Stanley. The ten helicopters which should have relayed the troops across the horrible peat moors, were lost when the *Atlantic Conveyor* carrying them was sunk. The greatest loss was three Chinook helicopters which could each transport underslung loads of 12 tons. Among other items, tents for 4,000 troops were lost.

The campaign is history now, but the large British garrison was still faced with transportation problems after the Argentine surrender. It was too expensive to continue routine supply with Chinook helicopters and caterpillar-tracked vehicles. A network of roads had to be constructed for day-to-day needs and in case Argentina made another attack.

I happened to be serving in a ship in Port Stanley at the time, and I noticed that all army transportation was carried out on water. The army had more boats than the navy and the harbour and surrounding waters were criss-crossed with the wakes of army speedboats, assault boats and powered-pontoons, all manned by khaki-clad soldiers. I wondered if I was witnessing the modern equivalent of the *Barcarii Tigrisenses*. Meanwhile, the Royal Engineers were constructing a new network of army roads.

The similarity of these British army roads to Roman ones was astonishing. Even the method of construction was the same. The Royal Engineers cut a deep trench across country and filled this with large boulders gathered locally or blown-up by explosives from rocky outcrops which abounded. Deep drainage ditches ran alongside the roads, following the Roman pattern. Where necessary, culverts, also in the Roman manner, ran underneath the British roads. The Romans crossed boggy land by laying bundles of faggots in the bottom of the excavated trench; the Royal Engineers used special rolls of wire-reinforced plastic. The British road surfaces, as were the Roman, were of rammed gravel.

Our historians have told us that, as the Roman army advanced, so the Roman engineers kept pace behind them with newly constructed roads. As an average Roman road has thousands of tons of stone per mile, I very much doubted this.

I was given permission to inspect the Royal Engineers' road construction works. The soldiers wondered why a sailor was taking so much interest in mundane road-building, but were intrigued to learn that their work was being compared with that of the Roman legions. Major Bradbury, R.E., gave me the specifications of the roads:

Roadway width, single carriageway   6 metres

Roadway width, double carriageway   10 metres
Average thickness   600 millimetres

Therefore quantities for 1 kilometre of road

= 1000 x .6   x 6 = 3,600 cubic metres, (single lane)

or 1000 x .6 x 10 = 6,000 cubic metres, (double lane)

The conversion factor for cubic metres to tonnes = 1.6 Therefore 5,760 tonnes are needed for 1 km of single lane road and 9,600 tonnes for 1 km of double lane.

The engineers were using six-wheel-drive Hydromatic dump-trucks which carried 6 to 7 tonnes at a time, which was 823 truck-loads for a kilometre of single lane road, and 1,372 truck-loads for a kilometre of double-lane. Forty loads per day was the average achieved in the Falklands, and it took 21 days to lay a kilometre of single lane and 35 days for a double. In addition, the Royal Engineers had a Chinook helicopter to move heavy equipment about.

Average Roman roads were the same width as single-lane Falklands roads but usually the Roman roads had deeper foundations than those built by the Royal Engineers.

Roman engineers would have needed 12,902 ox-wagon loads of stone per kilometre of road of the same dimensions as single-lane Falklands type. For a single-lane Roman road (18 ft wide) from Richborough to London, over a million ox-wagon loads of stone would have been needed.

How long was it before Roman roads could be used to supply an advancing army? Even when they were finished, their severe gradients still presented formidable obstacles to wheeled traffic.

In India and Burma, native bullock-cart-roads used a similar system to the seventeenth century wooden wagonways of Britain, except, instead of wooden rails, two strips of flagstones were utilised to lessen the friction. This technique could easily have been provided by the Romans but it was not done; why? Because obviously, the Romans had no need of heavy goods roads if they operated a much more efficient river-based system.

It is now time to examine further evidence, and suspected evidence, of Roman water transport in rivers not examined so far.

The River Tweed, with its mouth at Berwick upon Tweed, runs into the hinterland of Scotland. At Melrose, there is the Roman fort of Trimontium (NT 555 338). A wheel from a Roman vehicle and a sports-helmet with face-mask were found there. The steering oar from a Roman barge and a boathook were also found but these seldom get a mention as the authorities could not understand why these items were so far from the sea. There are many weirs which may have Roman bases and "funny river configurations" for field workers to examine in both the main Tweed and its tributaries. Roman pottery has been found at Norham Castle (NT 907 477). On the Whiteadder Water, the farm called "Chesterfield" (NT 941 539) looks as if it is sitting on a Roman-type fort platform. High up the Tweed above Peebles, and into the tributary of the Lyne Water, is the Roman fort of Hallyne (NT 187 405). To the south-east of the fort on the other side of the Lyne is an obvious Roman road (not mentioned in any documents), at NT 192 402. It heads for another Roman fort half a mile to the south at Easter Haprew. Further up the Lyne Water, the Tarth Water (NT 164 429) looked like an artificial channel from the air, similar to the Pow Water in Perthshire.

A blue line can be traced on the OS map all the way to the River Clyde via Castlecraig (two Roman marching camps), Newmill, the Garvald Burn, under the Roman road which approximates to the A702(T), into the South Medwin Water, and then into the Clyde via the Medwin Water (NS 973 443) not far downstream from Castledykes Roman fort (NS 929 443).

There is another possible Roman water-link between the Tweed and the Clyde via the Biggar Water. It leaves the Tweed at NT 133 353, follows the same gap through the hills chosen by the later railway engineers, through Causewayend to the south of Biggar, and splits into two mouths; one enters the Clyde at Wolfclyde (NT 018 365), the other beside a known Roman marching camp at Coulter (NT 014 350).

The Romans may have been far busier in Scotland than previously thought. It is now up to amateur historians, field walkers and detectorists to produce the evidence.

Now for the famous River Tyne, the Roman "Tinea Fl." At the river mouth, there used to be a shallow bar, and this has been used by some landlubberly historians and archaeologists to declare that the river was unnavigable in Roman times. In addition to the normal depth of the river, even if it was just a couple of feet over sand and shoals, the Spring tides would have provided an extra fourteen feet of water.

On the north side of the river entrance is the impressive rock upon which sits Tynemouth Priory and Castle. King Edwin of Northumbria erected a Christian temple here "175 years after the departure of the Romans." An early monastery was destroyed by the Danes in 865, and during later coastal defence works, Roman altars were found but unfortunately not recorded. The Romans could not pass a place such as this without putting a lighthouse, monument, trophy or temple on it.

On the south side of the river is South Shields and the Roman fort of Arbeia, where the Bargemen of the River Tigris were stationed. It is thought that, in Roman times, the fort stood on an island with a branch of the Tyne going down what is now Ocean Road. The fort has twenty granaries and was obviously a supply fort for either the Roman Wall or expeditions into Scotland, probably both.

Below the fort, and in the vicinity of the Milldam stream, according to the antiquarian Christopher Hunter, there existed: "an elevated pavement in the River Tine...proper for their safe landing at different times of the flowing and ebbing tide." A little further upstream, also on the south side of the river was the natural harbour of Jarrow Slake, now infilled. On the bank of the former haven is the Saxon church of St Pauls and the ruins of the monastery. The Ordnance Survey map marks a "Roman unspecified building" here. The Museum staff become quite rude when a Roman site is mentioned. Why is historical evidence concealed or distorted? The famous antiquarian, the Rev Hodgson was the parson here for many years and he was in no doubt about the church being on a Roman site. Quoted in *The Roman Wall*, Bruce, 1851, he said:

"At Jarrow, an oblong square of about three acres, with its corners rounded off, overlooking the estuary of Jarrow Slake, and fronting on the south, the bank of the navigable stream called the Don, is on good grounds, supposed to have been the site of a station or fortified town of the Romans. Underground foundations of a wall of strong masonry mark out its area on every side, and include within them the site of the present church and church-yard, and some ragged remains of the ancient monastery of Jarrow. In digging up part of the remains of these walls in 1812, a silver *denarius* of Aulus Vitellus was found embedded in mortar, in the heart of the wall; and when the road was formed past Jarrow-Row in 1803, two square pavements of Roman brick were discovered."

The *Notitia Dignitatum* lists a fort named, slightly doubtfully, "Danum" between Arbeia (South Shields) and Pons Aelius (Newcastle upon Tyne). The small River Don, which Hodgson quoted as navigable, intercepts the Roman road "Wrekendyke" just over a mile south-south-west of St Pauls, at NZ 334 634. Further south, the stream passes a farm with the significant name "Mount Pleasant." Close by, there is the tradition of an "old ship" having been seen during the last century. This was said to be the remains of a Viking ship, but it may be a Roman *codicaria*. After passing Wallsend (Roman Segedunum), Hadrian's Wall lies beyond the north bank, cutting off a bend in the river. As Newcastle is approached, the Wall gets closer to the river bank. The Swing Bridge is on the site of the Roman bridge, the mediaeval bridge which lost several arches during the Great Flood of 1771, and the later bridge, which was dismantled and replaced by the Swing Bridge to facilitate navigation. In 1772, when the wreckage of the mediaeval bridge was being removed, workmen found traces of Roman piers with embedded Roman coins, some reported as depicting Emperor Hadrian (Sykes, *Local Records*, Vol 1, 1833). The Roman bridge was built in AD 120 and lasted until 1248; over 1,100 years.

The Tyne is tidal for seventeen miles to Wylam where there are rapids. A couple of miles below Wylam, on the south bank, the skeletal timbers of a barge can be seen sticking out of the mud at low tide. Old wagonways meet the river in this area.

The name "Wylam" is thought to mean "barrier" (in the river) and the Spring tides reach the fast water just below the modern road bridge. Two miles above Wylam is the village of Ovingham with its Saxon church. The tower contains obvious reused lewis-holed stones.

A ferry operated here until the last century using the ruins of an old weir below the modern road bridge as a jetty. A few hundred yards upstream from this bridge, opposite the mouth of the Whittle Burn, the timbers of an old dam can be seen in the river bed during low river-levels. The grid of rough oak beams lies at forty degrees to the river flow, the downstream end to the north, and is thought to be of Roman origin. It looks as if this structure consisted of tree-trunk box-frames filled with rocks.

Rather than try to calculate the likely sites of Roman navigation weirs, which it seems were situated only where necessary rather than at precise intervals, it is better to mark the positions of known or suspected Roman forts, and also Saxon churches. The latter were invariably right on top of, or very close to Roman sites. After this has been done, pencil in possible missing locations at obvious places such as rapids.

As we progress up the river, the long-lost Roman Stanegate Roman road is now near the north bank. The next Saxon church beside the river is at Bywell, and the discovery of a Roman bridge and the excavation of a hitherto unknown Roman road network has been described in Chapter 6. The 1836 Bywell bridge is about a hundred yards downstream from the site of the three missing piers of the Roman bridge. The northern pier of the modern bridge has circular holes drilled into it, and these were for explosives to blow-up the pier if the Germans had invaded in 1940. Fortunately, the bridge did not suffer the fate of the last two piers of its Roman predecessor which were demolished by gunpowder in 1836.

Just opposite Bywell Castle are the remains of an old weir. Water-mills at Bywell are mentioned in 1278, and in 1637, there is a specific reference to the dam and the remains of the ancient bridge in *Camden's Britannia*:

> "Beneath the castle there is a very goodly weare for the catching of salmons, and two solid piles of most firm stone, which in time past supported the bridge, stand up in the midst of the river."

From Mackenzie's *History of Northumberland,* Vol 2, we get another description of the dam and ruinous bridge:

> "The appearance and situation of Bywell is affirmed to be the most interesting of any in this country. Viewed from the south side of the river, the landscape appears very beautiful. From the road near the brink of the river, the ruined piers of a bridge become the front objects, behind which, in a regular cascade, the whole river falls over a wear, extended from bank to bank, in height about ten perpendicular feet; a mill on the right hand, a salmon lock on the left."

A slightly later observer gives an account of the destruction of the remains of the bridge:

> "On the two piers, there was no spring of arches, so the superstructure must have been made of wood..... ...the piers, which stood near the dam, remained until August 10, 1836, when they were blown up by a charge of gunpowder, on the same day on which the foundations of the new bridge were laid, the latter a noble structure, erected farther down the river, was built at the sole cost of Mr T W Beamont."

Most of the dam was dismantled in 1862. The southern end survives and has modern additions such as iron bolts and cement repairs on the top. An iron-works and many corn-mills have used the structure over the centuries. At the southern end, the stonework springs from a natural rock projection of the cliff, and a narrow spillway, with slots for a lifting gate or stop-logs, has been cut through the solid rock close to the cliff face. Further out is a strange lock with slots for two sets of lifting gates. There is also a recess which may have housed the counterweight of a lifting-type bridge. The dismantled part of the dam (the northern three-quarters were taken down in July 1862) was curved as is evidenced by lines of square post-holes cut into the bed-rock of the river. An existing fish-trap has re-used the post-holes, but the fish-trap timbers are circular and are thrust into square holes. When we first examined the remains of the dam in 1982, we suspected that it could have had a Roman origin. Now that a major Roman road network and dozens of Roman coins and pottery have been found in the vicinity, a much more detailed examination will be necessary. Divers have discovered extra post-holes in the rock river bed below the dam, and there is an unexplained post hole in the floor of the lock, and this may pre-date the whole structure. The air-face of the remains of the dam-stub are stepped and the water-face sloped in the typical Roman manner. Just upstream, and right alongside St Peter's church, there is a large "V-cut" thought to have been a Roman barge-basin and through-channel to yet another dam-site, the latter located by divers at NZ 045 613 at the top end of the oversized leat. Piles survive on the river bed at the second dam-site. This dam was also curved downstream to the north bank and at one time has led water into the now dry cut which is far too large to have been designed as a mill-leat, although it may have been used as such at a later date. If filled with water, (and it would have been with the downstream dam intact), a very large barge could have negotiated it. The pattern which seems to be emerging, is that river barriers close to Roman forts were well engineered, while the intermediate ones were rough structures of timber and rubble. Also, at Roman sites, there often seems to have been a cascade of dams, as will be seen when we arrive at much firmer evidence.

St Peter's Church at Bywell once stood on a very Roman-looking platform (wood-cut of 1800), but landscaping has brought the surrounding fields up to the same level. A Roman altar was found at a depth of six feet in the churchyard in 1902. In 1750, a Roman silver cup was found in the Tyne close to the church.

The second Church, St Andrew's, is Saxon and the tower is built almost entirely of Roman stones. Investigations continue.

Five miles upstream is Corbridge, and the Roman fort and town of Corstopitum. A Roman bridge crossed the river at NY 980 647 and there were five piers in the river bed. Our divers have traced the remains of four, but on the spacing, a central one is completely missing. A Roman slave-chain, complete with barrel-lock was recovered from the bed of the river near one of the pier bases. In the north bank, fifty yards downstream from the Cor Burn, there is an old jetty at NY 981 646 from which I have taken Roman coins of Constantine. The timbers have been dendro-dated to the late Saxon period, so the structure has obviously been repaired after Roman times. When I first mentioned this jetty, I was told that it must be a "Victorian rowing club." At least the dendro-date (which I think is dubious), is getting a bit nearer the mark. A map of 1779 by Fryer shows that Corbridge once had a "funny river system" with suspected barge basins and a canal.

Three miles upstream is Hexham where a major Roman town is suspected. More will be said of this in Chapter 10 which deals with frontiers.

Round the next bend is the juction of the North Tyne and South Tyne. The North Tyne is the dominant river and has caused a shallow bar to form over the mouth of the South Tyne. We will turn north into the North Tyne, and a few hundred yards upstream is Howford where the Stanegate Roman road crossed. There may have been more than a ford here as there are still some very large worked stones lying in the river. It may well have been a combination of ford and weir. In the field to the east is the Saxon church at

A Norwegian PBY Catalina flying boat taxiing into the River Wear from Sunderland Harbour c1945. Behind is the old pilot house.

The old jetty at left has recently been replaced and many ex-Roman stones came to light. It is thought that the stones came from the massive Roman dam at Hylton when it was dismantled c1865. A further inspection of the area has revealed many more ex-Roman stones, some of them on the beach on the seaward side of the pilot house.

A suspected ex-Roman stone, revealed when the Sunderland Harbour inner jetty was replaced. Note the holes for butterfly cramps.

A stone in a Roman structure at Risingham (Habitancum) Roman fort. This stone is in the Chesterhope Burn. Note butterfly cramp holes for comparison with Sunderland stones.

An ex-Roman stone from the Sunderland jetty. Note lewis-hole.

Another ex-Roman stone, (dumped 1865?) on the inner mole at Sunderland.

Warden, once again with reused Roman stones in its structure.

At Warden Mill (NY 917 671), slightly further upstream, there are severe rapids, but an old woodcut shows a very rough dam constructed of unworked stones. Very little of this remains today, but the river was navigable even in recent years as an old map shows a "boat-house" upstream.

Half a mile further on, the remains of a weir can still be seen in the river bed at NY 916 682, and there are ruins of another, half a mile beyond that at NY 911 686. A branch of the Stanegate arrives here from the west around the north of Warden Hill and then turns south for reasons as yet unknown (E Sockett, *AA*, 1973).

We are now approaching the Roman fort of Chesters (Cilurnum, NY 912 702). The line of Hadrian's Wall crossed the North Tyne here and a magnificent bridge carried the roadway over. The abutments and three pier bases survive but, due to river movement, the easterly pier now lies under the river bank. The massive eastern abutment contains thousands of tons of stone and the pier of an earlier and smaller bridge has been encapsulated by the later work. There are several puzzling features about the bridge abutment. This eastern abutment, which is now high and dry, contains an integral mill-leat but it is at least ten feet above the present river-level, with no apparent means of being fed with water. The abutment is also asymmetric with a straight water-face and two angled walls which lead back from the river. The southern wall is far longer than the northern one and would have made an ideal jetty if the river were ten feet higher. One of the leading experts in Britain on the history of transport, MJT Lewis, came to the same conclusion independently and unknown to me. What he did not know, was that the base of a small Roman crane had been found in a purpose-cut hole in this "jetty." It was just a single-pole derrick-type crane and there was only one such hole in the entire abutment. The experts of course immediately decided that it must have been used during the building of the bridge, but you don't put a construction crane on a finished bridge, and in any case, its radius of action could have been only a few feet. The jib however would have overhung exactly, the position of a barge lying alongside the southern abutment wall. For this to have happened, the river needed to be ten feet deeper to lift the barge up to the "jetty."

The answer seems to be six hundred yards downstream where a rock sill across the river at about 45 degrees to the flow looks as if it has been used as a weir. A few huge rough stones remain on top of the western end of the natural barrier. The eastern river bank has been revetted with cobbles in a very neat manner, and this could be part of an old spillway. Such a weir would lift barges to the suspected jetty and derrick.

A short distance upstream from the Roman bridge is another "funny river configuration." Chollerford Island divides the river into two channels, and a curved dam deflects water into the smaller western arm. The whole layout smacks of Pommeroeul and other Roman river harbours.

In August 1913, Gerald Simpson investigated reports that stonework had been seen on Chollerford Island after severe floods of c1865. An excavation revealed the stonework (some of which is once again visible at time of writing) which, it was decided, must be the eastern abutment of a mediaeval

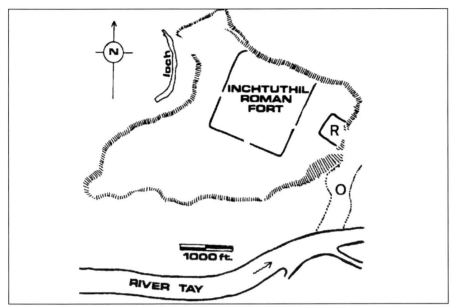

Inchtuthil Roman fort.

R = Three sided Roman camp known locally as the "Redoubt".
O = Old course of the river. Like Binchester in County Durham, Inchtuthil has had water all the way around it in Roman times.

The Roman fort at Bertha, near Perth.

F = Roman fort.
B = Site of Roman bridge across River Tay.
W = Old weir.

Once again, we have a bridge and a weir in close proximity to a Roman fort. This fort was at the Roman period tidal limit of the Tay.

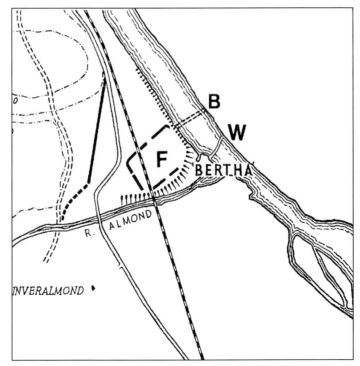

bridge. This entailed a postulated movement of the river to the east and right around the back of the bridge. Three angled walls were found and three courses survived with the top one chamfered and tied together with iron cramps. The interior was filled with rubble. This structure could be the remains of Roman harbour works. It is about 75 yards downstream from the Humshaugh Mill-dam.

The Humshaugh mill-dam, which leads water into the channel west of the island, may have had a Roman predecessor which would explain the high and dry mill-leat in the Roman bridge abutment downstream.

The remains of a genuine mediaeval bridge which was destroyed by the Great Flood of 1771, can be seen immediately downstream from the existing bridge which carries the B6318 over the river. At low river-levels, the base of a pier, complete with cutwater, can be seen in the water below the south side of the second arch from the eastern end of the later bridge. Tomlinson's famous *Guide* sugggests that these remains in the water, and old abutments at each end, are from Bishop Walter Skirlaw's bridge built, or rebuilt in 1394. If so, what is the strange stonework on the island? Also, the Humshaugh dam, or its predecessor, must have been built before the mediaeval bridge, as the surviving bottom course of the ruinous bridge-pier visible underwater, lies on top of the high level of silt and rubble accumulated by the dam.

There are further ruinous weirs upstream at Haughton Castle, Chipchase Mill, Glen Ridley (below Wark), and a strange island called Gold Island, all of which will have to be investigated by divers. The whole area abounds with Romano-British farmsteads, clearly visible from the air. Some up-dating of population figures for Roman Britain is necessary.

At NY 866 799, to the east of Lee Hall Farm, there are two curious configurations in the river. A stone cill, originally natural, but obviously shaped by the hand of man, crosses the river at right angles in a very neat manner. Just downstream are two natural rock abutments at either side of the river and a central rock-island. This is known as "Devil's Leap" and an obvious place for a bridge. Mother Nature has done half of the engineering already.

To the north, the River Rede joins the Tyne and up the tributary river are the Roman forts of Risingham (Habitancum), Blakehope (Latin name unknown) and High Rochester (Bremenium). Just under a mile downstream from Risingham, an RB farmstead, or perhaps a fortlet, was observed from the air on the south side of the river at NY 882 859, and the River Rede has old channels running right up to the Habitancum fort. These are said to be old courses of the Rede, but why do these strange loops always occur in the vicinity of Roman forts? Experts from the "ox-wagon brigade" declared the channels to be natural but they never even mentioned the massive stone dam just to the north-east which was dismantled last century because it was an obstruction to salmon. At NY 895 875, 900 yards north-east of West Woodburn, a legionary-size marching camp was observed from the air. A ground inspection shows that the Roman ditches are still visible on 2½ sides. Local experts declared that it was merely an old field boundary, but Mr Roy Farrar of the Royal Commission on Historic Monuments, London, found the *tuteli* (defensive earth banks in front of gates) and declared the site to be genuine.

At the Blakehope fort, NY 860 945, there is a possible rough dam in the river beside an old island, now dry, which is covered by mediaeval rig and furrow. The River Rede is now getting rather like the Tiber at Arezzo, the Roman limit of navigation of that river, so High Rochester (NY 828 988), may have been the top end of the water supply line with pack-animals continuing up Dere Street to the north, but meeting other pack-animals coming south from the barges which had negotiated the Tweed and its tributaries. The pack-animals would have had to travel no more than about five miles.

One other important river in north-eastern England remains to be discussed, but because of important evidence, the next chapter will concentrate entirely on the River Tees. Meanwhile, we must look at eastern England and the Fens, but before that let us look at some of the very strange Roman bridge remains found here and there.

Across the River Churn at Cirencester at SP 027 021, a massive curved Roman abutment a hundred feet long was found. In spite of the great size and peculiar shape of this abutment, what was thought to be the first pier was only twelve feet away from the abutment (*Antiquarian Journal* XLI, 1961). What a peculiar bridge! It is far more likley that this was a curved weir with a twelve foot wide canal channel or lock in one end. The official explanation talks about town ditch-systems being led through the bridge abutment. Near Worthing on the River Wensum at TG 004 202, the river divides into two channels around a small island. Two lines of Roman piles, dendro-dated to AD 130, eight feet apart, crossed the eastern channel. Nothing was found in the western channel and this was postulated as a possible mediaeval mill-leat. (Toynbee and Clarke, *Journal of Roman Studies*, XXXVIII, 1948) It is more likely that this was a Roman flash-lock with the fixed weir in the eastern channel and gates and a moveable weir on the western side of the island.

Over the River Arun near Alfodean at TQ 118 331, the stream is only twenty-six feet wide, but squared stones and oak stakes were identified as a possible Roman bridge with three stone piers only six feet apart. (Winbolt, *Sussex Arch Coll*, LXXVI). It is more likely to have served a navigation purpose.

In Wallasey Pool at SJ 322 894, a so-called Roman bridge, a hundred feet long, was found completely buried in silt. The report in *Chester Archit and Arch Soc Journal*, 1850, claims that four compound beams rested on two stone piers. This is not consistent with the drawings made in 1850 by the investigator of the structure, Rev W H Massie. These drawings show the beams above the remains of a longitudinal wall on the same alignment as the timbers. The four parallel beams were thought to have been the roadway, but these were ten feet below the level of high tide. A massive subsidence in antiquity was postualted but, remarkably, the timbers had remained perfectly level during the descent.

In *Popular Archaeology*, May 1985, Mr David Armstrong, B Eng, C Eng, says that the structure is far more likely to have been a Roman navigation cill over which vessels could pass at high tide and remain in navigable water when the tide ebbed. Armstrong points out that, according to J A Steers in his *Coastline of England and Wales*, the area in question is at a higher level now than in Roman times.

The Yorkshire rivers have witnessed much Roman water activity and I note from the *Cruising Guide to the North East Waterways*, compiled by the Ripon Motor Boat Club, that a Roman "paved ford" is a hazard to navigation on the River Ure at SE 364 664, opposite Mulwith. Even though much of it was removed by dredging in 1771 and 1930, it is still an obstruction at low river levels. It sounds more like the remains of a Roman weir than a paved ford. It looks as if the Romans were going up the river to Ripon, and points upstream.

Further downstream on the Ure, at the Roman town of Isurium (Aldborough), the *Cruising Guide* comments on the massive Roman jetty:

"Hall Arm Landing, Roman head of navigation, extending south by naturally navigable rivers and the Fossdyke and the Carrdyke to the cornfields of Lincolnshire and the Fens."

I have often looked at this stone jetty, built of huge stones, in the bend of the river at SE 412 669. It is obviously Roman but seems to be ignored by the establishment. It is much used by fishermen. A very straight cart track runs from this wharf into the Roman town. A mile downstream, the Ure is joined by the Swale which has come down from Catterick (Cataractonium). To get a name like this, there was obviously a very large waterfall at Catterick in Roman times. There is nothing there now, so it must have been an artificial waterfall and probably a weir with a massive spillway. Upstream from Catterick is a suspected Roman bypass canal at NZ 193 994 on the south side of the River Swale north-west of Colburn. There is a local tradition in Swaledale that the Romans first went there by water.

Back on the Ure, which has absorbed the Swale, the river does a very strange thing. It changes its name, not at the confluence with another river, but, in the middle of nowhere, (SE 473 604) it becomes the River Ouse. The reason is the tiny Ouse Gill Beck which joins the large river here. I suspect that this little stream has given the great river its identity because the little stream was an important Roman canal leading across to the Roman road Dere Street, just to the west. The stream has been dammed into an ornamental lake and this passes by Moat Hall (SE 452 610) which is built on Roman foundations. Many years ago, from the air I thought I saw the shape of a Roman fort just upstream, at Aldwark. This was naturally pooh-poohed, but now I find that there has long been a tradition of a Roman site there. I have now mislaid the negatives and will have to fly over again.

The former commodore, now vice president of the Ripon Motor Boat Club, Pat Jones, tells me that the volume of Roman river traffic on the River Ouse was sufficient to justify building an extensive dock at York in which to harbour the ships. The water in the dock was maintained at, or near, the high water level of the tidal river by a drainage channel cut from the water-logged Forest of Galtres, still known by a name which recalls its Roman origin - the River Foss.

It is fairly obvious from areas of intense Roman riverside activity, that the Romans navigated the Yorkshire Derwent. Stamford Bridge has been mentioned earlier as the probable site of Roman Derventio. The river configuration above Stamford Bridge at Buttercrambe would have lent itself ideally to Roman navigation works. I quote from Pat Jones' description of the river here:

"If the Romans did construct pound locks on the Derwent to improve its navigability, then Buttercrambe Mill may well have been the site of one of them. Evidence of the Roman occupation has been unearthed nearby and the head and tail races of the mill bypassed one of the river's particularly convoluted reaches. The head race alone was 400 yards long, virtually straight and almost as wide as the river. The Mill is situated on what would have been an ideal position for a pound lock, unlike the eighteenth century lock, which even the powered pleasure craft of the 1930's found difficult to enter or leave, due to the broad angle at which the upper lock cut joined the narrow river."

The level of the river bed at Buttercrambe is the same as the bed of the River Ure at Aldborough and there is a Roman jetty at the latter. Buttercrambe also had an Anglo-Saxon site which gives a Roman origin further credibility.

Further upstream is Kirkham Abbey and Mill where another river configuration with a natural island, has just cried out for a weir to be constructed on one side of the island, and locks on the other. As to be expected, the weir and locks are there. Does the weir have a Roman base? A mile upstream is the famous Roman pottery at Crambeck, from which the fourth century pottery gets its name. No doubt, thousands of tons of finished articles went up and down the Derwent.

Four miles upstream is the Roman fort at Malton which at the moment is labelled Derventio, but I am sure that its correct name is Delgovicia. Whatever its name, it was obviously sited on the navigable river for good reason. Also just over a mile downstream at SE 776 700, an old loop has been isolated from the main river, not by ox-bow action, but by the hand of man. Just opposite is the site of a substantial Roman building. On the south bank of the river at Malton, there was another major Roman pottery at Norton. The higher reaches of the Derwent and tributaries have yet to be searched, but the Ordnance Survey map of Roman Britain shows a profusion of finds along these watercourses.

 Don Billingham of Doncaster is convinced that his local "Danum" Roman fort was river supplied, and he brought my attention to the "odd" River Cheswold which makes a deviation from the River Don, past the Roman fort, and then back into the main river. He thinks that the Cheswold was a barge basin. I am sure he is right. All these "odd" river configurations in the vicinity of Roman sites cannot be coincidences.

Lincoln, with its legionary fortress, was obviously the centre of river navigation in Lincolnshire. The inland harbour of Brayford Pool shows us what the Romans could do.

Recent researches have shown that the Roman artificial canal, the Car Dyke, between the River Slea and Bourne, was not a through-navigation. In two places, uncut causeways across the canal are used as evidence to claim that the waterway was not navigated. If its prime function was a catchwater drain, it would still have been sailed on by the Romans who navigated drains all over their Empire. If a ditch held water and would float a boat, they would have used it. Even if they had to transfer their cargoes a dozen times, it was cheaper than road transport. Pliny the Younger, in his letter to Trajan, mentioned using an uncut section between two stretches of water as a safety device. The Romans even navigated a sewer underneath Rome. In the Fens, the Romans diverted rivers into so-called catchwater drains. Surely it should have been the other way round?

With regard to the mass of ancient, modern and unidentified waterways of the Fens, I must bring to the attention of readers, the best work I have ever seen on the subject: *The Black Fens* by A K Astbury, 1958, reprinted 1973. The author begins his account of years of research with the following fascinating paragraphs:

> "Of the unknown waterways of the southern Fens, the following must be accepted as Roman: the Car Dyke, Reach Slade, the Rodham Farm channel, Lark Slade, and those portions of the artificial Lark below and above the Slade. In addition, I suggest that the Fen course of the Little Ouse, that of the Ouse itself from Littleport to Stowbridge, Cnut's Dyke, and Colne Dyke are probably Roman too.

> We start therefore with the presumption that the other artificial waterways whose dates of origin are unknown, may also be Roman. Of these, the most important still in existence, are Whittlesea Dyke, the course (if it is artificial) of the Old Nene through March, the artificial courses of the Ouse at Ely, of the Cam north of Waterbeach, and all of those lodes which run from the chalk highland to the Cam-Ouse river - Bottisham, Swaffham, Burwell, Reach, Cottenham and Soham Lodes, with the New River south of Wicken and the eastern portion of the Old West River. In addition there are the extinct waterways which, with a stretch of the Old Nene north-east of March, led all of the way from the West Water south-west of Chatteris to the sea at Elm - the Leam and Elm Leam."

It is now time to return to the north of England where firm evidence of Roman river navigation is coming to light.

Chapter 9

A Bridge Too Far

"When a fact appears opposed to a long train of deductions, it invariably proves to be capable of bearing some other interpretation."
Sherlock Holmes, in Sir Arthur Conan Doyle's, *A Study in Scarlet*

When I first realised that the Romans had navigated our minor rivers, I flew over all the known (and a few suspected) Roman sites in northern England and southern Scotland, to see what they had in common. They were all situated on rivers and the sites had obviously not been chosen with defence as the first priority. A known Roman road usually crossed the river in the vicinity, but it was obvious from the air that other unrecorded Roman roads had also converged on the bridges in what Raymond Chevalier calls "bird's foot patterns." It was also obvious that more often than not, mediaeval water-mills had reused the Roman sites. The usual answer was that the mediaeval millers had been attracted by free ex-Roman building materials. Quite often Saxon churches had beaten the millers to it so there must have been other reasons. No doubt the Romans also had water-mills, but ground inspections showed that the mill-leats in the vicinity of Roman forts were huge. The Romans did everything on a grand scale and we are told that thirty thousand men were employed for twelve years digging a tunnel to drain Lake Celano in order to turn the lake bed into farmland. This does not tell us why they needed water wheels in Britain five sizes too big. If the mills were mediaeval originals, why were they always built on the same side of the river as the Roman forts? Were the associated river-barrages standing on Roman bases, and had those giant leats served some purpose other than to provide water power? As I looked at the easily navigable reaches above the dam/weirs, I wondered if this had been the main purpose of the barriers. At Ebchester, County Durham, the wild River Derwent is tamed by a mill-dam just below the fort, so much so, that a sports rowing club uses the river, transformed above the dam from little more than a mountain stream into an elongated lake. The mill-leat, now blocked-off and dry, has been large enough to take a boat through at one time.

My flights took me far and wide, but the establishment did not want any

Aerial view of Piercebridge.
The later three-arched bridge
on the site of the mediaeval
five-arched structure, is at top
right. The Roman fort is under
the village but the north-west
rounded corner can be seen
bottom centre. The excavated
north-east corner is in the
farmyard at left centre. The
Roman *vicus* is showing as a
crop mark in the Tofts Field
(top) and the main Roman
road, Dere Street, heads
towards the river. Another
Roman road leaves Dere Street
and enters the east gate of the
Roman fort.

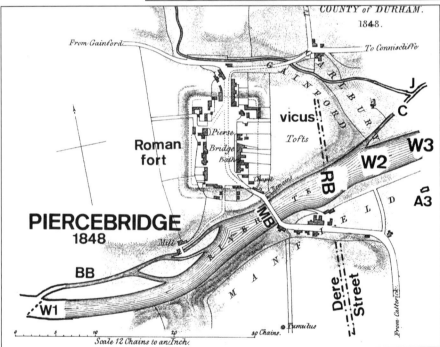

1848 map with recent information added.

W1 = Site of mill-dam which supplied mediaeval mill-leat BB.
This massive leat is suspected reused Roman barge basin.
MB = Three-arched modern bridge on site of five-arched mediaeval predecessor.
RB = Site of Roman bridge in line with crop mark of Roman road Dere Street through *vicus* in Tofts
Field. Roman bridge site is 260 paces downstream from modern bridge.
W2 = Old mill-dam which fed canal-sized leat (C), now (dry). Leat passed through Roman *vicus*.
J = Junction of canal/mill-leat with Piercebridge Beck.
A3 = Very small high-and-dry Roman plinth, found in 1972, which was mistaken for abutment of a
second Roman bridge. This caused the greatest confusion,as it was postulated that the first
bridge must have been washed away. In order to accommodate this theory, reports of old
antiquarians were questioned and massive river migrations and scouring actions were
necessary.

The crop mark of the Roman *vicus* in the Tofts field at Piercebridge. Even the foundations of the Roman houses can be seen. Roman Dere Street runs from lower centre to top centre. It is obvious where the Roman bridge (RB) was located, and remains were still visible just before the Great Flood of 1771, 260 paces downstream from the modern bridge. This distance is confirmed by the crop mark. There is a ruinous mediaeval mill-dam (W2) just downstream from the site of the Roman bridge, and a massive canal-sized leat (C), now dry. The *vicus* has produced many artefacts from the third and fourth centuries. During a drought in 1933, Roman piles were reported in the River at the position of the Roman bridge (RB).

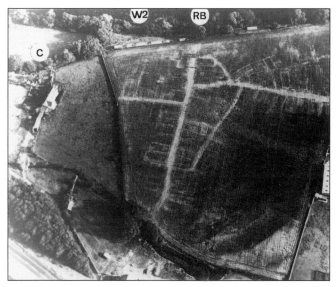

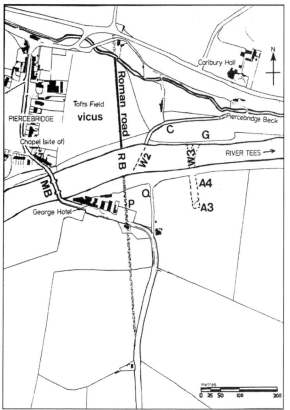

Map showing alignment of Roman road.

MB = Modern bridge on site of mediaeval bridge.
RB = Site of Roman Dere Street Bridge.
P = Roman wagon park in garden of Dere Street Cottage.
Q = Suspected Roman quarry.
W2 = Mediaeval mill-dam, possibly reused Roman structure.
C = Mill-leat of unusually large size.
A3 = Small Roman plinth, excavated 1972, identified as abutment of Roman bridge, even though it appeared to be complete and contained only about sixty tons of stone. (a Roman bridge abutment for a river of this size should contain several thousand tons).
A4 = Pile of stones (about thirty tons) identified as remains a Roman bridge pier? (A Roman pier should have 600 - 1,000 tons).
G = Large dry channel in river bank.
W3 = Suspected site of Roman weir.

new information. They already had the Roman period sewn-up, or so they thought. I was told that County Durham had been largely ignored by the Romans except for one major through-road and a few forts which housed second-line troops. All archaeologists worth their salt were beavering away on the Roman Wall to the north, and had been blinded by its magnificence. I got the distinct impression that meddling amateurs were merely tolerated but certainly not taken seriously.

I may have been an amateur archaeologist at that time but I certainly was not an amateur reconnaissance pilot. I had been a member of a flying team which operated a photographic survey aircraft in Central Africa. One of our tasks was for a French colonial government, and was to attempt to find out why the waters of Lake Chad were disappearing. There were many other projects all over Africa, and I realised that one of the great advantages of an aircraft was that it was quite easy to see where a river had altered its course, and on occasion where the hand of man had assisted Mother Nature.

Years later, as I flew my searches over northern Britain, my targets were signs of ancient occupations in general, and in particular, the possible remnants of Roman water engineering. The River Tees was one of the suspected rivers and a routine search was carried out. As I circled the Roman complex at Piercebridge I could see several large channels obviously associated with water-mills and the Roman road Dere Street could be seen arrow-straight stretching from northern to southern horizons. The village of Piercebridge sat right on top of the Roman fort. Just to the east of the village, the Roman civil settlement *(vicus)* was showing as a crop mark, and the foundations of all the Roman houses could be seen. The modern B6275 road which sits on top of Roman Dere Street for miles, deviated from its Roman foundations and swerved into the mediaeval and modern village but the crop mark of the Roman road continued straight ahead through the *vicus* in the cultivated Tofts Field to the now empty river bank. It was obvious where the Roman bridge had been, a couple of hundred yards or so downstream from the three-arched modern bridge. The latter is a modernisation of a five-arched mediaeval predecessor. The Roman bridge site was obviously and precisely in line with Dere Street, but there were no signs of any structures in the river. I had been told that the southern abutment of the Roman bridge had been excavated but perhaps it was invisible from my aircraft, under the trees on the south bank beside the George Hotel.

The westerly-deviated B6279 after crossing the Tees via the three-arched bridge, turned a right angle to the east, regained the Roman road line south of the village, and continued on an auto-pilot-straight course due south to Scotch Corner.

The antiquarian Edward Wooler of Darlington had commented in the early 1900's that he thought the various water-mills at Piercebridge must have had Roman origins as the leats were of such huge proportions that they could only have been constructed by slave labour. These opinions were not known to me during my first overflight, but I could see that there had been water-mills both upstream and downstream of the mediaeval village.

There was not much doubt about the location of the B6275 three-arched stone bridge on the same site as the mediaeval five-arched structure, as

Leland in 1536 mentions the reconstruction in his *Itinerary:*

"Persbrigg...sumtime of 5 arches but a late made new of 3 arches."

Furthermore, the mediaeval bridge followed the common practice of having a chapel at one end, and the remains of this have reused a wall of the Roman bath-house and can still be seen in the garden of "Tees View" at the north end of the B6275 bridge. William Camden mentions this chapel in *Britannia* (1586):

"Next upon the same river, lies Percbridge, which in the old Map of the North-riding of Yorkshire, is called Presbrigge, and according to Tradition; should be called Priestbridge, from two neighbours of that Order, who built it of stone, it having been of wood before; or from the Priests appointed to serve the Devotion of Travellers, as well as of the neighbourhood, in a Chapel, the ruins of which remain hard by the bridge." [The Roman bridge slightly downstream gets several mentions by antiquarians. Camden reported it in his *Britannia* (1586)]

"The Roman road comes immediately to the river a little lower than the present bridge, broad, strait and hard, the great original stone bridge not yet worn out."

The Roman bridge therefore contained stonework, at least in the piers if not the superstructure, as Camden saw this stonework; "not yet worn out" prior to 1586.

In 1785, the Roman bridge gets a further mention by W Hutchinson in his *History and Antiquities of the County Palatine of Durham (1785 -94).* [By this time the stonework has gone and even the timber pier-bases have been washed away]:

"The Roman Road passed a few paces to the east of the station extending in a line with the present way from Legscross towards Cathrick; an ancient bridge over the river lay in this direction; the timbers, piles or framings of the foundations were visible till the great flood of November 1771 when they were torn up and washed away; the present stone bridge now stands 260 paces higher up the river."

This 260 paces agrees exactly with the crop mark of the Roman road Dere Street, seen from the air. Furthermore, during a drought in 1933, a number of oak piles were seen in the river bed (P3) by C F Dixon at the afore-mentioned position of the Roman bridge which is just below Dere Street Cottage at the eastern end of the George Hotel (GH). Thus there were only two bridge-sites at Piercebridge, the mediaeval timber, then five-arched stone, both on the same site as the modern three-arched structure and in line with the remains of the mediaeval chapel. The other was the Roman bridge exactly in line with the Roman road Dere Street and 260 paces downstream from the timber/5-arch/3-arch crossing.

The mediaeval bridge-builders had chosen a better site for their bridge than the Romans and had selected two firm and high rock banks with exposed hard bed-rock in the shallow river between.

Two hundred and sixty paces downstream, the river was somewhat wider, and the river bed there changed from bare rock to boulders which meant that the Roman bridge would have had to use piles-and-rafts for the footings of the piers. These were the timbers reported by Hutchinson. The best possible site for any bridge is between two firm and high natural abutments and the mediaeval people selected such a site, which explains the deviation away from the Roman road and the siting of the mediaeval village beside the bridge. This selection of bridge sites was brought out in the film *The Bridge over the River Kwai* when the British prisoners of war selected such a site, whereas the Japanese had tried to erect a straggling unstable affair over a wide flood-plain.

Roman engineers had orderly minds and did not like untidy road deviations unless it was absolutely necessary. They could cope with most types of river bed so their bridge was erected exactly on the surveyed line of the road.

All the archaeologists were happy, except that the Latin name for the fort was not known (and still isn't) and a suspected earlier fort was as yet unlocated.

Chance finds by a mechanical excavator in 1972 (digger hit A3), two hundred yards further downstream, were to confuse the whole issue and throw everything into disarray but more of this shortly.

The Roman fort under the village was thought to have been built in the third century and I had been asked to look out for any signs of an earlier site, but was told that without much doubt, it must be on the high ground to the south of the river. My subsequent report that there was a suspected fort in exactly the opposite direction was listened to with polite but almost deaf ears, and my photograph of a faint rectangular crop mark with rounded corners in the hamlet of Carlbury, was greeted with shrugged shoulders. Official minds had already been made up.

It is an ill-advised general who takes no notice of a reconnaissance pilot's photographs, and the tragedy at Arnhem (A Bridge Too Far) was caused by a commander disregarding a flier's reports of a German panzer division exercising in the planned assault zone. The same holds true for archaeology, except nobody gets killed and professional reputations are the only casualties.

When I came to do my ground survey at Piercebridge, I had many things to look at, not least of which, were the massive mill-leats, which had been ignored by all archaeologists except Edward Wooler. As I had also been told that the southern abutment of the Roman bridge had been found, naturally I expected this to be in line with Dere Street and also to be of the typical Roman pattern.

The mill-leats were indeed massive and one of them was constructed with obvious Roman stones which did not seem to be in reused positions. While thinking hard about all that I had seen, I went into the grounds of the George Hotel looking for the recently excavated Roman bridge abutment, but was told that it was not on the line of Dere Street but several hundred yards downstream. I found this extremely puzzling but set off in an easterly direction along the southern river bank.

I was astonished at what I saw two hundred yards to the east of the line of Dere Street and in a field well south of the river. This excavated structure was

The strange stonework high and dry in the middle of a field on the south side of the Tees, 200 yards
downstream from the Dere Street crossing. The curious little plinth A3 has half a cutwater which
sparked off the "second bridge theory." The stones at A4 can be mentally reassembled to form a
mirror image of A3. The base of the A3 structure is ten feet above the present river level. A4 has
settled slightly probably due to subsidence.

not a Roman bridge. It did not even resemble a Roman bridge. It was high
and dry in the middle of a field, and although there was a small plinth (A3)
with half a cutwater, it was not part of a river bridge. Where was the expected
three-angled ten thousand ton structure? This small rectangular stone plinth
could only contain about sixty tons of stone and it stood on the southern end
of a seventy yard long slabbed pavement. There were no piers, and in any
case, the nine inch thick pavement which rested on natural soil would never
have supported Roman piers of the thousand ton type usual for this size of
river. Nor would the plinth have accommodated the sideways stress of a
Roman bridge arch. Roman piers were massive so that in the event of an arch
collapse, the whole bridge didn't go down like a row of dominoes. Each pier
was large enough to act as an independent temporary abutment. Neither
were Roman bridges built on pavements. Every Roman pier had independent
foundations on the river bed, and if these foundations could not be fixed
directly onto a hard rock bed, the following procedure was used. Scores of
foot-square iron-tipped oaken piles were driven into the river bed until firm
resistance was met. The tops of the piles were then sawn off level with the
river bed and a raft of massive oak timbers fixed to the tops of the piles. The
stonework of each pier was erected on top of the timber rafts. The whole
operation took place in the dry, in an evacuated coffer-dam.

This structure at Piercebridge had neither piers nor piles, and
furthermore, it was obvious, merely from looking at the site from the modern
flood bank close to the river side, that the pavement was about twice the

Top: Engineer Neville Andison beside the surviving A3 structure.

Bottom: Andison indicates cut-outs for tiny timbers (Roman bridge timbers were enormous). The pavement on which Andison is standing was incorrectly identified as the river bed in Roman times, which postulated that the river must have cut down ten feet through solid rock in 2,000 years. [The Colorado River (which is liquid sandpaper) has taken 2,000 years to cut down nine inches.] The cut-outs are only two feet above the postulated Roman river bed - very strange.

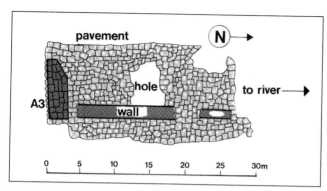

Plan of the A3 structure, the pavement, and a strange wall.

The A3 "abutment" is too tiny for a bridge and a Roman arch would merely push this structure over. Roman bridges were never built on pavements; each pier had an independent foundation on the river bed.

The strange wall would have blocked the river flow.

height of a man above the present river level. The plinth which formed the so-called abutment was also over a hundred yards from the river bank. It was another "bridge too far," this time a bridge *too far* away from the river, *too high* up the contours, with an abutment *far too small,* and the whole site *too far downstream* from the line of Dere Street.

Because of my researches, as soon as I set eyes on the structure, I knew exactly what it was. It was the high-level masonry flood-spillway (A3/A4) of a Roman weir (W3) and was at the expected ten to twelve feet or so above river level in order to perform its function. It was also a long way from the river because a spillway was usually at the end of a dam. The main dam structure (W3) across the river was missing, but on the north side of the river, there was a massive mill-leat (C) which was just in the right place to have been a by-pass channel containing some kind of lock to raise barges from the low level of water below the weir to the high level above. The leat was constructed of Roman stones and there were slots for a lifting-gate. A depth of about eight feet of silt had collected in the canal or leat since its last use by a water-mill, and the width at the suspected lock (inside the Roman *vicus*) was twenty feet.

In line with the spillway (W3), the river fell over shallow rapids and the bed was once again solid rock. The stonework of the dam had probably served as a free quarry for the villagers for hundreds of years, while the spillway lay concealed in the field well to the south until the mechanical gravel-digger operated by a very alert driver hit it.

A rescue excavation had taken place and a single coin of Hadrian and some second century pottery proved a Roman origin of the structure. The cut-water on the little plinth (A3), even though high and dry and an awful long way from the river, had signalled "BRIDGE" to all those present. Not only did this hypothesis necessitate a vast river migration to the north; it also meant that the river must have cut a much deeper channel since Roman times and through solid rock into the bargain. Why should there have been two Roman bridges? The only way to explain this was to assume that the first Roman bridge must have washed away, otherwise why build a second? Why put such a second bridge on a different line when it was known that the Romans did not like untidy thinking of this type?

Why did the Romans build a most unusual bridge on a thin pavement which lay on unreinforced soil? In the tiny A3 abutment, why were there slots

Top: A tiny Roman bridge abutment on the Cong Burn at Chester-le-Street. This abutment is the same size as the Piercebridge A3 structure but the bridge crossed a stream only ten feet wide and six inches deep.

Bottom: The Piercebridge A3 structure and the south end of the pavement, 100 yards away from the river bank and ten feet above level of river.

A normal 1,000 ton Roman bridge pier for a river of the size of the Tees, compared with the Piercebridge A3 structure, supposed abutment of a postulated second Roman bridge.

for angled six-inch timbers at only two feet above pavement level? These would have been damaged by floods if the pavement was the old river level. Why were the timbers only six inches when usual Roman bridge-timbers were about two feet square? These questions had all evidently been asked at the time of excavation and had been answered by a long string of suppositions. A guide-book had also been written, so when I mentioned that the structure was not a bridge at all, the information was not well received.

Had I managed to get the information across earlier, things may have been different, but too much publicity about the new bridge had gone out. I was given a handbook which explained the strange pavement. A drawing showed Trajan's bridge over the Danube sitting on a similar pavement, but I had just returned from an enforced sojourn of two months on the Danube, where I had been a temporary ship's officer on a merchantman which had experienced serious engine trouble. A friendly commissar who was interested in archaeology had provided me with much information and I knew that the piers of Trajan's bridge had been built inside coffer-dams in the normal Roman manner and that these were still in place on the bed of the Danube. A letter from Professor J J Wilkes of London University enclosing drawings of the construction of Trajan's bridge, clinched the matter and the guide-book was seen no more. It was said that the artist had made a mistake and drawn in a pavement instead of the water surface of the river.

The handbook also explained the absence of piers on the pavement by saying that the river must have moved north quickly in Roman times thus necessitating yet a third bridge, and the stone for this was robbed from the second bridge which had become high and dry and redundant.

There were a few tons of scattered stones on the downstream side of the spillway pavement but not enough to have been the remains of even a single pier, and seven piers were postulated on the drawings in the guide-book. On site, the fallen stones were just opposite a strange inscribed right-angled line on the north end of the pavement, and this obviously outlined the base of some kind of structure. The inscribed line was 65 yards from the small abutment at the southern end of the flagstones. Visitors from the Institute of Civil Engineers, Northampton, soon worked out the purpose of the inscribed line. Civil engineer Gordon Heald agreed that the pavement was a flood spillway and he calculated the probable dimensions of the missing main structure of the dam.

Mr Heald's research used records from the Hydrological Year Books which give the following figures for the Broken Scar Weir at Low Coniscliffe, NZ 259 137:

Mean Annual Flood	=	375.00 cubic metres/second
95 per cent of time flow exceeds...		1.35 cubic metres/second
10 per cent of time flow exceeds...		42.70 cubic metres/second

Mr Heald said that he could only guess the river flow figures for the Roman period, but it was his opinion that urbanisation, field drainage and river

The eastern abutment of the Roman bridge at Chollerford on the North Tyne. This abutment contains several thousand tons of stone and the North Tyne is the same size as the Tees.

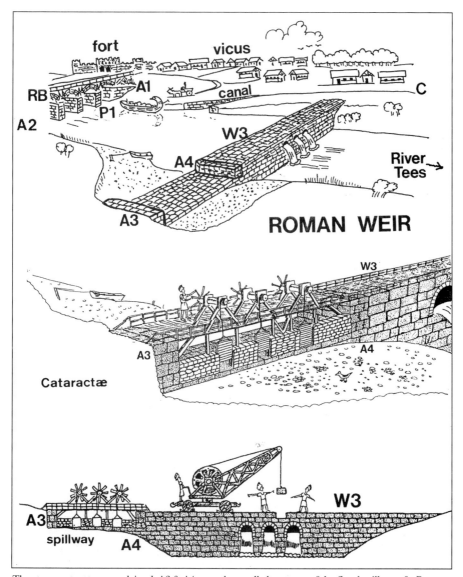

The strange structures explained. A3 & A4 were the small abutments of the flood spillway of a Roman weir, W3. Flood spillways were generally at the ends of weirs. This explains the long distance from the river and the height above river level.

The strange wall along the pavement was a balustrade which contained the *cataractae* flood level control mechanisms.

The purpose of the associated weir (W3) was to deepen the water upstream for navigation. The giant mill-leat (C) was probably a Roman canal and may have contained one or two locks, or may have been merely a "liquid ramp" to lift Roman barges from the low river level below the dam, to the high, above it.

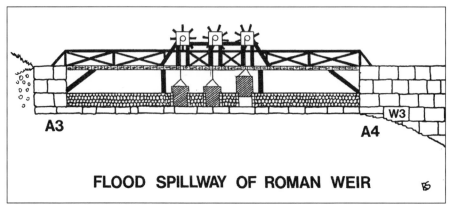

FLOOD SPILLWAY OF ROMAN WEIR

The drawing of a footbridge across the flood spillway explains why the cut-outs on A3 were for tiny timbers, and why they were placed so low on the structure.

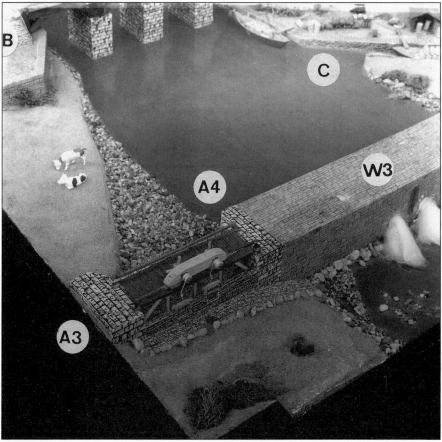

The model shows the principle of the flood spillway and the associated weir. The flood spillway is dry and the low level spillway in the centre of the dam is coping with the river flow.
Compare the size of the abutment of the genuine Roman bridge (B) with the A3 spillway abutment.

clearance had made flood flows increase and low flows decrease since Roman times. This would produce figures of, say:

Mean Annual Flood   =   200 cubic metres/second
95 per cent of time flow exceeds..   2 cubic metres/second

He estimated that there had been a four-metre-high weir (W3) right across the river, with a slightly lower flood spillway, (A3/A4) at the south end, and a low level outlet in centre of the missing barrier. His calculated width of spillway was seventy metres and main dam, a hundred metres. This fits almost exactly the measurements of the pavement between the southern plinth-abutment (A3) and the inscribed line (A4) and the present width of the main river.

The tumbled remains near the inscribed line had angled cut-outs for six-inch timbers, and the pile of stones could be mentally reassembled to form a mirror image (northern) spillway abutment (A4), of the surviving southern plinth-abutment (A3).

This undersized A3 abutment looks complete as the top stones contain no dowell holes to lock higher stones. Neither are there any pinch-bar holes for sliding stones of higher courses into place.

Along the downstream edge of the spillway's flagstones there is a peculiar low wall. You do not build a bridge and then block the flow with a wall. It was claimed that this wall was a causeway to replace the second bridge (A bridge too far) when the piers were removed by the Romans for the third bridge (A bridge far too far). With a width of only four feet, this "causeway" would have needed some sure-footed oxen. This so-called causeway is just in the right place to have been a balustrade in which the water-level control *cataractae* were installed. The holes for tiny timbers in the small abutment would have been for a timber footbridge, which allowed access to the top of the dam for operation and maintenance.

During the search for a redirected Roman Dere Street making a deviation to the east to use the so-called new bridge, a JCB excavator was used by archaeologists in the field on the north bank of the river. A trench was dug with the arm of the machine at full depth but no road was found. Remnants of this trench can still be seen from the air. On the south side of the spillway, it was claimed that a Roman road was found but only by dowsing. In any case, a road does not prove a bridge as all dams, ancient and modern have a road to at least one end of the structure.

It was obvious from my aircraft that the River Tees which runs on a straight course past the site, had not moved its channel. It was also extremely difficult to believe that the river had cut a four metres deeper channel mostly through solid rock, in fifteen hundred years. In the present Interglacial phase, rivers are depositing material, not cutting deeper channels as is evidenced by remains of Roman bridge piers in other rivers with even the Roman toolmarks on the stones surviving in pristine condition.

The most abrasive river in the world is the Colorado in the USA. It has cut the Colorado Canyon, but the river is almost liquid sandpaper and carries ten tons of water-borne sand past any point every second. Even so, it has taken the Colorado River 2,000 years to cut down one foot. How has the sand-free Tees cut a new bed at over ten times the rate of the Colorado? Why did the

The model of the A3 spillway abutment shows the arrangement of the timbers, and the balustrade/wall.

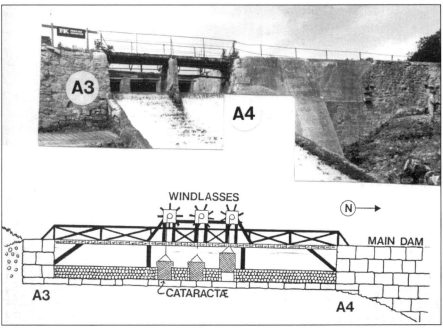

The spillway of a mediaeval dam in the West Country. This feature resembles the Roman A3/A4 flood spillway at Piercebridge.

View of model of Dere
Street Roman bridge
and Roman weir. Note
size of abutments of
Roman bridge.

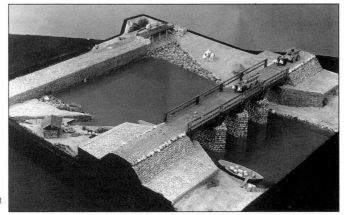

Model showing general
arrangement of the
Roman river complex at
Piercebridge.

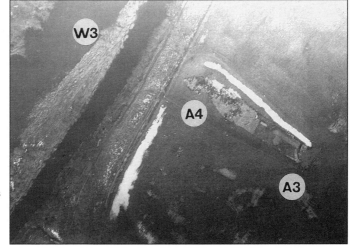

The Roman spillway
from 1,000 feet.
The island in the
river was caused by a
cliff collapse
upstream, some years
ago. It is not a
Roman feature. The
white marks are
snow-drifts.

cutting action just begin in the Roman period? If the Tees can cut a depth of four metres through rock in 1,500 years, where is the Piercebridge Canyon?

The only way to demonstrate that the spillway pavement could not be the base of a Roman bridge, would be to find the remains of the genuine Dere Street bridge, and try to elucidate if such remains lay on the *present* bed of the Tees and not some hypothetical river bed some four metres higher. From the reports of the Roman piles found opposite the George Hotel in 1933, it certainly sounded as if the Roman river bed and 1933 river bed were one and the same.

The river bed on the line of Dere Street had to be searched and this could be done only by skilled divers. My aerial photogrpahs clearly showed Dere Street as a crop mark, and this agreed with Hutchinson's position of 1785, Wooler's report of 1915, and C F Dixon's sighting of river-bed piles in 1933. Expert divers Bob Middlemass and Rolfe Mitchinson were briefed using aerial photographs, and they entered the river beside the George Hotel from the island which had formed some years ago after the collapse of a cliff upstream. This elongated deposit may have covered some of the piles reported in 1933, so the divers began their search at the north bank just a few yards south of where the crop mark of the Roman road ended at the top of the river bank in the Tofts Field. The divers used SCUBA and were equipped with an underwater metal detector. Within minutes they had located very large horizontal oaken timbers fixed to vertical piles. The piles had been driven into the river bed which consisted of medium and small boulders with clay between. Very significant was the fact that the piles had been sawn off level with the *present* river bed. If these timbers were part of the Roman bridge, the river had most definitely *not* cut a deeper channel since Roman times. One pile had been uprooted and its iron point was clearly visible. From the clay between the boulders, hundreds of pieces of broken Roman pottery were seen in the clear water and picked up. The Romans had been dumping garbage into the river from the bridge. The pottery types varied from samian to Crambeck Ware and spanned the whole four-hundred-year occupation period. Five fairly intact Roman boots, complete with hobnails, were also picked up and shortly after that, a Roman leather swimsuit. The artefacts were found on the line of the bridge all the way across the river and not just in the vicinity of the pier-raft near the northern bank. On the pottery evidence alone, the bridge had been in use for the whole Roman occupation period so, even at that early stage in the search, it was obvious that there had been no second Roman bridge.

The base of a second pier was found in the centre of the river and on the spacing, this indicated that there had been three piers in the water. On this spacing, the third is under the island formed by the spoil washed down from the cliff collapse. It was noted that the line of the bridge coincided with the section of Dere Street excavated in the garden of Dere Street Cottage a few years ago. In the same garden was a cobbled area believed to have been a wagon-park. Between the river's southern edge and Dere Street Cottage, there is a flat plateau, and there may have been a land-pier on this between the water and the high bank of the gardens. An excavation or radar scan is called for.

Aerial view of spillway and canal.
The snow-drift right centre marks the A3/A4 spillway. The curved hedge-line left centre is the suspected Roman canal. A thin white snow mark between the canal and the river bank is an infilled trench where a JCB was used by archaeologists to attempt to locate a Roman road from the north end of the supposed second bridge. Even though the arm was at full depth, no road was found.
At the south end of the spillway, a Roman road was "claimed" but merely by dowsing. In any case, a road does not "prove" a bridge, as all dams have roads to at least one end.

Above: Model of Roman A3/A4 flood spillway, showing balustrade/wall but no footbridge.

Right: Small post-hole in A3/A4 pavement, for tiny vertical timber of footbridge.

At the north end of the A3/A4 pavement there is an inscribed line (left) and tumbled stonework (right). The inscribed line has marked the position of the A4 spillway abutment and the tumbled stones can be mentally re-assembled to construct a mirror image of A3, complete with cut-outs for six-inch timbers.

Left: The official explanation for the balustrade/wall along the downstream edge of the pavement is that: "It was a causeway constructed because the second bridge was surplus to requirements because the river suddenly migrated to the north and cut a deeper channel at the same time. A third Roman bridge was built and the stone for this was taken from the second bridge." [which was the excuse for no piers being found]. The causeway was supposed to link Roman bridge number 2 and bridge number 3. [The river has not moved one yard since Roman times and bridges 2 and 3 never existed].
Right: View over the A3 spillway abutment, along the balustrade towards the tumbled A4 abutment. The river is over the hedge and down a sixteen foot drop.

Left: Engineer Andison stands on the so-called "causeway" (balustrade of flood spillway).
Right: As the so-called "causeway" is just wide enough for a dog, an ox-wagon would have had great difficulty negotiating it.

Top: The mediaeval mill-dam W2 which led water into the suspected Roman canal (later mediaeval mill-leat). The dam may have started life as a Roman wing-dam for the canal entrance. GH is the George Hotel on the south side of the river and at the southern end of the site of the genuine Dere Street Roman bridge (RB).

Bottom: The mediaeval dam W2, during a drought.

Left: The mediaeval mill-leat (and suspected Roman canal) in the Roman *vicus*. Without doubt the stonework at right is Roman.
Right: With the main river in flood, the water level simulated that which would have resulted with the Roman weir W3 intact with the canal flooded (even though silted up). A slot can be seen for a lifting-type *cataracta* gate.

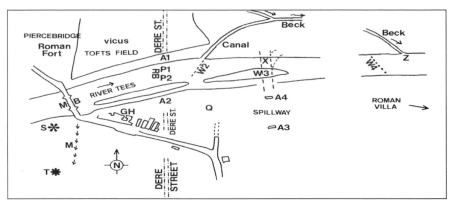

A further Roman weir (W4) has been found 500 yards downstream, just above the confluence of the Tees and the Piercebridge Beck.

A single row of post-holes, cut at an angle of thirty degrees to the flow, crosses the river bed-rock. Two coins of Hadrian were taken from hole number 9. Twelve holes are visible before they are obscured in mid-stream by heavy deposits of gravel. The excavated Roman villa at Holme House Farm is in the field to the south of this weir and on the same contour. W4 may have served a leat into the villa or it may have been part of the cascade of Roman barriers.

The Roman dam W3 may have been either straight or curved and future archaeological investigations should explore both possibilities. Large worked stones, complete with dowell holes lie on the river bed at (X). There is also an isolated Roman pile in the river bed at this spot.

S = Suspected Roman repeater signal station
T = Bronze Age *tumulus* reused by Oliver Cromwell as a cannon emplacement.
M = A mediaeval trackway.
A1 = North end of genuine Roman bridge.
A2 = Roman stonework peeping out of river bank, believed to be southern abutment of Roman
       bridge, or remains of a fourth pier.
Z = Mouth of Piercebridge Beck.

The Romans had not only thrown junk into the river. The river gods had been well supplied with offerings and the divers worked overtime. Coins and other artefacts were located between the boulders. Often several were taken from one piece of solidified mud and when this hard mud was cut open, the cross section showed stratified layers. The fairly swift flowing Tees had once been a stagnant pool at this point and the obvious reason was that, just downstream, there had been a dam across the river, probably for several hundred years. One extremely large stratified chunk of clay-mud had pieces of metal sticking out and this was X-rayed before it was cut open. The X-ray plate revealed a winged, Cupid-like statuette inside. It turned out to be a bronze figurine of "Harpocrates." Other bronze figurines found, included Attis, two dolphins holding a sphere between their noses, and a ram. All the while, Roman coins were being picked up, some visually and some with the aid of the metal detector. The search went on for several weeks and the divers reported that even when the river was running fast after rain, the current on the bottom was much reduced due to the resistance of the uneven boulders.

About three hundred Roman coins were recovered, a high proportion of them silver, which strongly suggested that they were votive offerings. They were examined by coin expert, Dr John Casey of Durham University. The dates were in the range from Juba II (King of Mauretania) AD 22, to Theodosius, 395-402 with only a few small gaps in the fourth century.

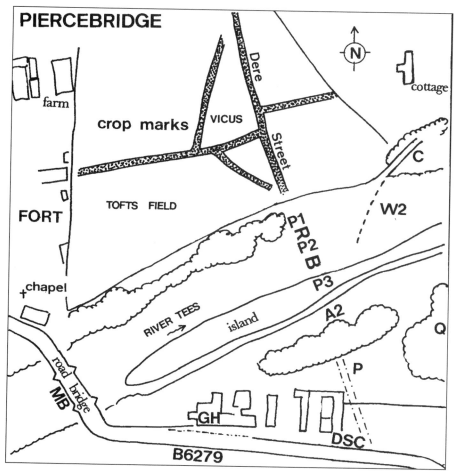

In order to prove that the river had neither moved to the north, nor cut a deeper channel since Roman times, it was essential to find the remains of the genuine Roman bridge. Expert divers Rolfe Mitchinson and Bob Middlemass entered the river in line with the Tofts Field crop mark of Dere Street. Within minutes they had discovered the timber rafts of two Roman piers, P1 and P2. On the spacing there should be a third, but this area is covered by the recently deposited island.

The huge two-feet-square horizontal pier-raft timbers were spiked to the tops of dozens of Roman piles. The latter were a foot square, and the tops had been sawn off level with the present river bed which was also the Roman river bed. One pile had been washed out of its seating and its an iron-shod tip was visible.

Several kilos of Roman pottery were picked up from the mud and silt between the boulders. The pottery spanned the whole four hundred year occupation period. Five fairly intact studded Roman army boots were also found, and a Roman leather swimsuit. The artefacts were picked up all along the line of the bridge and not just in the vicinity of bridge piers. The artefacts were just where the Romans had dropped them.

All manner of artefacts were found, many of them votive offerings. Three hundred plus, Roman coins covered the whole occupation period and dated from AD 22 to AD 402, with only a few small gaps.

A Saxon buckle dated c650 was also found, suggesting that the bridge was still in use in the Saxon period.

There had been only one Roman bridge and it served the entire occupation period, and beyond.

The numismatic evidence therefore confirmed that of the pottery: the bridge had been in use for the whole of the Roman occupation. All kinds of artefacts emerged before the winter floods forced operations to cease. Lucky charms, pins and brooches were found by the score. Other items were scales and weights, pieces of weapons, helmet straps, gold ear-rings and other jewellery, several rings, some inscribed; one solid gold ring has a ruby set in it; another has an exquisite intaglio showing a Roman lady milking a goat. Spoons, tweezers, a Roman razor, and a bronze stamp engraved 'FELIX' the wrong way round, were among hundreds of varied artefacts picked up.

Dr RSO Tomlin of Wolfson College Oxford, translated some of the inscriptions on rings such as AVE AMA (Greetings. Love[me]) and DM/ART (for deo Marti, 'to the god Mars'). Dr Tomlin also inspected some Roman military baggage seals which may throw some light on the units stationed at Piercebridge. A samian cup was identified from its stamp "ATILIANI," a central Gaulish (Lezoux) potter of the late Antonine period.

A Saxon buckle, picked up on the line of the bridge, was identified by Dr Martin Welch of the University College London, as a C2 square-headed type, dated c650. This suggests that the Roman bridge was still intact in the Saxon period.

The Saxon settlement may have been in the hamlet of Carlbury just to the north-east of Piercebridge. The name of the hamlet is evidently derived from the Old English *Ceorlaburgh*.

On 14th March 1990, a coroner's inquest was held in Bishop Auckland to determine the reason for the deposit of Roman artefacts across the river bed. Dr Casey gave evidence and as reported in the *Darlington and Stockton Times*, 17.iii.90, he said:

"A hundred of the coins contain silver.... they date from the first century AD to the end of the fourth century. They were probably thrown into

Photograph of model showing Dere Street bridge and Roman transport activity.

the river deliberately as offerings to the river gods.

We don't know the name of the deity of the River Tees but most rivers had them at that time. Some of the coins were bent, folded or pierced to take them into the next world."

The jury took only three minutes to decide that the artefacts were votive offerings thrown from the bridge during the entire period of Roman occupation.

The coins which were the subject of the inquest were identified by Dr John Casey who prepared a report entitled "*A Votive Deposit from the River Tees at Piercebridge, County Durham.*"

It is impossible to list here details of all the coins found, so only one or two from each emperor have been selected:

References: Mattingly & Sydenham (1923-81) [unless otherwise stated] Cun – Besley & Bland, *The Cunetio Treasure* (1983) LRBC – Carson, Hill & Kent, *Late Roman Bronze Coinage* (1976) MAZ – Mazard, *Corpus Nummorum Numidiae Mauretaniaeque* (1955) SS – Septimius Severus Issuer's name inside quotation marks indicates counterfeits.

Issuer	Denomination	Reference	Date
Juba II	[Mauretania]	AE 20mm	MAZ.286 22- 23
Nero	As	–	64- 68
Galba	Denarius	167	68- 69
Vespasian	Denarius	99	76
	Sestertius	460	71
Titus	Denarius	229	80- 81
Domitian	Denarius	149	90
Nerva	As	86	97
	Sestertius	–	96- 98
Trajan	Sestertius	as625	112-114
	Dupondius	as414	99-117
	As	393	98- 99
Hadrian	Denarius	118(a)	119-122
	Sestertius	751	134-138
	Sestertius	–	117-138
Antoninus Pius	Denarius(frag)	162	147-148
	Denarius	219etc	152-153
	Sestertius	751	144
	Dupondius	–	138-161
	As	as679	140-144
Faustina I	Denarius	394(a)	141-161
	Sestertius	1102(a)	141-161
Faustina II	Denarius	515(a)	145-161
M Aurelius, caes.	Sestertius	468	155-159
	As	1322	154-155
Ant.Pius, deified	Denarius	436	161-162
M Aurelius	Denarius	48	161-162
	Sest.(pierced)	as1205	161-180
'Faustina II'	Denarius(plated)	686	161+

Faustina II deified	Denarius	373	175-180
	Sestertius	1693	175-180
Lucilla	Sestertius	1732	164-169
Commodus	Denarius	as57	181-192
	Sestertius	441	183-184
Crispina	Sestertius	672	177
	Sestertius	–	177
Clodius Albinus	Denarius	7	193-196
Septimius Severus	Denarius	10	193-194
	Denarius	289	202-210
	As	716	195-196
'Septimius Severus'	Denarius(cast)	40	194+
	Denarius(plated)	–	193+
'Julia Domna'	Denarius	552	196-211
'Julia Domna'	Denarius(plated)	553	196+
Caracalla	Denarius	11	196-198
	Denarius	158	206-210
'Caracalla'	Den.(plated)	asSS150	200+
	Denarius	SS186	202+
Elagabalus	Denarius	49	221
	Den.(rolled, edges crimped)		218-222
'Elagabalus'	Den.(plated)	104	218+
Julia Maesa	Denarius	268	218-222
Julia Soemias	Denarius	241	218-222
Julia Paula	Denarius	211	218-222
Severus Alexander	Denarius	7(c)	222
	Denarius	133	233-235
'Severus Alexander'	Denarius(plated)	120	222+
	Denarius	–	222+
Julia Mamaea	Denarius	335	222-235
	Denarius	335	222-235
Gordian III	Antoninianus	38	238-244
'Gordian III'	Anton.(plated)	Treb.Gallus55	253+
Volusian	Antoninianus	168	251-253
'Trebonoanus Gallus'	Anton.(plated)	Gallienus17	253+
Gallienus	Antoninianus	18	252-258
Valerian II	Antoninianus	20	253-255
Valerian II, deified	Antoninianus	9	255
Salonina	Antoninianus	31	256-257
'Claudius II' deified	Antoninianus	266	270+
Postumus	Antoninianus	39	258-268
Victorinus	Anton.	asCun2537	268-270
'Victorinus'	Antoninianus	118	268+
Tetricus I	Antoninianus	98/9	270-273
'Tetricus I'	Antoninianus	141	273+
Victorinus/Tetricus	Antoninianus	–	268-273
'Victorinus/Tetricus'	Antoninianus	–	268+
Carausius	Aurelianus	880	286-290

Constantius II	Siliqua	Arles207	353-355
Valentinian, house	Sil(clipped)	asTrier(a)	378-383
Theodosius, house	–	LRBC.2.807etc	395-402
and hundreds more................			

I thought that the votive offerings were proof to the world that the Roman Dere Street bridge had existed for the whole Roman four hundred year occupation period. I was wrong. Bidwell and Holbrook in *Hadrian's Wall Bridges* (1989) claimed that the artefacts were merely wash-outs from the river banks and had been trapped by the bridge timbers. This is not so; the artefacts were found right across the river, most of them well away from the timber pier-rafts.

A few yards downstream from the Roman bridge are the remains of a mediaeval mill-dam (which has reused quite a lot of Roman stonework) [Weir No 2 or W2 on diagrams]. This weir still presents quite a barrier across the river. With Bidwell and Holbrook's theory, thousands of artefacts of all ages should have been trapped by this ruinous weir. The divers spent a whole day examining the upstream edge of this barrier and found only one isolated artefact – a stone inkpot of the 1920's. No establishment archaeologist came anywhere near our operations, in spite of invitations for them come and don diving gear and inspect the river bed themselves. New evidence was unwelcome.

Downstream from the mediaeval mill-dam (W2) is the Roman spillway (A2/A3) and site of the missing Roman weir (W3). It is not certain yet whether the Roman weir was straight or curved but there are obvious man-made disturbances in the form of a deep groove (G) in the northern river bank opposite the spillway. It continues for some distance downstream.

In the river bed under the north bank, directly opposite the spillway, two very large rectangular stones (X), lie on the river bed. Both have dowell-holes cut into the top surfaces. The river bed here is fissured-rock and the divers

The A2 abutment of the genuine Roman bridge, sticking out of the river bank below the George Hotel. This agrees with the old antiquarians' reports of the Roman bridge being 260 paces downstream from the modern bridge. It also agrees with the thousand artefacts found on the river bed and the crop mark of Dere Street in the Tofts Field.

carried out an intensive search for signs of the weir. No artefacts at all were found but hundreds of pieces of lead were picked up from cracks in the rock bed. It looks as if some giant structure has been tied together with cramps seated in lead. Excavations or electronic scans are needed in both banks in search areas which allow for either a straight or a curved dam.

The casting of offerings into the Tees at Piercebridge did not cease with the departure of the Romans. A local legend has it that a certain ghostly lady by the name of "Peg Powler" haunts the river there. The following quote is from *Durham,* Vol 2 by Sir Timothy Eden:

> "an Peg Powler wi' her green hair, she that rises out of the Tees so beautiful and draas the bonny bairns unto her for love of 'em."

There is a further mention of this lady in *Haunted Britain* by Antony D Hippisley Coxe:

> "You can enter County Durham by the A1 over the Tees. This river's goddess is Peg Powler, who lies in wait for victims at Piercebridge. She used to demand a sacrifice."

It is obvious that Piercebridge was a very complex place in Roman times. The Dere Street bridge could have served both a suspected early fort at Carlbury – the crop mark of which was seen from the air – and the later fort under Piercebridge village. A hitherto unknown major Roman road has also been identified from the air, approaching from the south-east from the Glebe Farm direction and passing some distance to the south of Holme House Farm (NZ 222 150) where Professor Dennis Harding excavated a Roman villa in 1969-70.

Another Roman road is thought to have approached from the west along the south side of the river from the known Greta Bridge fort (NY 084 132) and a suspected fort at Startforth, Barnard Castle (NY 045 160). Our main concern though at the moment, is the river, and it is time to detail the various features commencing a thousand yards upstream from the B6275 bridge.

At one time a curved dam deflected water into a massive leat on the north side of the river (Weir No 1 or W1 on diagrams). The mediaeval miller had to block most of it up as it was too large for his mill-wheel. The leat forms an island and there are other complex side-channels. With an intact dam downstream, these channels would have flooded and made an ideal barge basin (BB). As we proceed downstream, the Roman fort is under Piercebridge village on the left (north) bank, and the three-arched B6275 bridge which is on the same site as the mediaeval five-arched bridge (MB), is just ahead. Remains of the mediaeval chapel lie at the north end of this bridge near the south-east corner of the Roman fort.

As we pass under the B6275 (MB) bridge, the George Hotel (GH) is on the high bank on our right, as is the mediaeval road which is angling back to the east to regain the arrow-straight Roman line. Near the south bank of the river is the long strip-island which is a deposit of debris from the cliff collapse of a few years ago.

Two hundred yards (260 paces) downstream from the B6275 bridge is the site of the Roman bridge (RB) in line with Dere Street Cottage at the east

A piece of samian pottery, complete with potter's stamp "ATILIANI" picked up at (RB).

Some of the three hundred Roman coins found on the river bed along the line of the Roman bridge (RB).

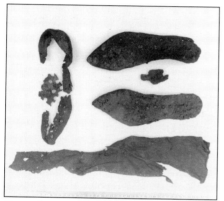

Roman boots and a leather swimsuit from the river bed on the line of the Roman bridge (RB).

Just part of the treasure picked up from the line of the Roman bridge (RB).

This ring is inscribed AVE AMA (Greetings Love [me])

Top left: Intaglio from ring showing Roman lady milking a goat.

Top right: Ram, possibly belonging to Roman God, Mercury.

Bottom: Saxon buckle, dated c650.

All from (RB)

end of the George Hotel. Remains of timber rafts for the bases of two piers (P1 and P2) lie on the river bed. A third pier (P3) almost certainly lies under the new island as this is where the piles were seen in 1933. A fourth pier, a land pier, (P4) may be buried in the plateau to the north of Dere Street Cottage. Right at the river edge, at time of writing, some large stones stick out of the bank-side. These may be part the fourth pier (P4), or perhaps even part of the bridge's southern abutment (A2).

Just a few yards downstream from the line of the Roman bridge, the remains of another mediaeval mill-dam (W2) curve into an old mill-leat which is once again of massive proportions. This leat (C) has been blocked-off and is now dry. It is right inside the Roman *vicus*. When I first saw this leat, it was 20 feet wide, and slots for a lifting gate survived in a few feet of stone-lining which looked like original Roman work. The ashlar facing stones had a rubble backing. My reports to the authorities produced no action and the stonework was later removed and used for repairs to farm buildings. There is about eight feet of silt in the leat so stonework and gate-slots should survive under this. A gentleman who tried to prove that this leat could never have been a Roman canal, placed his theodolite on top of the accumulated silt and postulated this as the bed of the leat. A local businessman who had assisted with the excavation of the A3/A4 spillway (Bridge too far), declared in the press that our discovery of hundreds of votive offerings on the site of the Dere Street bridge did not prove that the bridge had survived for the whole occupation. He claimed that after his postulated destruction of the Dere Street bridge, the Romans could have continued for hundreds of years to throw their offerings into the river at the former bridge site. I am certainly pleased that these gentlemen are not aircraft engineers.

The channel in the north bank, east of the Roman bridge is about 200 yards long and was cut across an isthmus to join the Piercebridge Beck; the latter then became an extension of the artificial leat. The Roman spillway (A3-A4) is on the south side of the river exactly opposite the artificial channel. The beck runs parallel to the river at a distance of about 70 yards and enters the river about 550 yards downstream at the site of a water-mill. The artificial cutting, together with the natural beck, would have made an ideal bypass canal to negotiate the Roman weir (W3). It has been quite large enough to take a barge and there is what looks like a "passing-place" (PP) at the half-way mark. If the suspected navigation had Roman origins, it is not known if the Romans had locks at both ends with a lift of about five feet each, or merely a lifting gate at each end thus using the whole length of canal as a pound. If the leat has been a Roman navigation, then the mediaeval mill-dam (W2) at the top end may have started life as a Roman wing-dam to the canal entrance, and the farthest upstream mill-dam (W1) may have served the same purpose for the suspected barge basin (BB).

There may not have been any locks at all as a drop of 10 ft in 1,000 yards is a gradient of 1:300 and the Romans may have used this as a liquid ramp. Any gates may have been for the conservation of water at times of no traffic. Excess water in the main river would have gone over the spillway A3/A4 at the southern end of Weir 3 (W3) [The Bridge too far].

Long mill-races are pointless unless the main river has a steep fall. If a race

Various artefacts picked up from line of Roman bridge (RB).

12 o-clock:
Ring inscribed
AVE AMA.

1 o-clock:
Gold ring with ruby.

5 o-clock:
Ring with intaglio of lady and goat.

9 o-clock
Ring inscribed
DM/ART
(for *deo* Marti, "to the god Mars."

Centre:
Roman disc brooch, stone missing.

Various artefacts found on line of Roman bridge (RB).

Centre top:
Harpocrates

Top right:
Atys expiring under a tree.
also; Saxon buckle, Roman and Celtic brooches, lucky charms and

Bottom:
hanging handle from Roman helmet.
It depicts two dolphins holding a sphere between their mouths.
This is almost identical to the Royal Navy submariners' insignia.
Do we have a Romanist in the British admiralty?

falls ten feet in half a mile, and the river falls twenty feet, then the miller has a head of ten feet with no need for a serious dam. If there is a dam, the best place for a mill is immediately below it and a long channel which commences at a dam is unlikely to have been built originally as a mill-race.

We are not finished yet with Roman civil engineering at Piercebridge. There are some strange holes cut into the rock bed of the river 550 yards downstream from Weir 3, and 135 paces above the point where the Piercebridge Beck has been diverted by an artificial cut, into the river. They are about a foot square and are cut into the bed-rock. There is only a single line of them and they lead a way from the north river bank in a downstream direction at 25 degrees to the river flow. Here is another dam (W4) but who were the constructors? It certainly looked like Roman handiwork. The divers soon solved the problem. There were twelve visible post-holes and Nos 11 and 12 still held oak stubs. From the ninth hole, two Roman coins had to be prised with a diver's knife, from the bottom of the hole to which they were welded by age. One coin is easily recognisable as a *sestertius* of Hadrian. Any holes beyond No 12 were obscured by gravel deposits; as I said earlier, the rivers are depositing material in the present interglacial; not cutting deeper channels.

We now have four dams at Piercebridge, two of which are known to be Roman (W3 & W4) with question marks hanging over the origins of the other two (W1 & W2). We also have a suspected barge basin (BB), canal (C) and possible length of navigable stream (Piercebridge Beck). The dams form a cascade in the river but by far the most important is the one which had the spillway (W3 & A3/A4). How can this evidence be put together? It looks as if the Romans not only navigated the beck and by-pass channel, but also the main river which seems to have been conveniently divided into pounds. The last dam (W4) discovered sits on exactly the same contour (50m) as the Roman villa at Holme House and this dam could have deflected water into a channel on the south side of the river. Did this Roman villa also have a canal leading into it? If so, there may a Weir No 5 downstream where the fifty metre contour bends back to the river. Investigations continue but here is a check-list with the main items found so far:

NZ 204 155	(W1)	Site of curved dam leading into suspected barge basin
NZ 205 155	(BB)	Very large mediaeval mill-leat and complex system of channels thought to have been the Roman harbour
NZ 210 157		Roman fort on north bank of river
NZ 211 155	(MB)	Mediaeval bridge, at one time of five arches, on same site as B6275 bridge of three arches
NZ 211 156		Remains of mediaeval chapel associated with bridge
NZ 212 157		Roman *vicus* and Dere Street in Tofts Field
NZ 213 156	(RB)	Site of Roman Dere Street bridge. Very large stones (possibly pier [P4] or abutment [A2]) stick out of south bank of river in line with Dere Street and Roman bridge remains on river bed
NZ 212 155	(GH)	George Hotel, suspected Roman well in courtyard
NZ 213 155	(DSC)	Dere Street Cottage. Roman road and suspected

		wagon park excavated (now infilled) in garden
NZ 213 155	(W2)	Remains of mediaeval mill-dam in river just downstream from Roman bridge site. Dam leads into mill-leat (now blocked, dry and partially infilled) which may be reused Roman canal
NZ 215 157	(J)	Junction of mill-leat and Piercebridge Beck
NZ 214 156	(Q)	Large crater which may be Roman quarry
NZ 215 155		Excavated flood-spillway of suspected Roman weir
NZ 218 160		Crop mark of suspected early Roman fort just to west of known *tumulus*. Inscribed Roman stone found in same field in eighteenth century. Roman burial reported when railway (now dismantled) built.
NZ 219 157	(W4)	Post-holes of Roman dam cut into river bed. Two Roman coins of Hadrian taken from ninth hole
NZ 220 157	(Z)	Mouth of Piercebridge Beck. Possible reused Roman stones in mill-channel
NZ 221 150		Roman villa excavated at Holme House Farm
NZ 224 142	(RR)	Crop mark of Roman road observed from air NZ 217 147
NZ 220 144	(F)	Romano-British farm on south side of above road
NZ 210 154	(S)	Earthworks of suspected Roman signal station in wood on top of hill above south end of B6275 bridge
NZ 210 153	(T)	Bronze Age *tumulus* which Oliver Cromwell converted into a cannon emplacement before a skirmish at Piercebridge

Upstream on the River Tees at Gainford at NZ 165 164, there is an artificial-looking dry channel to the south of a River bend. This is said to be an old course of the river; if so, the river has moved inwards (the wrong way) at the bend. There is a tradition that a Roman boat was found at this spot.

There are signs of Roman activity further up the Tees. At Winston, there is a single-arched bridge across the river, built in 1764 and claimed at the time as the longest single span in Europe. It survived the great flood of 1771. During the making of the television film *A Piece of Cake*, about the Battle of France prior to the Battle of Britain, a Spitfire pilot flew under a (supposed) French river bridge. This French bridge was actually the Winston bridge. The same bridge has genuine associations with 1940 as there is an anti-German invasion gun position above the southern end. The British soldiers of 1940 were not the first to select this spot as a defensive position; I was flying as Professor Harding's pilot many years ago when he spotted the crop mark of a Roman fortlet on the very edge of the cliff (NZ 143 162) above the bridge. The antiquarian Dr Gale said that a Roman road crossed here. He was right; this road can be seen on the north bank, east of the modern road and apparently heading for a crossing just upstream from the 1764 bridge. Whether there was a Roman bridge or a ford here has yet to be determined. The professor and I were on our way from Teesside Airport to Stornoway to carry out a survey of the Hebrides for Edinburgh University. As we flew up the Tees, a profusion of crop marks was showing and about forty unknown Romano-British farmsteads were recorded in half an hour. Our fuel situation forced us to cease circling and resume course to Stornoway and when we returned a couple of weeks later, rain had washed out all the marks by nourishing the entire crops to the same colour as those over the hidden ditches. There are therefore, still hundreds of as yet unrecorded sites in the Tees valley alone. Were the Roman barges taking exports of corn away from these sites?

Although not part of this story, our Hebridean search was to find and record small Iron Age Fortifications called *duns*. A favourite site for these was an island in a loch and the islands often had secret causeways out to them, hidden just below the surface of the water. The drought had reduced the levels of the lochs and the causeways were high and dry. It was possible to manoeuvre the aircraft into positions from which the professor captured photo-records of two or three unknown *duns* at a time. A couple of years previously, we had carried out a survey of the Orkney Islands and en-route from Durham, the professor had exposed all his ready-to-use film over Northumberland and southern Scotland. As we skimmed in over Scapa Flow towards Kirkwall Airport, the sea was mirror-calm and we were astonished to see the battleship *Royal Oak* lying on the sea bed. She had been sunk by a German U-boat in 1939. The battleship was lying almost upside down, bow to the east, stern to west. The green wreck-buoy which marks the ship's grave is just to the west of the ship's stern. A slight oil-leak could be seen leaving a propeller-shaft and rising to the surface where a small slick was forming. All our spare film was in the baggage compartment in the tail of the aircraft and the airport closed shortly after we landed. Next day, the Flow had returned to its normal rippled and opaque state and only the green buoy marked the grave of over 800 sailors.

Let us return to the River Tees. The Roman fort of Greta Bridge (NZ 084 133) is on the River Greta one mile south of the main river. At the confluence of the rivers, the Greta flows through a strange vertically-sided channel which may have been "improved" by the hand of man. A further tributary, the Tutta Beck, which runs right to the fort, has had its bed and banks paved. The Greta beyond Greta Bridge looks unnavigable but the Tiber in its upper reaches is similar and the Romans managed that river.

The head of navigation may have been at Bowes fort (Lavatris). Roman coins have been recovered from the foundations of the old watermill below the Roman fort and an easy-gradient Roman road leaves this mill-site and angles up the bank to the north. A Roman road continues westwards from Bowes, over the Stainmore Pass to Brough (Verteris) fort (NY 791 141), twelve miles away, where a mediaeval castle sits on top of its Roman predecessor. Verteris means "summit" but does this refer to the knoll which both Roman and mediaeval castles occupy, or was this the summit of navigation of the River Eden (Ituna Fl) and the Swindale Beck? A flat field to the south of the fort could well have been a barge basin. Pack-animals proceeding east from Verteris and west from Lavatris would have needed to travel only six miles to supply the various outposts and signal stations along the pass.

Assuming Roman navigation of minor rivers, the sensible and practical figure of five or six miles for pack-animal transport between summits of navigation in hilly areas, crops up time and time again. Where the lie of the

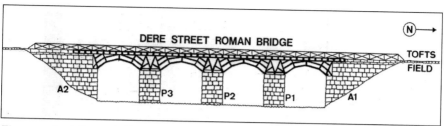

The one and only Roman bridge (RB), at Piercebridge at the Dere Street crossing, between the Tofts Field on the north bank and Dere Street Cottage on the south.

land was suitable, it looks as if the Romans linked the natural waterways together with artificial cuts thus dispensing with expensive pack-animals altogether.

This concludes the evidence at Piercebridge but investigations continue. It is hoped that readers will find signs of Roman river navigation in their home areas.

It is now time to move on to other subjects.

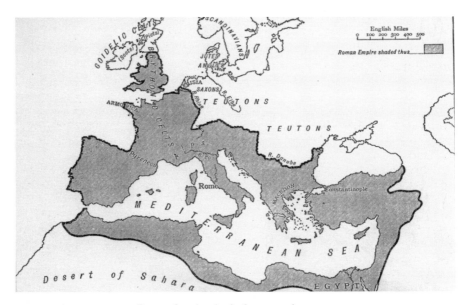

Roman frontiers in the late second century

Chapter 10

Roman Frontiers

"Britaniam petit in qua multa correxit, muramque per occtoginta milia passuum primus duxit, qui barbaros Romanosque divideret."
He went to Britain where he set many things right and was the first to build an eighty mile wall to separate the Romans and barbarians.

Spartianus (from his biography of Hadrian)

The conception of a scientific frontier was foreign to the government of the Roman Republic which preceded the Roman Empire. The Republic constantly extended its territory and sphere of influence and it got a bit out of hand.

With the advent of Augustus to power, all was changed. For the first time, it was recognised that a consistent frontier policy must be followed, and Tacitus tells us that one of Augustus' greatest achievements was that of confining the Empire within the limits of sea, ocean and distant rivers. To this could be added deserts. In his final conception, the Rhine and Danube formed the northern frontier (more or less) and it is here that we first meet with the earliest use of the term *limes,* which was in time, to describe a frontier, after a gradual change from the original meaning of a "military road" such as those the Romans constructed into newly conquered territories. These roads were intended to render the communications of an occupation force easy and secure.

In the later Trajanic period, we find the word *limes* used in the sense of "frontier." Thus a grid of frontier tracks developed into a clearly defined barrier with a network of roads behind it and a few more extending into "no man's land."

Claudius had withdrawn three legions from the right bank of the Rhine for his conquest of Britain, but a strip of land was still held on the "enemy" side of the river and no encroachment on this was permitted to the German tribes.

In Britain thirty-five years later, the beginnings of frontier defences were seen. Agricola, the Governor of Britain, reduced to submission a number of tribes hitherto independent of Rome. Tacitus tells us that at the close of Agricola's second campaign, he secured the conquered districts by a line of *praesidia* and *castella.* This line may have approximated to the line of Wall, which would be built between the Tyne and Solway some forty years on.

In AD 81, as mentioned in earlier chapters, Agricola reached the estuaries of the Forth and Clyde and here again, a line of *praesidia* was established. After Agricola's armies were withdrawn from Scotland because of the wars in the Balkans, some of his strategic positions would be used again sixty years later when Antoninus Pius erected a rampart between Forth and Clyde cAD 143.

Agricola had depended on seaborne supplies, so his fortified bases must have been located on waterways. The Rivers Carron and Kelvin were probably his supply routes from the Forth and Clyde. During his advance north, he also established the first of four forts at Newstead on the Tweed, and no doubt this was also river supplied.

Trajan reverted to a policy of expansion, but he lavished time and money on military roads along the frontier lines. The most famous of these was that which connected the Rhine frontier with the Danube. He also constructed a network of military roads in North Africa.

With the reign of Hadrian, there was a distinct change of policy with regard to frontiers. Not only was expansion halted; a systematic policy of erecting barriers around the Empire's boundaries was adopted. Palisades of split oak trunks, nine feet high plus deep ditches were his favourite boundary markers.

After modifying and strengthening his German frontier, he visited Britain and ordered the construction of the Tyne to Solway Wall. It is widely held that the predecessor to Hadrian's frontier was the Stanegate Roman road to the south, and it is not known if this road was constructed by Agricola or Trajan, but excavations have shown that this road had neither palisade nor ditch. The discovery of some of the last unknown stretches of this road have been described earlier in this book and this new evidence also throws doubt on the function of the Stanegate as a frontier. There is no fort at the crossing of the North Tyne at Howford, and even this crossing seems to have been a ford which relied on good weather.

There is no major fort between Vindolanda and Corbridge and east of Corbridge the unprotected road runs to Bywell and then hugs the river bank and forms a very poor defensive line. I think therefore, that pre-Hadrianic defences must be looked for on a totally different line.

Before that subject is discussed, let us look at the Roman Wall itself, constructed between about 122 and 128. There was a fort integral with the Wall every few miles, and at every Roman mile there was a milecastle. Between the milecastles were two turrets. To the north of the Wall, there was a ditch and behind the Wall, to the south, there was a complex earthwork known to us by the peculiar name *Vallum* (wall) although it consists of a deep ditch with earth ramparts either side. It bypasses the southern ends of some forts with angular alterations of heading, and some forts which are afterthoughts, overlie infilled sections of this *Vallum*. It is extremely difficult to obtain an official explanation as to the purpose of the *Vallum*. Opinions vary from customs barriers, to cattle fences.

The ditch would have been filled with very nasty things such as sharpened branches and thorns, as in a fairly similar earthwork described by Julius

The *Vallum* behind Hadrian's Wall where it makes a deviation around Downs Hill to the east of Halton (Onnum) fort.

Caesar at Alesia. The works at Alesia had three ditches and a single palisaded mound, and surrounded the city during the Roman seige. It faced inwards with the ditches towards the city and was intended to prevent the escape of the defenders.

The double mound of the *Vallum* has caused confusion but let us look at it from a military point of view. The Romans tell us that any wall less than seventy feet high could not prevent a determined enemy from surmounting it. Hadrian's Wall is estimated to have been fifteen feet high, so the Romans would have expected the enemy to get across now and again. The *Vallum* in this case would have made an excellent second line of defence with the Romans to the south of the south mound. The enemy having crossed the Wall would have had to present themselves as targets as they mounted the north mound of the *Vallum* while preparing to cross the ditch and its disagreeable contents.

A modern general fears an enemy armoured breakthrough of his lines, with tanks turning to attack his soft-skinned vehicles from behind. He therefore positions quite a lot of guns pointing to his rear for such an eventuality. If the enemy of the Romans achieved such a breakthrough of the Wall, then the Roman rear was defended by the *Vallum* and the Romans were in an elongated fort between Wall and *Vallum*.

After the surrender of Singapore to the Japanese in 1942, much criticism was levelled at the British military planners because the island's large guns could not turn to the north. They were deployed for an expected attack from the sea. An enemy advance down the jungles of the Malayan peninsula was not foreseen. Yet when we see the remains of a Roman system which faced both ways, it causes confusion.

As a matter of interest, the large British guns captured by the Japanese at Singapore were shipped to the Aleutian Islands in the North Pacific and installed there as a defence against the Americans. The Japanese had not learned the lesson they taught the British because the American marines came in over the back of the island and took those guns in the rear once again.

About AD 143, Hadrian's Wall was abandoned as Antoninus Pius decided a better offensive/defensive line would be between the Forth and the Clyde. This wall was of turf on a stone foundation. The forts were built of stone but there were no milecastles or turrets as on Hadrian's Wall. In 165 the Antonine Wall was abandoned and Hadrian's Wall reoccupied.

Towards the end of the second century, Hadrian's Wall was wrecked by invading tribes from the north, who caused havoc over most of northern Britain as far south as York and Chester.

The work of reconstruction of the Wall was carried out during the years 197 to 208. There were many modifications to the original design. The emperor Septimius Severus himself came to Britain in 208 and began a series of campaigns against the enemies in Scotland. These operations were costly in money and casualties. Before his programme was complete, he died in York in 211.

Now let us return to some time before Hadrian, when there must have been an earlier *limes* even though we don't quite know where. The evidence, for and against the Stanegate has already been mentioned.

The first clue in the chain of research which led to new evidence, was the reference in JC Hodgson's *History of Northumberland*:

"Heddon Law, Dewley Law, Turpin's Hill are all capped with *tumuli* cairns and other ancient works. Between these stations in 1728, there were six *castella*, in a series without interruption, measuring exactly 1,485 yards. In the nearest to Vindolanda on the east in 1766, an urn was found full of gold and silver coins."

When asked about their views on this reference, most Roman period experts said that: "the old antiquarians must have mistaken Romano-British settlements (native farmsteads) for Roman fortlets." This did not ring true, as groups of RB sites were not sited in straight lines, nor at equally spaced intervals. An investigation was called for.

Ordnance Survey 1:50,000 maps, numbers 88,87,86 & 85 were cellotaped together and a navigator's parallel ruler used to see if the sites mentioned by Hodgson formed part of a greater alignment. There was an extremely surprising result – with the rulers positioned on Turpin's Hill and Heddon Law, the extended line, when drawn between the North Sea and Irish Sea coasts, traversed several well known Roman sites, other suspected Roman sites and several findspots of Roman artefacts. The sites formed a near-perfect straight line from coast to coast on an alignment of 075/255 degrees True. Here and there, modern roads or cart tracks followed the line.

Navigator's dividers were then set to the distance mentioned by Hodgson – 1,485 yards, to see if this was the correct interval between the various sites.

There was a discrepancy, and I noticed with astonishment that the distance between the sites was 1,620 yards – a Roman mile. With the dividers still set to 1,620 yards, I marked Roman mile intervals on the maps all the way from coast to coast. Most of the following significant sites were exactly at the Roman mile intervals. Exceptions were suspected signal stations, major forts and river crossings:

St Mary's Island (NZ 352 755), Roman coins often found. Backworth (NZ 301 720), Roman treasure found many years ago. Newcastle Airport, line passes to south of runway. Callerton DMV (NZ 165 704), apparently unknown until this survey. Heddon Law (NZ 141 693), reuse of *tumulus* as signal station? West Heddon DMV (NZ 125 688), earthworks. Turpins Hill (NZ 108 685), gold & silver Roman coins found 1766. Whitchester Farm (NZ 099 683), suspected Roman fort under farm. Earthworks (NZ 094 683), suspected milefortlet in strip wood. Crossing of Hadrian's Wall (NZ 086 681), Welton DMV (NZ 063 676), pele tower built of Roman stones. Laker Hall (NZ 050 673), early Roman coins found. Shildon Hill IA hillfort (NZ 023 662), Square earthwork N end. Shildon Bog suspected fortlet (NZ 023 662), standing earthwork. Shildon Bog suspected fort (NZ 022 658), crop mark seen from air. Aydon (NZ 016 660), mound in field at correct interval. Red House Roman fort (NY 968 652), destroyed by A69(T). Hexham Abbey (NY 935 642), Roman town long suspected. Causey Hill (NY 925 637), long tradition of Roman road. Langley suspected Roman site (NY 837 622), seen from air.

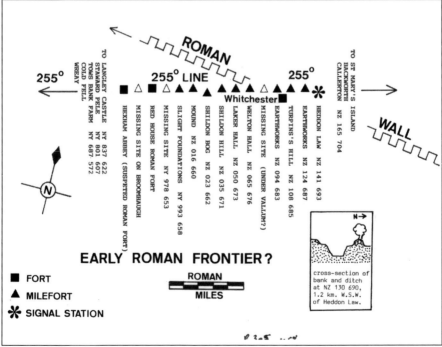

The recently discovered "255 degree Frontier Line" which is lined up on St Mary's Island, Heddon Ridge, Shildon Lough, Red House, Hexham, Staward Pele, Cold Fell and Wreay. This may be the pre-Hadrianic Roman frontier.

Staward Pele (NY 802 607), much reused Roman stone. Cypress Linn (NY 801 606), natural rock abutments, iron cramps. Beacon Hill (NY 764 594), possible signal station. Spot height 409m (NY 698 573), site of old currick (watch-tower). Tows Bank Farm (NY 687 572), Roman-type ditches, coins found. Cold Fell (NY 605 557), probable Roman survey point. Longdyke Farm (NY 538 536), significant name. Wreay Roman fort (NY 44 49). Old Carlisle Roman fort (NY 25 46). Heather Bank Roman fortlet (NY 07 41).

Not only was this line a Roman road, but it was also some kind of frontier.

The survey of the suspected frontier has hardly started, and any new information will be welcome especially from the western half of the country. There follows a summary of what is known so far and may make a starting point for interested field-walkers. All the sites mentioned lie on the 255 degree line from St Mary's Island to Maryport. The sites are mostly suspected fortlets at Roman mile intervals, and I often refer to them as "milefortlets" to distinguish them from the "milecastles" of Hadrian's Wall.

St Mary's Island is an islet just off the Northumberland coast, four miles north of the entrance to the River Tyne. Navigators of various ages have erected markers and lighthouses on it and Roman coins have been found there. The island is connected to the mainland via a causeway which dries out at low tide. It would have made an excellent eastern terminus for a frontier.

Four miles inland is the village of Backworth, and the findspot of a famous hoard. Historians have often doubted the discoverer's findspot because they could not conceive anything of Roman importance in the area. The finder of the hoard may have been telling the truth after all.

The 255 line runs across Newcastle Airport south of Runway 25/07 and converges on it towards the western end. Pilots landing and taking off have seen crop marks in fields on the south side of the eastern end of the runway.

Just after take-off from Newcastle's Runway 25 [252 degrees Magnetic which is 245 degrees True], if a climb is continued on runway heading for a minute or so, the aircraft passes over a line of low hills. The suspected frontier lies along the top of these. The excellent choice of line is obvious from the air and Tacitus mentions that Agricola had an keen eye for selecting the optimum military use of the lie of land. Maybe this is an example of his skill.

The first hilltop with a visible earthwork on it is at NZ 165 704, just to the south of the Callerton DMV. This DMV seems to have been unknown until our survey. A ground inspection shows a low rectangular earthwork, 40 yards x 30 yards on the hill to the south of the DMV.

Two miles further on is the prominent 500 ft high Heddon Law although I think it has also been known as "Penny Hill." There is an obvious *tumulus* on the top but it may also have been used by the Romans as a signal station. It is not at an exact Roman mile interval but its unique outlook would determine its use. The whole of southern Northumberland is visible from this point. Two trial trenches dug in 1925 revealed a four feet thick dry-stone wall around the peak at a depth of 18 inches. Penny Hill is probably derived from the Middle English *Pen-y-gwel* which means "Rampart on the Hill." The suspected Roman road runs along the line of hills under a farm track just below the crest to the south. This is known as a "military horizon" ie, out of sight of an enemy to the north.

At NZ 132 690, this farm track has become a tarmac road and turns a right angle from 255 degrees to south-south-east. A feature continues straight ahead on 255 degrees (NZ 130 689) and this is a deep *fosse*, far too large to be a drainage ditch. The ditch is lost at the bottom of a small valley, and the next items of interest are the earthworks of the West Heddon DMV at NZ 125 688. Another farm-track has now materialised on our suspected Roman line and can be followed to the junction with a north-south public road at NZ 114 686. This public road continues south to Hadrian's Wall and Rudchester Wall fort, a thousand yards distant. The 255 line is lost to sight across the fields to the south of Turpin's Hill Farm, but the site where the urn of gold and silver coins was found is marked at the time of writing by a lone hawthorn tree in the middle of a field at NZ 108 685. There is a possible Roman well in the field boundary just to the south of the tree.

A public footpath is picked up at NZ 105 685 and this leads to, and is aligned with, the Whitchester Farm road. This farm road is on top of the suspected Roman frontier road and Whitchester Farm sits on a prominent earthwork and may conceal a major fort. It is too large for a milefortlet and it is not situated at a Roman mile interval.

Some six hundred yards further down the farm road to the west is a strip wood on the north side of the road. There are slight earthworks in this wood very close to the road. At the end of this farm road is the crossing point with Hadrian's Wall. The latter is hidden under the B6318 road. If there was a 255 degree-line milefortlet at the next Roman mile, it has been lost under the later *Vallum* of Hadrian's Wall which crosses at exactly this point. Our 255 line is now to the south of Hadrian's Wall and *Vallum*.

Across to the west of the Whittle Dean reservoirs is Welton Hall and the Welton DMV. The B6309 coming south from Hadrian's Wall makes a right-angled turn to the west at the gates of the hall. After this turn, the B6309 is parallel to the central street of the DMV and just a few yards to the north. This DMV green track is on the suspected Roman frontier road. The pele tower incorporated into the buildings of Welton Hall is built of Roman stones previously thought to have been robbed out of the Wall to the north. They may have come from a 255 line milefortlet right on the same site.

Five hundred yards west of Welton Hall, the B6309 sidesteps slightly to the south and then continues on its previous heading, but now right on top of the frontier road. The B6309 turns south at Welton Farm but a minor road continues straight ahead on top of our 255 line.

Laker Hall is one Roman mile west of Welton Hall and, just to the east of Laker Hall, exactly at the 1,620 yard interval is a pile of stones in the field beside an electricity pylon. Early Roman coins have been found here.

Another Roman mile ahead along the same road is the Iron Age hillfort on Shildon Hill. On the north end of this, and just north of a brick reservoir, is a square earthwork believed to be a 255 milefortlet. The road on top of the 255 line divides just west of Shildon Hall. The southern fork which heads south-west is our Roman frontier road, and this sudden and typical Roman deviation was necessary because, straight ahead on the 255 alignment, is Shildon Bog which was a lake in Roman times. The Roman road has skirted

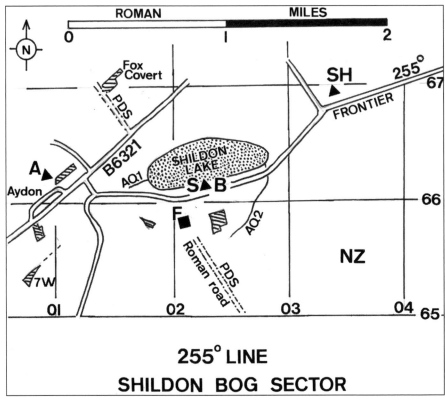

The Shildon Bog sector of the "255 Line" suspected early Roman frontier.

SH	=	Shildon Hill Iron Age hillfort, square earthwork north end.
SB	=	Shildon Bog suspected milefortlet.
F	=	Crop mark of fortlet seen from the air.
PDS	=	Proto Dere Street Roman road.
A	=	Aydon suspected milefortlet.
AQ1	=	Suspected aqueduct to Corbridge.
7W	=	Wood of the Seven Wells (on line of aqueduct).
AQ2	=	Suspected aqueduct to a Roman site at Bywell.

the lake with several angled straights.

On the north side of the road, at NZ 023 662, are suspected Roman earthworks with two prominent rounded corners. The road has bisected a suspected milefortlet. The half to the south of the road has been ploughed out. This is exactly one Roman mile (as the crow flies) from the Shildon Hill earthwork.

Just to the south-west, and halfway between two woods at NZ 022 658, the crop mark of a suspected Roman fort was seen from the air. Samian pottery and Roman coins have been picked up from this field. This crop mark was seen several years ago but its position not understood until now. The Roman road "Proto Dere Street" (from Ebchester and Bywell to Beukley) is now known to have crossed the suspected 255 frontier at this point. The small wood to the west of the crop mark contains a quarry. It is extremely likely that Shildon Lake was used by the Romans as the source of one of their aqueducts to Corbridge. A wood at NZ 007 653 is known as "The Wood of the Seven Wells" and this lies on the line of the suspected aqueduct (Corbridge seems to have had several aqueducts). Mackenzie's *Northumberland and Durham* of 1825 tells us about the draining of Shildon Lough:

"A great quantity of rain fell about a century ago, at the commencement of harvest time, when the lough overflowed and burst like a deluge to the westward, sweeping away not only the crops but also the fences. At Corbridge East Field, the water turned into the Tyne, leaving immense numbers of pike in every standing pool – when Sheldon Common was improved, the lough was drained."

The lough may have also been used by the Romans as a source for an aqueduct to Bywell. The Brock Hole Burn has its source at the east end of the lake and this stream runs all the way to Bywell. There is still an artificial cut at the east end of the lake but that may date from the final draining.

The Romans were not the first to use Shildon Lake. Dug-out canoes and stone axe-hammers have been found. Near Fox Covert plantation to the north of the lake, a cinerary urn was discovered, but this is likely to have been Roman as Proto Dere Street runs up the west side of this wood. This recently discovered Roman road must have crossed the western tip of the lake on piles as the *agger* can be seen just to the north of the swamp and is lined up exactly on Little Whittington and Beukley. The BBC radio mast at Beukley is an excellent marker for the road's heading, and no doubt the Roman surveyors used smoke signals at the same high point now occupied by the twentieth century signal station.

One Roman mile east of the Shildon Lake suspected Roman milefortlet is a mound in a field at NZ 016 660. Do not confuse this rounded mound with a mining spoil-heap just to the west. The farmer has removed a great deal of stone from this mound and has managed to plant his crops over the top of it. The stone lies at the field boundary to the west. A little further west at NZ 005 662 are unexplained channels which may be yet another one of the aqueducts to Corbridge. It has been estimated that the baths, latrines and dozens of fountains in the Roman town would have consumed two million gallons of water per day. When you think that a two-inch petrol pipe puts twenty gallons of fuel into a car in half a minute, it does not take long to calculate the amount of water flowing through a 3 ft wide x 1 ft deep aqueduct, and there were several such channels supplying the site.

A further Roman mile west of the Aydon "bump" are some earthworks on top of a hill at NY 994 659 just to the north of the Cor Burn and a gap in a wood.

A mile further on, the A69(T) may have removed evidence, just as it destroyed the Red House Roman fort which is on the line two miles to the west. As the latter was a major fort, it may not have been at an exact Roman mile interval. The 255 line crosses the Roman Stanegate here. Which one was the genuine frontier? Maybe both were and formed part a greater *limes* system. Only fieldwork will provide the answers.

There is a missing site on Broom Haugh to the north-east of Hexham, and a suggested search area is NY 953 647.

The next site is Hexham Abbey which has already been mentioned at great

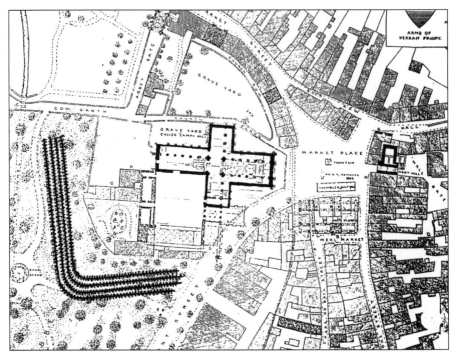

The old antiquarians were sure that there was a Roman town at Hexham. The 255 line passes right through Hexham Abbey. An expert dowser detected four parallel Roman ditches under the lawns of the Abbey. These will now have to be confirmed with scientific methods.

length as a probable Roman town and fort with a network of roads, some of which have been discovered only recently. The site would have been river supplied and would have formed the lynchpin of the whole system.

To the south-west of Hexham is Causey Hill, and tradition has long held that a Roman road passed here. If so, up to now, it has eluded survey pilots and field-walkers.

There is no doubt that the survey line of the suspected frontier continues on 255 degrees because we pick up more Roman sites on this alignment further to the west. There may have been a salient west of Hexham which approximated to the large northward bend of the River South Tyne. A suspected Roman road runs through Highwood Farm and the paving sticks out of the ground at NY 905 650. It can be seen again at Coastley at NY 895 656.

Back on the 255 line, there are earthworks at Blossom Hill farm (NY 903 633).

If there has been a salient to the north, the Roman line is back on the 255 degree line to the south of Langley Castle, where a suspected Roman fortlet was observed from the air at NY 622 837, on the north side of the dismantled railway line, and exactly on the public footpath which leads from Langley Castle, past Humbledon Cottage to the modern B6305 road. The railway has cut right through the ancient rectangular site, but one complete side and two rounded corners can still be traced at ground level. The site is in clear view of

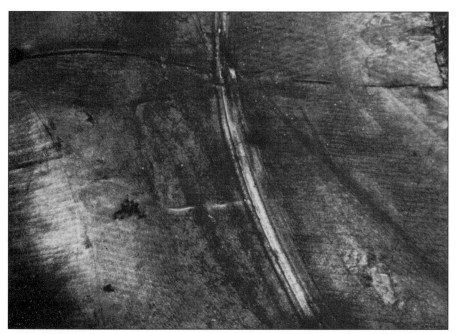

Exactly on the 255 Line and at a Roman mile interval, a suspected milefortlet was observed on the ridge to the south of Langley Castle at NY 837 622. An old railway line, now dismantled has cut right through the site.

Barcombe Hill, the position of the known Roman signal station to the east of the Stanegate fort of Vindolanda. This is five miles to the north-west.

The next visible evidence is at Staward Pele (NY 801 607) where the gatehouse contains many reused Roman stones. Professor Eric Birley, in his lecture read on 16.4.1950, said that he did not think the Romans stones had been transported very far in view of the wild terrain with its deep ravines and numerous streams. (it is more reminiscent of Canadian British Columbia than northern England). A Roman altar had been used as a quoin in the gatehouse but this altar fell down the sheer cliff into the Harsondale Burn in 1947. It has since been recovered and now stands in the garden of Staward Manor. The altar has an inscription which reads:

I O M
OH IIII GALL
I.PraEst.L.ll
GIVS PVDEN
.PRaEFECT
RAM pOSVIT
V V S

The altar is attributed to the Fourth Cohort of Gauls and the inscription restored and expanded reads:

"Iovi Optimo Maximo cohors IIII Gallorum cui praest Lucius....gius Pudens praefectus aram posuit ut voverat solvens libenter"

[To Jupiter Best and Greatest, the fourth cohort of Gauls, in command of which is Lucius ——gius Pudens, prefect, set up this altar, as it had vowed to do, willingly fulfilling its vow.]

The Fourth Cohort of Gauls served at Vindolanda during the third century, but had been at Templebrough in the first century and at Risingham at the time of Antonius Pius. (E Birley in "A Roman Altar from Staward Pele and Roman Remains in Allendale" in *Archaeologia Aeliana* 1950).

Many other Roman stones, including one with a lewis hole, lie in the Harsondale Burn at the foot of the cliff below the gatehouse. The most likely site for the Roman fortlet was the mediaeval pele tower which has probably reused Roman foundations. This site is on a high promontory with steep cliffs on three sides. The River Allen is to the west and the Harsondale Burn to the north and east. The only access to the pele is from the south via a path along a narrow ridge, and this is guarded by the gatehouse. The path is interrupted by a ditch and there are steep cliffs on both sides. The selection of this site and the whole line must have been carried out by a professional soldier who had a keen eye for the best military use of topography. With alterations of heading of only a degree or two, the 255 line has traversed ridges, spot heights, lake shores and, as will be seen next, even a "natural bridge."

To the west of Staward Pele, in the deep ravine of the River Allen, there are two remarkable natural rock abutments, one at each side of the river, at a waterfall called Cypress Linn (NY 802 605). The river tumbles through a deep and narrow cleft between the natural rock platforms. A few timbers between the flat rocks would have made an instant bridge. It is likely that a bridge has existed at some time in the past, as there are iron cramps in the rocks. On the west side of the river, a farm track follows the 255 alignment to Haining Hall (NY 785 598) and a little further west, a public road continues on the correct line to the south of Beacon Hill (NY 765 594). As will be gathered from the name, this would have made an excellent site for a signal station. The hill is covered in thick heather which may conceal archaeological evidence. Two miles to the south is Whitfield where Roman artefacts have been found. There is a complex of suspected Roman roads here. One has left Whitley Castle Roman fort (NY 695 487), crossed the River South Tyne at NY 699 493, where a small and very ruinous Roman bridge abutment can be seen in the west bank of an old course of the river, opposite Underbank Farm. An inscribed Roman stone has been used as a lintel in one of the farmyard buildings. To the east of the farm, the Roman road zig-zags up the steep slope. The Roman road continues north-east under farm tracks past Moscow (NY 735 502) and a section of A688 road (NY 745 516), to Whitfield Hall (NY 778 564) and then possibly joins the 255 line. The crossing of the West Allen has not yet been found but the road looks as if it is heading for the confluence of the Carr's Burn and West Allen (NY 782 558). At Bearsbridge (NY 780 575) a suspected Roman subsidiary road heads north-west up the steep hill in the direction of Whitfield and Beacon Hill.

Back on the suspected frontier, at NY 743 587, the modern road leaves the 255 line and bends to the north, but straight ahead across the moors to the west, it can be seen that the road prior to the bend is lined up on the distant Cold Fell (NY 605 557) on the west side of the River South Tyne. Before the

Reused Roman stones in the gatehouse of Staward Pele, (NY 802 607) This mediaeval building is also on the 255 Line and at an exact Roman mile interval.

The Roman altar which fell off the Gatehouse of Staward Pele, down into the Harsondale Burn. It is now in the garden of Staward Manor.

gorge of the South Tyne is reached, there is a spot height of 409m at NY 698
573 which is the site of a "currick" (watch-tower) of unknown age. It may have
had a Roman predecessor.

One mile further west, and right on the eastern rim of the South Tyne
gorge, is Tows Bank Farm (NY 687 572) and it is obvious from the air, that
this farm has a typical Roman ditch on its north side. When I visited the farm,
I mentioned to the farmer that I had reason to believe that his farm was on a
Roman site to which he replied: "That must be why I am finding Roman coins
in the kitchen garden." Below the farm, the suspected Roman road zig-zags
down the steep cliff to the river but a search for the crossing has not yet been
carried out. Neither has the line been surveyed to the west of the South Tyne.

Beyond Cold Fell, the theoretical 255 line crosses Longdyke Farm (NY 538
536) and this area should be searched. A Roman road has been found
recently at Cumwhitton but this runs north-east/south-west from NY 540 504
through Cumwhitton (NY 505 523) and then along the north edge of High
Wood, and is lined up on Wetheral Priory. This is very interesting, but it is
not the 255 road, which remains to be found in the area.

The Roman fort of Wreay (NY 44 49) is on the line, and it may well be that
this name has a Viking origin. It is possible that the name is derived from the
Old Norse *hreyrr* which means "cairn" or "heap of stones forming a
boundary."

The original 255 line heads for Old Carlisle fort and Heather Bank fortlet
but searchers should be prepared for tactical deviations.

So much for new evidence of a suspected early frontier but many mysteries
still surround features of the well known Hadrian's Wall. A brief history of the
Wall may assist those to whom the whole subject is new:

AD 43	Claudius' successful invasion of Britain.
AD 71	Romans occupying Pennines.
AD 81	Roman governor Agricola's campaigns in Scotland.
c 96–90	Roman withdrawal from much of Scotland.
c 117	Uprisings in Britain.
122-130	Building of Hadrian's Wall.
AD 139	Roman reoccupation of southern Scotland. Antonine Wall between Forth and Clyde built. Small garrisons left on Hadrian's Wall.
AD155	Reoccupation of Hadrian's Wall. Antonine Wall temporarily evacuated.
AD165	Antonine Wall finally abandoned.
193-211	Rebuilding of Hadrian's Wall by emperor Severus after severe damage.
208-211	Scotland briefly reoccupied. Extra outposts built north of Hadrian's Wall.
AD 296	Further damage to Hadrian's Wall.
c300	Rebuilding of Wall by Constantius Chlorus.
AD 367	Further attacks on Wall.
AD 369	Rebuilding by Count Theodosius.
c400+	Wall ceases to be manned and the Dark Age begins...

There are large gaps in our knowledge and new information, instead of answering questions, often poses more. Here and there, evidence has been twisted to suit historians. In the central sector the double-faced *Vallum* runs extremely close to the Wall for miles, which destroys the theory that the strip, only a few yards wide between Wall and *Vallum,* was a Roman cattle compound. The *Vallum* deviates around the southern walls of some Roman forts, and at others the *Vallum* has been infilled by the Romans themselves.

At Chesters (Cilurnum) at the North Tyne crossing, it is widely claimed that the *Vallum* deviated around the fort, yet Professor Haverfield, who excavated this area in 1904, said that the *Vallum* originally ran into the southern fort ditch. Haverfield's reports have been disregarded but nevertheless, he was right. Aerial photographs clearly show the infilled *Vallum* running into the fort's southern ditch. Furthermore, as well as levelling the *Vallum* mounds, the Romans have used the infilled ditch as a burial ground. Archaeologist Tom Wright found nineteen Roman graves along the line of the infilled *fosse.* They are clearly visible as circles of random rubble (crazy paving), similar to two known graves by the riverside some 200 yards further downstream. The gravestones of the latter are now in the Museum of Antiquities, Newcastle upon Tyne. Close by the two recorded graves, at the time of writing, the river has uncovered what looks like a stone jetty in the west bank. This is several feet above the present water level and is further proof that the Romans had a weir downstream.

One of the aqueducts, which fed the baths and latrines at Chesters, can be traced from the north-west. The source appears to be a spring at NY 896 712, about 450 yards north-east of Turret 28B. A second aqueduct commences at a small dam at NY 903 717, 350 yards north-west of Leazes Farm. The *specus* (water channel) can be seen leaving the dam and winding around the hill at a lesser rate of fall than that of the source-beck.

Two-and-a-half miles along the Wall to the west of Chesters is Limestone Corner, the most northerly point of the frontier. The ditch to the north of the Wall has not been completed. The OS map refers to this section as: "Ditch unfinished owing to the hardness of rock," yet a few yards to the south, the Romans have cut the *Vallum* ditch with apparent ease, through the same outcrop.

A possible Roman road runs south towards the Tyne from this point. An old quarry (NY 876 713), believed to be Roman, has an uncut causeway across it in line with the suspected road. Perhaps the Romans decided to build a fort at Limestone Corner and left the ditch unfinished, and then changed their minds again. There were several changes of plan and afterthoughts during the Wall's construction.

Just to the north of Limestone Corner, there are outlying earthworks of suspected Roman origin, overlooking a steep slope. Also a possible Roman patrol road runs east-west, two miles north of the Wall, from Townhead (NY 877 741, north-east of Simonburn) across Standard Hill (NY 826 752) on Broadpool Common, to Whygate (NY 770 757), past Great Watch Hill (NY 702 749), and then to Butterburn (NY 676 744). This could well be part of an unknown *limes.*

A little over a mile west of Limestone Corner is Carrawbrough fort (Brocolitia) where thousands of Roman coins were found in the famous

Coventina's Well. Traces of the well can be seen in the dip to the west of the fort. The aqueduct which fed the fort was spotted from the air and appears to have had its source at a small pool 1,200 yards to the north-east of the fort at NY 866 722. If the Romans threw thousands of coins into the well close to the fort, perhaps they also threw some into the aqueduct's source-pool. On our ground search, we picked up some sherds of pottery and two Roman coins at the edge of the pond.

For me, the most fascinating of all the Wall forts is Housesteads (Vercovicium), which is perched on a cliff. The Roman service road, the Military Way, which tracks along between Wall and *Vallum* is prominent here. This road *does* seek out easy gradients, so obviously it was used for supplies as well as for troop movements. The fort's north wall coincides with the frontier Wall and the latter continues along the crest of the crags to the west. To the south of the fort, the gentler slope is covered with cultivation terraces. What were the Romans growing? The terraces are perfectly level which hints at irrigation. When I suggested that perhaps the Romans grew rice here, I was shouted down and told that rice would not grow in Britain. I had seen it growing in northern China in a climate much worse than that of Britain, so I carried out an experiment.

Treated supermarket rice is sterile so during a spell of overseas duty, I brought some rice seed back from Sierra Leone in West Africa. A member of my archaeological society, Elizabeth Anderson, is a lady with "green fingers" and she was given the job of conducting the rice-growing experiment. She planted rice in several pots and kept some indoors and some outside. The remainder, she threw onto her patio for the birds. The potted seeds germinated and then died, but, from the cracks between the paving slabs of the outside patio, an excellent crop of rice appeared. The crop was almost ready for photography when the gardener paid a visit while Elizabeth was out. He removed all the "untidy grass" from the patio, so our experiment will have to be repeated. We know however, that rice will grow in Sunderland.

The Romans mention rice (*oryza*) in their price lists as being double the price of wheat. At one period, the Roman unit stationed at Housesteads was the Syrian "Hamian Archers." Maybe these middle-eastern soldiers constructed the cultivation terraces. Another piece of evidence points towards combined irrigation and manuring of the terraces. During excavation it was not understood why the drain from the latrines, instead of running down to the stream in the normal Roman manner, apparently curved round into the terraces. This type of fertilization is still used in some eastern countries.

The soil is acid in the Housesteads area and I am told that this favours pollen analysis. I shall welcome any advice on the subject.

To the west of Housesteads, a walk along the Wall on the crest of the escarpment is a remarkable experience. There is a marvellous view of unspoilt countryside, and at the same time, one receives an insight into the workings of the Roman military mind. In the valley to the south-west is Roman Vindolanda on the Stanegate Roman road, and on the other side of the Wall immediately below the north face, is a steep cliff. One-and-a-half miles west of Housesteads the cliff drops into the beautiful Crag Lough. This

Top: A Roman road leaves Whitley Castle Roman fort to the east and crosses the River South Tyne at Underbank Farm. On the east side of the river, the road can be seen zig-zagging up the steep slope.

Bottom: On the west side of the South Tyne, exactly opposite Underbank Farm, there is a small Roman bridge abutment on an old and now dry course of the river. This road may have connections with the Roman frontier.

lough is drained from the eastern end by the Bradley Burn which passes
through a cleft in the cliffs called Milking Gap. The Wall descends into this
defile, and the stream passes under the base of the stonework via a culvert of
Roman rectangular shape. What a marvellous reservoir this lake would have
made for Vindolanda in the valley to the south. The Romans would not have
missed such an opportunity. They tell us that an aqueduct gradient of 1:250
was ideal and if one traces this out across the contours, it will be seen that the
line intercepts Brackie's Burn at NY 767 806. There are old iron-stone mines
here and an industrial tramway has crossed the stream on an earthwork
which may have started life as a Roman aqueduct embankment. To the south
of the stream, the now dismantled narrow gauge line ran all the way to the
Stanegate road and terminated exactly at the Vindolanda bath-house. This
narrow-gauge tramway on top of a suspected aqueduct is not to be confused
with the dismantled standard gauge railway line which ran north to south and
crossed the Stanegate to the east of Vindolanda and the Bradley Burn.

Brackie's Burn itself also seems to have been a Roman aqueduct source, as
there is a cistern hewn out of solid rock at NY 762 806 at the junction with a
smaller stream coming down from the north. The latter is fed from an
artificial well and a spring just south of the Wall. The upper reaches of
Brackie's Burn should be searched for paving and signs of troughs or
cisterns.

With the requirements of millions of gallons of water per day, all Roman
forts would have had extensive aqueduct systems. Very few of these have been
identified. Large viaduct-type *arcades* were not necessary in Britain. The
aqueducts were, in the most part, covered channels which approximated to
the contours. They are easy to find because the searcher can look at the
landscape through a Roman engineer's eyes. Using only maps, the likely
courses of Roman aqueducts can be plotted at home or in the office. Out in
the field, it is most rewarding to find that one's calculations have forecast the
exact positions of genuine Roman handiwork.

Earlier this century, the town clerk of Corbridge was looking for extra
sources of water supply for the town. When he investigated springs in the
surrounding hills, he noted that the Romans had beaten him to it, leaving
traces of their stone channels and earthwork-dams. Unfortunately, he did not
record the map references.

Much research work on the Wall remains to be done and many false
assumptions need to be corrected. West of the River Irthing, the Wall was
orignially built of turf and later rebuilt in stone. This was discovered because
the Romans built a section of the replacement wall on a slightly different line
to the original turf construction. Remains of this survive to the west of
Birdoswald (Camboglanna) fort. The official explanation is that the Wall west
of the Irthing was built originally of turf because there were no lime outcrops
to provide a necessary ingredient for mortar. These outcrops cease at the Red
Rock Fault which is just to the west of Lanercost Priory. How is it that the
previously mentioned section of Turf Wall is well outside the Red Rock Fault
area? The mystery remains unsolved. Also, the Wall changes in character at
the Irthing. From Wallsend, it has used every military advantage and, except
at isolated points, the patrolling soldiers would have had an excellent view to

In one of the farm buildings at Underbank Farm, a Roman inscribed stone has been used as a lintel

the north. To the west of the Irthing, the Wall follows a very poor defensive line. A better tactical line would have been along the ridge to the south of the Irthing, but was the Irthing the barge supply route which had to be defended? The same argument holds for the rest of the Wall. Why was it built to the north of the Tyne instead of along the south bank. The southern banks of the Rhine and Danube were used as Roman frontiers; why not the Tyne? Compared with the Rhine and Danube, the Tyne, away from the estuary, is a narrow river and barge traffic could have come under fire from the northern shore during periodic enemy incursions into the frontier area. The next best defence line to the north was the one actually selected; the Wallsend-Irthing line.

At both ends of the Wall, at the Tyne and Eden estuaries, the defence line was placed along the southern shores. No actual traces of a barrier have been found at the eastern end, but there is a fort at South Shields and a high probability of another at Jarrow. The five-mile length of southern river bank from opposite Wallsend to South Shields is covered with industrial development, and chances of further finds are slight. Jarrow is the critical site but all mention of the Roman handiwork there has been censored for reasons unknown.

Although millions of words have been written about the Roman frontiers of Britain, very little is actually known. The field is wide open for new search technology and operators with uncluttered vision.

All armies and navies have had efficient methods of communication even in the most difficult circumstances. This photograph shows a Royal Naval Air Service airship on convoy escort duty c1916. In order to preserve wireless-telegraphy silence, the observer is signalling to another airship by semaphore.

A later generation of aviators also used visual signals between aircraft in addition to the well known "Aldis' morse-lights. During the 1939-45 War of the Atlantic, Royal Air Force Coastal Command anti-U-Boat patrol bombers flew alongside each other on such occasions as taking over escort duties. In order to communicate while maintaining radio silence, the art of "zogging" was developed. This was a form of semaphore but it used the morse code and needed only a hand and forearm. A dot was a short flick of the wrist and a dash was a movement from the elbow. Crewmen of the two aircraft in formation communicated extremely well with this simple system. Although Romans soldiers and sailors lacked modern technology, their intellect and skills quite equalled those of the twentieth century servicemen, and expertise at visual communications would have been well within their capabilities.

Chapter 11

Roman Signal Stations

GLD DE GBTT QRV K

(Landsend radio from RMS Queen Elizabeth 2, I am ready to receive your message, go ahead)

The large number of Roman signal stations found in Britain indicates that they played an important part in the military occupation, but very little is known about the signalling techniques employed.

We know that the Romans *did* use signal stations, as a relief on Trajan's Column shows a Danube frontier-tower. A boom with a burning torch at the end extends from an upper window. Beside the tower are what look like two emergency signal bonfires, ready to be ignited. The boom on the tower certainly looks like a semaphore arm and elsewhere there is a Roman mention of: "the flailing arms of a signal station." Therefore, it is safe to say that in addition to emergency flares, the Romans used some form of semaphore.

Various other references tell us that the ancients were well acquainted with the art of transmitting information by visual signals – in 458 BC, Aeschylus heard of the fall of Troy and this news was conveyed to Greece by a chain of beacons.

In the second century BC, Polybius described actual methods of transmitting elaborate messages by light-signals, and in the fourth century AD, the military historian, Vegetius, mentioned fire, smoke and semaphore codes as employable for signalling.

In these days of modern telecommunications, we tend to think of old systems such as semaphore, as unweildy and inefficient but until the 1950's, semaphore was still used extensively at sea, and seamen of all nations were experts in its use. A better visual signalling system was the use of the morse code with a signal light, usually known as an "Aldis lamp." This had a longer range than semaphore and could be used by day or night. The development of VHF (Very High Frequency) radiotelephone meant that seamen could talk to their opposite numbers on other ships, many miles away and in bad visibility, at the touch of a button. The art of visual signalling deteriorated. These skills had to be learned again very quickly during the Falkands War of 1982, because the enemy could pick up radio signals. Even if radio signals are in code, an enemy can measure the direction from which they are coming and two direction-finding stations can take cross bearings and plot the location of the transmitter. Many a German U-boat met its death during the 1939-45 War because an efficient network of D/F stations, operated by the Royal Navy, pin-pointed their positions as they transmitted reports back to Germany.

For those of us who are used to modern radiotelephone communications, the older systems of morse and semaphore may seem to take a lot of skill and training, but messages transmitted by these methods are less prone to garbling as every letter is spelled out one by one. British naval morse radiotelegraphy was usually carried out at twenty-five words (125 letters) per minute which was just about as fast as the receiving operator could write. Visual messages by signal lamp were somewhat slower, at about eight words (40 characters) per minute. During the 39-45 War, radiocommunications were divided into two main categories, radiotelephony (human speech) and radiotelegraphy (morse). In order to differentiate between the two, radiotelephony was given the abbreviation "R/T" and morse transmissions, the older one, "W/T" (wireless telegraphy).

A story used by military instructors illustrates the comparative reliability of the two systems:

It is said that a general sent a radiotelephone message back to his rear:

"Send reinforcements, we are going to advance."

These reinforcements did not materialise because the message was received as:

"Send three-and-fourpence, we are going to a dance."

If the message had been transmitted in morse, it would not have been garbled and the general would have received his troops.

If the Romans used visual signalling codes, then they had a system which was just as efficient as any modern one up to the invention of wireless telegraphy.

We are sure that the Romans used light and/or semaphore systems but the use of long distance speech in the case of frontiers cannot be ruled out. There are vague references from historians of the nineteenth century, to "speaking tubes" being found in a Roman Wall milecastle. Unfortunately, we will probably never know the truth of this matter as any metal tube embedded in the Wall between milecastles would have been in the long-disappeared upper courses. Modern historians say that such a system wouldn't work, but when I was a boy, a new system of fencing was developed. This consisted of concrete posts with two holes and two continuous tubes which ran for thousands of yards without breaks. We often used to talk to each other through these tubes over distances of half a mile. Of course even if the Romans had thought of this, the system would only work in a wall. An exposed pipe would have been too easy for an enemy to cut.

The information between signal stations would have been transmitted letter by letter, but oft-repeated routine messages may have just consisted of a code number such as:

1 = ALL'S WELL
2 = SUSPICIOUS MOVEMENTS TO NORTH

3 = SUSPICIOUS MOVEMENTS TO EAST .....and so on....
7 = WE ARE UNDER ATTACK
8 = OUR RELIEF HAS NOT TURNED UP, PLEASE INVESTIGATE

Negative signalling may have been used – if a routine message was not received at the appointed time, troops would be dispatched to investigate.

The whole Roman alphabet which includes Roman numerals, could have been transmitted with a pattern of three lights, such as two movable torches switched to various positions around a fixed reference light.

We know that the Romans had knowledge of secret codes as one of Hadrusbal's couriers was captured when trying to pass from Carthaginian occupied northern Italy, through Roman central Italy to Hannibal's army in the south. The Romans thought that because the letter was in plain language, it was a "plant" and intended to be captured to mislead them. They did in fact take action but the absence of codes caused them to deliberate on the matter for some time.

Polybius devised a system of secret signalling using torches which showed two numerals at a time. Each double number represented a letter selected from an alphabet displayed on a grid. The first number was from a vertical line at the side of the grid, the second from along the top. This also formed the basis of a German cipher used during the 1914-18 War.

Roman signal stations were usually positioned so that they had a good all-round view, but on occasion, they were screened from certain directions. Was this because the Romans did not want an enemy to see the signals? Even if an enemy can't read the codes, he knows that something is going on. During the

A Roman watch-tower on the Danube frontier as depicted on Trajan's Column. The two stacks on the left look like signal fires ready to be ignited in an emergency. The boom with a torch on the end looks like a semaphore arm.

39-45 War, the Germans always knew when the British were going to mount a night bombing attack, because during the day, the RAF radio mechanics went along the aircraft dispersals checking the radio of each aeroplane in turn. Although the transmissions were merely tests and the radiomen had no knowledge of the details of the forthcoming attack, the increase in volume of traffic picked up by German monitoring stations alerted anti-aircraft defences.

Some of the highest Roman signal stations in Britain may tell us a little about the climate of Britain in Roman times. For example, the highest hill in my home area, is the Cheviot Hill in Northumberland which is just over 2,600 feet high. Its fairly flat top has no known Roman signal station, whereas the Eildon Hill, just a few miles away near Melrose, does have one although the hill at just over 1,300 feet is only half the height of Cheviot. What is the reason for this as both hills were in an area of intense Roman activity? Surely a signal station on Cheviot would have had a far greater range than the one on Eildon. The answer is, I think, the British weather – the average height of the cloud base in Roman times must have been the same as it is now, about 2,000 ft. Only about one day in seven can we see the top of the Cheviot Hill as it usually has a tablecloth of cloud on it.

The top of Eildon is in cloud only in bad weather. Does this tell us that the British climate was exactly the same in Roman times as it is now?

Evidence from wells seems to confirm this. Remains of *flora* and *fauna* taken from Roman wells have been examined. Insects and plants were identical to those of today. This also suggests a similar climate to the present even if there was a temporary deterioration in the mediaeval period.

The tablecloth which hides Cheviot's summit cost many a wartime airman his life when flying in cloud at 2,000 ft. A few flyers strayed north from England's eastern coastal plain and there are at least twelve aircraft wrecks up there. The tangled remains of a Boeing B17 Flying Fortress of the American Army Air Force can still be seen beside Braydon Crag, West Hill, Cheviot at map ref NT 894 214. This aircraft was a victim of bad weather and false signals. The aircraft, B17 No 44-6504, left Molesworth in 1944 to bomb Ulm in Germany. Bad weather caused the formation to break up and the aircraft were recalled to their bases. The navigator of 44-6504 was lost, and the radio operator asked the RAF for radio bearings (in morse). He was answered by German stations using false British call-signs and these bearings were of course incorrect ones. The navigator plotted a false position from this information and decided that the aircraft was being blown south of track by an increasing northerly wind. A course alteration was made to north-west and, instead of crossing the East Anglian coast at the safe height of 2,000 ft, the bomber flew into Northumberland and 2,000 ft was certainly not a safe height in that area. In Cheviot's tablecloth, the aircraft struck a relatively flat plateau and the navigator and bombardier, who sat in the nose, were killed. The rest of the crew escaped from the burning aircraft before the bombs exploded. Sheila, a sheepdog from Southerknowe Farm, was awarded the Dicken Medal (the animal VC) for finding the survivors.

False signals in all wars, ancient and modern, have been a legitimate weapon.

I will shortly suggest how a slight knowledge of modern radiocommunications can help us find unknown Roman signal stations but first I must ask readers to bear with me while I describe technology which may seem irrelevant to archaeology.

It is not usually appreciated that radio waves, infra-red rays (heat), visible light, ultra-violet light, X-rays, and Gamma rays are all *electro-magnetic* waves. The only reason they differ from each other is their various *wavelengths* which cause them to have different properties. Mother Nature has chosen that part of the spectrum known as "visible light" for the use by the eyesight of all her creatures. We can feel the longer wavelength infra-red waves but not see them and radio waves are of a much longer wavelength and need special apparatus to detect them.

In very simple language, a radio transmitter can be described as an "electron pump." Free electrons in a (usually) vertical piece of wire are forced to the top of the wire, and this is an imbalance of nature, so a strong downwards force is felt all around in space and it just so happens that this force travels outwards at 300 million metres per second, (186,000 miles per second), 670 million mph, or 300 metres in a microsecond (millionth of a second). We think that this is nature's absolute speed limit. The radio transmitter then reverses its pump action and forces the free electrons down to the base of the wire. This again is an imbalance of nature and an upward force is sent out at 186,000 miles per second by which time the downward force has gone a considerable distance. The distance between two consecutive down-waves or up-waves is known as the *wavelength,* and it will be seen that the faster the pump action of the transmitter, the shorter will be the distance between wave crests. Frequencies are usually expressed in *Megahertz* (millions of cycles per second) or *Kilohertz* (thousands of cycles per second). One megahertz gives a wavelength of 300 metres. The radio wave/frequency spectrum goes from the very long waves (Low Frequency or LF) through the medium waves (Medium Frequency or MF) to the short waves (High Frequency or HF) and to the metric waves (Very High Frequency or VHF) and on to the centimetric waves which are used for radars, then on to the microwaves, X-rays, heat and light.

Although all radio waves are exactly the same type of stress passing through space, the various frequencies/wavelengths cause them to propagate in three different manners. The Low Frequencies (long waves) follow the curvature of the earth and the feet of the waves even penetrate water as they pass over the surface of the sea. These are the only frequencies which can be picked up by (shallowly) submerged submarines. Such messages are broadcast to submarines which cannot reply while submerged. The practice is to acknowledge messages when operations allow. The boat (submarines are referred to as "boats" and not "ships") comes to periscope depth and deploys an antenna, periscope-fashion, and acknowledges receipt of the message on a high frequency. A tremendous amount of power is needed by shore stations to propagate the long wave broadcasts. It has been known for all the lights to come on in an aircraft while flying near these stations, even though all the light switches were off.

Next come the Medium Frequencies (medium waves) and these are used for broadcasting and marine and aeronautical radiobeacons. These waves also follow the curvature of the earth and although the range is not as great as that of the Low Frequency waves, less power is needed to propagate them. A greater range is obtained at night because of reflections from the ionosphere which rises in height during the hours of darkness.

Further along the spectrum are the High Frequencies (short waves) and the ionosphere affects these greatly. Round-the-world communications can be achieved with very little transmitter power, as these waves are reflected alternatively between the ionosphere and the Earth's surface. The high end of the band is suitable for positions which are both in daylight (low ionosphere) and the low end of the band between points both in darkness (high ionosphere). The centre of the band can be used for both day and night communications.

What has all this got to do with Roman signal stations? Please bear with me a little longer...

When we get to the VHF (Very High Frequency) and UHF (Ultra High Frequency) bands, the propagation properties change again and 99 per cent of the waves go straight through the ionosphere and are lost into outer space. Only one per cent is reflected, therefore unless we have tremendously powerful transmitters and sensitive receivers, VHF, UHF and centimetric waves can only be used between communicators who are in line-of-sight of each other. This does not matter very much in the case of VHF communications between the ground and an aircraft, as an aircraft at 10,000 ft has a VHF range of 100+ miles and at 20,000 ft, 200+ miles. At 30,000 ft, the VHF range is 300+ miles and so on. An aircraft down at one thousand feet will be lucky to manage a VHF range of twenty miles.

Even though VHF and UHF are restricted in range by line of sight, the great advantage is that the frequencies are static-free – all nature's transmissions of crackles and hisses caused by thunderstorms and static are in the low and medium frequencies. Also for television transmitters, VHF/UHF bands are essential because the change of coded intelligence and modulations needed to form the lines, frames, and pictures, is so fast that this information is a high frequency in itself and needs an even higher frequency to carry it.

A television transmitter is therefore always placed on high ground so that the greatest number of receivers can be in its line-of-sight coverage. All kinds of other VHF/UHF transmitters also use high ground, and examples of these are: police repeater stations, post office telecommunications links, fire service control etc.

Our modern engineers and surveyors have therefore selected many vantage points because of the limitations of range of line-of-sight frequencies. If we eliminate those high points which are often in cloud (cloud does not affect radio transmissions) and concentrate on those which we think may have been clear of cloud in Roman times, then our modern engineers will have done part of our archaeological fieldwork for us and pin-pointed possible sites which the Romans may have used for that part of the electro-magnetic frequency spectrum that they used for signalling – visible light.

As it is useless to search high mountains for Roman signal stations, it is also a waste of time to search around the radio stations which use lower frequencies and do not rely on line-of-sight coverage. These stations which are of no value to our search are the ones with forests of masts and interconnecting wires. They are seldom built on high points. Our useful telltale stations are usually single masts with short antennae at the top, or merely poles with telecommunications "dishes."

Now that I have got over all that dreadful (but essential) information, it is time to put the knowledge to work. The Romans liked to line up their roads on high points, but quite often the road alters course many miles short of the high point. The latter is then merely a survey point and evidence now shows that the Romans used some form of triangulation. If a straight parish boundary is lined up on a VHF mast, then the chances are that a Roman road has been found. If there is also a Saxon church on the line, then there is probably a fort close by. If the line crosses a river with a mediaeval water-mill in the vicinity, then a major river supplied fort may have been found.

Other technical aspects must be studied before we look further at a few Roman signal stations which seem to be placed quite uselessly on low ground. Because of their seemingly unsuitable positions for communications, they have often been misidentified as fortlets.

Although VHF/UHF radio systems are static-free and ideal for radiotelephone communications, the line-of-sight propagation restricts the range. With modern technology, this has been overcome by "bouncing" signals off a satellite. It is not quite that simple of course; the signals are not "bounced" but retransmitted, quite often on a different frequency, by the satellite. The satellite is in geostationary orbit over the equator. The closer a satellite is to Earth, the faster it orbits but at a height of 25,000 miles, the orbit keeps pace with Earth's daily spin and the satellite apparently remains fixed in one place. Any satellite in its swift flight is actually in free-fall and is trying to drop back to Earth but the radius of curvature of the trajectory created by the launching rocket is greater than Earth's radius, so the satellite's forward horizon constantly dips away inside the line of fall. The communications satellite is kept at the right height for geostationary orbit by small adjustments from internal "puffer" rockets. Thus a sailor on a ship in the South Atlantic can talk to London by telephone on clear UHF frequencies and is in line of sight with London via the Atlantic satellite in orbit 25,000 miles above the equator near Ascension Island. The apparently fixed geostationary satellite is actually falling through space in its curved path around the Earth, at 7,600 mph, the centrifugal force balanced by Earth's gravity. There are two geostationary martitime communications satellites over the Atlantic and one each over the Pacific and Indian Oceans.

Now, let us return to a typical Roman fort situated not on a hill-top like the conquered Iron Age hillforts, but beside a river in a valley for reasons discussed earlier at great length. How did the Roman fort signal to its neighbours, when it was usually out of sight of the main chain of Roman signals stations along the ridges and rolling hills? The answer is, repeater-stations. Every Roman fort hidden in a valley had a local signal station on a suitable knoll within a mile or so. Although the fort itself was out of sight of the nearest high ground station of the main chain, the repeater-station on the knoll was not. Signals were sent from the fort to the repeater and then up to the main system. It is easy to find these relay links as the Roman planning engineer in his fort had only a limited number of options. To find a repeater-station, stand on a Roman fort site, and look for a hillock which you think would be in sight of the uplands and then go and check it out.

At Greta Bridge Roman Fort mentioned previously, there is a possible repeater-station on the crest of a slope just to the south-east of the fort at NZ 087 127.

The Roman complex at Chew Green in Northumberland has a known signal station on the higher ground at NT 790 097.

Whitley Castle fort has a possible repeater-station on the eastern slope of Great Heaplow at NY 690 484.

The Roman Stanegate fort of Vindolanda sits in a hollow but there is a signal station (NY 783 668) perched on Barcombe Hill just to the east.

The Roman fort at Corbridge is in the Tyne Valley and hidden from the nearby Roman Wall. I strongly suspect a farmhouse called Mount Pleasant, built on a very obvious artificial mound, to be on the site of Corbridge's relay station. This position (NY 975 668) is in sight of both Corbridge fort and the Wall. To the south of Corbridge there is another possible satellite station at NY 984 628, on the south side of the Tyne and to the east of Dilston.

Here in my home town of Chester-le-Street, we have a typical river valley Roman fort (Concangis, NZ 276 513). There is a recently discovered Roman road and possible signal station on the very prominent escarpment of Sacriston Heugh (NZ 234 486) to the west. This is out of sight of the fort. An ideal position for a repeater would be the knoll on which now sits the mediaeval Lumley Castle (NZ 288 511). Dr Hunter's Roman road, mentioned c1750, has been recently identified passing right by the castle, and a close inspection shows that the bottom course in the castle's north-east tower contains reused Roman stones.

In foggy conditions it seems that Roman signalling was carried out by horn signals. Hadrusbal who was encamped close by the enemy Roman lines knew that Roman reinforcements were arriving because he could read their trumpet calls and he also noticed that some signals were repeated thus indicating two lots of troops.

The recently-found Roman road, which runs from Lanchester, County Durham (NZ 160 469) eastwards to Sacriston Heugh near Chester-le-Street, is under the "Long Edge" farm road for two miles. It is lost in open-casted land at the spot height of 232m at NZ 223 480. There is a radiocommunications pole & dish at this point and it is interesting to note that the very straight Roman "Dere Street" north-west of Ebchester fort (NZ 103 555) is also lined up on this point. The line passes over the hill occupied by the Pontop Pike television transmitter. A Roman road has obviously passed along this line. Unfortunately, most of the line has been open-cast mined. The line continues to Seaton Carew at West Hartlepool, where there have been significant Roman finds. Near the previously mentioned 232m spot height and radio dish, an inspection of an old map entitled *Map to Elucidate the Roads Before the Conquest,* in *History and Antiquities of Northumberland,* Vol 1 (Durham University Library No L942.82) shows: "paving recently removed" at this point. The line on the old map passes through "entrenchments" at Old Durham Farm (NZ 288 420). A Roman bath-house was excavated to the east of this farm in 1945. From the air, the farm looks as if it is sitting on a Roman fort platform. The map also marks Dr Gordon's road leaving Old Durham and heading towards South Shields, but an aerial survey suggests that it is lined up on Sunderland and en-route traverses the hill with the VHF transmitter at Stony Gate (NZ 355 510). Roman artefacts have been found here and there is an unidentified square earthwork on the hillside at NZ 351 511.

If the line of Dr Gordon's road from Sunderland to Old Durham is extended to the south-west, it traverses the Roman fort of Vinovia (NZ 210 313) at Bishop Auckland.

Two known Roman roads transit the County Durham town of Sedgefield, one north-east/south-west and the other north-west/south-east. A third has recently been identified running west-east and it ends up at Hartlepool like the Ebchester/Pontop Pike/232m spot height/Old Durham line. The "new" Sedgefield road runs from the church eastwards to Beacon Hill Farm (NZ 380 290), over the spot height of 97m at NZ 402 297 and then through Three Gates Farm (NZ 457 308) to Hartlepool.

Another Roman road left Vinovia and proceeded north-easterly through Kirk Merrington (NZ 262 315), Thrislington DMV (NZ 305 333), the radio transmitter at NZ 362 344 east of Greenside Farm, and then to Hartlepool via the hill with a vast telecommunications array at NZ 440 342.

The Romans just had to have had a road down the coast of County Durham, and this eluded us for many years. We were searching too close to the cliffs. The road is a mile and a half inland presumably to avoid the steep denes which run down to the sea. This north-south road also transits the transmitter-capped hill at NZ 440 342. The road commences in South Shields and crosses the prominent Tunstall Hills (NZ 392 545), then east of Dalton-le-Dale (NZ 413 477), through the Saxon village of Yoden (NZ 431 418), just to the west of the Saxon village of Sheraton (NZ 441 350) and probably to Billingham where a Saxon church should be investigated. The Sheraton Saxon village looks as if it could have reused a Roman fortlet in the centre. It seems that yet another Roman road has branched off from Sheraton, this time to the north-east. The farmer is obviously sick of it as he has placed markers in his fields proclaiming "ROAD" to stop his ploughmen hitting it.

The well-known Roman road Wrekendyke left South Shields and, once it rounded the Jarrow Slake (a large natural harbour, now infilled, beside Jarrow Monastery) it headed south-west in such a straight line that it is obvious that the Roman surveyors had their eyes on a distant marker. The survey point was probablly a fire signal on a suspected Roman fort on the Wrekenton Golf Course. Most of the outline of this recently discovered site (NZ 269 591) can be seen from the air just north of the point where the Wrekendyke met Cade's Roman road (from Chester-le-Street to Newcastle upon Tyne). It so happens that this is a high point and only a few hundred yards north of the junction, is a VHF transmitter-mast.

Modern history books tell us that the Wrekendyke stopped at this junction but old antiquarians said that it continued to the west. It looks as if they were right as the alignment is on the church on top of the hill at Stanley (NZ 196 533) several miles to the west. This church will figure in yet another alignment to be mentioned shortly.

The suspected fort platform in the Wrekendyke Golf Course is a few yards to the west of a now dismantled railway. At this spot, according to Mackenzie and Ross' *Historical, Topographical and Descriptive View of the County Palatine of Durham,* Vol 1, 1834:

> "A quantity of very ancient gold, silver and copper coins was found on Feb 10, 1809, by some workmen who were forming a wagon-way on the Fell."

The line of the Wrekendyke west of Cade's road to Stanley Church has yet to be investigated but there is a tradition of a Roman site at Stanley. The Roman road network in County Durham, plotted with the help of reports of old antiquarians, the siting of VHF transmitters, and lines drawn between churches, is now beginning to look more like the road map of a fairly heavily populated province. The maps, which depict Durham as a Roman backwater with two supply trails across it, can be consigned to the waste bin. Some critics of new evidence are aghast at the mileage of Roman roads being discovered. Let us not forget that industrious Roman civil engineers were in Britain for over four hundred years. Many more Roman roads remain to be found.

I was certain that the Romans would have had a road between the Chester-le-Street (Concangis) and Ebchester (Vindomora) forts. I was astonished to find that a line drawn on the map between Ebchester church (on top of the Roman fort) and Chester-le-Street church (also on top of a Roman fort) cut right through the afore-mentioned Stanley church upon which the Wrekendyke from South Shields (Arbeia) was also aligned. The extended line to the south-east of the Ebchester/Stanley/Chester-le-Street line also cut Houghton-le-Spring and Dalton-le-Dale churches. Our newly discovered Roman coast road passes close to the last-named church. The whole jig-saw was fitting together. While walking the Chester-le-Street to Stanley line, I found the lower courses of a very small bridge abutment (NZ 260 517) in the north bank of the Cong Burn (Roman "Con") and was given permission to excavate. Buried in the south bank was a matching abutment. Eight Roman coins were taken from the northern abutment and one from the southern. There was much iron slag in the Roman road approaches to the bridge and further down the valley is the site of an eighteenth century furnace. I assumed that the Roman road had been reused and repaired by these ironworkers but William Fordyke in his *History of Durham,* 1857, tells us:

> "The well-known Whithill forge was worked in the dene between Whithill and Chester, where iron ore is supposed to have been worked by both the Romans and the Danes, as great quantities of scoriae, or slag, are found on the fells for many miles westward."

There were also signs of the corner of a Roman building beside the northern bridge abutment, but the walls of this extended beyond the area in which we had permission to excavate. It is there for future investigators. Perhaps it is a Roman ironworks.

This is getting away from Roman signal stations and modern radio station sites, so let us move to the now very familiar Piercebridge area. The very straight Roman road north, from Scotch Corner, is lined up precisely on the Roman bridge site at the George Hotel, and as Piercebridge is a riverside site, it would have needed a repeater signal station. A likely place is the earthwork on the wooded hill at NZ 210 154.

The Roman surveyors approaching Piercebridge from the south have had their eyes on a distant target well beyond the concealed valley of the Tees. After crossing the Tees bridge without the slightest deviation, the road proceeded to the spot height of 222m above Brusselton Wood (NZ 204 249), fourteen miles north of Scotch Corner and seven miles north of Piercebridge. A modern radio mast occupies this position which would have made an ideal site for a Roman signal station. From just south of this point, a suspected Roman road has branched off from Royal Oak to the north-west. It is quite obvious from the air at NZ 203 245. This road may have originated in Darlington, passing known earthworks at Archdeacon Newton (NZ 255 173) en-route.

A mile south of Royal Oak, Roman Dere Street passes the enigmatic "Legs Cross Stone." Any inscriptions have been worn off by weather and cattle-rubbing, but it is said that it once carried the letters "LEG XX."

From the spot height above Brusselton Wood, Dere Street takes a dive down the east side of the wood and the Roman surface is exposed in places. If Roman ox-wagons went down this incline, they must have had good brakes. The Roman fort of Vinovia is ahead but not on the alignment of the road. Below Brusselton Wood, at Fieldon Bridge (NZ 206 267) the Roman road does a peculiar thing; it alters course at the bottom of a valley. Normally, alterations are on high points. The change of heading is to the fort at Binchester (Vinovia) and this fort must have been an afterthought. The new heading transits the main street of Bishop Auckland and then runs around the east end of the large river loop south of the Roman fort. There are roadside Roman burials in Bishops Park beside the confluence of the Rivers Wear and Gaunless.

The wide loop of the River Wear has caused many wild goose chases among archaeologists searching for a double river crossing. One school of thought was that the river bend had migrated eastwards thus washing away the Roman road. Another was that there must have been two bridges. Both were wrong. Aerial photographs clearly show Dere Street deviating around the outside of the river bend. The curved feature in the field east of the fort which caused the problem is not a Roman road at all, but an old plantation boundary. This is clearly shown on Taylor and Hooppell's excavation plan of c1890 which has been ignored by modern researchers.

There is a possible Roman signal station to the east of Vinovia at NZ 219 313, a hundred yards or so to the south-east of Lodge Farm. A small ditched square earthwork sits in a small copse. Another possibility is that it is a Roman *tumulus.* If so, it must be the grave of a very important person.

Dere Street traversed the fort and headed north-west back to the original line, and crossed the River Wear via a known bridge at NZ 204 318. Another Roman road went round the east side of the fort and crossed the Bell Burn at NZ 211 320.

Dere Street rejoined the original survey line at NZ 196 323. There seem to be traces of the pre-Vinovia road up this line in which case there must have been a Roman bridge in the vicinity of Toronto, just upstream from the B689 bridge over the River Wear. Close to this suspected early road is the Saxon church of Escomb (NZ 189 302). This church is built mostly of Roman stones and all of our history books positively state that these stones were robbed from Binchester. There is not the slightest proof of this. Why do grave-diggers at Escomb find Roman coins and broken Roman pottery? Did the Saxon monks as well as removing Roman stones also take away the Roman garbage? Were the Saxon monks the binmen of Binchester? Whenever our experts cannot explain the presence of Roman stones, the latter were always robbed from the nearest known fort or on occasion "washed down the river."

There are no further obvious signal station positions ahead, nor telltale radio masts, but this is an appropriate place to mention the strange alteration of heading of Dere Street from north to almost west at Rag Path Wood (NZ 205 423) just to the south of Flass Hall and east of Esh Winning. It is obvious that a Roman road, lined up on Newcastle upon Tyne, has gone straight ahead from this corner. It was discovered north of Flass Hall at NZ 206 434 and again down "Groove bank" at Langley Park (NZ 210 443). The surrounding area is thick with Romano-British farmsteads, visible from the air as crop marks. Flass Hall may hide something more important than a farmstead as there is a link Roman road which joins the north and west arms of Dere Street together, forming a triangle. The resident of Flass Hall, Princess Helen of Roumania, was intrigued by all this former Roman activity around her house, as she can trace her ancestry back to the Eastern Roman Empire.

At the alteration of heading of Dere Street to the west at Rag Path Wood, the Roman descent is so steep that ox-wagons would have needed more than good wheel-brakes; a tail-parachute may have been of more use.

Point-to-point signal stations and fort's signal link-ups have been mentioned at length, but the Romans had another type of station which served a different purpose and that was for ship-to-shore communications. There was a string of them up the Yorkshire sea cliffs and they probably extended up the Durham coast and beyond. Unfortunately, Durham's coastal cliffs have eroded considerably since the Roman period and if the stations were near the cliff edges, they will have gone.

These stations are not to be confused with Roman lighthouses though some of them may have served in a dual capacity. Their main function seems to have been the control of warships but no doubt they handled point to point messages also, as they formed a continuous visual chain.

A Roman cliff-top signal station was excavated many years ago at Castle Hill, Scarborough. About a third of the site has fallen down the cliff at an unknown date. This collapse may have actually happened in Roman times as, just to the north, in dry weather conditions, the faint parch mark of a second station, set slightly back from the cliff edge, is visible from the air. Both stations can be seen in a photograph on page 82 in *Roman Britain from the Air*, by Professors SS Frere and JKS St Joseph. No mention is made in the caption about the parch mark.

If the Romans built a second station close to the cliffs, there must have been a good reason for them pushing their luck like this, and the reason must have been that this position was critical for a clear line of sight to an adjacent station.

With the information on signal stations and survey points added, the Roman road network makes more sense. We can now look at Roman roads in a totally different light. The severe gradients and evidence of river navigation proves that they were not heavy goods routes. Their main purposes were:

1 All weather routes to enable troops to quell native uprisings or any other disturbances, in a very short time.

2 Pack animal trails. No Roman animal would have had to travel more than five miles from a river or stream. Even the lesser waterways would have been negotiated by small barge or punt.

3 In frontier areas, part of *limes* grid systems which used defence in depth.

4 Lines of communication for the Roman postal system, the *Cursus Publicus*.

5 The backbone of lines of signal stations located at high points.
These signal stations probably commenced life as survey points during the construction of the roads.
Some survey points never actually had a road constructed over them, but they served as part of a some kind of Roman triangulation pattern.

6 A military network to overawe the native population. (Two thousand years later, I am one of the natives and I am still impressed).

7 In the vicinities of forts, there *were* roads for the famous ox-wagons and other types of vehicles. These were short lengths between jetty and fort or between fort, *vici* and villas. They took easy gradients and have therefore not usually been recognised as Roman. Present-day farmers use them because their modern heavy vehicles can negotiate the gentler gradients designed for Roman wagons.

Only the Roman roads and signalling systems of Northumberland and Durham have been discussed in detail in this book, but every county in England, Wales and southern Scotland should contain similar undiscovered networks. The main aim of this book is to persuade hundreds of enthusiasts to scour the countryside in order to help fill in all those blank spaces on the maps of Roman Britain.

This concludes the main theme of this book but I would like to stress that time spent in the countryside is *never* wasted. Invariably, if one is searching for evidence of the Roman occupation, items from other periods are also found. These can range from prehistoric burials to early wagonways, lead workings, and old coal mines. The final chapter will include a few examples of these "bonus-finds."

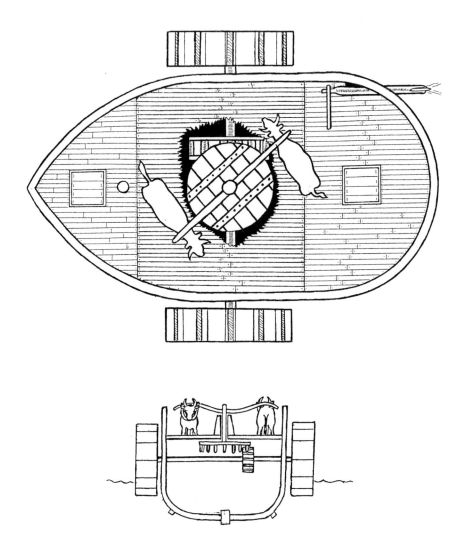

At the end of the fourth century AD, an unknown writer, speaking on the subject of warfare, described an oxen-powered paddle-ship. Two oxen walked in a circle on the deck of the ship and turned a capstan which was connected by gears to the paddles. many modern historians have dismissed this ship as the figment of an ancient imagination with the argument that such a ship simply would not work. There is no proof that such ships did exist but the system certainly works as there is a reference in the Penny Magazine 1840, to a similar ship, worked by two horses, which operated across the Niagara River between Canada and USA. (see pages 336-338).

Chapter 12

Further Research

Give us the tools, and we will finish the job.
Winston Churchill, 1941

When I was a schoolboy, I thought that it would be wonderful to be an explorer but it looked as if all the remote territories had already given up their secrets. I did not realise that only two or three feet down, and occasionally sticking out of the ground, were the remnants of an empire of two thousand years ago. Also by the time the Romans arrived, the landscape already contained tombs, habitations, fortifications and religious circles erected from Neolithic times onward.

How fortunate we are, that in our spare time, we can search our own land which has no steaming jungles, boiling deserts or frozen wastes; nor are there any dangerous beasts and the only poisonous snake is the adder.

I hope therefore that the guidelines in this book will assist with the discovery of many miles of Roman roads and scores of Roman river-sites. Valuable information on the latter would be:

Are the old mediaeval mill-leats too large for water-mills?

Are the suspected reused channels always on the same side of the river as the Roman fort?

Is there a known or suspected Roman road approaching the river?..etc, etc. (use all the other guidelines previously mentioned)

I am very grateful to Elizabeth Waller of Piercebridge, who told me about the single line of post-holes cut into the rock-bed of the Tees at an angle to the flow. These holes have proved to be of Roman origin and are part of a suspected weir, six hundred yards downstream from the scene of all the intense archaeological activity of recent years.

Those readers fortunate enough to spend holidays wandering around the continent may like to look for Professor Grenier's "paved fords" which I am sure will turn out to be Roman weirs. I have a holiday guide-book which shows an ancient mill-dam in Brittany. It is a typical Piercebridge-type structure. Unfortunately, there is no caption to the picture.

As one is being conducted around a known Roman fort by a sage who confidently points out a well as having been the main Roman water-source, estimate roughly, the millions of gallons needed per day for the bath-houses, latrines and fountains, all of which used constant flows. Then look at any high ground for a suitable sparkling stream which the Romans loved, and judge where a simple Roman contour-hugging aqueduct-channel would have intercepted it. A small eroded dam and long-dry leat should be fairly close to this point. Searching for aqueducts is great fun. If possible, have a look at a couple of known ones first. The stone settling-tanks have often been reused as water troughs for animals by generations of farmers, but, because of their weight, are seldom far from original positions.

Library research should be pursued whenever possibe. Old and obscure books often produce excellent clues to old problems and an example follows.

At the end of the fourth century AD, an unknown writer, speaking on the subject of warfare, described a ship which was driven by paddle-wheels, and the power for these wheels was provided by two oxen. These oxen walked in a circle on the deck of the ship and turned a capstan which was connected by primitive gears to the paddles. Many modern historians have expressed the opinion that this ship was just the figment of some ancient inventor's imagination, and that such a propulsion system just would not work. Indeed, there is no proof that ancient ships of this type were ever built, but historians are completely in error when they say that ship-borne, animal motive power wouldn't work; I have found a reference to a similar ship, driven by two horses, which was in use in USA/Canada c1835. The reference was in *The Penny Magazine,* 1840 and it is such a delightful little story that I quote it in full:

What were the Romans growing on these cultivation terraces at Housesteads on the Roman Wall?

"ANECDOTES OF AMERICAN HORSES

(From a Correspondent)

"There are various instances on record fully establishing the courage and sagacity of that noble animal, the horse. The following incidents I am about to relate occurred in America, to horses bred in that country.

A short distance below Fort Erie, and about a mile from where the River Niagara escapes over a barrier of rock from the depths of lake Erie, a ferry has long been established across that broad and there exceedingly rapid river, the distance from shore to shore being a little over one-third of a mile. On the Canada side of the river is the small village of Waterloo, and opposite thereto on the United States side is the large village of Blackrock – distant from the young and flourishing city of Buffalo two miles. In completing the Erie Canal, a pier or dam was erected – up and down the river, and opposite to Blackrock, at no great distance from the shore, for the purpose of raising the waters of the Niagara to such height that they might be made to supply an adjoining section of the Erie Canal. This pier was (and is) a great obstruction to the ferry boats; for previous to its erection, passengers embarked from *terra firma* on one side of the river, and were landed without any difficulty on the other; but, after this dam was constructed, it became necessary to employ two sets of boats – one to navigate the river, and the other, the basin; so that all passengers, as well as goods or luggage, had to be landed upon this narrow wall or pier, and re-shipped.

Shortly after the erection of the pier dam, a boat propelled by horses was established between this pier and the Canada shore. The horses moved upon a circlar platform, which consequently was put in motion, to which other machinery was connected, that acted upon paddle-wheels attached to the sides of the boat. The boat belonged to persons connected with the ferry on the American side of the river; but owing to the barrier formed by the pier, the horses employed on the boat were stabled at night in the village of Waterloo. I well recollect the first day this boat began to ply – for the introduction of a boat of that description, in those days, and in such a situation, was considered an event of some magnitude. The two horses (for that boat had but two) worked admirably, considering the very few lessons they had had (upon the tread-mill, as it was called) previous to their introduction upon the main river.

One of the horses employed on the new ferry-boat had once been a dapple-grey, but at the period I am speaking of, he had become white. He was still hale and hearty, for he had a kind and indulgent master. The first evening after the horses had been a short time in the stable, to which they were strangers, they were brought out for the purpose of being watered at the river, a common custom at that place. The attendant was mounted upon the bay horse – the white one was known to be so gentle and docile that he was allowed to drink where he pleased. I happened to be standing close by, in company with my friend

W– – – –, the ferry contractor on the Canada side, and thus had an opportunity of witnessing the whole proceedings of old Grizzle, the name that the white horse still went by. The moment he got round the corner of the building, so as to have a view of his home on the opposite side, he stopped – and gazed intently. He then advanced to the brink of the river – when he again stopped and looked earnestly across for a short time – then waded into the river until it had reached his chest – drank a little, lifted his head, and with his lips closed, and his eyes fixed upon some object upon the farther shore, remained for a short time, perfectly motionless. Apparently having made up his mind to the task, he then waded further into the river until the water reached his ribs – when he shot into deep water without a moment's hesitation.

The current being so strong and rapid, the river boiling and turmoiling over a rocky bed at the rate of six miles an hour, it was impossible for the courageous and attached animal to keep a direct course across, although he breasted the waves heroically, and swam with remarkable vigour. Had he been able to steer his way directly across, the pier-wall would have proved an insurmountable barrier. As it was, the strength of the current forced him down to below where the lower extremity of the long pier buts upon an island, the shore of which being low and shelving, he was enabled to effect a landing with comparative ease. Having regained *terra firma*, he shook the water from his dripping flanks, but he did not halt over a few minutes, when he plunged into the basin and soon regained his native shore.

The distance from where Grizzle took the water to where he effected a landing on the island was about seven hundred yards; but the efforts made to swim directly across, against the powerful current, must have rendered the undertaking a much more laborious one. At the commencement of his voyage, his arched neck and withers were above the surface, but before he reached the island, nothing but his head was visible to us.

He reached his own stable-door, that home for which he had risked so much, to the no small astonishment of his owner. This unexpected visit evidently made a favourable impression upon his master, for he was heard to vow, that if old Grizzle performed the feat a second time, for the future he should remain on his own side of the river, and never be sent to the mill again. Grizzle was sent back to work on the boat on the following day, but he embraced the very first opportunity that occurred of escaping, swam back in the way he had done before, and his owner, not being a person to break the promise he had once made, never afterwards dispossessed him of the stall he had long been accustomed to, but treated him with marked kindness and attention."

During Agricola's campaigns in Scotland he fought a battle against the Caledonians at Mons Graupius. Ten thousand enemy tribesmen were killed. The Auxiliary troops fought the battle while the crack troops of the legions watched. The Graupian Mountain has not been positively identified but it is likely to prove to be Benachie, about seven miles west of Inverurie.

In 1975, Professor St Joseph of Cambridge photographed a legionary-size marching camp (NJ 699 572) at Durno. The camp is close to the River Urie and is thought to have been Agricola's base for the battle.

A limited excavation was carried out in 1977, and I quote an interesting paragraph from *Britannia*, Vol 9, 1987, which describes part of this excavation:

"A gentle sinuous crop mark was observed from the air in 1977, near the edge of a small terrace on the north side of the Urie, by Strathorn Farm. Two trenches dug in September 1977 showed this to represent a shallow feature 1.85m wide, with steep sides and a flat bottom 0.70m below the surface. An early boundary of arable land, or an open leat for water are possible explanations. The feature extends between NJ 6853 2725 and NJ 6895 2721."

It looks as if Agricola's supplies were arriving by punts or other flat-bottomed craft. The Urie flows into the Don which reaches the sea at Aberdeen. This suggests that Agricola's ships used Aberdeen as a port and trans-shipped cargoes into barges there. All the Scottish rivers should be searched for traces of Roman navigation.

The eighteenth century antiquarian, the Rev Dr Stukely, drew a map in 1755 of Roman Britain. This is widely held to have been compiled from false and forged information. If so, Stukeley's forgers were quite prophetic as he marks the Roman fort at Brough on Humber with its correct name "Petuaria." This was not known until fairly recent excavations and some Ordnance Survey maps still mark it incorrectly as "Praetorio." Stukeley also marks our "Dere Street North" Roman road, from the peculiar corner at Rag Path Wood, south of Flass Hall, near Esh Winning, Durham. This was found from the air only recently. Perhaps Stukeley's map contains other genuine and useful information.

He also marks a waterway right across Scotland on the line of the Caledonian Canal but this artificial waterway was not constructed until 1803. Was there a Roman navigation which connected the seas to Loch Ness and Loch Lochy? There have been Roman finds at Fort Augustus.

In the West Country, Stukeley's map also marks a water route between the English Channel and the Bristol Channel. This appears to be on the Ilchester/Dorchester line. Did the Romans connect the Rivers Parrett and Stour? Searchers in the area should look at the watersheds of these rivers and others in the area, very carefully.

Wherever he finds himself, on duty or on holiday, the amateur archaeologist can always find things to explore and even make new discoveries. In my own case, my duties have often taken me to places beyond the limits of the former Roman Empire and I have amused myself with investigations into the local areas.

On one occasion, I was a crew-member of a new ship on delivery from Alabama, USA to Sierra Leone, West Africa. We were bunkering in Antigua in the West Indies prior to crossing the Atlantic. Outside the harbour area, a scrub-covered conical hill seemed too regular to be natural. A closer look through binoculars showed a line of discoloration in the hill's foliage. It

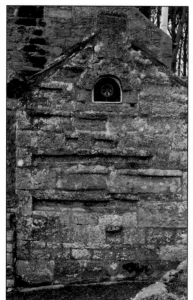

The author in the Falklands inspecting a wrecked
Argentine air force "Pucara" ground attack aircraft.

In this old building near the main road at
High Rochester(Bremenium) Roman fort,
ex-Roman aqueduct-channel stones have
been incorporated into the wall.

The locomotive found at Navy Point, Port
Stanley, by Major Allen and the author.

The Falkland Islands stamps which resulted from the discovery of the old locomotive.

seemed to form a helical line around the hill. When time allowed, I inspected the hill on foot and found that it had been one of Nelson's cannon positions. The helical line was a mule-track up which the animals had carried the cannon-balls and powder. Nobody knew about this, and nobody seemed interested, but it was a useful little exercise.

The following is not intended to be a war yarn. It refers to a fairly recent lesson I received in military supply lines. I had long known that all warfare can be described as the use of a large logistical wedge with a sharp point. If you don't have the wedge, the point is useless. I was to gain an extra practical lesson in the subject and this is how it came about.

In November 1990, I was asked if I could do a few weeks temporary duty as an officer on a Dutch merchant ship which was due to leave Lisbon, call at Casablanca and other north African ports, and then return to Rotterdam. I would be home by Christmas (or so I thought) after a pleasant little paid holiday in the sun. Dutch law requires all seamen to hold Dutch certificates of competency so a hectic 24 hours ensued. A flight to Amsterdam was followed by a medical and X-ray in Rotterdam, the issue of Dutch identity papers in the Hague, a longer rail journey to Groningen for an inspection of British qualifications and an issue of Dutch equivalents. All this would have taken at least a fortnight in England but I was on a flight from Amsterdam to Lisbon the next day to join the *Singelgracht* (named after an Amsterdam canal). I thought that I would be replacing a crew member who had gone sick but this was not the case. The ship was taking on extra personnel which was rather strange for a short run around North Africa and back to Holland. Unknown to me, a large logistical plan was under way for the forthcoming Gulf War.

After a few relaxing days at sea, and a couple of runs ashore in ports like Casablanca, we set course for Rotterdam with a now empty ship. This was very strange for the Dutch who always seem to find a cargo to pay for the voyage. All was explained when, in the Bay of Biscay, we received a radio message ordering us to divert to Marchwood, Southampton. The captain and Dutch officers had never heard of Marchwood but I had been there. I knew that it was the British army port where military equipment was loaded. It was obvious that we were bound for the Gulf and the forthcoming war.

As we entered the port, this was confirmed when we tied up alongside the fleet auxiliary "*Sir Tristram*" which was loading sand-camouflaged tanks. When I enquired of an army warrant officer if my ship was also to load tanks, he replied: "Oh no sir, that is your cargo over there" as he pointed nonchalantly to a large shed stacked high with bombs and rockets. His next comments did not improve my sinking morale when he said: "After you have taken on a thousand tons of bombs, we will move you for reasons of safety, out into the river to load a further thousand tons from lighters. After that you will be proceeding to Emden in Germany to load laser guided bombs." As an afterthought, he added: "you will also be taking on two machine-gunners here as extra crew members."

I had quite a lot of experience in the moving of military equipment and personnel both by sea and air, but I did not enjoy the prospect of sitting on top of 5,000 tons of bombs, rockets and ammunition in a war zone where the enemy air force was equipped with Exocet and other anti-ship missiles.

I had long been a student of military logistics and it looked as if this lesson might prove to be a nasty one.

We sailed from Emden on 23rd December 1990 into dreadful weather and our two gunners, an RAF sergeant and a corporal were bedbound for a week. They missed their Christmas dinners. As Lord Nelson said, the only cure for seasickness is: "Sit under a tree."

Our orders were to proceed to the Suez Canal and expect further orders there from the Royal Navy. We were to maintain radio silence and all mention of our ship's name disappeared from *Lloyds List.*

The deadline for Iraqi forces to leave Kuwait was 2400 hours, New York time, on 15th January, 1991. I worked out on the chart table that we should just be entering the Gulf at the Straits of Hormuz about then.

On arrival at Port Said, we anchored while waiting to join a south-bound convoy for the transit of the canal. Our two gunners constantly patrolled the decks looking down into the clear water to make sure that no terrorist, operating from one of the hordes of bumboats, stuck a limpet-mine on our plates. A Royal Navy lieutenant-commander in *mufti,* gave us our orders which were to proceed to the Straits of Hormuz and there contact the admiral on board the British naval auxiliary *Orangeleaf.* He also told us that if any suspicious craft approached us in the Straits of Bab-el-Mandab or Hormuz, we were to open fire on it.

In the Red Sea and Arabian Sea we were intercepted several times by patrolling coalition warships of the Dutch, Belgian, Canadian, Spanish and Italian navies. The initial call was the standard flashing signal-lamp morse "AAA" but when I answered in morse with our own searchlight, a radio call on the international calling-frequency, channel 16, said: "Merchant ship being flashed, please come up on channel 9 and report your international call letters." The various European navies had lost the art of visual signalling. Only the Royal Navy which had re-learned the art in the Falklands, were competent with morse-lamps.

Just as some historians doubt that the Romans used fast visual communications, so future historians will doubt the now largely-lost skills of naval conversation by searchlight.

In the Red Sea, we were also intercepted by a low-flying Lockeed Orion patrol bomber of the US Navy. I noticed that he was on three engines with number one (left outer) stopped and propeller feathered, no doubt to lessen fuel consumption and improve endurance. He read our name as he flashed past and called us on channel 16 to report our signal letters. Satisfied, he departed for another unidentified radar blip.

Down the Red Sea we had listened to Radio Baghdad and a lady announcer with an American accent, known to us as "Baghdad Rose." She played music and then told us what the Iraqi Air Force was going to do to allied ships if hostilities began. As we approached the Straits of Hormuz, we knew that the war had started when "Baghdad Rose" went off the air in mid-sentence. A bomb had either hit the studio, or the power supplies.

Our captain was sure that, as we entered Hormuz, we would receive an escort of destroyers and minesweepers. He was most put out when we

Top: The problems of operating an army without roads. A track over a peat bog leads to an Argentine anti-aircraft gun, WirelessRidge, East Falkland. Bottom: The wreck of the sailing ship *Lady Elizabeth* in Port Stanley. Wireless Ridge in background.

reported to the admiral on *Orangeleaf* and received the reply:

"YOUR DESTINATION IS BAHRAIN STOP EXERCISE CAUTION
DUE FLOATING MINES STOP THERE IS DANGER OF AIR ATTACK
STOP PROCEED INDEPENDENTLY STOP"

We were on our own. How do you exercise caution because of floating
mines, in foggy weather? We placed an RAF gunner as a look-out up in the
bows and he reported on a walkie-talkie that he could not even see the water!

A few days later, as we approached Bahrain, the area to the west had come
under attack by Scud missiles. As we tied up, the air raid siren sounded and
this was followed by the transit of a missile across the sky to the west. The
Scud was destroyed by an intercepting American anti-missile rocket.

I was extremley pleased to see our bombs going ashore but it was going to
be a slow job. We had about five hundred lorry-loads (ten thousand ox-wagon
loads) for the RAF base at Muharraq and the USAF airfield at Dahran.
Perhaps this shows the advantage of sea transport.

The reason Iraq was given such an extended deadline was purely logistical.
The strongest nations in the world still needed quite a few weeks to assemble
the mass of equipment necessary to defeat a relatively minor nation like Iraq.

Why were the bombs, rockets and ammunition not airlifted to Saudi
Arabia and Bahrain? Transport aircraft are the modern military equivalent of
ox-wagons. They carry relatively small cargoes, are tremendously expensive
and need more fuel than the weight of cargo carried. Hundreds of large
aircraft, refuelling at remote airfields en route, will soon dry up fuel supplies
and extra has to be flown in, so we end up with an ever increasing number of
aircraft – like the camels for the invasion of Afghanistan. Ships and rivers,
assisted by railways where necessary, are the only answer to large logistical
problems.

The Berlin Airlift is often quoted as an example of a successful airborne
logistical supply operation, but the Russians did not shoot at the aircraft; they
had merely closed the border. Berlin was at peace. The aircraft did not
deliver military supplies; only food, fuel and medical supplies for the civilian
population.

A better example of an attempt to supply an army completely by air was at
Stalingrad in January 1943, when the Red Army surrounded a German army
of 300,000 men. In spite of using 500 transport aircraft, the *Luftwaffe*
delivered only 20 per cent of the required stores. The starving German army
surrendered to the Russians after a siege of three weeks. The transport
aircraft were merely flying ox-wagons and could supply only a fraction of the
trapped army's requirements.

Back in the Gulf, we were most disheartened when, after discharging only
half of our cargo, we were told that we had filled up all the bomb dumps of
the RAF and USAF for miles around, and that, as we were a danger to the
whole city of Bahrain, we would have to leave the Gulf and go and hide in
some place of our own choice until called back into the war zone. Unlike our
inward voyage, the departure was in clear weather with a visibility of forty
miles. The captain and I were on duty on the bridge when a voice on VHF
channel 16, from a ship close by, the Bermudan *Trader,* announced: "Two
missiles have just missed us by a hundred yards."

It was 24th January 1991, the only day the Iraqi Air Force got through. There was no sign of any enemy aircraft. The missiles had been released from miles away. The two Mirages which launched them were shot down before they got home but the escorting Mig 23 escaped.

We left the Gulf and hid at anchor behind the rocky Masirah Island for two weeks before being called back in. Instead of getting home for Christmas, I just made it back for Easter. I had learned an excellent lesson in military logistics but my seat had been too close to the stage.

The ultimate military logistical exercise is of course a nuclear weapon. A nation has to use much of its workforce, industry, transport and finances to provide the football-sized critical mass of uranium which will eliminate the capital city of an enemy state in a few seconds. The whole of the bomb-producing country has become the wedge, and the bomb the point. The more complex hydrogen bomb needs an even bigger logistical wedge as it needs a uranium bomb merely as a detonator to trigger off the fusion of hydrogen in a similar process to that taking place in our parent Sun.

Let us leave such a dismal subject and return to archaeology. I was offered the interesting temporary job of helping to take a cable-laying ship from the Tees to its new Italian owners in Naples. During my flying career, I had often made quick visits to Naples and often looked down into the crater of Vesuvius, the volcano which had destroyed Pompeii and Herculaneum in AD 97, but I never had time to visit these excavated Roman towns. Now, I was to spend a few days in the area where we were to hand the ship over to its new crew and help them prepare for an expedition to South America. I had provided myself with guide-books to both Pompeii and Herculaneum in anticipation. The voyage was uneventful and in the Mediterranean there was a lot of naval activity. The American Sixth Fleet was on exercises. To the north of Sicily, we were playfully engaged by US Navy destroyers and we were also treated to the spectacle of a huge nuclear-powered aircraft carrier close by, catapulting and recovering awesome-looking jet aircraft.

Two hundred miles from Naples, we received a radio message which informed us that the berth reserved for us in Naples harbour was still occupied by a US Navy cruiser and we were ordered to anchor off the Italian coast for twenty-four hours and await further instructions.

It was midnight when we anchored half a mile off the islet of Nisida, about six miles west of Naples and although it was too dark to see the beach, the radar picture showed that the islet was in fact a peninsula connected to the mainland by a narrow causeway. The radar picture also showed that Nisida had a large almost circular hole on the south-western side and it was obvious from the chart, that this was an old volcanic crater, now flooded by the sea.

The islet of Nisida is just across the bay from Misenum, the headquarters of the ancient Roman navy. The remnants of Roman canals which linked inland lakes to the sea can still be seen in the area. It was from this naval base that the commander of the Roman fleet, administrator and encyclopaedic writer Pliny the Elder, sailed on a rescue mission in AD 79 when Vesuvius blew its top. Pliny lost his life in the operation.

At dawn, almost two thousand years later, I looked from my ship across the bay at the majestic but menacing slopes of the mountain which had caused so much death and destruction. It was hard to believe that the Romans had been taken by surprise by the eruption, but surviving records suggest that the Romans did not know that Vesuvius was an active volcano. A wall-painting from an excavated Roman villa shows that instead of a cratered summit, the mountain had a normal pointed peak. The explosion must have blown over a thousand feet off the top. The Roman city of Pompeii was soon covered by volcanic ash while further north, Herculaneum was engulfed by boiling mud and lava.

Closer to hand, just half a mile from my ship, was Nisida and I examined the island through binoculars. An old fortress, now a prison, occupied the highest point. Below this fort was the sea-filled volcanic crater. With the main Roman base at Misenum so close by, I was sure that the Romans would not have ignored this natural haven. I could imagine two war-galleys lying concealed in this perfect lair and I scanned the crater's sides for signs of ancient occupation.

The steep slopes were covered with dense scrub but my binoculars picked out a discoloration in this thick vegetation. There was a disinct line of brown foliage against a background of green. This line descended the crater in a spiral and ended at the northern arm of the entrance to the natural harbour. I wondered if this was a Roman road but only a close inspection would establish this. I resolved to escape from my shipboard duties at the first opportunity and make my way along the coast from Naples by taxi, bus, tram, or on foot if necessary. As it turned out, I was to use none of these methods of transport.

Plans for an archaeological expedition were temporarily forgotten when a radio message instructed us to proceed immediately into Naples harbour and tie up alongside the prestigious passenger terminal, usually reserved only for cruise liners.

After the first twenty-four hours of hustle and bustle in our new surroundings, the captain sent for me and announced that as I was an archaeologist, he had decided that I should organise visits for the crew, to Pompeii and any other places of historic interest. I was to accompany the sailors and make sure that they did in fact visit the archaeological sites. I then brought up the subject of Nisida and he informed me that the ship's "Z-boat" which was capable of 40 knots had been installed with a new engine and the chief engineer required the engine to be "run-in." I was given the running-in job. I could take the boat to Nisida – or anywhere else that took my fancy – but I was to attend to the cultural education of the crew first.

In the Naples Sea Terminal are the headquarters of the American Sixth Fleet, and a quick visit to the padre's office furnished me with telephone numbers of bus companies which would undertake tourist trips to places of interest. The ship's crew was divided into two, and the first "liberty-men" were to proceed to Pompeii in the morning, and, in the afternoon, the bus would climb the tortuous road to the observation station just below the rim of the crater of Vesuvius. The itinerary was to be repeated on the following day with the second half of the crew.

Most of the sailors were fascinated with Pompeii, and it was certainly preferable to painting the ship.

While I was delivering my very basic lecture in the Pompeii *forum*, I noticed that my class had increased in size. One of the extra students was a young lady who turned out to be a doctor of archaeology at an American university. She asked if she could accompany our expedition for the rest of the day so we took her with us to the summit of Vesuvius. She was intrigued to know whether or not, the carriage of archaeologists was standard practice on British ships.

During a short stop at a museum on our way to Vesuvius, our sailors recruited another young lady, this time an Australian teacher of history.

After the bus had creaked and grinded its way up the zig-zag road on the flank of Vesuvius, we had to complete the last few hundred feet on foot to the crater rim, up a rough path across cinder and lava scree. The view from the top, across the Bay of Naples, was magnificent, but the yawning crater of the volcano looked sinister. Smoke still issued from fissures in the vertical walls and there was a strong smell of sulphur.

There is a little inn near the summit, and it is traditional for visitors to the mountain top to drink a certain type of sweet wine. This met with the wholehearted approval of the sailors who duly complied with the local custom. On our return to the ship, the one-day-students of Roman history staggered up the gangplank and the captain who was in the offing observed that the volcanic fumes of Vesuvius must be quite stong! He must have decided that he was missing out on something, as he informed me that he would lead the second day's expedition himself, and could he borrow my guide-books? I was therefore released to my Z-boat duties and my exploration of the coastline.

Next morning found me entering the Naples Museum just as the doors opened, and a discussion with an official provided the information that, although the old volcanic crater in Nisida was called "Porto Paone," it was not a known Roman harbour and there were no known Roman roads in the vicinity. I was warned though, that because Nisida had a prison on it, I might encounter problems with the security authorities.

My short stay in Naples was drawing to a close and I could not afford to waste time seeking out officials, so on the same afternoon, we lowered the Z-boat into the water and with one seaman at the helm and another operating the VHF radio, we sped along the coast at 30 knots as recommended by the chief engineer. The sparkling spray from our stern provided miniature rainbows in the bright Mediterranean sunshine and it took us only quarter of an hour to arrive off the islet of Nisida. We reduced speed to a couple of knots, edged through the narrow entrance into the crater and ran the boat up onto a shelving lava shore. The suspected Roman road was quickly located. It was covered with vegetation but the *agger* was quite prominent, and close to the beach, it emerged from the foliage and became a distinct trackway cut into the rock. Beside the road, close to the "harbour" was some very Roman-looking stonework. Our exploration was cut short by the arrival of several armed Italian prison guards. They were quite friendly but insisted that landing on the island was strictly prohibited. I had no time to request official permission for a further search as next day, my relief took over and I was ordered to fly back to UK.

Prospective explorers of the possible unknown Roman harbour and associated road system should seek permission well in advance from the Department of Justice, Naples.

During my searches for the Romans, I chance across all kinds of evidence from all periods of history. In addition to visible evidence from ancient times, Britain's fairly recent wars, from the Napoleonic to the present day, have left their marks on our countryside. These are mixed up with a vast amount of industrial relics such as mines, quarries, lime-kilns, mills, wagonways and railways. Before I reach the final subjects of this book, I must return to the subject of military logistics.

After the surrender of Argentina's forces in the Falkland Islands, I found myself on duty as a merchant ship's officer in Port Stanley. I have already mentioned the construction of the British army roads and have compared them with Roman handiwork. I have also stressed the use of water transport by the army.

Britain was converting the islands, not into a "Hitler type fortress" as described by some journalists and politicians, but into islands criss-crossed with good roads, and therefore easily defendable. A floating harbour, with jetties constructed on giant oilfield barges, was planned for the army. The supply ships would then be able to discharge cargoes at any state of the tide. A long bridge with a hinged span would link the floating jetties to the shore and the new road system.

A new airport at Mount Pleasant was to be constructed to replace the inadequate Stanley airfield. The RAF was operating ex-Fleet Air Arm Phantom jet fighters on the old airfield and these aircraft had at one time served on the old *Ark Royal* and had tail-hooks for deck-landings. The fairly short runway at Stanley had been hastily equipped with navy-style arrester-wires which were lowered flush with the runway for landings by normal aircraft.

Not only would the new airfield be able to operate jet fighters, it would also be able to handle long range fast jet-liners which could bring troops in from southern England at a few hours notice. It costs less to keep a parachute brigade in Surrey than in the Falklands because supplies do not have to be transported eight thousand miles.

The only heavy transport aircraft able to use the Stanley runway was the Lockheed Hercules. Rather unkindly, I have called transport aircraft the equivalent of ox-wagons, because of their tiny cargoes compared with those of ships, and the high fuel consumption and therefore high cost of operations. You can air-freight cement down to the Falklands or to central Africa, but by the time you get it there, a bag will cost several hundred pounds.

I have talked about Roman ox-wagons achieving little more than five miles per day with hungry oxen having eaten a great deal of their own cargo at the end of the day's work. So it was with the Hercules aircraft plying the four thousand mile ocean transits between Ascension Island and the old Stanley airfield.

With a maximum *payload* of 45,000 lbs (20 tons) the Hercules can carry enough fuel to fly 2,100 nautical miles with 5 per-cent reserve plus fuel for 30 minutes loitering at sea level.

With maximum *fuel* (9,680 US gallons/ 8,065 Imp gals/ 36,636 litres) the range is extended, with the same fuel reserves, to over 4,100 miles but the payload is cut by more than half to 20,000 lbs (9 tons). It will be seen that in the second case the fuel load is three times the weight of the cargo (we are getting back to the equivalent of the Roman ox-wagon problems). In the first case the Hercules can make it only half-way to the Falklands.

"In-flight" refuelling was therefore essential for the four thousand mile Ascension-Falklands "Air Bridge."

Before the heavily loaded cargo-Hercules left Ascension's Wideawake Field, a Hercules flying tanker took off, followed by a Victor tanker. After a couple of hours, the Victor tanker topped-up the Hercules tanker by in-flight refuelling, and the Victor returned to Wideawake. The Hercules tanker then flew in loose fomation with the cargo-carrying Hercules. After six of the thirteen hour flight, the Hercules tanker then refuelled the cargo-carrier. After this operation, the tanker did not go back to Ascension but continued to Stanley in case the Falklands weather deteriorated – as it is prone to do – forcing the cargo-Hercules to overshoot and either hold off, awaiting weather improvement, or return to Ascension.

In the event of sudden bad weather and no prospect of improvement in the time limit imposed by fuel remaining in tanker and cargo-carrier, both aircraft would have to return to Ascension and be met en route by more tankers. It is the old "Afghanistan Camel Calculus" all over again.

Normally, when bad weather blots out a destination airfield, the pilot diverts to the nearest airport with reasonable weather. In the case of the Falklands, the nearest airports were four hundred miles away and in enemy territory. Montevideo, in neutral Uruguay, was a thousand miles to the north, and a landing there could have involved the impounding of military equipment.

[How are the Romans supposed to have managed enormous ox-wagon supply lines? Maybe the ox-carts carrying large *amphorae,* depicted on reliefs, were not on short trips between farm and town, but actually Roman "in-flight refuellers" for the long journeys postulated by some of our historians.]

This brings me to the end of all discussion on military logistics. The ancient problems are still with us today and can be summed up thus: All transport costs money. Water transport is very economical, rail transport is moderately expensive, road transport over long distances is extremely expensive and the cost of air cargo for bulk cargoes is prohibitive.

With serious studies behind us, we can now relax and look at some of the very interesting features and artefacts (some of them very large), of periods other than Roman, and which can still be found in unusual places.

During my afore-mentioned duty on board ship in Port Stanley, I listened to Patrick Watts, the local radio station announcer, asking for details of the old narrow-gauge railway which ran from Navy Point to Moody Brook during and after the 1914-18 War. The request was on behalf of the Falkland Islands Philatelic Bureau.

Postage stamps of the Falkland Islands are usually beautiful and have featured birds, animals, butterflies and moths, flowers, ships, aircraft and military uniforms. The designer thought that a picture of one of the old narrow-gauge locomotives would be a suitable subject for a new stamp. Patrick was asking on the radio if anyone had old photographs of the railway, as the only sign of it was a rough farm track along its former route. The fate of the locomotives and rolling stock was unknown.

The line, along the northern shore of the inner harbour had been operated by the Royal Navy and its purpose had been to transport coal from the jetties at Navy Point to the RN wireless station at Moody Brook. Presumably the generators for this station had been coal-fired.

On board my ship, we had an army liaison officer, Major Allen of the Royal Engineers. I knew the major was a railway enthusiast and mentioned the broadcast to him. He took immediate action and informed me that when I came off duty the next day, an army support boat of the Royal Corps of Transport would arrive at our anchored ship at 1330 hrs and transport us to Navy Point.

We disembarked at Navy Point and walked along the jetty where a strange black-painted ship was flying the white ensign. This was the captured Argentine tug, *Yehuin,* renamed HMS *Falkland Sound,* but known to all and sundry as the *"Black Pig."* Her mundane duty now was to ply around all the ships in the harbour collecting their refuse which was suitably packaged in black plastic bags.

Major Allen and I began our search for signs of the old railway, in and around the collection of huts at Navy Point. After only a few minutes, he called to me from behind an old hangar and I was pleased to see that he had had located a right-angled rail-crossing sticking out of the turf. A closer inspection after a little more turf-kicking, showed that the crossing was a wagon turntable and a little more "excavation" exposed the direction of the main track which appeared to have been of 2 ft or 60 cm gauge. The track passed right through the naval yard and underneath several buildings.

We located two sidings but the central track seemed to head for the eastern breakwater of the small harbour. The inshore end of this breakwater was covered by a large scrap dump. There were old hawsers, rusty ships' plates, hundreds of oil drums and all manner of junk. As we probed into this mass of debris, we couldn't believe our eyes – underneath the top layer was an almost complete 0-4-0 narrow-gauge steam engine. It was lying at an angle of 45 degrees with its cab invisible under heaps of scrap iron. The front of the smoke-box was missing but the locomotive looked as if it was well worth recovering. We also found a wagon in the shallow water nearby. Feeling very satisfied with ourselves, we decided to walk the full length of the line to Moody Brook about four miles away.

Outside the navy yard, no further rails were found but here and there, remains of wooden sleepers could be seen. The route ran along the shore under Wireless Ridge. There were many Argentine bunkers close to the track and here and there, abandoned 30 mm anti-aircraft guns pointed forlornly at the Albatrosses and Turkey Vultures which slope-soared along the ridge. The Argentine anti-aircraft guns carried manufacturer's plates marked with the beautiful flying-stork insignia of the Hispano-Suiza company. One gun had taken a direct hit and there was a soldier's grave beside it. The body had been removed recently to the central Argentine cemetary but the sad little wooden cross, with the soldier's name written on it in biro, was still in place at the head of the empty hole.

A few of the Argentine bunkers had roofs of corrugated iron covered with turf and several had used old railway lines as rafters. Ammunition, weapons and uniforms were scattered around and caution had to be exercised because of minefields. When we strayed off the hard track-bed, we made sure that we followed tank-tracks or landrover tyre marks through the peat and heather.

Close to Moody Brook, we found a pair of wagon wheels and were satisfied that we had discovered all that remained of the long-lost railway.

Moody Brook camp was operated by an army unit of the REME and all that was left of the naval wireless station were the concrete bases which had anchored the guy-wires of the masts.

From Moody Brook, a captured Argentine Mercedes jeep took us back into Port Stanley along the south side of the harbour. Every army unit seemed to have a captured jeep and even the town peat-wagon was a camouflaged ex-Argentine six-wheel truck.

The locomotive was recovered and identified as a Kerr Stuart "Wren" saddle-tank type. Others researchers revealed that the Royal Navy had operated "wind-driven trucks" complete with masts and sails.

An excellent set of stamps was printed and when I look at my collection, I am reminded of that afternoon's archaeological expedition in the remote South Atlantic.

Port Stanley is a paradise for nautical historians. There are dozens of old wrecks lying around the harbour. Some had limped into this harbour over a hundred years ago and are still there. Two or three have been returned to museums in their countries of origin.

The SS *Great Britain,* Brunel's famous iron ship lay for many years in Sparrow Cove. She was launched in Bristol in 1843 and was the largest iron ship of the period. She was the first transatlantic liner to be driven by a propeller.

She was not built in the normal fashion on a slipway but in a similar manner to that described by the Romans – in a dry-dock which was flooded when the ship was completed.

Great Britain sailed the North Atlantic for nine years and after a major overhaul and alterations, she was put on the England to Australia run. This lasted until 1876 when she was laid up. In 1882, her engines having been removed, she returned to the Australian run as the world's largest full-rigged ship. Four years later, she put into Stanley after damage off Cape Horn.

She was used as a storage hulk and during the 1914-18 War, refuelled the British cruisers which took part in the Battle of the Falkland Islands. On April 12th 1937, she was beached in Sparrow Cove.

In 1970, the ship was rescued and towed back to Britain on a purpose-built pontoon. She now occupies the same Bristol dry-dock that was built for her construction.

The *Egeria* now has a corrugated iron roof over her decks and is moored to the Falkland Islands Company's East Jetty. She is used for storage but was originally a barque of 1,066 tons, built in Quebec in 1858. On a voyage from London to Callao in 1872, with a cargo of cement, ninety-five days out, she had to put back into Stanley in a leaky and damaged condition.

The *Jhelum* was built in Liverpool in 1849, and fetched up in Port Stanley in 1870 in a leaky state with a cargo of guano and a mutinous crew. She is still moored to a jetty but has broken her back and sits on the mud in a very poor condition.

The most graceful ship in Port Stanley is the three-masted barque, *Lady Elizabeth,* built by Robert Thompson in Sunderland and launched in 1879. She was damaged rounding Cape Horn in 1913 and four seamen were lost. She later struck rocks off Volunteer Point and put into Port Stanley on March 13th 1913, with a damaged keel and a hole below the waterline.

The ship lies in Whalebone Cove just off the western end of Runway 26 at Stanley's old airfield. A cable runs out to the ship to power red obstruction lights on her masts, as they are a hazard to arriving and departing aircraft. During most of the Argentine occupation, an observation post manned by the SAS was hidden in the ship and all enemy aircraft movements were reported. It is possible to wade out to the ship at low tide but because of Argentine mines on the beaches, we boarded her from a ship's boat.

The *Golden Chance* lies beached at the Canache at the extreme eastern end of the harbour. She was a steam drifter of 90 tons and was built in Lowestoft by Messrs John Chambers Ltd in 1914. She arrived in the Falklands in 1949 for service as a sealer but the operation was not a success. Her engine was built by Messrs Crabtree of Great Yarmouth and is described as a "compound surface condensing direct acting inverted cylinder."

The hulk of the steam tug *Samson* lies close to the *Lady Elizabeth* and was built in Hull in 1888. She arrived in the Falklands in 1900 in order to assist the many vessels which were damaged in the Cape Horn area.

The *Snow Squall* was an American clipper, built in 1851 at Cape Elizabeth USA. She put into Stanley on 2nd March 1864 after suffering much damage trying to round Cape Horn and was fifty-nine days out of New York to San Francisco with a general cargo. During the American Civil War, she had a narrow escape off the Cape of Good Hope. She sighted an unidentified ship which ran up the Stars and Stripes but when the vessels were very close, the stranger – which turned out to be the *Tuscaloosa* – hauled down the Stars and Stripes and replaced it with the Confederate flag. The *Tuscaloosa* opened fire but the *Snow Squall* managed to outsail the enemy and escaped. I believe that her remains, which used to lie at the Falklands Islands Company's East Jetty, have now been returned to USA.

There are several more wrecks and I counted about twelve during my spell of duty in Port Stanley.

Eight thousand miles to the north and back on my home airfield at Usworth, I was astonished to learn that three strange underground wartime gun emplacements had been found. I could hardly believe this and thought that Captain Dennis Ord was joking when he pointed out a circle of concrete, flush with the grass at the side of the main runway. I had taxied aircraft over the top of this dozens of times, and because of the manhole-cover set into the concrete, I had assumed that it was part of the airfield drainage system. While trying to trace a blocked field drain to get rid of a swampy patch, Dennis had opened the iron lid and gone inside. Below ground level was a pill-box with machine-gun slits and a central mechanism which looked like a large jack. It did not take him long to work out that when required, the whole gun-turret used to rise out of the ground like a Jack-in-the-box.

We discovered that these devices were called "Pickett-Hamilton forts" and had been manned by five men. It took four seconds to lift the turret from its sunken to raised position and it could be lowered back into the ground in ten. There were three of these down the side of our Runway 05. When a car factory was built on the airfield, one turret was rescued by the North East Air Museum. They were installed c1940 at airfields at Bury St Edmunds, Hawkinge, Honington, Hornchurch, Ipswich, North Weald, Silloth, Stapleford, Stradishall, Usworth and Wattisham. An example at Silloth at NY 112 536 was restored to working order a few years ago.

Before my retirement from professional aviation and my subsequent return to occasional sea duties, I spent several happy years at the RAF radar station at Boulmer in Northumberland, where I was a Civil Aviation air traffic control officer, attached to the air force. The head of the air traffic control unit was a wing commander who decided that it would be convenient for him to fly to his many conferences in various parts of UK. We all had secondary jobs in addition to control duties, and one of mine was "station expedition officer." I also got the extra job of flying the wing commander around. Although most of of the RAF controllers were ex-pilots, I seemed to be the only one in current flying practice. As Boulmer's wartime runways had been taken up, recycled, and used in the Alnwick bypass, we used the nearby RAF airfield at Acklington for our flying operations. One day, my duty was to take the wing commander to a conference in Northern Ireland. We used an Usworth based aircraft and a few minutes flying took me from there to Acklington where the CO was to board.

On final approach at Acklington, as I skimmed over the railway line just prior to touch-down, I noticed a strange vehicle in a swamp. It looked like a cross between a lorry and a concrete pill-box. On our return from Ireland, a ground inspection showed that the strange object was a Leyland lorry which had had its engine and cab protected by concrete, and on the back was a concrete turret. No wonder it had sunk into the swamp. Research showed that these vehicles, known as "Bisons" were of 1940 vintage and were intended for airfield defence.

I informed the RAF Museum at Hendon who in turn told the RAF Regiment at Catterick. The latter sent a tank-recovery vehicle and dragged the Bison out of the swamp. It was refurbished and placed in the Regimental Museum.

There are many Small forts called "Martello Towers" in the south of England and these were built in case of an invasion by Napoleon. Although I don't know of any in the north of England, we have remnants of isolated gun batteries of the same period. One of these was close to the radar station at Boulmer. An inspection of an old map showed "target" marked in the sea at the outer end of the Boulmer reef. Curiosity took me to the end of the rocks at a low spring tide and, cemented to the rocks by age, and covered in seaweed, were scores of cannon balls. An expedition force of young airmen volunteers recovered them all and they were auctioned at the village fete. The

"Bison" concrete armoured vehicle
1940

Top: The "Bison" concrete armoured car of 1940 vintage, as the author found it in a swamp at Acklington, Northumberland.
Bottom: The Bison being re-furbished in the RAF Regiment Museum, Catterick.

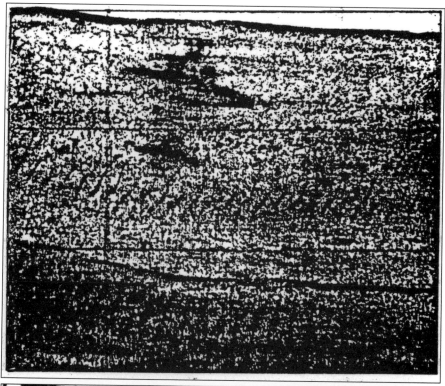

Modern technology is about to revolutionise archaeology. The Sidescan Sonar read-out of a PBY Catalina flying boat lying on the bed of Loch Ness.

proceeds went to the Boulmer lifeboat fund.

A more ambitious scheme got under way when an inspection of local records told us that:

"On December 23rd 1565, a ship en route from France to Scotland was wrecked on Heulle Carrs, off Seaton Point. The ship was among other things, conveying a chest of gold to Mary, Queen of Scots."

This rocky point was just below our radar station. We were poised to mount a diving operation when further documentary research saved us the trouble. In *A Survey of the Manor of Longhoughton,* 1567, it said:

"My Lord claims as in the deeds of Aylnmowth, wrecks that chance upon the coast of this Lordship as in other manors. There chanced on December 23 1565, a ship of Flushing in Sealand to be broken and wrecked on the Hullie Carr beside Boulmer. A passenger was Frances Yeakslayd, an Englishman who was a servant of Mary, Queen of Scots, and who was conveying from Flanders to the Queen, a great amount of gold.

The gold was found in one chest, washed up on the rocks, by Thomas Shippert, of Houghton and the fishermen of Boulmer."

We were four hundred years too late.

As the station expedition officer at Boulmer, I had used the airfield's fishing boat to investigate all the inlets and islands of the Northumberland coast. This coastline had been part of a Roman frontier zone. The Roman navy must have used some of these inlets. I noted that there had been Roman finds at the picturesque Howick Haven (NU 260 165). A circular Iron Age hillfort overlooked the inlet, but where was the Roman fort? I wondered if the Romans had merely reused the Iron Age camp, ignoring the fact that its shape did not comply with the Roman Army handbook instructions. An Iron Age hillfort to the south of Ingram in the Cheviots, curiously, has remains of square buildings in it instead of the normal circular huts.

When I carried out my aerial survey of the area, my suspicions were heightened when I discovered two suspected Roman roads converging on the Howick Haven IA circle. Frequently, long stretches of Roman roads in the frontier zone run for miles without any sign of square or rectangular Roman forts but they pass right by the Iron Age circular ramparts of the defeated natives. The reuse of enemy positions and equipment has always been a bonus in any war. The first ship I served in was a captured German minelayer, the *Linz,* renamed by us *Empire Wansbeck.* There was a feeling of victory as we ate our meals from plates which carried the eagle-and-swastika insignia of the *Kriegsmarine.*

The Nazi insignia were obviously designed by admirers of the Roman army. The *Luftwaffe* pilots' and observers' badges were almost exact replicas of a Roman relief of an eagle on a laurel wreath. The Messerschmitt 109's of the *Luftwaffe* carried Roman insignia. The *Gruppen Adjutant's* aircraft had a centurion's insignia in front of the black cross on the side of the fuselage. This is a "V" on its side. The *Gruppen kommandeur's* fighter had a double insignia with a small "V" inside a larger one. I notice that some modern Israeli tanks also use the centurion's mark. The wartime Italian *Reggia*

Aeronautica naturally used old Roman insignia and the national emblem on their aircraft was three Roman *fascis* (a bundle of whipping rods with protruding axe-head which was carried before a Roman magistrate to signify his powers of punishment). Roman influence is all around us.

The zig-zag thunderbolt insignia of the Romans has been copied by most modern fighting services.

The Roman practice of placing forward-facing gods' and animal figures on their ships' sterns gave way in later periods to a crucifix in the same place. On a modern warship of the Royal Navy, an officer reaching the top of the gangway turns aft and salutes. This was the direction of the crucifix in years gone by.

Most historians are interested in insignia, and much can be learned from them. Pilots are astonished when I tell them that the insignia on British military aircraft have French revolutionary origins. In 1914, the insignia on the aircraft of the Royal Flying Corps was the Union Flag (Union Jack) but the British ground troops mistook the red English cross for the black German one and friendly fire resulted. The French air force used Napoleon's red, white and blue roundel so the RFC adopted the same insignia but reversed the colours.

The British were the first to use "wings" as a pilot's badge and this was copied by most of the world's armed forces. Everyone seems to think that RAF pilots' wings are those of an eagle. That is not the case. Although the badge of the RAF is an eagle (*volant & sinister*) [flying to the left], the pilots' wings are those of a *swift*, and this was decreed by King George V when he selected the bird's picture from his handbook on ornithology.

The double-dolphin Roman insignia found by our divers on the bed of the River Tees, is almost identical to the modern Royal Navy's submarine badge. The Roman dolphins always have three flukes on their tails whereas the living creature has a horizontal tail with only two. The two dolphins on our recovered Roman insignia are holding a sphere between their noses. Does this sphere represent the Earth? The Romans knew that it was round.

We cannot move around our cities without seeing the influence of the Romans: the columns in front of the law courts and other public buildings and the winged statues of Victory on the war memorials. Our merchant ships still have their names on the bows, and our modern sailors, like the Romans, thought that it was bad luck to sail on a Friday.

When A Roman ship was in danger, the passengers would wear any jewellery available so that if they drowned and washed up on shore, a stranger would have the money to pay for a decent funeral. If the weather was good, no cutting of hair or nails was permitted, but if the weather was bad, nail clippings and locks of hair could be tossed overboard as an appeasement to the gods. Dancing was forbidden on board, and no blasphemies were allowed, – it was considered bad luck if a blasphemy was even received in a letter on board.

Our modern word "biscuit" is derived from the Latin *biscocus* (twice cooked) and refers to ships' stores which saved the Roman cooks from baking bread at sea.

We speak of an "opportune moment" and few realise that *opportune* is a

Among the Iron Age hillforts of Northumberland, pieces of wrecked aircraft lie in the peat bogs.Top: a radial engine and bottom, a wheel, both on Cairn Hill,Cheviot.

Roman nautical expression. Each year, on August 17th, the Romans held a feast in honour of Portunus, the god who protected the harbours. Before (*ob*) the ship enters the port (*portus*), it is a happy time; an opportune moment.

The word "fathom" meaning a depth of six feet, comes from the Latin *patene* which became the Saxon *faehom and* meant the distance spanned by two outstretched arms.

The word "cargo" is taken directly from the Latin *cargo* or *carga* which means a load, or freight.

Captain is derived from the Saxon *caput* (head or chief) and *thane*, a title of honour. The list is endless and the ancients are still with us in our everyday language.

As well as exploring the Northumberland coast, my expeditions with young airmen and Waafs took us into the heart of the Cheviot Hills where we examined scores of Iron Age hillforts with great interest. I am sure that some of the old Drove Roads across these hills, hide Roman roads, and much fieldwork remains to be done. My own calculations forecast that a Roman settlement will be found at Alwinton (NU 921 063).

On occasion we came across wrecked aircraft of the 39-45 War. One was a Handley Page Hampden, of RAF Bomber Command. It lay on Windy Gyle at NU 848 155, a couple of hundred yards into Scotland. The aircraft was based at Topcliffe in Yorkshire and was returning from over Germany, in a damaged condition. All the crew were killed. A wing still carried a red and blue roundel (the white was left out on the top surfaces, during the war). Later when the RAF Museum needed a wartime Bristol Pegasus engine, I was able to guide an RAF helicopter and Landrover to this wreck and an engine was lifted out and taken away.

There are many other very large artefacts lying around; everybody read about the Vickers Wellington bomber which was recovered from Loch Ness, but a sidescan-sonar picture shows a PBY Catalina flying boat also lying on the bed of the loch. Modern technology is revealing a lot of secrets and that is why I say to the scientists: "give us the tools and we will finish the archaeological search."

During my airline career flying: Yorks, DC3 Dakotas, DC4 Skymasters, Vikings, Doves, Herons, Bristol 170's etc, we did not need to fly at the heights required by modern jets (jet engines just gobble up fuel at low altitudes), I had noticed an old locomotive lying in the Saudi Arabian desert north of Medina. The engine and tender lay on their sides beside the dismantled Hejaz Railway. I discovered that this locomotive had headed a train which was blown up by Lawrence of Arabia in 1917. A couple of years later, I looked for the wreck again but the engine had disappeared; the tender remained. I was told that the locomotive had been recovered and sold to Indian Railways where it was refurbished and put into service.

The world is full of interesting artefacts. A wrecked Arab dhow in the Persian Gulf contained a reused engine from a London bus!

I hope that my introduction to simple navigation in Chapter 7 will encourage further research on the subject. I am amazed at some unconventional methods which come to light now and again. I met a yachtsman in San Francisco who navigated regularly to Hawaii and he never bothered with expensive navigation equipment. He said: "I just follow the vapour trails." Some of the ancient navigators followed migrating birds so there is nothing new.

The explorer Dr David Livingstone used a marine sextant to fix his position in central Africa. In order to use a sailor's sextant, one must be able to see both the heavenly body and the sea horizon at the same time, and the angle between the two can be used to calculate a position line. Dr Livingstone was surrounded by jungle and mountains and had no level horizon but he overcame the problem; he poured golden syrup into a frying-pan and meaured the angle between the Sun in the sky and the Sun's reflection in the treacle. He then divided by two. I wonder if this is the reason why the treacle tins have the Royal coat of arms on the side. If it isn't, then it should be!

The captain of a cruise liner received a report that a passenger was missing, presumed overboard. He turned the ship onto a reciprocal course and after two hours, spotted the passenger in the water and rescued him. When the captain was congratulated on his magnificent feat of navigation, he said: "I just followed the beer tins."

This brings me to the end of this book and I hope that many amateur historians will be encouraged to get out into the countryside and continue the search all over Britain and further afield if possible. Some of the field-workers who have assisted me over the last few years gained their initial interest in history and archaeology with artefacts found with metal detectors. I note that over the years, their eyes have become tuned in, and they are reading the the landscape. The metal detectors are now used only for specific tasks such as verifying paved fords, scanning spoil heaps etc. The detectorists have become true archaeologists.

If this book encourages readers to become archaeological trackers and pathfinders, then I shall be well satisfied. I also hope that all who take up the exploration of the countryside will get as much pleasure from their expeditions as I have had from mine. I wish you all:

"Good Hunting."

Addendum

Since the main script of this book was finished, more important information has come to light, hence this addendum.

That Hylton Dam again...

Fairly recently, repairs to the north inner mole at Sunderland Harbour (photo p256) revealed dozens of stones which appear to be reused Roman material and it is highly likely that these very large blocks came from the great Roman dam at Hylton when it was dismantled in 1865 (p210). The stones have wedge-shaped horizontal recesses for iron butterfly-cramps and remains of Roman structures elsewhere have produced similar handiwork. The abutment of the Roman bridge at Risingham is one example. Also, in Glasgow's Hunterian Museum, a stone almost identical to the Sunderland stones is on display to the public. This stone was removed from the remains of a Roman bridge which had spanned the River Kelvin north of the Antonine Wall near Balmuidy.

In the eastern abutment of the Roman bridge at Chollerford (Chesters), similar butterfly-cramp holes can be seen in the pier of the earlier bridge. This pier base has been encapsulated in the later abutment. The stones of this later abutment have not used butterfly-cramps but most have lewis-holes.

Some of the stones at Sunderland also have lewis-holes (p257). Butterfly-cramped stones were found in the Roman bridge at Carlisle and also at Chester-le-Street. The latter were found in the bed of the River Cone when it was cleaned out and cemented in 1930. The findspot of the Cone bridge was in line with the north gate of the Roman fort.

More documentary evidence has also been brought to my attention regarding the Hylton structure. *The Proceedings of the Society of Antiquarians,* 1884, Vol 1, p134, tells us that:

"Mr Lister (shipyard owner) saw hundreds of tons of stone taken out nineteen years ago and hundredweights of lead taken by apprentices during dinner hours. There was an oak frame underneath and he was convinced of a bridge. A lighter loaded with stone sprang a leak, the stone landed on the quay reached a height of ten feet."

The Sunderland harbour engineeer's report of 1881 has also come to light:

"Gentlemen,

I beg to report that a cut of from 90 to 100 feet in width and from 12 to 15 feet in depth below zero level, has now, by means of the dredger Hercules, been completed through the 'Brigg Stones' at Hylton, and the

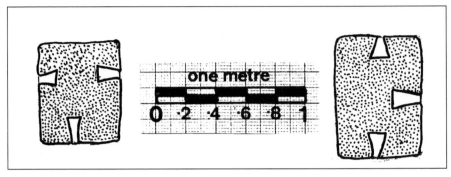

Stone from Roman Bridge over River Kelvin on   Sunderland Stone (from Hylton Dam?). Several
display in Hunterian Museum, Glasgow   lying at Roker

result is that the low water of an Ordinary Spring tide has been lowered
from the level of a similar tide of 8' 4½" on the Hylton tide gauge in
1870, to 3' 0" on the same gauge in 1881, thus giving a vertical tide gain
of 5' 4½" at Hylton. It is satisfactory for me to state that this is the result
which I anticipated in 1870 would be accomplished by the dredging of
the River when carried up to Hylton. I am not yet in a position to state
definitely what the actual amount is of tidal gain at Ordinary Spring
tides but I do not consider it to be less than 390,000 cubic yards. The
dredger *Hercules* is at present engaged cutting through a sand bank
above the Hylton Ferry and on the completion of this cut, I propose
that she shall commence to remove the projecting point of rock and
sand at Parks Nook.

Your obedient Servant,
(signed) Henry H Wake."

Deeds respecting the Manor of Offerton have also been brought to my
notice. These refer to a parcel of land known as the "Damflatt":

*"In le Westridding qatuor siloes. In Weststrotheracris septe silioes & vnu
heuedland. In Est strotheracris octo siloes. In le damflat qatuor silioes. In le
schortflat qatuor siliones & dimid."*

In the Westridding, four selions; in Weststrotheracres, seven and one
headland; in Eaststrotheracres, eight selions; in the Damflat, four
selions; in the Shortflat, four selions and a half

The above tells us that in the "Damflat," there were four selions, (strips of
rig & furrow).

A photograph of one of the suspected Roman stones at the mouth of the
Wear, appeared in the *Sunderland Echo* on 5.12.94 and further reports were
received about several Roman stones lying at Hylton North Farm which is
very close to the dam site. These stones turned out to be of the lewis-holed
variety.

A geology student at Sunderland University has offered to try to find the
quarry which the harbour's reused stones came from, and he will use the
information for his degree dissertation.

The curator of a local museum has claimed that the Hylton dam was a figment of Victorian antiquarians' imaginations. Mr Maude would not have agreed with him as he was drowned in 1753 while trying to cross the river via the structure. Another "expert" claims that the massive stone construction was a mediaeval fish-trap in spite of its Roman inscriptions. The structure could have trapped a fish the size of one of Hitler's U-boats, let alone a salmon. Although all the ramshackle wicker fish-traps are recorded in mediaeval documents, there is a stony silence about a fish-trap at Hylton. The same historian claims that the Wear was not navigable in Roman times due to shoals at the river mouth. What an astonishing comment! Even if the bed of the river dried out completely, the fifteeen feet tides sweeping in every 12½ hours could hardly be termed un-navigable. Shoals do not rise and fall with the tide. I noted that "Time Team" on television ITV CH4 on 29,i.95, mentioned that Roman ships came up the shallow Thames on the tide and then dropped anchor in the deep pool which later became the Roman port of London. I am sure that is exactly what happened at Hylton.

Information comes in all the time about more recent river navigation. Mr Thursby who is a native of Catterick informs me that when he was a boy (he is

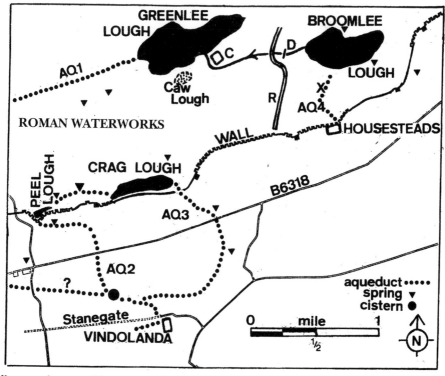

Known and suspected Roman reservoirs in the Roman Wall's "Mini-Lake District"
AQ1 = Known Roman aqueduct from Greenlee Lough to Aesica.
AQ2 = Suspected Roman aqueduct fom Peel Lough to Vindolanda.
AQ3 = Suspected Roman aqueduct from Crag Lough to Vindolanda.
AQ4 = Suspected Roman aqueduct from Broomlee Lough to Housesteads,
C = Roman temporary camp.
D = Site of suspected Roman dam
R = Roman road north from Rapishaw Gap.

Armstrong's map of 1769 which shows the lakes in the central Roman Wall sector. The now-disappeared Caw Lough is shown, also the suspected Roman patrol road from Sewingshields to Rose Bower via Keming's Cross.

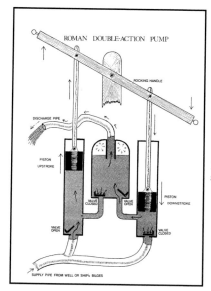

Roman double-action pump of the type used in Roman ships' bilges and Roman wells

now 73), the timbers of an old staunch (flash-lock) could still be seen in the River Swale at Catterick. Navigation of the Swale (said by some historians to be un-navigable) continued up to and beyond Catterick until the turn of this century. Mr Thursby also informs me that 30 feet was taken from the top of the "motte" to the north-east of Catterick airfield c1940, as the earthwork was a hazard to aircraft.

Hadrian's Wall Mini-Lake District.

In the central area of the Roman Wall, there is an interesting group of lakes to the north of Housesteads and Vindolanda. Usually, only the beautiful Crag Lough is seen by Wall walkers, as the others are hidden by ridges. The largest lake is Greenlee Lough, a mile north of Crag Lough and the Wall. A Roman temporary camp sits on a ridge to the south of Greenlee Lough and there are signs of Roman quarries close by.

Roman engineers used Greenlee Lough as a reservoir for the Wall fort of Great Chesters (Aesica), and the Caw Burn which drains the lough was intercepted at "Fond Tom's Pool" (NY 741 688), south of Swallow Crags, by a six mile contour-following aqueduct. Long stretches of the open leat can be traced across the rough moorland. A precedent has been set - a known Roman aqueduct has used one of the lakes as a source of water. How about the other lakes? A search was called for.

Four members of the Northern Archaeology Group of County Durham formed an aqueduct hunting team and to begin with, they inspected the Greenlee - Aesica channel in order to familiarise themselves with Roman water engineers' handiwork and to try to see the various problems through long gone but very capable eyes.

The team was led by Norman Cassidy, a recently retired RAF sergeant-engineer. Norman has often flown as my co-pilot and he is quite familiar with the Wall area. His three enthusiastic assistants were Doug Moar, an insurance assessor, Doug's son David, a recently graduated surveyor, and Beverley Pemberton, a civil servant. It was known to the searchers that Roman forts and towns seldom had just one aqueduct as this would have allowed for neither planned maintenance nor accidents.

After inspecting the known *specus* (water channel), they found another, this one completely unknown. Whereas the known channel arrives at the fort from the east and is north of the Wall, the newly discovered leat approaches from a spring-source to the west of the fort and the entire length is below the Wall ridge to the south. It looks as if the two aqueducts joined in a hollow about two hundred yards west of the fort, just south of the Wall and Military Way. From this point, it is assumed that the combined aqueduct followed the contours south-eastwards to the bath-house which was situated a hundred yards or so, south of the fort's SE corner.

A further interesting point emerges: the low ground to the south of the Wall and well below the aqueduct levels, contains vast areas of swamp. Are these waterlogged expanses the remnants of Roman period lakes? They are too low down to have served as reservoirs but they would have made excellent rear-facing defences for the Wall system. The Vallum skirts the north side of the swamps in just the right place for the sheets of water to have augmented this earthwork against an attack from the south. Evidence will be produced shortly to show that there was much more water around in Roman times.

In my book *The Piercebridge Formula* of 1983, I suggested that Crag Lough may have been used by the Romans as a reservoir for Vindolanda. The lough is drained by the Bradley Burn which runs under the Wall at Milking Gap via a rectangular culvert in typical Roman fashion. The stream runs right past the Vindolanda (Chesterholm) fort. It would have been a fairly simple task for the Roman engineers to divert the multi-million-gallon-per-day flow of water, into the bath-houses, inns, latrines, forges, smithies and ornamental fountains. Just to the east of the fort, the Bradley Burn is joined by Brackies Burn and I strongly suspect that this latter stream has also been harnessed by the Romans. An earthwork, later used by a narrow-gauge industrial tramway, leaves the burn to the north-west of the fort and ends up at the Roman bath-house right in line with its water intake!

My search of 1983 located a suspected cistern hewn out of the solid rock at the point where a small stream joins Brackies Burn from the north (NY 763 667), just to the west of an old limekiln. This was the starting point for our search party and the team followed the small stream to the north, crossed the *Vallum* and the B6318 road and then climbed the ridge along the top of which runs the Wall. On the southern slope, the stream was fed by an artificial east-west channel and this cutting showed traces of paving. The channel was followed past a spring and then up to the Wall at Peel Gap. Peel Gap is a defile into which the Wall descends and makes a southerly kink at the same time. Two square culverts, now dry, were observed low down in the stonework of the Wall. Unlike drainage culverts, they are not in the bottom course. On the north side of the Wall there is a swamp which looks as if it has been a lake at one time; if so, the Wall has dammed it.

Beside the culverts, (now suspected of being aqueduct feeders), there is a spurious tower attached to the Wall. It is not a milecastle as Milecastle 39 is half a mile to the east and Milecastle 40 a similar distance to the west. Nor is it a turret as Turret 39A is on top of Peel Crags to the east and Turret 39B on the hill to the west. It is said that this tower was an extra defence against an ememy trying to rush Peel Gap, but my colleagues are of the opinion that it was a control post for the Roman operators of the waterworks. These gentlemen are mentioned in antiquity and evidently the job held low status and was usually a position into which a Roman soldier was demoted.

The usual critics demand to know why the missing Peel Lough has vanished into thin air, leaving only a swamp behind? The answer to that is: the same place where Caw Lough just to the north-east has gone. This is marked as a lake on the 1850 OS map but there is no trace of it today.

Springs used by the Romans were usually faced with a short low wall, and a centrally placed stone trough collected the water, with the overspill feeding an aqueduct. Quite often, the Roman stone tanks have been broken or removed but farmers have replaced them with modern ceramic vessels which are in constant use as animal drinking-troughs. Such a revetted spring sits on the north side of the site of the missing Peel Lough.

From the eastern end of the Peel swamp an old incoming water-channel can be followed eastwards to another Roman-style spring. The latter is halfway between "Peel Lough" and Crag Lough and is on a rise above the level of both loughs. From this spring (NY 758 679), a second channel runs in the opposite direction, down to Crag Lough.

Next, our team investigated Crag Lough. It is obvious that the lake has been much larger at one time. The old shore-line is obvious. More springs on the high ground to the north feed the lough. At the east end of the lake, a line of large boulders, now high and dry and almost completely covered with grass, may have been the original Roman dam which either caused the lake to form, or increased the size of an existing one. The Bradley Burn leaves this end of the lake as previously described.

We now have three reservoirs, one known to be Roman and two strongly suspected. There is still another lake in our "mini Lake District" and a large one too - Broomlee Lough which is tucked out of site beyond the hill to the north of the Housesteads Roman Wall fort. Although many archaeologists including myself have searched long and hard for the Roman water supply to this fort, the investigations have always ended in failure. The fort sits on a crag above and to the west of the Knag Burn Gap, but the fort's main bath-house was down in the gully beside the Knag Burn. The Knag Burn Gap is another break in the natural defensive line of the Whinstone escarpment which the Wall has utilised. The Romans placed a gateway in the Wall here for reasons as yet unknown.

In winter the Knag Burn would have kept the bath-house amply supplied with water, but what about the summer? In the summer of 1994, no water at all flowed down the burn for over two months. When this question was put to a Roman Wall guide, his reply was: "perhaps the Romans didn't wash in the summer!"

The answer was there somewhere and I am delighted to report that my friends solved the mystery. Although Broomlee Lough is out of sight from Housesteads, on the other side of a hill to the north, the lake is at a slightly higher level than the Knag Burn culvert in the Roman Wall. The lough is just six hundred yards north of the Wall but there is no valley in the high ground which a contour-following aqueduct could utilise. Our team knew that in Italy, France, Spain, North Africa and elsewhere, Roman engineers penetrated hills with aqueduct-tunnels. Maybe the hill between Broomlee Lough and the Knag Burn culvert had been pierced by just such a tunnel. On a large-scale map, the lowest point on the high ground between Wall and lough was plotted and earmarked as a search area. The team duly proceeded through the Knag Burn Gate and up the gentle slope to this position. They were astonished to find that exactly at the location plotted on the map, there were the remains of a large cutting, like those excavated for railways. It was mostly infilled but its purpose was suddenly crystal clear. The Romans had not used a tunnel; they had put a cutting through the hill. The channel was found at both ends of the cutting. The southern end would have fed the Knag Burn and once we knew where it was, the aqueduct could be traced, heading for the culvert. There was a problem at the north end of the cutting; the suspected northern inlet was about fifteen feet above the level of the lake. Engineer Neville Andison who had joined the expedition observed that the lough had at one time contained far more water and he pointed out a raised shoreline. Had the water level dropped some fifteen feet by natural causes or had the level been artificially increased by the Romans? The ruins of an old stone boathouse and jetty, probably about two hundred years old from the design, is now high and dry near the Jenkins Burn which drains the lake. This shows that the lake had decreased in size but not by as much as fifteen feet since the old boathouse was in operation. A modern boathouse on the north side of the lake has been built on the present day shore-line. The Jenkins Burn flows through a narrow gorge before meandering into the larger Greenlee Lough which it enters close by a Roman temporary camp. If the Romans had dammed Broomlee Lough, the dam must have been in this narrow gully. An investigation revealed two rocky outcrops, which could have served as abutments, scattered stones and small grass-covered quarries at NY 783 696. Is this the dam site? A north-south farm road in the vicinity proved to be a Roman road. A branch leaves this road and terminates at the suspected dam site. The farm road is the track which crosses the Roman Wall at the Rapishaw Gap and was reported as Roman by eighteenth century antiquarians. They were correct. This north-south road joins a north-east to south-west road beside Greenlee Lough at NY 782 700. Both roads may form part of a Roman grid of patrol tracks, but more of this shortly. On the north side of the junction, a rock has a strange carving on the top. A large hole (a bit like the cup-and-ring central hole) has a smaller one a few inches away and the two are joined by a sinuous channel. Does this represent Broomlee Lough, Greenlee Lough and the Jenkins Burn? Who carved it?

At long last, the main source of water for the Housesteads bath-house had been found but how did the Romans get the water from the Knag Burn up to the fort on the crag above. It is obvious that stone gutter channels excavated in the fort collected rainwater but this together with water from wells would have formed only emergency supplies inadequate for normal needs which included the large latrine complex in the fort's south-east corner.

With the strong gush of water from Broomlee Lough which we now know was connected to the Knag Burn, a large undershot or overshot water-wheel could have been installed above the bath-house without affecting in the slightest, the supply to that essential amenity to Roman life. The large diameter water-wheel could have driven a double acting Ctesibian-type piston-pump of the kind installed as bilge-pumps in Roman ships. Similar pumps have also been found in Roman wells. These Roman pumps closely resemble the emergency fuel-transfer hand operated pumps which were installed in case of electrical or engine-driven pump failure in some World War II American aircraft.

When the bronze twin-cylinder assembly of the Roman pump is examined, one realises how close the Romans were to inventing a steam engine. An example of a Roman pump is on display in London in the British Museum's Roman rooms.

Below the Knag Burn bath-house, the bed of the burn is paved and this must have formed the main drain for the fort and bath-house although a subsidiary sewer did curve into the cultivation terraces. The burn runs down to the Grindon Lough which sits in a hollow beside Stanegate road, a mile to the south-east. Grindon Lough is peculiar in that it has no visible outlet. Water seeps away through its porous bed and emerges via the various springs further south. This lough must have collected all the sludge from the Housesteads fort and *vicus*. In the valley immediately below Housesteads to the south, we once again get those peculiar swamps which look like former lakes. Could they have been paddy fields where the Roman garrison, for a period known to have been the Syrian "Hamian Archers," grew this crop, usually associated with eastern countries? I once suggested that the cultivation terraces at Housesteads might have been used for rice-growing. We now know that there was a plentiful water supply. My suggestion of rice-growing was vetoed by the "experts" but I now find that the Queckett Microscope Club have identified rice grown by the Romans at the Lunt fort, Coventry. The acid soil at Housesteads would have been suitable for rice cultivation.

Is it not strange that the extensive Roman waterworks and aqueducts are north of the Wall, in territory liable to have been overrun from time to time by hostile tribes? In the trenches of France in the 1914-18 War, no soldier dare drink from a stream which originated from beyond the German trenches. Likewise, the Germans would have been foolish to drink water which had passed through Allied held territory. The Romans must have been in firm control of the area to the north of the Wall and new evidence to this effect will be discussed shortly. Before that however, let us look at one more Roman reservoir which is further to the east, close to Corbridge: Shildon Lough is now dry but it was a large lake in Roman times (see map p308)

Expert field-walker Andy Davison was searching the area between the Lough and the Wall, looking for signs of the Roman stone-lined spring-channels mentioned generations ago by the Corbridge town clerk. Andy found an unknown Roman aqueduct with several feeders, only a short distance south of the Wall near Halton Shields to the north-east of Corbridge. He had been walking along the farm track between Greenleighton (NZ 023

673) and Halton Shields (NZ 016 687) when he realised that the track was an unknown Roman road. Several aqueduct-feeders and springs were found in the vicinity of the road. The work of plotting them is now in progress. A further search of the road traced it to the south of the B6321 road, and it continued south to the eastern end of the former Shildon Lough. Yet another Roman road has been revealed.

Andy does not wait for our survey aircraft to provide aerial photographs; he carries a large kite and associated equipmenmt in his car boot. This kite, fitted with specially developed elastic bungee anti-shake mounts, carries a video camera aloft, thus providing instant air reconnaissance. He is assisted in the field on occasion by our photographer and dark-room technician, Steve Marchant. Steve is also our expert on churches and ancient religions including Mithras, but of late, he has been impressed as a kite-handler and road-searching foot-slogger.

Also in the team is Neil Pattison, a ship's chief engineer and a very useful man to have around. He is no newcomer to inland navigation and took his ship, a converted tank landing craft, up Russia's River Don, through the Don/Volga lock system and down the Volga to Astrakhan and into the Caspian Sea, where the ship is engaged on oilfield exploration.

Let us not forget researchers like Jack Shaw. In addition to the Roman roads of Durham, Jack is building up a picture of the lost roads of Scotland which he comes across on his many fishing expeditions into Caledonia.

No man's land?

Yet a third field-team has commenced operations at my call for assistance. A group of highly experienced metal detectorists laid aside their electronic tools and became cross-country field archaeologists. The main targets were the suspected Roman patrol roads of the area north of the Wall.

Ken Brown is a retired executive but at one time was an aircraft engineer in the RAF; Captain Harry Whitelaw is a master mariner; Peter Harvey, an expert wood-carver, is a former miner (and expedition's unofficial geologist). John Jenkins is now a businessman but was formerly a helicopter engineer with the Army Air Corps. With colleagues like this, how could I fail in my search? The first target area was the area to the north of Limestone Corner to elucidate the problem of complex and vulnerable waterworks systems in territory which according to tradition, was little more than a "no man's land."

During a search for an aqueduct to the Roman fort at Chesters (Cilurnum) in my preparation for *THE PIERCEBRIDGE FORMULA*, I chanced across an east-west track along a ridge (NY 870 722) to the north of Limestone Corner. The track had associated earthworks which looked like Roman handiwork. Was this part of a forward patrol network? The team's task was to find such a grid and with the main script of this book completed, I joined the team.

A good starting place was a possible Roman road described by the Rev G R Hall in the *Proceedings of the Society of Antiquarians of Newcastle upon Tyne*, 1865. Little or no attempt seems to have been made over the intervening 130 years to verify Rev Hall's report. It was time to see what our erstwhile detectorists could do. Hall's report was studied first and he tells us that: [map refs etc inserted by author] "at various times, farmers and gentlemen in the hunting field had noticed the course of an ancient road on both sides of the River North Tyne. The road had originated on Hadrian's Wall at a point [NY 856 712] to the west of Carrawbrough   [Brocolitia] and was followed by a very straight farm road [on a heading of 340 degrees]. Mr Allgood of Nunwick Hall reported very large Roman stones in the road below [east of] Goatstones. The road crossed Ward Lane [NY 845 752] and proceeded to Moralee Mill [NY 845 761]."

Our survey confirmed the route and showed that the Roman line, described by Rev Hall, turned a right angle at the top of the cliff (NY 843 760), south of High Moralee Farm. The Roman road avoided a descent of the cliff but the turn to the east still negotiated a very severe gradient. What Rev Hall did not mention was a mirror image road, now a grass covered hollow-way, which angled down the severe slope to the west. One must look over a field wall to observe this feature. The Roman road had divided here. A continuation of this westerly arm will be picked up in due course.

The next position mentioned by Hall is the river crossing at Wark Ford [NY 863 769, about 200 yards downstream from the present bridge]. At the west side of the ford, a Roman altar was found c1793 at the foot of Wark Mote Hill ["*Moat* Hill" on 1769 map], Scyteceastre before that. This altar is in the possession of the Newcastle Society of Antiquarians.

Hall's notes tell us that on the east side of the North Tyne, the route of the Roman road was:

1 Up Wark's Haugh Bank [NY 865 773], north side,
2 In Birtley village, through the north of "Cow's Grasses,"
3 Past a stile on the Buteland Road,
4 A little to the south of Pitland Hills Cottage,
5 Somewhat to the south of Tone Hall,
6 Crossed Watling Street [Dere Street],
7 Thence on the Whiteside ground, north of Carey Coates Hall,
8 On the north side of Sweethope Lough.

[Birtley Church stands on a rectangular earthwork and two prominent rounded corners can be seen in the churchyard on the eastern side of the church] (observed 1994)

Our survey located the agger and other features exactly on the line mentioned by Rev Hall. In some fields, there are no visible traces whatsoever but at NY 901 785, a thousand yards east of Bog Shield Cottage and five hundred yards north of Rushey Law Farm, the Roman road is intact and is on a heading of 065 degrees. Mediaeval rig & furrow has used the grass-covered stone *agger* as a boundary between furlongs. On the spot-height of 258M at NY 903 794, there is the outline of a square building which could have been a Roman signal station. Close by is a possible Romano-British farmstead. A standing-stone leans at a drunken angle just south of the site. Four hundred yards to the east-north-east, at the foot of the hill, the remains of a small bridge or paved ford can be seen in a small stream. Slightly downstream, a farmer has reused some of the large stones to make a farm crossing which utilises a concrete pipe as a culvert. On the east side of the stream, the Roman road is followed by a field boundary. A very short distance up the bank and on the south side of the hedge-line, are the grass-covered remains of a small square building.

If this building proves to be a Roman turret, then the Roman road was fortified at short intervals and must have traversed untrustworthy territory. Further east, at the top of the hill, the Roman road is overlain by a modern estate road which leaves the A68 (Dere Street) at the Tone Inn and proceeds to Tone Hall. Rev Hall's road joins this estate road at the right-angled turn at NY 912 798 where the minor road turns north to Tone Hall. It is extremely likely that the Tone Inn (NY 915 800) stands on top of a Roman fortlet. A distinct earthwork can be seen in the garden on the south side of the inn. The suspected signal station or watch-tower on the spot height of 258M is exactly one Roman mile (1620 yards) from the Tone Inn.

Rev Hall tells us that his Roman road possibly ran along the north side of Sweethope Lough. If this is the case, it would explain the name "Knowsgate" at the crosssing of the A696(T) (NY 989 857). A mile further east, the suspected Roman road, at NZ 005 863, becomes very straight and it looks as if the Roman surveyors have picked up a distant survey point. This is obviously the Rothley Crag at NZ 043 885. It is interesting to note that a back bearing on this road is lined up on the Tone Inn. Several other Roman and suspected Roman roads are lined up on the Rothley Crag. One is the recently discovered "Rothley Road" which runs all the way from the Roman Wall area. Armstrong's map of Northumberland of 1769 marks Rothley as "Roadley" which adds fuel to the argument for it being associated with ancient roads.

A Roman *Limes* (defensive grid system)

There is a strong possibility that the modern "Ward lane" across Broadpool Common lies on top of a Roman outlying patrol road to the north of the Wall. A glance at the map will show that this road follows the same pattern as the alteration of heading of the Wall complex at Limestone Corner. The Broadpool Common road obeys Roman rules: it alters course with sudden angles at high points such as the turn towards Simonburn at NY 861 751, and it follows a ridge which has an excellent view to the north. This "early warning" could have been augmented by a signal station on Ravensheugh Crag (NY 832 748) where the 1850 OS map marks a "currick" (watchtower). The farm-track which runs south to the crag from opposite a small roadside pig farm, is paved with large sandstone blocks whereas the local stone in the crag is whinstone.

Further west, Ladyhill Farm (NY 801 751), on the south side of the Broadpool Common road, stands on a very Roman-like rectangular platform.

If the road is Roman, surely Standard Hill, on the high point, at NY 821 751, must have been a Roman site. Once again, it is on a platform and hundreds of tons of stone can be seen on the north side. Exactly one Roman mile (1620 yards) north of Standard Hill and the Broadpool Common road, is a very straight east-west bridle-track called Longlee Rigg. It is lined up on a high point (Birk Hill, NY 789 769) to the west. This bridle-track is yet another suspected Roman patrol line along a ridge. The track follows a "military horizon," i.e. just below the crest, so that an enemy to the north would not see troop movements. At NY 822 767, on the north-eastern corner of a conifer plantation, (and exactly one Roman mile north of Standard Hill), is a suspected Roman fortlet which has been bisected by the bridle-track. It is marked on the six-inch OS maps but has probably been regarded as an RB site until now. The southern ditch and two prominent rounded corners are still in good condition. The remainder of the outline can be traced as a slight depression in the cultivated field to the north of the track. Very large square stones lie in the ditch at the south-western corner of the site.

The Rev Hall's road traverses the whole suspected Roman *limes* and the westerly bound mirror image of his right-angled easterly turn at High Moralee needs further investigation to see if it is part of the grid system.

On Armstrong's map of 1769, the farm "Goatstones" is marked as "Gatestones" which has a totally different meaning and could indicate a Roman road. The farm gets its name from the four Neolithic? stones at NY 831 748. To the south of Great Lonbrough Farm, the wooded slope looks as if it has been defended with a patrol track. At NY 822 733, a Roman-looking zig-zag climbs the escarpment.

Armstong's map of 1769 shows a suspiciously Roman looking road heading north from our previously mentioned Roman Wall Lake District. The track runs north from Sewingshields Crags (NY 810 703 and passes Kemming's Cross (Comyn's Cross, NY 799 737) and arrives at Rose's Bower (NY 799 769) where the 18th Century antiquarians reported square fortifications. The name "Bower" frequently occurs on Roman roads in Northumberland.

Further north, yet another suspected Roman patrol road was picked up and this is lined up precisely on Risingham (Habitancum) Roman fort (NY 891 862) to the west and the peculiar bend of the Devil's Causeway Roman road near Longhorsley (Devil's Corner NZ 122 923), to the east. The initial clues which led to the discovery of this road, for reference purposes, termed the "Fairnley Road," were: near Fairnley Farm (NZ 005 890), a liner east-west wood and ruler-straight bridle-track coincided with a parish boundary. This combination of features was lined up with the folly "Codgers Fort" on a hill to the ENE. The line also joined up with the modern B6342 road at NZ 018 894. The B6342 sits on top of an enclosure road which was preceded by a drovers' way. All three may be on the line of a Roman predecessor. The cobbled surface and heavier foundation stones of the "new" Roman road can be inspected along the ridge to the south of the Ottercops Burn (which becomes the Hart Burn), to the north of Fairnley Farm at NZ 006 893. Yet another Roman road is thought to cross the above Fairnley Roman road at right angles and this last mentioned north-south road transits Chesters (NZ 008 877), Fairnley, and Harewood (NZ 001 904). It seems incredible that so many Roman roads exist in the area but it looks as if even more will shortly come to light as the grid is obviously incomplete. Three thousand yards to the west of Fairnley Farm, an earthwork just to the south of the Fairnley suspected Roman road is covered in deep heather. This site is marked as a "settlement" on the OS maps but it may be of greater importance than a mere homestead. It is perfectly rectangular with rounded corners. Three sides (west, south & east) are single-ditched but the north side is double-ditched. Romano-British settlements were never double-ditched and usually had only a single entrance on the eastern side. The major axis of the above site is parallel to the Roman road. There are entrances with ditch infills on east and west sides.

The Roman road divides at NY 978 884 with the staight-ahead length (WSW) proceeding to the Risingham fort and the SW arm lined-up on Redesmouth. A large rectangular wood is marked on most OS maps north of this junction and this may cause confusion as the wood has been felled. At the north end of the former wood, a prominent rocky outcrop contains cup & ring marks (prehistoric patterns of unknown date and meaning).

The newly discovered roads are quite often lined up on circular Iron Age fortifications and it looks as if the Romans were using friendly or possibly mercenary native tribes, to police the area to the north of the Wall.

Let us return to Ward Lane across Broadpool Common. At the eastern end at NY 861 761, the road makes an alteration of heading to the south-east. The modern road terminates at its junction with the B6320 at NY 877 741 but it will be seen that an extension would take it across the grounds Nunwick Hall. On the south bank of the rivulet at NY 883 739 is a suspected Roman road which has obviously crossed the North Tyne's tributary at this point. The suspected Roman road can be picked up again at NY 892 733 where a prominent *agger* runs up the hillside towards a quarry. The *agger* enters the quarry where it is lost. The road can be seen again a mile north-west of Chesters (Cilurnum) at NY 904 717 and the *agger* up the field boundary is obviously bound for the Chesters fort.

A missing aqueduct to Chesters is also in this area with a suspected dam and raised *specus* at NY 903 717, to the north-west of Leazes Head Farm and thence around the contours to the east of Lincoln Hill and then into the Roman fort. The upper reaches of this aqueduct are at the bottom of the slope below the patrol road at NY 870 722, north of Limestone Corner.

Conclusion

It looks as if the Roman Wall was not a "Maginot Line" type defence; its purpose seems to have been a safe retreat for Northumberland's occupation forces and patrolling allied tribes should military policing operations north of the barrier have taken a turn for the worse.

Air and ground searches for similar patrol grids are now being organised along the whole length of the Wall and the Roman and allied occupied area to the north. No doubt a search for these roads will also produce some more unknown aqueducts.

And we have one....

Not only our waterworks experts can find aqueducts - the roadfinders decided to have a look at the area around the Roman fort at Risingham (Habitancum) at West Woodburn. After looking at the fort and its enigmatic water channels, (which are described as old river courses, but which I am sure served Roman inland navigation requirements), we climbed to Cragg Farm to view the surrounding countryside. On the highest point at NY 887 851, a *tumulus* is marked on OS maps. It looks more like the remains of a Roman signal station to me, though of course it is not unknown for the Romans to have adapted a burial mound for such purposes. Many high points around Nortumberland can be see from the site.

A few yards to the east, at the side of a wood which contains a hidden (Roman?) quarry is a shepherd's hut, built of stone and decorated with an

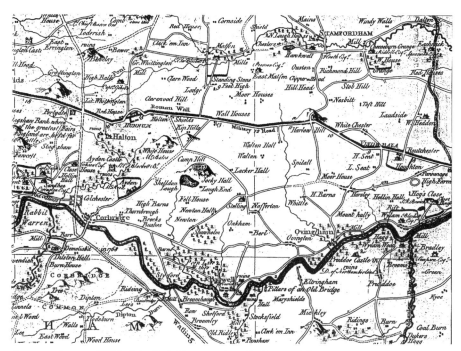

Armstrong's map of 1769 of the Corbridge area. A newly discovered Roman road is under a farm track which runs south-east from Halton Shields towards Camp Hill and Shelldon Lough (Shildon Lough).

old millstone. Built into the drystone-wall behind the building are about thirty aqueduct channel stones of distinct Roman type. There was an aqueduct in the vicinity, and a swampy area was a possible reservoir site. After a few minutes Peter attracted my attention to a rabbit burrow into which the resident had hastily taken cover. Peter remarked that this particular rabbit must be an excellent stonemason as the burrow's entrance had stone walls with a little lintel across the top. The missing aqueduct had been found and its orientation was up to the afore-mentioned swamp.

There must be more than one aqueduct to the fort and a projected search area for the principal one is Chesterhope Common. One of our Roman roads transits this area on its way from Fairnley to Redesmouth and can be seen at NY 923 854 where it joins a modern road at a right-angled bend. A suggested search area for the aqueduct and reservoir is NY 915 842 where a public footpath crosses the source of the Chesterhope Burn.

The 255 Frontier Line

More information is being revealed from old maps. Armstrong's map of Northumberland, 1769 gives us two further clues. Tows Bank Farm (NY 687 572, p314) which sits on a suspected milefortlet on the eastern rim of the South Tyne gorge is marked as "Tower Bank." All of a sudden, the name makes sense.

Just to the south of the Callerton DMV at NZ 165 704 (p305) the hill with the suspected milefortlet is shown on the map as "Brough Hill" (Fortified

Hill).

The lynchpin of the suspected 255 Frontier Road is Hexham where the 18th century antiquarians were sure that a Roman town had existed. Modern fashion is to ignore the reports of these 18th century antiquarians. The thousands of reused Roman stones in Hexham are said to have been transported from Corbridge. How about the coins and pottery that keep turning up at Hexham? In order to stick to the Corbridge story and explain the increasing amount of finds in and around Hexham, a lady has said that the Corbridge *vicus* may have extended as far as Hexham! A four mile-long Roman *vicus* would have been quite something even for the Wall area. In spite of the official line, we are all certain that Hexam was a Roman town and I am grateful to Dr. John Chapman of High Shield, Hexham, for supplying the following information on two Roman altars which were found in *undisturbed* soil when a new street was being constructed in the town in 1864. In *THE ABBEY OF ST ANDREW, HEXHAM*, 1888, by Charles Clement Hodges, p3, the author has this to say:

"In 1864, two Roman altars were found when the new street between the Market Place and Battle Hill was being made. One of them is quite plain, having neither sculpture nor inscription but it is of a large size and finely moulded. The other bears an inscription which has been read by Dr Bruce as follows:

> Apollini
> Mapono
> Terentius
> filius Oufentina
> Firmus Saena
> Prefectus castrorum
> *legionis sextae victricis piae fidelis donum dat*

Dr. John Chapman tells me that the "new street" is Beaumont Street and that altars which fit this description are in the west end of the abbey nave. He also tells me that "Apollini Mapono" also occurs on a reused altar stone in the crypt.

I can recall only one occasion when our local museums admitted defeat: a few years ago, Hilda Harvey was on holiday at Woolaw Farm in Redesdale and she had been shown by the farmer's daughter, Louise Chapman, a strange inscription on a rock beside a waterfall. It said:

LAT = ZEN DIS + DEC

The local museums and archaeological departments gave up in defeat so Miss Harvey turned to The Northern Archaeology Group. For the fliers and sailors in our society, the meaning was perfectly clear. The inscription meant:

LATITUDE = ZENITH DISTANCE + DECLINATION

This is a standard formula in astro-navigation (see p171/172)

Local people thought that a German officer at a nearby prisoner of war camp in the 1914-18 War had carved the letters because a German name appears on another rock close by. A senior German officer had given his parole and was allowed to roam freely over the surrounding countryside. The German name on the rock has figures beside it and the inscription reads:

KEPLER
$$DIST^3$$
$$= K$$
$$PERIOD^2$$

Kepler was a German but he was not a POW. He was an astronomer who died in 1630. The formula on the rock summarises "Kepler's Third Law of Planetary Motion" which says:

"The time taken by any planet in its revolution about the Sun has a definite relation to its distance from the Sun, the square of its time being in exact proportion to the cube of its distance."

Who carved the inscriptions? If a German officer had carved the navigational formula, surely he would have written it in his native language and not the language of the enemy:

Latitude = die Breite,
Zenith = Zenit,
Distance = Distanz
Declination = Deklination.

The formula in German should read:

BRE = ZEN DIS + DEK

Who then carved the inscriptions? I favour a local boy who lived in the next valley and I quote from *TOMLINSON'S GUIDE TO NORTHUMBERLAND*, p343:

"Wreighill has its celebrity in the person of George Coughron, a mathematical prodigy, who was born here on August 12th 1752. His powers of calculation were indeed extraordinary, and during his brief career (he died in the twenty-first year of his age), he obtained no fewer than ten prizes for answering questions in fluxions alone. He challenged all the mathematicians of this time to answer the prize question in the Gentleman's Diary for 1772. His challenge was not accepted and he gave the solution himself. The most difficult problems were submitted to his decision and at the time of his death he held the appointment of calculator to the Astronomer Royal."

He was in the habit of taking his calculations out into the quiet countryside. Maybe he was the mysterious rock-carver. The map ref of the inscribed rocks is approx NY 824 980, beside a waterfall on a small stream which joins the River Rede a few hundred yards to the south-east.

We will shortly examine evidence in central Durham but first, some new evidence close to one of our modern radio antennae has come to my notice. If a Roman road continued south-east of Ebchester (Vindomora) on the same heading as Dere Street to the north-west, it would have crossed the prominent hill and excellent survey point on which now stands the giant Pontop Pike television transmitter antenna (NZ 149 528, spot height 312m). A conversation with the farmer revealed the following information: yes, an old road thought to have been a drove road did cross his land on a north-west to south-east heading but his father had removed the stones in order to reuse the material in field walls. The marks across the fields can still be seen. This former road is lined up exactly on the Roman survey point at NZ 222 480 which is also on the "Long Edge" Roman road from Lanchester to Chester-le-Street.

The conclusion is that another important road in addition to Dere Street has departed from Ebchester. Durham seems to be its destination.

Before we move to the Durham area, let us look at a question repeatedly asked and that is: "Did the Romans drive on the left or right-hand side of the road?"

In the north of England, the cambers of the Roman roads are so pronounced that if wagons had been used, they must have stuck to the crown or fallen off! Opposite direction traffic could not have passed without serious risk of overturning. The agger of the main Roman Dere Street just north of Corbridge in a field at NY 984 655 is a typical example. The roads were suitable only for pack-animals. Around forts and towns, wagons were used but the streets were wider and lacked the exaggerated cambers of the cross-country routes. Around the farms and villas, the journeys were short and ample fodder was available for the animals.

"In the wider streets of Roman Italy, it seems that the Romans kept to the left. There is a reference (which I have mislaid) but I remember that the Roman writer advised travellers that traffic entering Rome via a certain bridge over the Tiber should keep to that side nearest a prominent landmark, a tower I think it was. Interested researchers should be able to locate the reference.

At the Roman circus, the charioteers went round the *spina* in an anticlockwise direction which means that the shortest distance around the circuit was by keeping to the left. We know of this anticlockwise direction because the line of starting chambers *(carcares)* was angled and aslo slightly concave so that it aimed the competitors at a focal point in the centre of the track to the right of the *spina*. Was ancient Rome like modern Britain, a left-hand orientated nation? Now, we come to the final part of this addendum which is a close look at the Cathedral and University City of Durham and its mostly ignored evidence of a Roman presence. The city has all the ingredients described earlier. The river curves around a high rock forming a peninsula which is occupied by the Norman cathedral and castle. Tradition has it that the narrow neck of land was pierced at one time, thus forming an island. Defence immediately springs to mind but the cut could have served a navigation purpose. A mediaeval dam allows the 150-passenger riverboat *Prince Bishop* to ply the river for a couple of miles upstream from Prebend's Bridge (p218). You can charter this riverboat and hold a dance on it if you wish - very strange for a so-called un-navigable river!

Both upstream and downstream from Durham are Roman forts with a strong suspicion of having been associated with river transport. There is Chester-le-Street (Concangis) downstream and also the giant Roman dam at Hylton near the river mouth. Binchester (Vivovia) is upriver. Roman tiles found at Binchester are stamped "*Num Con*" (*Numerus Concangios*) which was the Roman unit stationed at Chester-le-Street for a time. Did the tiles make the 23 mile river trip by ten ton *codicariae*? The alternative was a vast number of pack-animals, or ox-wagons balanced on those Roman *aggers*, not to mention the impossible gradients.

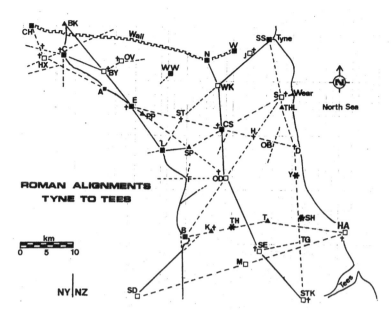

ROMAN ALIGNMENTS
TYNE TO TEES

**THE EMERGING ROMAN ROAD SYSTEM
BETWEEN TYNE AND TEES**

Known Roman Roads shown as solid lines.
Suspected Roman roads in broken lines

A = Apperley Dene, Romano-British farm, road junction
B = Binchester, fort, road junction, bridge
BK - Beukley, road junction, survey point, radio mast
BY = Bywell, bridge, road junction, fort? Saxon church
C = Corbridge, fort, town, bridge, road network, Saxon church
CH = Chesters, Wall fort, bridge
CS = Chester-le-Street, fort, road network, Saxon church
D = Dalton-le-Dale, road junction, old church
E = Ebchester, fort, road junction, old church
F = Flass Hall, road junction
H = Houghton-le-Spring, road, old church, Roman artefacts
HA = Hartlepool, Suspected Roman port
HX = Hexham, road network, fort? abbey, Roman artefacts
J = Jarrow, Saxon church, Roman artefacts
K = Kirk Merrington, old church, survey point
L = Lanchester, fort, road junction, old church
M = Mordon, road, artefacts found

N = Newcastle upon Tyne, Wall fort, bridge, road junction
OB = Old Burdon, road found (Sunderland - Sedgefield?)
OD = Old Durham, fort? bath-house, road junction
OV = Ovingham, Saxon church, Stangate
PP = Pontop Pike, road? Survey point NZ 150 528, TV mast
S = Sunderland, suspected Roman port
SD = Staindrop, road junction, old church
SE = Sedgefield, road network, old church
SH = Sheraton, road, Saxon village, radio mast
SP = survey point, NZ 222 480, 232m, road, radio mast
SS = South Shields, fort and port?
ST = Stanley, road? church on survey point
STK = Stockton-on-Tees, road? Saxon tower, Roman artefacts
T = Trimdon, road, survey point, radio mast
TG = Three Gates, road junction, significant place name
TH = Thrislington, road, DMV
THL = Tunstall Hills, road, survey point
W = Wallend, Wall fort, Wall terminus
WK = Wrekenton, suspected fort seen from the air
WW = Washing Wells, early fort? & temporary camp
Y = Yoden, road, Saxon village

Lubberly attempts have been made by advocates of long distance ox-wagon transport, to show that an impossible number of dams would have been needed in our rivers to support Roman navigation. They have taken the elevation of destination and divided by ten feet (estimated average height of

Top: an aerial view of Brinkheugh Farm (NZ 122 984) near Brinkburn Priory. Tradition has it that a Roman road, a branch of the Devil's Causeway, crossed the River Coquet here. Modern archaeologists disagreed and hoping to find nothing, succeeded. Txvheir trench must have been in the wrong place or too shallow.

Bottom: The Roman road was found north-west of Brinkheugh Farm by members of the Association of Northumberland History Societies; Janet Brown, Carole Ross, BA (Hons), Bob Robson, Chris Hudson and David Patterson.

Roman minor river dams) to give the number of barriers required. This assumes that dams stem the rivers into level pounds. They do not: the rivers retain a considerable slope thus reducing the theoretical number of barrages by over 50%. Furthermore, we know that the Romans could handle shallow and difficult water so the number of dams is even further reduced. From Sunderland to Durham, dams would have sufficed at Hylton, Chester-le-Street, Lumley Mill, and Finchale Priory. There have been finds of Roman material at all of these locations.

Durham Cathedral stands on the site of the Saxon "White Church" and we now know that there is a high probability of earlier Roman occupation on later Saxon religious sites. Numerous Roman artefacts have been found on the peninsula. This includes finds in the Cathedral gardens.

Although the Normans did not use lewis devices to raise their large stones, there are some reused stones with lewis holes in the Cathedral's walls. These were spotted by schoolboy Andrew Duff, a keen student of Roman engineering. The stones are in the wall nearest the entrance close to the Cathedral's bookshop.

A mile to the south-east of the cathedral, at Old Durham, a Roman bath-house was excavated in 1940. This was a rescue operation when gravel quarrying hit Roman walls. How many other features had been destroyed in the past? Close by, Old Durham Farm looks as if it is standing on a typical Roman fort platform. Roman coins have been found there (Cade, *Archaeologia vii*, 1785). John Cade investigated the Roman road from the Tees to Chester-le-Street. He mentions the site of Old Durham:

"This station I imagine, was formerly thought of great consequence, but at length suffered the fate of many others in northern parts, when William the Conqueror made that horrid devastation between York and this place, and erected his *castrum* in the new city; the fortifications were then partly levelled, but enough is left to point out its former magnitude and importance; it being in my opinion much larger than Dr Stukeley has described; and the rivulet Pidding has, with great labour and ingenuity, been diverted from its original channel, where it ran into the Wear, near Shinkley Bridge, to answer the purpose of the *Fosse* along the southern and western sides of it."

Stukeley, Hutchinson and Surtees all refer to the massive Iron Age hillfort of Maiden Castle on the opposite side of the river but Cade makes no mention of it and concentrates on the Roman features.

The 1940 excavation at Old Durham produced an almost complete domestic bath-house but clearly there must be, or have been a large associated fort or settlment close by.

Both Cade and Surtees mention two supposed Roman bridges in Durham. Cade refers to a Roman bridge at Kepier:

"A gentleman with whom I am acquainted has carefully surveyed the old road from this place [Old Durham] by Kepyre hospital [the mediaeval leper hospital] and he assures me that, in the dry season, the piers of a bridge are obvious in the bed of the river, seemingly of Roman construction."

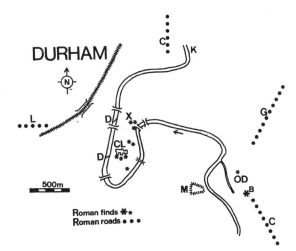

Map of Durham

Asterisks mark findspots of
Roman material.
Dots mark Roman roads,
known or suspected
CL = Durham Cathedral
D = Mediaeval dams in River
Wear
X = Tradional site of channel
short-circuiting river loop
M = Maiden Castle Iron Age
hillfort
OD = Old Durham, suspected
Roman site
B = Roman bath-house,
excavated 1940
K = Kepier mediaeval leper
hospital
C = Cade's Roman Road
G = Gordon's Roman road
L = Possible Roman road from
Lanchester

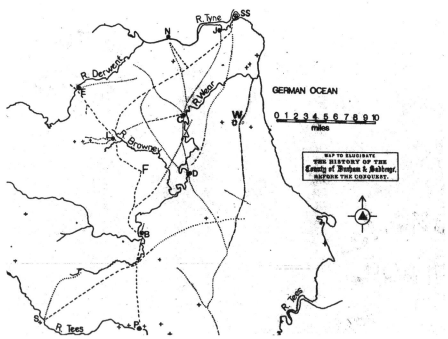

Map to elucidate the History of the County of
Durham & Sadberge, before the Conquest
SS = South Shields (Arbeia?)
J = Jarrow (Danum?)
N = Newcastle upon Tyne (Pons Aelius)
E = Ebchester (Vindomora)
L = Lanchester (Longovicium)
F = Flass Hall
C = Chester-le-Street (Concangis)

D = Durham
B = Binchester (Vinovia)
S = Startforth
P = Piercebridge
W = Warden Law
+ = findspots of Roman artefacts
dashes = observed Roman roads
dots = reported Roman roads
dots and dashes = Salters' road

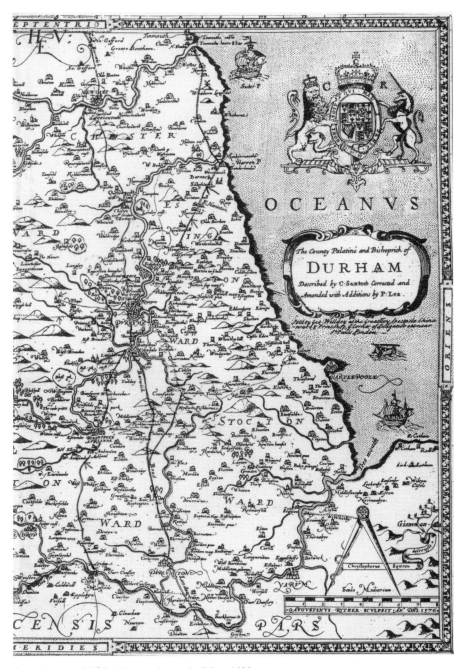

Saxton's map of 1576 with amendments by P Lea, 1686

The Corbridge Eagle
While inspecting the tower of St Andrews Saxon church, Corbridge, for reused Roman stones, a stone with half an eagle, lying on its side, in a coffer, was observed high up on the north face of the tower, with binoculars. It was thought to be an ex-Roman stone but archaeologists who had failed to spot the stone said it was merely a stone which had been washed by the rain into that shape. However, Professor Richard Bailey, of Newcastle upon Tyne University, one of Britain's leading experts on Saxon history identified the shape as St John's Eagle (Saxon). This indicated that there had been an earlier Saxon church in the vicinity and this upset the dating of the present church. The rainwashing theories vanished like the mythical phlogiston of long disproved academic arguments.

Surtees, also in *Archaeologia vii,* 1785, mentions another Roman bridge, this time a timber one at Old Durham:

"During the late dry summer, the wooden piers of a bridge over the Wear, leading exactly to the station at Old Durham, were not only visible, but those very piers, left high and dry, were taken up, consisting of long trunks of trees, squared and bored, and mortized together so as to form a strong foundation on each side of the river. At the same time, from the same state of the river, the piers of solid masonry were discovered on the North side of the Wear below Kepyer Hospital, confirming, it would seem, the old tradition, that a great road passed this way across the Race-ground, and so by Kepyer Northwards...."

Surtees also reported that in the same summer, there were: "vestiges of a mill-dam across the Wear, formed by stakes and large stones, a little below Old Durham."

Thus, there was a dam and a bridge at Old Durham.

The inference is that there was a considerable Roman settlement at Durham with major sites under the cathedral and at Old Durham.

There is a strong possibility of Roman river navigation and a network of Roman roads converging on the capital city of the county. A closer examination of the road system is called for.

A known Roman northbound road investigated by the afore-mentioned John Cade, crossed the River Tees at Pountey's Bridge near Middleton St George, and passed by Stainton-le-Street (Great Stainton) and then via Sedgefield to Shincliffe and Old Durham. A map little used by researchers is *Saxton's Map* of 1576. During this period, most of the roads in use were ex-Roman.

Dr Gordon's Roman road shown as a sinuous line from South Shields to Old Durham on the *Map to Elucidate the History of the County of Durham & Sadberge before the Conquest,* is marked as a very straight and definite line on *Saxton's Map* between Sunderland and Durham. The main alignment is on Old Durham but it suddenly bends towards Kepier. On the *"Elucidate Map,"* Gordon's road terminates at Old Durham but on Saxton's it is picked up again, still on the previous Sunderland - Old Durham alignment, but now west of the River Wear and presumably heading for Binchester (Vinovia). The line crosses the River Wear to the north of Tudhoe and heads for Whitchurch (Whitworth) where a Roman road heading north from Vinovia was mentioned by 19th century observers. The Sunderland - Old Durham - Whitworth - Binchester road has passed close by Croxdale and crossed the Browney near its confluence with the Wear. Many Roman artefacts have been found at Croxdale.

On Saxton's map, the Roman road Dere Street through Lanchester (Longovicium) is marked but instead of turning south at Flass Hall, Saxton marks it running by Vffhaw (Ushaw) and thence via Aldwinedge (Aldin

The author's book THE PIERCEBRIDGE FORMULA, 1984, won a Rolex International Prize for exploration. Hundreds of enthusiastic letters of support from readers were also received. One reader, Mr Peter J R Wheatley of

Felixstowe, sent the author the model van depicted here. The author values this gift as much as the gold Rolex watch with which he was presented by Sir Vivian Fuchs, the Antarctic explorer, on behalf of the Rolex Company of Geneva.

Grange) to Durham. A further road is shown coming in from the west (from Salter's Gate?) to Flass Hall and then following the River Browney to Croxdale. This is all food for thought.

Much has been said about Roman roads but in the minds of many people, their purpose is still obscure. A television programme talked about Roman roads two hundred feet wide but the gentleman was confusing the road *zone* with the actual road. The zone was the area cleared of scrub as a deterrent to ambushes. The actual paved road surface was very narrow, with a marked camber and occasionally, as we have seen in Northumberland, there were grass tracks at both sides for unshod animals.

I hope this book encourages readers to carry out archaeological fieldwork. It is often hard work and one must frequently cross territory which is very hard going. After a long and difficult cross country slog, over moorland and swamps, up and down gullies and in and out of streams, with aching muscles, an occasional farm track is a luxury and a metalled road becomes sheer bliss. As one marches down the last mile or so of modern road, back to the parked car, where tea and sandwiches wait, the walking pace increases from the rough terrain rate of one-mile-per-hour to about four; the morale soars; the aches and pains are eased and the reason for the Roman all-weather network becomes clear. Our knowledge of its purpose makes the roads easier to find.

I have not intended to rewrite part of Roman history with this book, in fact I have merely scratched the surface. The work is intended as a pathfinder flare to help guide amateur historians across the dark two thousand years.

Bibliography

Adam, J P	Le Chantier Antique, in *Dossiers de l'Archeol.* 1977
anonymous	Anecdotes of American Horses, in *Penny Magazine,* 1840
Astbury, A K	*The Black Fens*
Bailey, R, et al	*Dowsing and Church Archaeology*
Baines, T	*Yorkshire Past and Present,* 1870
Baradez, J	*Fossatum Africae - Vue Aéienne de l'organisation romaine dans le sud-Algérien,* 1949
Bede	*A History of the English Church and People*
Birley, E	*Corbridge Roman Station,* & A Roman Altar from Staward Pele and Roman Remains in Allendale, in *Archaeologia Aeliana,* 1950
Boyles	Jarrow Church and Monastery, in *Archaeol. Aeliana,* 1885
Bruce, J C	*The Roman Wall,* 1867, & Roman Hexham, in *Archaeologia Aeliana,* 1861
Burton, A	*The Changing River*
Camden	*Britannia,* 1637
Campbell, J, et al	*The Anglo-Saxons*
Casey, J	A Votive Deposit from the River Tees at Piercebridge, County Durhm, in *Durham Archaeological Journal 5.*
Chevalier, R	*Roman Roads*
Churchill, W	*A History of the English Speaking Peoples*
Cintas, P	*Manuel d'Archéologie Punique*
Codrington, T	*Roman Roads in Britain,* 1919
Crawford, O G S & Keiller, A	*Wessex from the Air,* 1928
Deuel, L	*Flights into Yesterday*
Dickinson, G	*Allendale and Whitfield*
Duckham, B F	Inland Waterways, in *Amateur Historian,* vol 6 No 1
Eckholdt, M	Navigation on Small Rivers in Central Europe in Roman and Medieval Times, in *The International Journal of Naut. Archaeol. & Underwater Expl.* 1984
Eden, T	*Durham*
Engels, D W	*Alexander the Great and the Logistics of the Macedonian Army*

Fordyce   ***Local Records of Northumberland and Durham***
Forster, R   ***History of Corbridge***, 1881
Frere, S S   ***Britannia***
Frontinus   ***The Strategems and Aqueducts of Rome***
Garrett, W E   George Washington's Patowmack Canal, in ***National
                           Geographic Magazine***, Vol 171 No 6, June 1987
Glover, M   ***Invasion Scare 1940***
Graham, F   ***Bridges of Northumberland and Durham***
Grenier, A   ***Manuel D'archéologie Gallo-romaine***
Hall, G R   Roman Way Across Wark's Ford, in ***PSAN, 1866***
Hildyard, E J W   A Possible Roman Road, in ***Archaeology of Weardale***, 1948
Hersey, J   ***A Single Pebble***
Hippisley Coxe, A D   ***Haunted Britain***
Hodges, H   ***Technology in the Ancient World***
Hodgson, J C   ***A History of Northumberland***, 1839
Horsley, J   ***Britannia Romana***, 1732
Hoskins, W G   ***Fieldwork in Local History***
Hutchinson, W   ***History and Antiquities of the County Palatine of Durham***
                           1785,& ***Views of Northumberland***
Johnston, D E   ***Roman Roads in Britain***
Jones, P   Flash Locks and Flashing, in ***Waterways World***, Apr.'91
Longstaffe   ***Before the Conquest***, & ***History and Antiquities of
                           Northumberland***
Mackenzie, E   ***History of Northumberland***, 1825
Mackenzie & Ross   ***Durham***, 1834
Maclauchlan, H   ***Survey of the Watling Street***, 1852
Margery, I D   ***Roman Roads in Britain***, 1967
Massie, W H   A Roman Bridge at Birkenhead, in ***Journal of the
                           Architect. Archaeol. & Hist. Soc. of Chester***, 1850
Mitchell, W C   ***History of Sunderland***, 1919
Mócsy, A   ***Pannonia and Upper Moesia***
Moore, R W   ***The Romans in Britain***
Mothersole, Jessie   ***Agricola's Road into Scotland***
Murray   ***Handbook for Travellers in Durham and Northumberland***
Nelson, R B
& Norris P W   ***Warfleets of Antiquity***
Ordnance Survey   ***Roman Britain***
Palmer   ***The Tyne and its Rivers***, 1862
Pliny the Elder   ***Natural History***
Pliny the Younger   ***Letters to Trajan***
Poidebard, R P A   ***La Trace de Rome dans le désert de Syrie***, 1934 ***Le Limes
                           de Chalcis***, 1945, & ***Le Limes de Trajan Ä la conquete arabe***
Pollen, J H   ***Trajan's Column Described***
Ripon Motor
Boat Club   ***Cruising Guide to the North East Waterways***
Rivet, A L F
& Smith, C   ***The Place-names of Roman Britain***
St Joseph, J K S
& Frere, S S   ***Roman Britain from the Air***

Salzman, L F	***Building in England Down to 1540***
Selkirk, R	***The Piercebridge Formula, 1983***
Shirley Smith, H	***The World's Great Bridges***
Sitwell, N H H	***Roman Roads of Europe***
Smith, N A F	***A History of Dams***
Society of Antiquarians of Newcastle upon Tyne	***Proceedings,*** 1839
Stukeley, W	***Itinerarium Curiosum, Centuria 11***
Summer	***History of Sunderland***
Surtees	***History of the County of Durham***
Sykes	***Local Records,*** 1866
Tacitus	***Agricola, Annals, & Histories***
Testaguzza, O	Port of Rome, in ***Archaeology,*** Vol 17 No 3
Tomlinson, W W	***Comprehensive Guide to Northumberland***
Tudor, D	***Les Ponts Romains du Bas-Danube***
Vegetius	***De Re Militari***
Venedikov	***Trakijskate Kolesniza***
Von Hagen, V	***Roman Roads***
Warburton	***Vallum Romanum,*** 1753
Willan, T S	***River Navigation in England 1600-1750***
Wright, R P	The Wrekendike and Roman Road Junction on Gateshead Fell, in ***Archaeologia Aeliana,*** 1940

Index

For ease of reference, the index has been subdivided under the following headings:

An asterisk before a page number indicates an illustration

1. Aerial searches

aerial photography, 2,3,5,7-12,18
aircraft operating techniques, 9,11-13,18-20
balloons, 1,18
crop/shadow/snow marks,
    1-9, *2,*3,*5 *9,14,*19,34,38,39, 69,122
identification of sites,
    2-4,21,22,34,40
infra-red photography, 11
kites, 14,
stereoscopic photography, 9-11

2. Aircraft

Auster,
    operated by Cambridge Univ, 19
Avro Anson, over Roman Wall, 97
Avro Lancaster,
    fuel consumption, 144
Avro York & other airliners,
    author, crew member of, 359
Catalina (PBY), Consolidated,
    in Sunderland harbour, *256,355
    on bottom of Loch Ness, *355,359

Cessna 150, 11
Cessna 172, 11
Cessna 337 Skymaster,
    operated by Cambridge Univ, 20
Chinook helicopter, Boeing,
    logistics support, 250
De Havilland Dove, photo recce,
    flown by author in Africa, 240
De Havilland Puss Moth,
    flown by Major Allen, 18
De Havilland Rapide,
    over Roman Wall, 98
DFS 230 assault glider, 45
Fairey Gannet, radar picket, 156
Flying Fortress, B17, USAAF,
    wreck on Cheviot, 324
Focke Wulf 200 Condor,
    maritime recce, 149
Handley Page Hampden,
    wreck on Windy Gyle, 359
Handley Page Victor,
    tanker, Ascension Island, 349
Hawker Hurricane,
    Battle of Britain, 45
    merchant ship catafighter, 149

7. Dams/weirs

10. Logistics

Roman sea transport;
    see "ships and sea transport"
South Africa,
    difficulties of ox-transport,
    trekpads (ox-roads), 52
    use of easy gradients, 52
South America,
    aviation fuel supplies,*205
Stalingrad,
    Luftwaffe airlift 1943, 344
Wade's military roads, 120, Intro.

11. Ships and sea transport

admiral's flag (Roman), 161
animal-powered paddle vessels,
    *334,336-338
artemon (sail), 187,199,201
Atlantic Conveyor, 250
Battle of Atlantic 1942, 148,149
bireme, 152,*160,161
Blackfriar's Ship, 227
Boulogne Roman lighthouse, 165,*166
Caligula's super-ship, 164,*166
camouflage of Roman ships, 161
Carthaginian navy, 149
Cheop's Ship, 184
corvus (raven) assault bridge,
    *142,149,154-156
County Hall Ship, 227
dhows, 203,359
Dover Roman lighthouses, 165
dry-docks *(navalia),* *201,204,205

Falkland Islands wrecks

Egeria	351
Golden Chance	352
Great Britain	351
Jhelum	352
Lady Elizabeth	*343,352
Samson	352
Snow Squall	352

floating corn-mills, 82
fuel consumption of ships, 144
General Belgrano, 250
Golden Hind(e), 20,153,*186,187
Graf Spee, 45
Guy's Hospital Ship, 227
Harrapans, 203,204
heptere, 152
Hercules, dredger,
    hit Roman dam at Hylton, 214
HMS *Ajax,* 45
HMS *Ark Royal,* 156,348
HMS *Audacity,* ex-*Hannover,* 149
HMS *Falkland Sound,* ex-*Yehuin,* 350
HMS *Hermes,* 250
HMS *Invincible,* 250
HMS *Royal Oak,* 298
HMT *Empire Wansbeck,* ex-*Linz,* 356

insignia of marines, *150, navy 357
insignia of merchant ship, 161
Isis, very large grain carrier,
    163,164,187
Kreigsmarine, 43,44,159
La Coruña, lighthouse, 165
lateen sail, 187,199,201
lead lines, 184,228
liburnae, 158,220
lighthouses (ancient), 164-167,
    *166,*167
Lothal, Bronze Age port, 203,204
Louisiana, 240
marines, 149-152,154,159,161
Marques,
    lost in Tall Ships Race, 20
merchant seamen in Roman army,
    159,161
Naviculari, 220,231
Netherby ships, remains of, 229
Pharos (lighthouse), 155,164,165
Pisa Constitutum Usus, 167
Portus, 164
pumps, 201 & Addendum
quinquereme, 152,154,157
Roman invasion fleets, 43,45-50
Roman merchantmen,
    50,161,*162,*163,167,168,185-
187,199,200
Roman naval bases, 159
Roman navy,
    organised as auxiliaries, 159
Roman regional war fleets,
    159-161,219,220
Roman sailors' uniforms, 161
Roman sea trade with China, 168
Roman transports,
    45,46,50,161,165,200
Roman voyage durations, 167,187
Saxon ship *(cyul),* 207
ship construction;
    Roman/Celtic, 227,228,
Singelgracht, 341
Sir Tristram, 341
sounding pole in Cheops' ship, 184
square rig, 185,187,199
Trader, 334
trireme, 152,154,155,161
Tuscaloosa, 352
U-boats, 148,149,298
USS *Nevada,* 45
USS *Phoenix,*
    (later General Belgrano), 250
Viking longships, 185,207

12. Navigation and astronomy

astro-compass, 62,66,*169,*170,*171
astronomical navigation,
    66,168,*169,172-178,180-183
    & Addendum

13. Armies

14. Fortifications

15. Frontiers

16. Environment & cultures

20. Signalling and postal services

21. Surveying

22. Water supplies & aqueducts

23. People (individuals)

25. Addendum, sequence of subjects:

Hylton Roman dam
navigation on River Swale
aqueducts on Hadrian's Wall
Rev Hall's lost Roman road
Roman patrol roads north of the Wall